THE HANDBOOK
OF JEWISH THOUGHT

The
HANDBOOK
of Jewish Thought

By
Rabbi Aryeh Kaplan

MAZNAIM PUBLISHING CORPORATION
NEW YORK / JERUSALEM

For information write:

Maznaim Publishing Corporation
4304 12th Avenue
Brooklyn, New York 11219
Tel. (212) 438-7680   853-0525

Printed in Israel

נכרך במפעלי ה. וגשל, ירושלים, ישראל

CONTENTS

ONE

FOUNDATIONS

1:1   The foundation of Judaism and the basis of all true religion is the realization that existence is purposeful, and that man has a purpose in life.[1]

1:2   Both man and nature have meaning because they were created by a purposeful Being. It is this Being that we call God.

1:3   If there were no Creator, then the universe would be purposeless, human existence pointless, and life devoid of meaning and hope.[2]

1:4   The existence of a purposeful Creator is indicated by the fact that the inorganic universe contains every ingredient needed to make organic life possible. The world exists as an arena for life, and the probability that this is entirely due to chance is infinitesimally small.[3]

---

1. *Mesilath Yesharim* 1. Cf. *Zohar Chadash* 70d; Introduction to *Kalach Pith'ch. Chokhmah.*
2. *Cf.* Psalms 127:1.
3. The essence of the argument is that mathematically the more complex an ordered structure, the less the probability of its structure being due to chance. The chemistry of life is by far the most complex process in our experience, and yet we find that the inorganic matter of the universe can support this process. Since there is only one type of matter in the universe, the chances of its having all the chemical and physical

1:5   In recognition of this, the Psalmist said, "I will give thanks to God, for I am awesomely and wonderfully made" (Psalms 139:14). It is also written, "From my flesh, I will see God" (Job 19:26). That is, God's handiwork is discernable from the very fact that human flesh can exist.[4]

1:6   It is likewise taught that even inanimate things praise God. Their very existence is a hymn, demonstrating God's handiwork. It is thus written, "The heavens declare God's glory, the firmament tells of His handiwork" (Psalms 19:2).[5]

1:7   It is as unthirkable to conceive of the universe as arising by chance without a purposeful Creator, as it is to conceive of a beautiful poem written with a random splash of ink.[6]

1:8   The first of the Ten Commandments reads, "I am God your Lord, who brought you up out of the land of Egypt, from the house of slavery" (Exodus 20:2). This is a positive commandment to believe in God.[7] This commandment depends on thought and can be fulfilled at any time.[8]

properties needed to support life are remotely small, unless we take into account a purposeful Creator. In essence, it is the properties of the electron that make possible the existence of the human brain. For the classical argument, see *Emunoth VeDeyoth* 1:3, ninth opinion. Also see *Bereshith Rabbah* 12:1; *Koheleth Rabbah* 2:14. *Sifri*, Deuteronomy 307.

4. *Chovoth HaLevavoth* 2:5; Rabbi Abba Mari (ben Yosef) HaYarchi don Estrok, *Minchath Kenaoth* 7 (Pressberg, 1838), p. 8; Rabbi Yosef (ben Yehudah) ibn Aknin, *Sefer Mussar* on Avoth 3:17 (edited by Binyamin Zeev Bacher, Berlin, 1910); Rabbi Moshe de Leon, *Shekel HaKodesh* (London, 1911), p. 5; Rabbi Yehudah Chayit, *Minchath Yehudah* on *Maarekheth Elohuth*, Chapter 11 (Mantua, 1558), p. 161b; quoted in *Sh'nei Luchoth HaB'rith, Shaar HaGadol* (Lvov, 1860) 1:46b; Rabbi Shneur Zalman of Liadi, *Likutey Torah, Pekudey* (New York, 1973), p. 4b; Rabbi Menachem Mendel of Lubavitch, *Derekh Mitzvothekha* (New York, 1956), p. 45a; *Noam HaMitzvoth* 467. Cf. *Bereshith Rabbah* 48:2.

5. *Moreh Nevukhim* 1:4.

6. *Chovoth HaLevavoth* 1:6, end. Cf. Rabbi Elchanan Wasserman, *Kovetz Maamarim* (Jerusalem, 1963), p. 13.

7. Yad, *Yesodey HaTorah* 1:6; *Sefer HaMitzvoth*, Positive Commandment 1; *Sefer Mitzvoth Gadol*, Positive Commandment 1. Also see *Zohar* 2:25a, 3:256b. However, the Ramban on *Sefer HaMitzvoth*, loc. cit., disputes this, arguing that it is inappropriate to regard the foundation of our faith as a mere commandment. Since it is a commandment, however, it may be rewarded. Also see *Teshuvoth Tashbatz* 1:139; Abarbanel, *Rosh Amanah* 7.

8. *Sefer HaChinukh* 25.

1:9   From its wording, it is evident that this commandment includes an injunction to believe in God both as the God of creation, and as the God of history.[9]

1:10   Judaism therefore rejects the deistic concept that God created the universe, and then abandoned it with neither ruler, guide nor judge.[10]

1:11   The existence of God as the ethical Power and motivating Force behind the universe is indicated by the experience of men and nations that only the good is stable, while evil tends to destroy itself. It is thus written, "There are many thoughts in man's heart, but it is God's counsel that shall endure" (Proverbs 19:21).[11]

1:12   The second of the Ten Commandments reads, "You shall have no other gods before Me" (Exodus 20:3). This is a negative commandment not to believe in any deity other than the one true God, Creator of the universe.[12] This commandment also depends on thought and can be observed at all times.[13]

1:13   This commandment forbids us to accept any being, entity or object as a deity and call it a god.[14] This is true even if one still believes in the one true God.[15]

1:14   This commandment also forbids us to accept any being, entity or object as a mediator between God and man. This is also considered idolatry.[16]

---

9. Ramban on Exodus 20:2; *Sefer HaChinukh, loc. cit.*
10. See *Kuzari* 1:1,2. *Cf.* Commentaries on Ezekiel 8:12, 9:9.
11. *Avoth* 4:11, 5:17.
12. *Yad, Yesodey HaTorah* 1:6; *Sefer HaMitzvoth*, Negative Commandment 1; *Sefer Mitzvoth Gadol*, Negative Commandment 1.
13. *Sefer HaChinukh* 26.
14. Ramban on Exodus 20:3, from *Sanhedrin* 7:6 (60b).
15. *Cf. Sanhedrin* 63a, *Tosafoth ad loc. s.v. Kol; Sefer Mitzvoth Gadol*, Negative Commandment 1. Also see *Mekhilta*, Ibn Ezra, on Exodus 22:19.
16. *Yad, Avodath Kokhavim* 1:1; *Moreh Nevukhim* 1:36.

1:15   It is for this reason that Judaism utterly rejected the Christian concept of a mediator between God and man.

1:16   Most authorities extend this prohibition to Jew and non-Jew alike.[17] Others, however, maintain that a non-Jew may accept another being as a deity or mediator, as long as he does not actually worship it as an idol, and also believes in God.[18] They base this on the verse, "Lest . . . you be drawn astray and worship them, the ones God your Lord has allotted to all the gentiles . . . (Deuteronomy 4:19).[19] According to the second opinion, Christianity may be a permissible religion for non-Jews, and it may be in fulfillment of God's ultimate purpose.[20]

1:17   Of all the Ten Commandments, only these first two are written in the first person. According to tradition, only these two commandments were given to us directly by God, while all the others were transmitted by Him through Moses.[21]

17. See *Yad, Melakhim* 9:3, where no exceptions are made. Also see *Teshuvoth Nodeh BeYehudah*, Tinyana, *Yoreh Deah* 148; *Teshuvoth Meil Tzadakah* 22; *Teshuvoth Shaar Ephraim* 24; *Pith'chey Teshuvah, Yoreh Deah* 147:2; *Pri Megadim, Eshel Avraham* 156:2, *Sifethey Daath (Yoreh Deah)* 65:11; *Chatham Sofer* on *Orach Chaim* 156:1; *Minchath Chinukh* 86.

18. *Tosafoth, Bekhoroth* 2b, s.v. *Shema, Sanhedrin* 63b, s.v. *Assur; Orach Chaim* 156:1 in *Hagah; Rosh, Sanhedrin* 7:3 (but see *Pilpula Charifta ad loc.*); *Darkey Moshe, Yoreh Deah* 151; *Sifethey Cohen (Shakh), Yoreh Deah* 151:7; *Machtzith HaShekel, Orach Chaim* 156:2; *Teshuvoth Tashbatz* 1:139; *Teshuvoth VeShev HaCohen* 38; *Mishnath Chakhamim* on *Yad, Yesodey HaTorah*, quoted in *Pith'chey Teshuvah, loc. cit.*; Rabbi Tzvi Hirsh Chajas (Maharatz Chayoth) on *Horioth* 8b. There is another opinion that non-Jews are only forbidden to make use of a mediator in the Land of Israel, see Ramban on Leviticus 18:25; Yaakov Emdin, *Mor U'Ketziah* 224; Maharatz Chayoth on *Berakhoth* 57a.

19. Cf. Rashbam *ad loc.; Derekh Mitzvothekha* 59b.

20. Cf. *Yad, Melakhim* 11:4 (only in Rome, 1475, and Amsterdam, 1703, editions); quoted in Ramban, *Torath HaShem Temimah* (in *Kithvey Ramban*, Jerusalem, 1963) p. 144; *Teshuvoth Rambam* 58; *Kuzari* 4:23; *Teshuvoth Rivash* 119; *Akedath Yitzchak* 88.

21. *Makkoth* 24a, top. In *Shir HaShirim Rabbah* 1:13, however, there is a dispute regarding this, and some maintain that all the Ten Commandments were given directly. See Ramban on Exodus 20:7, and on *Sefer HaMitzvoth*, Shoresh 1. Also see *Pirkey Rabbi Eliezer* 41, Radal *ad loc.* 41:77. Cf. *Moreh Nevukhim* 2:33; *Teshuvoth Radbaz* 817, that the very fact of revelation demonstrated these two commandments. Cf. *Shemoth Rabbah* 42:7.

Regarding this, it is written, "God has spoken once, two of which I heard" (Psalms 62:12).[22]

1:18   If a person denies the existence of God, or accepts any other being as a deity, he is denying the very essence of Judaism,[23] and is totally rejected by God.[24] This is the only case in which one can be punished for mere thought.[25]

1:19   We are commanded always to be aware of God and not to forget Him and His miracles, as it is written, "Beware, lest you forget God, who brought you out of the land of Egypt, from the house of slavery" (Deuteronomy 6:12). We are likewise warned not to forget God by ignoring His commandments, as it is written, "Beware, lest you forget God your Lord in not keeping His commandments, His decrees and His laws" (Deuteronomy 8:11). Some authorities count this as a negative commandment.[26]

1:20   One should therefore constantly be aware of God's presence, and the Psalmist thus said, "I have set God before me at all times" (Psalms 16:8).[27]

1:21   We are similarly enjoined not to forget the revelation at Sinai where the Ten Commandments were given. It is thus written, "Take the utmost care, and watch yourselves scrupulously, so that you not forget the things that you saw with your own eyes, that they not fade from your mind as long as you live. Make them known to your children, and to

22. Rashi, *Makkoth* 24a, s.v. *MiPi*; *Moreh Nevukhim, loc. cit.*
23. *Yad, Yesodey HaTorah* 1:6, *Avodath Kokhavim* 2:4. Cf. *Kiddushin* 40a.
24. *Tosefta, Shevuoth* 3:5. In Hebrew, the term is *kofer ba-ikkar* (כּוֹפֵר בָּעִיקָר). See *Yad, loc. cit.*
25. *Emunoth VeDeyoth* 5:8; *Kiddushin* 39a; from Ezekiel 14:5, see *Radak ad loc.*
26. *Ramban*, additions to *Sefer HaMitzvoth*, Negative Commandment 1, quoting *Halakhoth Gedoloth, Sefer Mitzvoth Gadol*, Negative Commandment 64; *Rabbenu Yonah, Shaarey Teshuvah* 3:27; *Cheredim*, Negative Commandment 1:6.
27. Rashi, *Radak, ad loc.*; *Moreh Nevukhim* 3:51,52; *Orach Chaim* 1:1 in *Hagah.* Cf. *Sanhedrin* 22a; *Reshith Chokhmah, Shaar HaYirah* 1 (Munkatch, 1896), p. 8d.

your children's children: The day that you stood before God at Horeb . . ." (Deuteronomy 4:9,10). This is stated in the most emphatic terms, and it is counted by some authorities as a negative commandment.[28]

26. Ramban, additions to *Sefer HaMitzvoth*, Negative Commandment 2, and commentary on Deuteronomy 4:9; *Sefer Mitzvoth Gadol*, Negative Commandment 13; *Sefer Mitzvoth Katan* 15; Rabbenu Yonah, *Shaarey Teshuvah* 3:28. Cf. *Menachoth* 99b.

TWO

GOD

2:1   God is defined as the Creator of the universe, as the opening verse of the Torah states, "In the beginning God created the heaven and the earth" (Genesis 1:1). God likewise said, "I am God, I make all things" (Isaiah 44:24).[1]

2:2   As Creator of the universe, God must be distinct from the world. Judaism therefore rejects the philosophy of pantheism.

2:3   As Creator of the universe, God's existence cannot depend on any of His handiwork. Judaism therefore rejects any definition of God as an abstract ethical force or social convention.[2]

2:4   As Creator of all, God is on a higher plane than His handiwork. He is therefore referred to as the Supreme Being.[3]

1. Also see Jeremiah 10:12, Zechariah 12:1, Psalms 33:6, 89:12, Nehemiah 9:6. Cf. *Emunoth VeDeyoth* 1:1; *Yad, Yesodey HaTorah* 1:1,5. When God reveals Himself, He does so as the Creator; cf. *Mekhilta* to Exodus 6:2; *Sifra* on Leviticus 18:2.
2. Thus, God cannot be defined as love, truth, justice, goodness, or in any other human terms. While these are attributes of God, they are not God Himself. See *Pardes Rimonim* 3:1; *Tikuney Zohar Chadash* 115c; *Zohar* 1:22a. Also see *Yad, Yesodey HaTorah* 1:4; Rabbi Avraham Yonah Yevnin of Gorodno, *Nimukey Mahari* ad loc. Cf. Radak on Jeremiah 10:10; *Yerushalmi, Berakhoth* 1:5 (9b) (in Vilna edition); *VaYikra Rabbah* 26:1 (in Warsaw edition).
3. Ibid. Also see Numbers 24:16, Deuteronomy 32:8, 2 Samuel 22:14, Psalms 7:17,

2:5   As Creator, God is absolutely different from anything else that exists. He is therefore totally unknowable.[4]

2:6   Although God himself is unknowable, we can, to some degree, understand His relationship to the universe. In this manner, we speak of God through His "attributes of action." Also, although we cannot know what God *is*, we can learn much by realizing what He *is not*. In this sense, we speak of God using "negative attributes."[5]

2:7   It is a foundation of our faith to believe that God is One, and that He is a most perfect and absolute Unity.[6]

2:8   It is written, "Hear O Israel, God is our Lord, God is One" (Deuteronomy 6:4). This is a positive commandment to believe in God's unity.[7] This commandment depends on thought and can be fulfilled at any time.[8]

2:9   Although the universe contains many galaxies, each consisting of innumerable stars and planets, there is one God who is Author and Creator of them all.[9] It is absolutely impossible to conceive of more than one Absolute Being.[10]

2:10   Although there may be many other universes, both physical and spiritual, God is One over all. It is thus written,

Radak ad loc. God is called the "highest of the highest," see *Tikuney Zohar* 17a; *Pardes Rimonim* 3:1.
4. *Shomer Emunim (HaKadmon)* 2:11, sixth principle. See below, 2:49.
5. *Moreh Nevukhim* 1:58; *Kuzari* 2:2; *Ikkarim* 2:22. Thus, defining God as Creator, or saying that He is good, merciful or just, involve "attributes of action." Saying that His is one (nonplural), incorporeal, or unknowable, involves "negative attributes." Since two different methods are used to speak of God, there are times when the two conflict, giving rise to theological paradoxes.
6. Thirteen Principles of Faith 2. See Rambam on Mishnah, *Sanhedrin* 10:1.
7. *Yad, Yesodey Hatorah* 1:7; *Sefer HaMitzvoth*, Positive Commandment 2; *Sefer Mitzvoth Gadol*, Positive Commandment 2; *Tur, Orach Chaim* 61.
8. *Sefer HaChinukh* 417.
9. Cf. *Moreh Nevukhim* 2:1 (end). See 1:4.
10. *Moreh Nevukhim* 1:75. There can not be more than one Creator of *all things*.

"Your kingdom is a kingdom of all worlds" (Psalms 145:13).[11]

2:11   Judaism emphatically rejects any concept of plurality with respect to God.[12] It therefore rejects the Christian concept of the trinity, in which God is depicted as three persons in one, corresponding to His manifestation in creation, redemption and revelation.[13]

2:12   Since any additional quality would add an element of plurality to God's essence, we conceive of Him as being absolutely simple. His simple essence, however, implies every attribute with which He created and rules His universe.[14]

2:13   As Creator, God's power in His universe is unlimited. We therefore speak of God as being omnipotent, and refer to Him in our prayer as "King of the universe." It is likewise written, "All that God wishes, He does, in heaven and earth, in the seas and all the deeps" (Psalms 135:6).[15]

11. *Metzudoth David ad loc.* Cf. *Reshith Chokhmah, Shaar HaYirah* 1 (9a); *Teshuvoth Radbaz* 2116.
12. With regard to the Sephiroth, see *Pardes Rimonim* 4. The charge of pluralism was even leveled against the Kabbalists by those who did not know their interpretation of the Sephiroth; see *Teshuvoth Rashbash* 189; *Teshuvoth Rivash* 157; Rabbi Avraham Abulafia, *VeZoth LeYehuduh* (in A. Jellinek, *Ginzey Chokhmath HaKabbalah*, Leipzig, 1853), p. 19.
13. *Emunoth VeDeyoth* 2:5-7; Rambam, *Iggereth Techiyath HaMethim* (Warsaw, 1926), p. 3; *Moreh Nevukhim* 1:50; *Teshuvoth Meil Tzadakah* 22; *Teshuvoth Shaar Ephraim* 24; *Chatham Sofer* on *Orach Chaim* 156:1. See Chapter 1, note 17. Similarly, although God is called the "Knower, the Knowledge, and the Known," this does not contradict His unity, since He and His knowledge are one; *Yad, Yesodey HaTorah* 2:20; Rabbi Moshe Cordevero (Ramak), *Shiur Komah* 13:12 (Warsaw, 1883) 14a; *Pardes Rimonim* 4:3. Regarding such "essential attributes" as knowledge, will and ability, see *Emunoth VeDeyoth* 2:1 (44a); *Pardes Rimonim* 4:9. Cf. *Moreh Nevukhim* 1:53,56; *Zohar* 2:42b; *Zohar Chadash* 34d; *Tikuney Zohar* 17b; *Derekh HaShem* 1:1:5.
14. *Or HaShem* 1:3:4: (Vienna, 1860), p. 26a; *Sh'nei Luchoth HaB'rith, Beth David* (note) 1:42a; *Derekh HaShem* 1:1:5; *Yad, Yesodey HaTorah* 2:10. This paradoxical situation develops because when we speak of God through negative attributes, we speak of Him as being simple, while when we speak of Him through attributes of action, we speak of Him as having every possible perfection. See note 5.
15. Cf. *Bereshith Rabbah* 28:2, 48:22; *Tanchuma, Shemoth* 18, *Korach* 9; *Midrash Tehillim* 62:1, 107:3; Rav Nissim Gaon on *Berakhoth* 32a.

2:14   We do not, however, ascribe to God the power of doing that which is categorically impossible, such as duplicating, annihilating, corporifying, or changing Himself.[16] Judaism therefore rejects the possibility that God could have ever assumed human form.[17]

2:15   Since God is the Creator of all matter, it is obvious that He does not consist of matter.

2:16   Because of God's antithesis to all material attributes, He is called Pure[18] and Holy.[19]

2:17   As Creater of *all* things, God is also the Creator of space and time. He therefore does not exist in space and time.[20]

2:18   It is therefore taught that God is given the appellation "Place," *Makom* (מָקוֹם) in Hebrew. The universe of space and time is a creation of God, and does not contain Him.[21]

16. *Moreh Nevukhim* 3:15. Also see *Pardes Rimonim* 2:7; *Shefa Tal* 1:3. This is not a definite statement, however, since we cannot ascribe any impotence to God; Rabbi Aaron Marcus, *Keseth HaSofer* 9a. Here again, however, we see God's omnipotence as an attribute of action, while the impossibility of His duplication, annihilation, corporification, and alteration involves negative attributes. See note 5. Moreover, any of these "impossible tasks" would involve a change of "mind" on the part of God, which is also impossible. See 2:29. Also see *Moreh Nevukhim* 3:25. This is closely related to the commonly asked paradoxical question as to whether or not God can create a stone that He cannot lift.

17. *Yerushalmi, Taanith* 2:1 (9a), from Numbers 23:19. The incarnation, of course, is a basic tenet of Christianity.

18. Cf. *Berakhoth* 10a; *VaYikra Rabbah* 4:8; *Devarim Rabbah* 2:26; from Habakkuk 1:13.

19. *Kuzari* 4:3. Cf. Leviticus 19:2, 21:8, Isaiah 6:3; *VaYikra Rabbah* 24:9; *Tosafoth, Kiddushin* 2b, s.v. *DeAssar*.

20. *Emunoth VeDeyoth* 2:11,12; *Sh'vil Emunah ad loc.* 2:11:10; *Moreh Nevukhim* 2:8, 2:30; *Ikkarim* 2:18; *Asarah Maamaroth, Choker Din* 1:16; *Derekh Mitzvothekha* 57b. Moreover, if God existed in the space-time continuum, then He could be assigned a position in this continuum. It would then be possible to speak of two concepts with relation to God, namely, His essence and His position. This would introduce an element of plurality which is not permissible.

21. *Bereshith Rabbah* 68:10; *Shemoth Rabbah* 45:6; *Midrash Tehillim* 50; Rashi, *Baaley Tosafoth*, on Exodus 33:21; *Pesikta Rabathai* 21 (104b); *Radak* on Psalms 90:1; *Nefesh HaChaim* 3:1-3. If each letter of the Tetragrammaton (YHVH, יהוה) is squared, their sum is 186, the numerical value of *Makom*. Abudarham on Haggadah, s.v. *Barukh HaMakom* (Jerusalem, 1963), p. 224; *Shiur Komah* 20 (35b). [Also see *Sefer Yetzirah* 1:5.]

2:19   The human mind can only deal with physical concepts, and it is therefore virtually impossible for it to picture any existence outside of space and time. This is but another reason that God's Essence is unknowable.[22]

2:20   Body, shape and form are all attributes of space. It is therefore obvious that God has neither body, shape nor form.[23]

2:21   It is a foundation of our faith to believe that God is absolutely incorporeal. The Torah therefore states, "Take good heed of yourselves, for you saw no manner of form on that day that God spoke to you at Horeb . . ." (Deuteronomy 4:15).[24]

2:22   God is therefore not to be compared to any of His creatures, even to the highest angels. The prophet thus declared, "To whom will you then liken God? To what likeness will you compare Him?" (Isaiah 40:18). It is likewise written, "There is none like You, O God" (Jeremiah 10:6).[25] The Psalmist similarly said, "There are none like You among the Powers (angels), O God, and there are no works like Yours" (Psalms 86:8).[26]

2:23   In many places, the Torah speaks of God as though He had a human body, using anthropomorphisms such as, "the hand of God" (Exodus 9:15), and "the eyes of God"

22. *Emunoth VeDeyoth* 1:4.
23. *Yad, Yesodey HaTorah* 1:8, 1:11; from *Chagigah* 15a; *Moreh Nevukhim* 1:35, 2:1 (end); *Kuzari* 5:18 #6. Cf. *Tanna DeBei Eliahu Rabbah* 1 (with commentary *Ranathayin Tzofin*, Warsaw, 1881), p. 9a.
24. Thirteen Principles of Faith 3; *Yad Teshuvah* 3:6; Raavad *ad. loc.*; *Ikkarim* 1:2; *Iggereth Techiyath HaMethim*, p. 4.
25. *Yad Yesodey HaTorah* 1:8; *Moreh Nevukhim* 1:35, 1:55; *Zohar* 3:225a in *Raya Mehemna*; *Reshith Chokhmah, Shaar HaYirah* 1 (9a).
26. Cf. *Targum ad loc.*; *Emunoth VeDeyoth* 2:1. See *Mekhilta* on Exodus 14:29; *Bereshith Rabbah* 21:5; *Shir HaShirim Rabbah* 1:46; *Sefer Chasidim* 605; *Makor Chesed ad loc.* 605:20.

(Deuteronomy 11:12). In doing so, the Torah is in no way asserting that God has a body, shape or form. Rather, it borrows terms from God's creatures[27] allegorically to express His relation to His creation.[28]

2:24 Similarly, when the Torah states that God created man in His image (Genesis 1:27), it by no means implies that God looks like man. What it means is that man partakes of the same attributes that God uses when He interacts with His world.[29] It also implies that God gave man the ability to use the same logic with which He created the universe.[30]

2:25 Moses asked God, "Let me behold Your Glory" (Exodus 33:18). In making this request, he did not actually wish to see God, since that would be impossible. In an allegorical manner, he was merely requesting that God grant him a prophetic comprehension of His greatness. God replied that this is impossible for any living creature, saying, "You cannot see My Face, for man cannot see Me and live" (Exodus 33:20). He did allow Moses the greatest comprehension of God ever granted to any human being, but even this was not a perfect understanding. This is what God meant when He allegorically told Moses, "You shall see My back, but My Face shall not be seen" (Exodus 33:23).

---

27. *Mekhilta*, Rashi, on Exodus 19:18; *Tanchuma, Yithro* 13; *Bereshith Rabbah* 27:1; *Koheleth Rabbah* 2:24; *Midrash Tehillim* 1; *Pesikta* 4 (36b); *Yad, Yesodey HaTorah* 1:9; *Moreh Nevukhim* 1:26, 1:47; *Emunoth VeDeyoth* 2:10; *Chovoth HaLevavoth* 1:10; *Kuzari* 4:3 (18a).
28. Ramban on Genesis 46:1; Maharal, *Tifereth Yisrael* 33. Cf. *Tikuney Zohar* 17a; *Avodath HaKodesh, Chelek HaTachlith* 26; *Pardes Rimonim* 22:1; *Sh'nei Luchoth HaB'rith, Beth Yisrael* (1:15b); *Nefesh HaChaim* 2:2, 2:5, note s.v. *VeZehu*.
29. *Nefesh HaChaim* 1·1; *Avodath HaKodesh, Chelek HaYichud* 18. Also see *Mekhilta* on Exodus 14:29; *Bereshith Rabbah* 21:5; *Shir HaShirim Rabbah* 1:46; *Yad, Teshuvah* 5:1.
30. God was not restrained to create the world with the logic that it now has. If He were, He would be subservient to logic, which is unthinkable. See *Kalach Pith'chey :hmah* 30 (22b). Therefore, if the universe seems logical to us, it is because God us the same logic that He used in creation.

The same was true of the other "visions" of God experienced by the prophets.[31]

2:26   When the Torah speaks of people hearing God's "voice,"
it usually refers to a prophetic voice within the individual's
mind. At other times, God might actually create sound
waves to convey His message.[32]

2:27   God is always referred to as "He" in the masculine
gender. This is because there is no neuter in the Hebrew
language, and the Hebrew word for God is masculine. The
feminine gender is not used because God is an active force in
the universe.[33]

2:28   God is spoken of as being "eternal," that is, as existing
outside the realm of time. Time as such does not apply to
God Himself, only to His creation. God therefore has neither
beginning, end nor age, since these concepts would imply
existence within a framework of time.[34]

2:29   God Himself is therefore absolutely unchangeable and
unchanging. He thus said, "I am God, I do not change"
(Malachi 3:6).[35]

2:30   As Creator of time, God can make use of it without
becoming involved in it. He can therefore cause change in
the world without being changed Himself. God is thus called
the "unmoved Mover."[36]

31. Yad, Yesodey HaTorah 1:10; Moreh Nevukhim 1:5, 1:54, Emunoth VeDeyoth 2:12; Kuzari 4:3 (23a).
32. Moreh Nevukhim 1:21, 1:65; Kuzari 1:89, Shiur Komah 32; Avodath HaKodesh 4:31,33; Rabbi Eliezer of Garmiza, Sodi Razia (Bilgorey, 1936), p. 42.
33. Cf. Berakhoth 32a; Bereshith Rabbah 13:14; Ikkarim 2:11; Akedath Yitzchak 4 (36b); Shiur Komah 18.
34. Yad, Yesodey HaTorah 1:10; Emunoth VeDeyoth 2:10; Kuzari 5:18 #5; Ikkarim 2:18,19; Pardes Rimonim 3:1. Cf. Bereshith Rabbah 81:2; Mekhilta on Exodus 22:3; VaYikra Rabbah 19:2 (end); Ibn Ezra on Ecclesiastes 3:15.
35. Yad, Yesodey HaTorah 1:10,11; Moreh Nevukhim 1:11.
36. Cheredim 5 (Jerusalem, 1958), p. 42; Anonymous Commentary on Yad, Yesodey HaTorah 1:1,5.

2:31   There are statements in the Torah that may seem to contradict this. Thus, the Torah appears to ascribe emotions such as joy and anger to God. But here too, it is merely speaking of God's interaction with man. We perceive God's actions, and ascribe to Him the same emotions that we ourselves would feel if we were performing a similar act. Thus, for example, when God punishes, we say that He is "angry." None of this, however, is meant to imply any change in God Himself.[37] Even the creation of the universe did not change God in any way. Similarly, it did not involve any change of God's mind. It cannot be said that at a particular moment He suddenly decided to create a world. A statement such as this has no meaning, since time, and hence, the very concept of change, were among the things created by God.[38] Therefore, both before and after creation, God was absolutely the same.[39]

2:32   Creation therefore did not fill any need in God's being. God is inherently perfect, and does not have any need for the universe.[40]

2:33   In absolutely no way can it be said that God was compelled to create the world.[41] Hence, creation was nothing less than an act of absolute altruism on the part of God.[42]

2:34   God is called "living" because He performs acts that are normally ascribed to living things.[43]

37. *Yad, Yesodey HaTorah* 1:11; *Moreh Nevukhim* 1:54; *Emunoth VeDeyoth* 2:11; *Ikkarim* 2:15,16. Cf. *Pardes Rimonim* 4:3.
38. *Shomer Emunim (HaKadmon)* 2:17.
39. *Cheredim* 5 (p. 40); *Sh'nei Luchoth HaB'rith, Beth HaShem* (note on 1:6a). Cf. *Pirkey Rabbi Eliezer* 3.
40. *Yad, Yesodey HaTorah* 1:2,3; *Moreh Nevukhim* 3:13; *Emunoth VeDeyoth* 1:4; *Sh'vil Emunah ad loc.* 1:4:9; *Reshith Chokhmah, Shaar HaYirah* 1 (8d). Cf. *Pesikta* 6 (57b); *Moreh Nevukhim* 3:25.
41. *Akedath Yitzchak* 4 (35b); *Likutey Moharan* 52. Cf. Rabbi Yitzchak Adarbi, *Divrey Shalom, Derush* 9.
42. *Emunoth VeDeyoth* 3:0; *Shevil Emunah ad loc.* 3:0:1.
43. *Kuzari* 2:2, 5:18 #8; *Emunoth VeDeyoth* 2:1; *Yad, Yesodey HaTorah* 1:11, 2:10. Cf.

2:35   Our understanding of God's relationship to the world is twofold, namely, that He is both immanent and transcendental.[44] Thus, He both fills and encompasses all creation.[45] This duality, however, is only due to our imperfect understanding of God, since He Himself is the most absolute Unity.[46]

2:36   This twofold concept is expressed in the song of the angels. They sing, "Holy, holy, holy is God of Hosts, the whole world is filled with His Glory" (Isaiah 6:3). This indicates that God is immanent, filling all creation. However, they also sing, "Blessed is God's Glory from His place" (Ezekiel 3:12). Here they are speaking of God in His transcendental sense, where even the highest angels cannot comprehend His "place."[47]

Deuteronomy 5:23, Ibn Ezra *ad loc.; Jeremiah* 10:10, *Hosea* 2:1, *Psalms* 42:3; Radak *ad loc.; Tosefoth Yom Tov, Tamid* 7:4; Rav Nissim Gaon, *Berakhoth* 32a;
44. Cf. *Megillah* 31a; Ibn Ezra on *Psalms* 113:5.
45. *Raya Mehemna, Zohar* 3:225a; *Reshith Chokhmah, Shaar HaYirah* 1 (9a); *Nefesh HaChaim* 3:4; *Likutey Amarim (Tanya), Shaar HaYichud VeHaEmunah* 7 (83b).
46. *Sh'nei Luchoth HaB'rith, Beth HaBechirah* (1:44a), *BaAsarah Maamaroth* (1:64b); *Likutey Amarim (Tanya)* loc. cit. (84a). An example is a three dimensional space surrounding a two dimensional plane. The space both surrounds the plane, and at the same time, touches every point on it. Similarly, God, who transcends all space and dimension, both saturates and encompasses the space-time continuum. It is also taught that God "removed" His essence from a certain domain, forming a "vacated space" in which He created the space-time continuum; *Etz Chaim, Derush Egolim VeYosher* 2; *Mavo Shaarim* 1:1:1; *Likutey Moharan* 49; also *Pardes Rimonim* 4:9, 6:3; *Shefa Tal* 6:1 (89b, 90d), 6:8 (101a); *Bahir* 14; *Zohar HaRakiu* on *Zohar* 1:16a. This "removal" or constriction *(tzimtzum)* involved God's "light," and not His essence; *Shaarey Gan Eden, Orach Tzadikim* 2:1; *Pelach Rimon* 4:3; *Derekh Mitzvothekha, Emunath Elokuth* 6 (51a), *Shoresh Mitzvath Tefillah* 34 (136a). Also see *Shomer Emunim* 2:49; *KaLaCh Pith'chey Chokhmah* 24; *Likutey Amarim, Shaar HaYichud VeHeEmunah* 7. A paradox is raised, since after the "removal," we must say that God is absent from the "vacated space," but on the other hand, this cannot be said; *Likutey Moharan* 64. But from a viewpoint of attributes of action, God is removed from the "vacated space," but from a viewpoint of negative attributes, we cannot say that He is absent from any place. From the viewpoint that He is in the vacated space, God is imminent, while from the viewpoint that he is absent, He is transcendental; *Likutey Moharan* 64:2.
47. Cf. *Chagigah* 13b; *Pirkey Rabbi Eliezer* 4 (end); *Moreh Nevukhim* 1:8; *Nefesh HaChaim* 3:6.

2:37   This is also expressed in the Sh'ma, which states, "Hear O Israel, God is our Lord, God is One" (Deuteronomy 6:4). Before declaring that God is an unknowable transcendental Unity, we declare that He is "our Lord" — accessible to us at all times. Similarly, in every blessing, before addressing God as the transcendental "King of the universe," we also call Him "our Lord." In the prayer, "Our Father, our King" (*Avinu Malkenu,* אָבִינוּ מַלְכֵּנוּ), we likewise liken God to both an immanent Father and a transcendental King.

2:38   God's immanence implies that there is no place in all creation that is devoid of His being. He is therefore spoken of as being omnipresent. The Torah thus says, "All the earth is filled with God's Glory" (Numbers 14:21). It is likewise written, "His Glory is in heaven and earth" (Psalms 148:13).[48]

2:39   In a number of places, the Torah speaks of God as being in a certain place at a given time. This does not mean that God is in that place and not elsewhere. Rather, it means that God wishes to bestow special honor and attention to that place, or, alternatively, that His action is particularly visible there. Thus, God was said to "dwell" in the Holy Temple (*Beth Hamikdash,* בֵּית הַמִּקְדָּשׁ) because He bestowed special honor and attention to this edifice. God was said to "lead" the Israelites at the Exodus because His activities were particularly visible in relation to them.[49]

2:40   Nothing can exist unless God wills it to exist. If God were to stop willing anything's existence, it would

48. *Berakhoth* 10a; *VaYikra Rabbah* 4:8; *Devarim Rabbah* 2:26; *Midrash Tehillim* 24:5 (103a); *BaMidbar Rabbah* 12:4; *Pesikta* 1 (2b); *Yalkut Shimoni* 2:986; *Raya Mehemna, Zohar* 2:42b; *Shiur Komah* 33; *Reshith Chokhmah, Shaar HaYirah* 1 (7a, 8c, 8d); *Radak* on Jeremiah 23:24.
49. *Mekhilta,* Ibn Ezra on Exodus 13:21; *Emunoth VeDeyoth* 2:11; *Kuzari* 2:7,8; *Moreh*

instantaneously cease to exist. God's will must therefore permeate all creation. But since God is an absolute Unity, His will must be identical with His essence. Since God's will must fill all creation, the same must also be true of His Essence.[50]

2:41   The existence of all creation thus continuously depends on God's will and creative power. If this power were removed from creation for even an instant, all things would instantly cease to exist. It is thus written, "You have made the heaven . . . the earth and all that is on it . . . and You give life to them all" (Nehemiah 9:6). God constantly gives "Life Force" and existence to all things. In the morning prayers, we likewise say, "In His goodness, He daily renews the act of creation."[51]

2:42   Although God's presence fills all creation, His existence is absolutely undetectable. The prophet therefore said to God, "Certainly, You are a God who hides Himself" (Isaiah 45:15).[52] If God would reveal His true Glory, all creation would be nullified before it.[53]

2:43   Furthermore, God cannot be seen because there is no place empty of Him. The reason is very much like the reason that the air cannot be seen; it is an integral part of our

Nevukhim 1:19, 1:27; Ramban on Genesis 46:1; *Ikkarim* 2:17. Cf. *Sukkah* 53a; Rashi ad loc, s.v. *Im.*; *Shiur Komah* 23.

50. Cf. *Moreh Nevukhim* 1.69.
51. *Ibid.*; *Kuzari* 4:26; Ibn Ezra on Exodus 3:2; Ramban on Genesis 1:4; Ralbag on Nehemiah 9:6; *Yad, Yesodey HaTorah* 2:9; *Zohar* 3:31a, 3:225a; *Pardes Rimonim* 6:8; *Tosefoth Yom Tov, Tamid* 7:4; *Reshith Chokhmah, Shaar HaYirah* 1 (9b), *Shaar HaAhavah* 5 (63d); *Nefesh HaChaim* 1:2; *Likutey Amarim, Shaar HaYichud VeHaEmunah* 2 (77b). Cf. *Midrash Tehillim* 119:36, from Psalms 119:89; *Berakhoth* 10a; *VaYikra Rabbah* 4:8, from Isaiah 46:4; *Devarim Rabbah* 2:26; *Pirkey Rabbi Eliezer* 7; 18; 34; Radal *ad loc.* 7:6, 18:9, 34:75, 48:5. Also see *Kiddushin* 32b; *Avodah Zarah* 3b; *Mekhilta* on Exodus 18:12.
52. Cf. Isaiah 45:15. See *Berakhoth* 10a; *VaYikra Rabbah* 4:8; *Devarim Rabbah* 2:36; *Midrash Tehillim* 103:1; *Pirkey Rabbi Eliezer* 34. See below, 3:9.
53. *Chullin* 60a, top; *Yalkut Shimoni* 1:396. Cf. Exodus 33:20.

environment, and this is all the more true of God. The reason we cannot see God is not because He is too transcendental, but because He is too immanent. The only time we are aware of the air is when the wind blows. Similarly, we are only aware of God when He acts to manifest His presence. This is why the same word, *ruach* (רוּחַ) denotes both wind and spirit.[54]

2:44   It is a foundation of our faith to believe that God knows all our deeds as well as everything else that occurs in the universe.[55]

2:45   God is therefore spoken of as being omniscient. He fills all creation and gives it existence, and therefore, He is aware of all that takes place in it. God thus said, "Can a man hide himself in secret places so that I will not see him? . . . Do I then not fill heaven and earth?" (Jeremiah 23:24). It is likewise written, "God's eyes are in every place, beholding the evil and the good" (Proverbs 15:3).[56]

2:46   God knows man's thoughts, as it is written, "God probes every heart and perceives every urge of thought" (1 Chronicles 28:9). It is likewise written, "[God] knows the secrets of the heart" (Psalms 44:21).[57]

2:47   Since God exists outside of time, He knows the future exactly as He knows the past. This precise concept is expressed in His words to His prophet, "I call the

54. See *Moreh Nevukhim* 1:40; Raavad on *Sefer Yetzirah* 1:9.
55. Thirteen Principles of Faith 10.
56. *Tanchuma, Naso* 5; *Yalkut Shimoni* 2:305; *Mekhilta* on Exodus 12:13; *Bereshith Rabbah* 9:3; *Kuzari* 5:18 #7; *Yad, Yesodey HaTorah* 2:9,10; *Teshuvoth Rivash* 439. Cf. Psalms 33:13,14; 94:9, 139:12; Job 28:24; 2 Chronicles 16:9.
57. *Bereshith Rabbah* 9:3; *Shemoth Rabbah* 21:3; *Yerushalmi, Rosh HaShanah* 1:3 (8a); *Tanna DeBei Eliahu Zuta* 23 (50b).

generations from the beginning; I, God, am the First, and
with the last I am the same" (Isaiah 41:4).[58]

2:48   God's knowledge is identical with His infinite Essence,
and it is therefore also infinite. It is thus written, "[God's]
understanding is infinite" (Psalms 147:5). God can therefore
know what is happening to every single atom in the universe
at every given instant. No matter how great the number of
simultaneous events, it is nothing compared to God's
infinite knowledge.[59]

2:49   Above and beyond all this, God is so high above us that it
is utterly impossible to comprehend Him in any manner
whatsoever. It is thus written, "Can you by searching find
out God? Can you probe the Almighty to perfection?" (Job
11:7). God's Essence transcends our very powers of
thought, as He told His prophet, "My thoughts are not your
thoughts, nor are My ways your ways" (Isaiah 48:17).[60]

2:50   It is thus taught, "No thought can grasp Him at all."[61]
Just as an abstract thought cannot be grasped by the
physical hand, so the essence of God cannot be grasped even
by thought.[62] Even the highest spiritual beings cannot
comprehend God's true essence.[63]

2:51   Therefore, every name and every description that we
may give to God can only apply to His relationship to His

58. Cf. *Sanhedrin* 90b; Rambam on *Avoth* 3:15; *Bereshith Rabbah* 2:5, 26:4, 27:7;
Bamidbar Rabbah 16:22; *Tanchuma, Shelach* 5; *Pirkey Rabbi Eliezer* 36, 38, 48;
Tanna DeBei Eliahu Rabbah 1 (5a); Rashi on Genesis 6:6, Psalms 139:16. *Cf.* Isaiah
41:26, 46:10. Also see *Yerushalmi, Rosh HaShanah* 1:3 (7b).
59. *Yad, Yesodey HaTorah* 2:10. Cf. *Bereshith Rabbah* 9:3; *Tanchuma, Yithro* 12;
Tosefoth Yom Tov, Rosh HaShanah 1:2.
60. *Yad, Teshuvah* 5:5; *Emunoth VeDeyoth* 2:0; *Zohar* 1:103a; *Cheredim* 5 (p. 37).
61. *Tikuney Zohar* 17a. See *Pardes Rimonim* 4:5.
62. *Likutey Amarim, Shaar HaYichud VeHaEmunah* 9 (86b).
63. *Yad, Yesodey HaTorah* 2:8; *Chagigah* 13b; *Sifra* on Leviticus 1:1; *BaMidbar Rabbah*
14:37; *Midrash Tehillim* 18; *Pirkey Rabbi Eliezer* 4; *Tanna DeBei Eliahu Rabbah* 31
(123a); *Reshith Chokhmah, Shaar HaYirah* 2 (11c).

creation.[64] Even the Tetragrammaton (YHVH, יהוה), which is called God's "proper name" (*Shem HaMeforash,* שֵׁם הַמְפֹרָשׁ) only denotes His highest emanation in creation.[65] God Himself, however, is absolutely unknowable, unnamable, and innominate.[66] Words do not exist that can describe Him or tell all His praises.[67]

2:52   Although God is incomprehensible, we know Him through our traditions of the past and our hopes in the future. We know Him through our prayers for life, health and prosperity, as well as our hopes for mankind. In the *Amidah* (עֲמִידָה) recited three times each day, we address God and say, "Blessed are You, O Lord, our God and God of our fathers; God of Abraham, God of Isaac, and God of Jacob; Great, mighty and awesome God, Highest One, Giver of love and goodness, Master of all, who remembers the love of the fathers, and brings a redeemer to their children's children, for His name's sake, with love. King, Helper, Deliverer, and Shield." This prayer expresses our most basic feelings toward God.

64. *Shemoth Rabbah* 3:6; *Cheredim* 5 (p. 40); *Nefesh HaChaim* 2:3.
65. *Pirkey Rabbi Eliezer* 3; *Radal ad loc.* 3:10; *Zohar Chadash* 6a; *Tikuney Zohar* 17b; *Avodath HaKodesh, Chelek HaYichud* 2, 12, 15; *Pardes Rimonim* 4:5, 11:1, 19:7; *Sh'nei Luchoth HaB'rith, Beth HaShem* (1:4b); *Nefesh HaChaim* 2:2; *HaGra* on *Sefer Yetzirah* 1:1:3. This was not universally recognized by the earlier philosophers; see *Moreh Nevukhim* 1:61; *Kuzari* 2:2, 4:1; *Ibn Ezra* on Exodus 3:15, 33:21; *Ikkarim* 2:28.
66. *Zohar* 2:42b; *Tikuney Zohar* 17b; *Nefesh HaChaim* 2:3. Even such expressions as *Ain Sof* (אֵין סוֹף), "The Infinite One," or the "Limitless One," used to denote God, are actually negative attributes, and not true names; *Pardes Rimonim* 3:1.
67. Cf. *Berakhoth* 33b; *Megillah* 18a; *Makkoth* 10a; *Pirkey Rabbi Eliezer* 3; *Moreh Nevukhim* 1:59; *Yad, Tefillah* 9:7; *Teshuvoth Rashba* 4:29; *Turey Zahav, Orach Chaim* 113:7.

THREE

MAN

3:1   For man to fulfill the purpose of creation, he must be aware of that purpose.

3:2   Understanding the purpose of creation obviously does not mean fathoming God's internal reasons. Since we cannot understand God, we certainly cannot understand His motivations.[1]

3:3   Still, we can look at God's creation, and seek to comprehend the reason for its existence. We can also study what God Himself has taught about the purpose of creation.[2]

3:4   Since God is absolutely perfect in Himself, it is obvious that He had no inner need to create the universe.[3] It must

---

1. *Moreh Nevukhim* 3:13. Cf. *Avoth* 6:14, from Isaiah 43:7; *Yoma* 38a, from Proverbs 16:4; *Avoth DeRabbi Nathan* 41:16.
2. *Moreh Nevukhim* 3:25,27; Abarbanel, *Shamayim Chadashim* 4:6 (Roedelheim,1828), p. 47ff; quoted in *Shevil Emunah* (on *Emunoth VeDeyoth*) 1:4:9 (41b); *Shomer Emunim* 2:13. Thus, for example, if one examines a building, one can discern its function. Nevertheless, one may still not know that builder's motives in constructing it.
3. Above, 2:33. Some sources state that God made the world to attain the status of "Creator." See *Raya Mehemna, Zohar* 3:257b; *Sefer HaYashar* 1; Rabbi Meir Aldebei, *Sheveiley Emunah*, beginning of 3; *Pardes Rimonim* 5:4; *Etz Chaim, Derush Egolim VeYosher* 1; *Reshith Chokhmah, Shaar HaTeshuvah* 1 (101b). This,

therefore be concluded that God's creation of the universe was a most perfect act of altruism and love. It is thus written, "The world is built of love" (Psalms 89:3).[4]

3:5 God thus created the world to bestow good to His handiwork. It is thus written, "God is good to all; His love is on all His works" (Psalms 145:9).[5] God Himself called His creation good, as it is written, "God saw all that He made, and behold it was very good" (Genesis 1:35).[6]

3:6 Even things that appear contrary to this purpose are all part of God's plan. It is thus written, "God has made everything for His own purpose, even the wicked for the day of evil." (Proverbs 16:4).[7]

3:7 God's ability is limitless, and it therefore follows that His love and altruism are unlimited, resulting in the greatest benefit for all creation.[8]

3:8 God defines all good. Therefore, the greatest possible benefit is that which comes most directly from God Himself.[9]

3:9 In order for something to be appreciated, or even detected, some degree of contrast is required.[10] Thus, in order for the universe to experience God's presence, it must

---

however, was only true after God had brought forth the concept of "Creator" and creation. Also see *Likutey Moharan* 52.

4. *Emunoth VeDeyoth* 1:4 (end), 3:0; *Or HaShem* 2:6:2; *Sefer HaYashar* 1; *Reshith Chokhmah, Shaar HaTeshuvah* 1 (101b); *Sh'nei Luchoth HaB'rith, Beth Yisrael* (1:21b); *Shomer Emunim* 2:13; *Derekh HaShem* 1:2:1; *Likutey Moharan* 64. Also see *Zohar* 1:10b, 1:230b, 2:166b; *Sefer HaB'rith* 2:1:3.

5. *Emunoth VeDeyoth* 3:0 (53a). Cf. *Sanhedrin* 39b, Rashi *ad loc.*, s.v. *Oder*; *Menachoth* 53b; *Esther Rabbah* 10:15; *Akedath Yitzchak* 60.

6. *Moreh Nevukhim* 3:25.

7. Rashi *ad loc.*; *Shemoth Rabbah* 17:1; *Tanchuma, VaYikra* 7; *Akedath Yitzchak* 35. See below, note 32.

8. *Teshuvoth Chakham Tzvi* 18; *Likutey Amarim, Shaar HaYichud VeHeEmunah* 4 (79a).

9. *Derekh HaShem* 1:2:1. Also see *Shiur Komah* 13:3; *Yad, Teshuvah* 8:2.

10. *Likutey Amarim (Tanya), Shaar HaYichud VeHeEmunah* 7 (81b). See above, 2:42.

first experience His absence. In order to provide the greatest possible contrast, God thus created the universe as an environment where His essence would be undetectable.[11]

3:10 To fulfill His goal, God created the universe as an environment for a creature capable of partaking of His goodness. The creature would be capable of understanding, joy, and happiness, as well as of communing with God. This creature is man.[12]

3:11 Everything in the world is thus a means through which man becomes able to attain God's goodness.[13] It is thus taught that upon completing His creation, before creating man, God said, "If there are no guests, what pleasure has the King with all the good things He has provided?"[14]

3:12 Man was therefore created as a creature capable of to some degree understanding, and ultimately experiencing, the greatest possible good, which is God Himself.[15] It can therefore be said that God's purpose in creation was to allow Himself to be experienced by a creature far removed and much lower than Himself. It is thus taught that God created the universe because "He desired an abode in the lower world."[16]

3:13 God caused man to have a psychological makeup with which he would experience the greatest possible pleasure in

---

11. See *Chullin* 60a.
12. *Mesilath Yesharim* 1 (3b); *Derekh HaShem* 1:2:5. There is, however, a question as to whether the world was created for man alone, see *Moreh Nevukhim* 3:13. There is also a question as to whether there are other inhabited worlds; see Rabbi Yehudah Barceloni, Commentary on *Sefer Yetzirah* (Berlin, 1885), pp. 171-174; *Or HaShem* 4:2 (86a); *Matteh Dan (Kuzari Sheni)* 2:136-144; *Sefer HaB'rith* 1:3:4.
13. *Derekh Hashem* 1:2:5.
14. *Bereshith Rabbah* 8:5. Cf. *Sanhedrin* 38a; *Yerushalmi, Sanhedrin* 4:9 (23b).
15. Cf. *Bereshith Rabbah* 5:1; *Eikhah Rabbah* 1:59; *Pirkey Rabbi Eliezer* 3 (5b). Also see *Emunoth VeDeyoth* 1:4 (end), from Psalms 145:12.
16. *Tanchuma, Naso* 16; *Likutey Amarim (Tanya), Sefer Shel Benonim* 36 (45b).

doing something that he knew to be good and beneficial. This pleasure is enhanced according to the importance of the authority declaring that a given action is good. Since God Himself is the highest possible authority, there can be no greater pleasure in performing a job well done than in knowingly obeying the expressed will of God.[17]

3:14   For this reason God revealed His will to man. God thus said, "I am God your Lord, who teaches you for your profit, who leads you by the way you should go." (Isaiah 48:17).[18]

3:15   Obedience to God's will therefore fulfills His altruistic purpose in creation.[19] The Psalmist thus said, "You let me know the path of life; in Your presence is the fullness of joy, in Your right hand, eternal bliss" (Psalms 16:11).[20]

3:16   In order to enjoy the pleasure of such accomplishment, it is imperative that man know that his accomplishment is a matter of his own free choice, and not the result of his nature of compulsion. So that all choices of action be up to the individual, God gave man absolute free will.[21]

3:17   Free will is required by God's justice. Otherwise, man would not be given or denied good for actions over which he had no control.[22] Beyond this, however, it is also required by the very purpose for which He created the universe, namely, that He give man good through the pleasure of his own accomplishment.[23]

17. Cf. *Avoth* 4:7; *Kiddushin* 31a; Ritva *ad loc.* s.v. *DeAmar Bava Kama* 38a, 87a; *Avodah Zarah* 3a; *Sotah* 21a. The pleasure is to some degree derived from spiritual closeness to the authority. Where God Himself is the authority, the pleasure is derived from spiritual closeness to Him.
18. *Emunoth VeDeyoth* 1:4 (end). See below, 5:46.
19. Cf. *Shabbath* 31b; *Yalkut Shimoni* 2:1069; from Ecclesiastes 3:14. Also see *Bereshith Rabbah* 1:6, 12:2; *Zohar* 2:42a; Rashi on Genesis 1:1; *Reshith Chokhmah, Shaar HaTeshuvah* 1 (101b).
20. Ibn Ezra *ad loc.*; *Emunoth VeDeyoth* 3:0.
21. Yad, *Teshuvah* 5:1; *Moreh Nevukhim* 3:17; *Emunoth VeDeyoth* 4:4 (64b). Cf. *Pirkey Rabbi Eliezer* 15 (35a); *Menachoth* 29b.
22. Yad, *Teshuvah* 5:4; *Moreh Nevukhim, Emunoth VeDeyoth, loc. cit.*
23. *Zohar* 1:23a; *Emunoth VeDeyoth, Reshith Chokhmah, loc. cit.*

3:18   Since the ultimate good is God Himself, the greatest possible good that He can bestow is Himself. There is no greater good than achieving a degree of unity with God, the Creator of all good. Since God desires to give man the greatest good possible, He gave him the ability to resemble Himself.[24]

3:19   This is another reason that God gave man free will. Just as God acts as a free Being, so does man. Just as God acts without prior restraint, so does man. Just as God can do good as a matter of His own free choice, so can man.[25] Man is therefore spoken of as being created in the image of God.[26]

3:20   In order for man to have true free choice, he must not only have inner freedom of will, but also an environment in which a choice between obedience and disobedience exists.[27]

3:21   So that such a choice can exist, God created a world where both good and evil can freely operate.[28] He thus said, "I form light and create darkness; I make peace and create evil; I am God, I do all these things" (Isaiah 45:7).[29]

3:22   God made man's psychology so that the more difficult an accomplishment, the more satisfaction there is in doing it. God then created the world so that it should present man with the greatest possible challenge.

3:23   The world was therefore created as a place where it would be possible, but very difficult, to obey God. God

---

24. *Derekh HaShem* 1:2:1.
25. *Ibid.* 1:2:2.
26. Cf. *Mekhilta* on Exodus 14:29; *Bereshith Rabbah* 21:5; *Shir HaShirim Rabbah* 1:46; *Yalkut Shimoni* 1:34; *Yad, Teshuvah* 5:1.
27. *Derekh HaShem* 1:2:2. Cf. *Midrash Tehillim* 36:3; *Reshith Chokhmah, Shaar HaYirah* 7 (22b).
28. Cf. *Moreh Nevukhim* 3:10; *Sefer HaYashar* 1; *Sh'nei Luchoth HaB'rith, Beth Yisrael* (1:22a). Also see *Sanhedrin* 39b.
29. Cf. *Bereshith Rabbah* 9:12-14; Rabbi Yaakov Emden (Maharibatz) on *Bava Bathra* 16a; *Etz Chaim, Shaar HaMelakhim* 5.

allows evil and temptation to exist, even though they may
cause people to abandon Him and ignore His teachings.[30]
Although some may stray through their own choice, this is
the price that must be paid so that the reward for those who
choose good will be maximized. It is thus taught that for the
sake of the righteous the world was created.[31]

3:24   Therefore, even the evil and temptations of the world
serve the divine purpose of enhancing the satisfaction of
accomplishment of those who overcome them. They thus
serve an important function in man's ultimate reward, and
hence, in God's purpose.[32]

3:25   The greater the barriers that must be overcome, the
greater the satisfaction and reward in overcoming them. It is
thus taught, "Reward is according to suffering."[33]

3:26   God may have created the possibility of evil, but He
created it in order that man should overcome it. It is thus
written, "Behold, the fear of God, that is wisdom, and to
depart from evil, that is understanding" (Job 28:28).[34]

3:27   There is an important dichotomy between the environment required to serve God, and that required for the
satisfaction and reward for such service. In order to gain the
maximum satisfaction of accomplishment, one must obey
God's will in an environment which presents the maximum
allowable challenge for the individual. It must therefore be

30. *Mesilath Yesharim* 1 (4a). Cf. *Eruvin* 13b; *Tosafoth, Avodah Zarah* 5a, s.v.
    Shellmale; Rabbi Aaron Shmuel (ben Moshe Shalom) of Kreminetz, *Nishmath
    Adam* (Pieterkov, 1911), p. 32d ff; *Avodath HaKodesh, Chelek HaAvodah* 22.
31. *Emunoth VeDeyoth* 4:5 (66a). Cf. *Sifri* on Deuteronomy 11:9; *Yalkut Shimoni*
    1:872; *Reshith Chokhmah,* Introduction (2a).
32. *Tana DeBei Eliahu Rabbah* 16 (77a); *Tana DeBei Eliahu Zuta* 12 (17a); *Zohar*
    2:163a; *Sefer Chasidim* 155; *Likutey Amarim Tanya, Sefer Shel Benonim* 36 (46a).
    Also see *Bereshith Rabbah* 9:9; *Midrash Ne'elam, Zohar* 1:138a. See above, note 7.
33. *Avoth* 5:23. See *Sh'nei Luchoth HaB'rith, Beth Yisrael* (1:21b).
34. Cf. *Emunoth VeDeyoth,* end of 4:1 (63b).

an environment in which neither God Himself, nor the divine nature of God's commandments is obvious. On the other hand, both God and the divine nature of His commandments must be as obvious as possible in the environment where man is to enjoy the fruit of his deeds. The more obvious this is then, the greater will be the satisfaction and reward for man's accomplishment.[35]

3:28   God therefore created two levels to existence. He created the present world (*Olam HaZeh*, עוֹלָם הַזֶּה), as an environment of challenge and accomplishment, where man earns his ultimate reward. He also created a second level, the World to Come (*Olam HaBa*, עוֹלָם הַבָּא), as the world of ultimate reward. This will be a world where the true nature of all our deeds is perfectly obvious.

3:29   The existence of these two worlds thus resolves the dichotomy. This present world exists as the place of maximum challenge, while the World to Come is the environment of the greatest possible realization of accomplishment.[36]

3:30   The principle that man has absolute free will, with the ability to choose between good and evil, is therefore a foundation of our faith. The Torah thus says, "I call heaven and earth to bear witness this day, for I have set before you life and death, the blessing and the curse. Therefore, choose life, so that you and your children may live" (Deuteronomy 30:19).[37]

3:31   Every person can therefore choose his own path in life, whether good or evil. Each individual has the ability to

---

35. *Derekh HaShem* 1:3:4.
36. *Ibid.*
37. Ramban *ad loc.*; *Yad, Teshuvah* 5:3; *Moreh Nevukhim* 3:17; *Emunoth VeDeyoth* 4:4 (64b). *Cf.* Deuteronomy 11:26.

attain the highest human perfection, or to sink to the lowest levels of evil and degradation. If a person chooses evil and fails to heed the call to righteousness, he has no cause to complain, for the decision is his alone. It is thus written, "Evil and good come not from the mouth of the Most High. Why then should a living man complain, a strong man, because of his sins?" (Lamentations 3:38).[38]

3:32   A person cannot always determine his circumstances and natural capabilities, and these may limit his sphere of activity.[39] Still, every person has the ultimate choice whether or not to serve God according to his ability.[40] It is thus taught, "All is in the hand of Heaven, except for the fear of Heaven."[41]

3:33   The very indeterminacy inherent in the quantum nature of matter indicates that the universe was created as an arena for a free-willed creature. It is this freedom of will that gives man a wider choice than merely to react to his surroundings. Therefore, although a person's actions may be influenced by his heredity and environment, neither of these absolutely determines his actions.

3:34   When we understand God's purpose in creation, we can also understand why an omnipotent God does not force man to do good and obey His commandments. If God would force man to obey His commandments, their entire purpose would be negated. God may want us to do good, but only as a matter of free will.[42]

38. *Yad, Teshuvah* 5:2; *Sefer Chasidim* 33. Cf. Rashi *ad loc.*; *Eikhah Rabbah* 3:31; *Devarim Rabbah* 4:3; *Tanchuma, Re'eh* 3.
39. *Emunoth VeDeyoth* 4:4 (65a); *Shevil Emunah ad loc.* 4:4:2; *Kuzari* 5:20:6 (54a); *Akedath Yitzchak* 28.
40. *Niddah* 16b; *Tanchuma, Pikudey* 3. Also see Maharsha, *Bava Bathra* 17a, s.v. *Al*; Maharatz Chajas, *Gittin* 66a; *Rambam, Shemonah Perakim* 8.
41. *Berakhoth* 33b; *Megillah* 25a; *Niddah* 16b; *Yalkut Shimoni* 1:455, 2:302; *Zohar* 1:59a; *Tikuney Zohar Chadash* 121b,c; *Bahir* 187; *Sefer Chasidim* 33; *Teshuvoth Meil Tzadakah* 7. "Heaven" denotes God, see *Bahir* 100, from 1 Kings 8:6.
42. *Yad, Teshuva* 5:4; *Moreh Nevukhim* 3:17; *Emunoth VeDeyoth* 4:4 (65a); *Kuzari*

3:35   All ethics and morality only exist for the benefit of man, and this benefit is only attained when man acts as a free agent. Morality as such does not affect God in any way, nor does He derive any benefit from our good.[43] Similarly, evil may ultimately harm its perpetrator, but it can never actually affect God. God thus said, "Am I then the one they anger? . . . Is it rather not they themselves, for their own shame?" (Jeremiah 7:19). God therefore has no intrinsic reason to force man to do good or refrain from evil.[44]

3:36   Since free will is a prime ingredient of God's purpose, He does not do anything in this world that might destroy or diminish man's choice between good and evil. Therefore, He does not openly reward the good or punish the wicked in this world; it would diminish man's freedom to sin. Similarly, God does not permit any manifest miracles where they would determine one's freedom of choice.[45]

3:37   The fact that God is omniscient and knows the future does not contradict the principle of man's free choice. This apparent paradox stems from the fact that we cannot understand precisely how God knows anything, much less how He knows the future.[46] As long as man is bound to this physical world, and his mind is limited by the bonds of time, he cannot see beyond time where the resolution of this paradox exists.[47] However, to the limit of our understanding, we know that God somehow restricts His knowledge of the future in order to give man free will.[48] The

5:20 (47a); *Chovoth HaLevavoth* 3:8. Cf. *Bereshith Rabbah* 22:22; *Yalkut Shimoni* 1:38; *Tosefoth Yom Tov, Avoth* 3:15.
43. *Shomer Emunim* 2:11 #4.
44. *Radak ad loc.; Emunoth VeDeyoth* 4:4 (65a).
45. Rabbi Yitzchak ibn Latif, *Shaar HaShamayim* 1:22 (Munich, ms. 45); quoted in *Menorath HaMaor*, end of 3 (237); *Tosefoth Yom Tov, Avodah Zarah* 4:7. Cf. *Berakhoth* 20a; *Bereshith Rabbah* 9:6; *Ikkarim* 4:12, from Ecclesiastes 8:12.
46. *Yad, Teshuvah* 5:5; *Moreh Nevukhim* 3:20; *Shemonah Perakim* 8.
47. See *Likutey Moharan* 21.
48. *Or HaChaim* on Genesis 6:2; *Meshekh Chokhmah* on Genesis 1:26. Also see Rabbi Moshe Cordevero (Ramak), *Elemah Rabathai, Eyn Kol* 2:18. This is the same as the

main point is that, although we might not understand how, God's knowledge of the future in no way deprives the individual of his own free choice.[49]

3:38   We know that God exists outside of time. Therefore, His knowledge of the future is *exactly the same* as His knowledge of the past and present.[50] Just as His knowledge of the past does not interfere with man's free will, neither does His knowledge of the future.[51]

3:39   As Creator of time, God can do with it as He wills.[52] Moreover, time was not created because God Himself needed it, but because it was required to make the world an arena of action, for man's own ultimate benefit. It is thus taught, "All is foreseen,[53] but free choice is given; the world is judged for good, and all is according to one's works."[54]

paradox of the "vacated space" discussed above, Chapter 2, note 46. God's knowledge is the same as His essence, as pointed out in *Yad, Teshuvah* 5:5 in the discussion of this very question. Therefore, since God's essence is in the future, His knowledge must also be there. In order to allow man free will, He must then restrict His knowledge and essence from the future. But still, it is impossible to say that it is not there. But here too the paradox is related to the twofold way in which we look at God (Chapter 2, note 5). If we look at Him through attributes of action, He is not in the future, but if we look at Him through negative attributes, He is there.

49. *Emunoth VeDeyoth* 4:4 (65b); *Kuzari* 5:20 (47b); *Chovoth HaLevavoth* 3:8; *Milchamoth HaShem* 3:4; *Ikkarim* 4:3; *Akedath Yitzchak* 21; *Teshuvoth Rivash* 119; *Sh'nei Luchoth HaB'rith, Beth HaBechirah* (1:43a); *Tikuney Zohar Chadash* 89b; *Pardes Rimonim* 4:9; *Asarah Maamaroth, Maamar HaMiddoth* 4 (216a); Maharal, *Gevuroth HaShem* 2; Bachya on Exodus 15:18; *Or Sameach* on *Yad, Teshuvah* 5:5. See below, note 52.

50. *Ikkarim* 2:19.

51. Rabbi Moshe Almosnino, *Pirkey Mosheh* on Avoth 3:15; quoted in *Midrash Shmuel, Tosefoth Yom Tov,* on *Avoth* 3:15; Rabbi Barukh Kasover, *Yesod HaEmunah* 2; *Shevil Emunah* (on *Emunoth VeDeyoth*) 4:4:1. Also see *Tana DeBei Eliahu Rabbah* 1; *Ramathayim Tzofim ad loc.* 1:8. Also see *Kol Yehudah* (on *Kuzari*) 5:20 (47b), s.v. *Ki; Otzar Nechemad* (on *Kuzari*) 1:1 (11b), s.v. *Kol.* Cf. *Tanchuma, VaYeshev* 4.

52. Moreover, as discussed earlier (Chapter 2, note 30), all logic is a creation of God. Therefore, where His purpose requires it, God can suspend logic.

53. Some interpret this phrase differently, see Rashi, ad loc. But there are other sources where the phrase *ha-kol tzafuy* (הַכֹּל צָפוּי) unequivocally denotes God's knowledge of the future; see *Pirkey Rabbi Eliezer* 26 (61b), 36 (83a), 38 (88a), 48 (114b).

54. *Avoth* 3:15, according to interpretation of Rambam; Rabenu Yonah; Bertenoro (second explanation); *Tosefoth Yom Tov.*

Both time and the apparent paradox were created so that God would attain His ultimate purpose: to "judge the world for good." It can then be an environment where "all is according to one's deeds."[55]

3:40   There are occasions where God reveals the future actions of an individual to a prophet.[56] Nonetheless, such prophecy is contingent upon the individual's free choice, and is not absolutely binding.[57] God merely reveals to the prophet the most probable course of events based on the individual's nature. This does not bar the individual from going against his nature; such a change of mind is by no means precluded by the prophecy.[58]

3:41   Similarly, there are cases where God reveals to a prophet that those not yet born will be wicked.[59] Here too, He is merely revealing their most likely future, based on heredity and environment, but the ultimate choice is still up to the individual.[60]

3:42   Even when God does reveal to a prophet that an individual will do evil, He does not reveal the extent of this evil. Therefore, the fact that their evil has already been predicted does not exempt them from punishment.[61]

55. Cf. *Otzar Nechemad* (on *Kuzari*) 1:1 (11b), s.v. *Kol.* Also see Abarbanel, *Nachlath Avoth* on *Avoth* 3:15.
56. Cf. Rashi on Deuteronomy 34:1; *Sefer Chasidim* 1159, from 2 Samuel 16:21,23, Amos 7:17.
57. *Yad, Yesodey HaTorah* 10:4. Cf. Jonah 3:10, 2 Kings 20:1-6; *Yoma* 73b; *Yerushalmi, Sanhedrin* 11:5 (56b); *Tanchuma, VeYera* 13; *Yalkut Shimoni* 2:308; Rashi, Mahari Kara, Radak, on Jeremiah 28:7; Radak on *Pirkey Rabbi Eliezer* 10:4.
58. *Tosafoth, Yevamoth* 50a, s.v. *Teyda*; Maharsha, *ibid.*; *Sh'nei Luchoth HaB'rith, Beth HaBechirah* (1:45a). Cf. Rashi on Genesis 21:17.
59. Cf. *Berakhoth* 10a.
60. *Tosafoth, Niddah* 16b, s.v. *HaKol*; Maharsha, Maharshal, *ad loc.*; *Tosafoth HaRosh, ibid.* Cf. Ramban on Deuteronomy 31:21.
61. Ramban; *Or HaChaim;* on Genesis 15:13; *Tosefoth Yom Tov, Avoth* 2:6, s.v. *Metifcha.*

3:43   Thus, God told Abraham, "Know for sure that your offspring will be foreigners in a land that is not theirs . . . and that nation will afflict them . . . But I will then punish the nation whom they shall serve" (Genesis 15:13,14). Although there had been a decree that the Egyptians subjugate the Israelites, individuals would be judged for their actions. The Egyptians were also punished for maximizing the suffering of the Israelites.[62] God thus said, "I am sorely displeased with the nations . . . I was a little displeased, but they helped add to the evil" (Zechariah 1:15).[63]

3:44   Although God does not determine the conduct of individuals, He does determine the large scale course of history. Therefore, the collective wills of nations and societies are largely determined by God. Still, each individual retains free will to overcome his environment.[64]

3:45   To influence the course of history, God often guides the wills of kings and other important leaders. It is thus written, "As streams of water, the king's heart is in God's hand, He turns it wherever He wills" (Proverbs 21:1).[65]

3:46   Although God does not influence a person's action directly, He does occasionally plant thoughts in one's mind to lead him along the path He wills.[66] The individual,

62. Ibid.; Raavad on Yad, Teshuvah 6:5.
63. Radak ad loc.; BaMidbar Rabbah 10:5; Ramban on Genesis 15:13; Raavad, loc. cit.; Rabbi Yaakov Emden (Maharibatz) on Shemonah Perakim 8:2. Also see Isaiah 47:6, Radak ad loc.
64. Yad, Teshuvah 6:5; Moreh Nevukhim 2:48.
65. Rabbenu Yonah, Ralbag, Metzudoth David, ad loc.; Yalkut Shimoni 2:959, Rabbenu Yonah on Avoth 2:3. Cf. Berakhoth 55a, Rashi ad loc., s.v. Tzerikhim; Yalkut Shimoni 1:860, 2:306; Emunoth VeDeyoth 4:7 end (68a); Maharatz Chajas, Megillah 11a; Radak on Jeremiah 20:23. If a stream is deflected even a little, it can take an entirely different course. Similarly, a slight change of mind on a ruler's part can have a major impact on history. See Malbim ad loc.
66. Tanchuma, Re'eh 12; Pesikta 11 (97b).

however, has the free choice whether to follow these thoughts or not.

3:47   It is thus taught that God leads a person along the path that he has chosen to follow.[67] God may plant ideas in his mind that are conducive to helping him follow the correct path, or may otherwise bring about events to encourage him. It is taught, "One who comes to cleanse himself is helped [by God]."[68] The Psalmist thus prayed, "Teach me Your ways, O God, that I may walk in Your truth; dedicate my heart to revere Your name" (Psalms 86:11).[69]

3:48   God may similarly bring about circumstances which will be conducive for a righteous person to do good.[70] Likewise, He gives the wicked every opportunity and circumstance in which to continue doing evil.[71] It is thus taught, "When one comes to defile himself, the door is opened for him."[72] In all such cases, however, the final choice is with the individual.[73]

3:49   A person may occasionally be so wicked that the ultimate benefit of humanity requires that the choice be taken away from him, and that he lose the power to repent.[74] An example of this occurred when God told His prophet, "Make the heart of this people fat, make their ears heavy, and shut their eyes, so that they will not . . . return and be

---

67. *Makkoth* 10b; *BaMidbar Rabbah* 20:11; *Zohar* 1:198b, 2:50a, 3:47a, 3:207a. Cf. *Avoth* 4:2; *Mekhilta* on Exodus 15:16; Maharsha, *Avodah Zarah* 5a, s.v. Mi.
68. *Shabbath* 104a; *Yoma* 83a; *Avodah Zarah* 55a; *Menachoth* 29a; *Yerushalmi, Peah* 1:1 (5b); *Yalkut Shimoni* 2:936; from Proverbs 3:34; *Yad, Teshuvah* 6:5; *Kuzari* 5:20 (49b).
69. *Yad, Teshuvah* 6:4; *Emunoth VeDeyoth* 4:6 (86b); *Zohar* 1:59a.
70. *Shabbath* 32a; *Sanhedrin* 8a; *Bava Bathra* 119b; *Tosefta, Yoma* 4:11; *BaMidbar Rabbah* 13:17; *Sefer Chasidim* 45, 1159; *Sh'nei Luchoth HaB'rith, Beth HaBechirah* (1:44a).
71. Cf. *Sifra* on Leviticus 18:2; *Yalkut Shimoni* 1:586 (end); Raavad, *Teshuvah* 6:5.
72. See note 68.
73. Cf. *Sh'nei Luchoth HaB'rith, Shaar HaOthioth, Biyah* (1:157b); *Sefer Chasidim* 352, *B'rith Olam ad loc.* Cf. *Yad, Teshuvah* 6:4.
74. Cf. *Chagigah* 15a.

healed" (Isaiah 6:10).⁷⁵ This is also the significance of God's word to Moses, "I will harden Pharaoh's heart, and thus multiply My signs and wonders in the land of Egypt" (Exodus 7:3).⁷⁶ In all such cases,⁷⁷ God does not initially decree that the person be wicked, but once his wickedness surpasses certain bounds, free choice to repent is taken away from him.⁷⁸ It is thus taught that God first warns the sinner three times, but if the warning is not heeded, then the gates of repentance may be closed.⁷⁹

3:50   Ultimately, then, all of life is a test. However, there are times that God puts an individual through an especially difficult test (nisayon, נִסָּיוֹן). In such a case, a person is placed in a situation where his devotion and faith are tested.⁸⁰

3:51   God does not put a person to a difficult test unless He knows that the person will pass it. It is thus written, "God tests the righteous, but His spirit hates the wicked" (Psalms 11:5).⁸¹ It is taught, "The potter does not tap vessels that are easily broken, but only vessels that are strong. God similarly does not test the wicked, but the righteous."⁸²

3:52   Since God is omniscient, He has no need to test people to see what they will do. When He tests a person it is to bring out his latent potential and allow him to express it in action.⁸³

75. Rashi ad loc.; Akedath Yitzchak 36.
76. Ramban ad loc.; Shemoth Rabbah 11:2; Maharal, Gevurath HaShem 31.
77. Cf. Deuteronomy 2:30, Joshua 11:20.
78. Yad, Teshuvah 6:3; Shemonah Perakim 8; Rambam, Tosefoth Yom Tov, on Avoth 5:18.
79. Shemoth Rabbah 13:4.
80. For a general discussion, see Rabbi David Luria (Radal) on Pirkey Rabbi Eliezer 31:2.
81. Rashi ad loc.; Shemoth Rabbah 2:2; Emunoth VeDeyoth 5:3 (70b).
82. Bereshith Rabbah 32:3, 34:2, 55:2; Shir HaShirim Rabbah 2:35; Midrash Tehillim 11:4; Tanchuma, VaYera 20; Yalkut Shimoni 2:350, 2:654; Menorath HaMaor 5:3:1:3 (300); Alshekh on Genesis 22:1.
83. Kuzari 5:20 (48b); Ramban on Genesis 22:1, 22:12, Exodus 16:4, Deuteronomy 13:4.

3:53   God therefore sometimes tests a person in order to reward him.[84] This is because there is no reward for potential alone, as it is written, "Your *work* shall be rewarded" (2 Chronicles 15:7).[85] A test may also make a task more difficult so as to increase its reward.[86]

3:54   Moreover, a test is often needed to make a person's potential and ability known to himself so as to increase his self-confidence.[87] In some cases, God also tests a person in order to make his good qualities known to others.[88] It is for this reason that God often tests a person before choosing him for greatness or leadership.

3:55   Although God might guide or test man, the final choice between good and evil ultimately rests with the individual. Whether a person does right or wrong, it is totally up to him. Every normal person can always control his actions, if he only tries hard enough. Man was created to be master of his fate, and as such, he bears the full responsibility for it.

84. Ramban, *Torath HaAdam, Shaar HaGamul* (Jerusalem, 1955), p. 72a,b.
85. Radal on *Pirkey Rabbi Eliezer* 31:2. Cf. *Mekhilta* on Exodus 12:6; *Yalkut Shimoni* 1:195.
86. *Shemoth Rabbah* 31:2; *Torath HaAdam*, loc. cit. Cf. *Mekhilta*, Rashi, Ramban, on Exodus 20:17.
87. *Pirkey Rabbi Eliezer* 31; Radal *ad loc.* 31.2. Cf. *Sanhedrin* 107a.
88. *Avoth* 5:3; *Avoth DeRabbi Nathan* 33:2; *Bereshith Rabbah* 55.1; *Tanchuma*, VaYera 23; *Midrash Ne'elam, Zohar* 1:106b; Rashi on Genesis 22:12.
89. *Shemoth Rabbah* 2:3; *Sefer Chasidim* 13. Also see *Sefer Chasidim* 106, 161.

FOUR

ISRAEL

4:1   The recipient of the good for which God created the universe was destined to be man.[1] However, it was initially not determined whether the entire human race or only part of it would be the recipient of this good.[2]

4:2   The group that would be the recipient of the divine good was defined as Israel (*Yisrael*, יִשְׂרָאֵל).[3] These people would

---

1. See above, 3:10.
2. See note 13. The identity of "Israel" could not be determined since even the Patriarchs had free will. In the sense that God knows the future, however, He obviously knew who "Israel" would be. The question of the election of Israel therefore involves the paradox of God's foreknowledge and free will, see above, 3:27; *Yeffeh Toar* on *Bereshith Rabbah* 1:4 (Vilna). Also see *Likutey Moharan* 21:9, who also discusses this within the context of the paradox, cf. 21:4. This also explains the juxtaposition where first Rabbi Akiba states that although all mankind was created in "God's image," only Israel are considered His "children," immediately after which he presents the above paradox; *Avoth* 3:14,15. Adam raised a similar question, see *Tanchuma, VaYeshev* 4; *Teshuvoth Radbaz* 1:256. Also see *Zohar* 3:14,15. According to the Kabbalists there are spiritual levels where time does not exist and the future is known, and lower levels where free will has an effect; *Pardes Rimonim* 4:9, 18:3. Thus, on the higher level, the identity of Israel was determined, while on the lower one it was not. See below, note 10. Also see Maharal, *Derekh Chaim* on Avoth 3:14.
3. Thus, the name "Israel" (יִשְׂרָאֵל), is interpreted to mean *SheRoeh El* (שֶׁרָאָה אֵל), "he who sees God;" or *Ish Roeh El* (אִישׁ רָאָה אֵל), "a man who sees God;" *Tanna DeBei Eliahu Rabbah* 27 (107b). The name Israel (יִשְׂרָאֵל) is also seen as having the same letters as *Li Rosh* (לִי רֹאשׁ), "I have a head," or "I have a beginning," indicating Israel's pre-eminence; see *Shemonah Shaarim, Shaar HaPesukim, VaYishlach* (Tel Aviv, 1962), p. 82; Rabbi Shneur Zalman of Liadi, *Likutey Torah, Shelach* (48b);

be the ones who would perceive the divine and become the recipients of God's goodness. It is thus taught that the concept of Israel was God's very first thought in creating the universe.[4] It is thus written, "Israel is God's holy portion, the first of His harvest" (Jeremiah 2:3).[5]

4:3   Besides creating the concept of "Israel" as the recipient of His good, God also created a means through which this "Israel" would receive this good.[6] This means was the Torah, which, as such, was God's blueprint for creation.[7]

4:4   The Torah is the way to God's good, as He said, "I have given you a good teaching, My Torah, do not forsake it" (Proverbs 4:2). It is thus taught that, "There is no good other than the Torah."[8]

4:5   The Torah was thus among the prime ingredients of creation. The Torah itself allegorically says, "God made me as the beginning of His way, the first of His original paths" (Proverbs 8:22).[9] Still, the Torah did not assume its present form until it was given.[10]

Kedushath Levi, VaYetze (Jerusalem, 1958), p. 59. Also see Degel Machaneh Ephraim, VeEthChanan (Yosefof, 1883), p. 68d. See below, notes 83, 84.
4. Bereshith Rabbah 1:5; Zohar 1:24a. Also see Shemoth Rabbah 38:5; BaMidbar Rabbah 20:2; Zohar 2:108b, 2:119a (end), 2:275b, 3:229b (end, in Raya Mehemna), 3:306b; Tikuney Zohar 6a, 6 (23b), 40 (80a), 67 (99b), 69 (100a, 102b); Zohar Chadash 37a, 88d, 100a, 108d, 120c, d.
5. Rashi on Genesis 1:1.
6. Derekh HaShem 1:4:5; Pirkey Moshe on Avoth 3:14. Cf. Pesachim 54a; Bereshith Rabbah 1:5.
7. Bereshith Rabbah 1:2. Cf. Pirkey Rabbi Eliezer 3; Zohar 1:5a, 1:24b (end), 1:47a, 1:134a, 1:205b (top), 2:161a, 2:200a (top), 3:35b, 3:69b, 3:178a.
8. Avoth 6:3; Berakhoth 5a; Mesechta Kallah 8; Yerushalmi, Rosh HaShanah 3:8; Tanchuma, Re'eh 11; Tana DeBei Eliahu Zuta 17; Eikhah Rabbah, Pesichta 2.
9. Rashi on Genesis 1:1.
10. Ramban, introduction to Commentary on Torah; Mabit, Beth Elohim, Shaar HaYesodoth 25. Thus, before it was given, the Torah was likened to water, while after it was given, it was likened to stone; Bahir 165. This also involves the paradox of God's foreknowledge and human free will; see note 2. The primeval Torah can be seen as a "computer program," which produces a specific result for every particular event. Thus, the "program" was determined before creation, but its "output" was not determined until after the Torah was given.

4:6   The Torah was created for the sake of Israel.[11] God's purpose in creation required that Israel accept the Torah. If not, all creation would have lost its reason for being, and would have ceased to exist.[12]

4:7   If Adam would have been worthy and would not have sinned, then all of his descendants would have been worthy of the Torah. If not for Adam's sin, all mankind would have had the status of Israel."[13]

4:8   Because of Adam's sin, however, the Torah was restricted to the small portion of humanity who would eventually be worthy of receiving it. The rest of humanity were given seven commandments, binding on every human being. They are:[14]

1. Not to worship idols.[15]
2. Not to curse God.
3. To establish courts of justice.[16]
4. Not to murder.
5. Not to commit adultery or incest.
6. Not to steal.
7. Not to eat flesh from a living animal.

---

11. *Tana DeBei Eliahu Rabbah* 14; *Koheleth Rabbah* 1:9; *Sifri* on Deuteronomy 11:21. Some authorities, however, dispute this; see *Nefesh HaChaim* 4:11.
12. *Shabbath* 88a; *Avodah Zarah* 3a; Rashi on Genesis 1:31.
13. *Derekh HaShem* 2:4:2. Cf. Maharal, *Tifereth Yisrael* 17; *Tosefoth Yom Tov* on *Avoth* 5:2; *Beth Elohim, Shaar HaYesodoth* 19.
14. *Sanhedrin* 56b; *Tosefta, Avodah Zarah* 9:4; *Bereshith Rabbah* 16:9; *Devarim Rabbah* 2:17; *Shir HaShirim Rabbah* 1:16; *Pesikta* 12 (100b); *Zohar* 1:35b; *Yad, Melakhim* 9:1; *Moreh Nevukhim* 1:2; *Kuzari* 3:73 (75b). These seven commandments can be remembered by a mnemonic: The first four letters of the Hebrew alphabet, Alef (א) is *aver min ha-chai* (אֵבֶר מִן הַחַי), flesh from a living animal; Beth (ב) is *birkath haShem* (בִּרְכַּת הַשֵׁם), cursing God; Gimel (ג) is *gezel* (גֵּזֶל), robbery; and Dalet (ד) is *dayanim* (דַּיָּנִים), judges. The final three are the three cardinal sins for which a Jew must give his life rather than commit: idolatry, murder, and sexual crimes (*giluy arayoth*, גִּלּוּי עֲרָיוֹת).
15. See above, 1:16.
16. Rambam, in *Yad, Melakhim* 9:14, writes that this is a positive commandment to set up courts of justice. Others dispute this, however, and maintain that it is a commandment not to pervert justice; see Ramban on Genesis 34:13. See *Teshuvoth HaRama* 10.

4:9   Of these commandments, the first six were given to Adam himself.[17] The seventh commandment would have been redundant for him, since the eating of all animal flesh was forbidden until the generation of Noah, following the Great Flood.[18] Thus, the final commandment, prohibiting the eating of flesh from a living animal, was given to Noah and his sons.[19] Since this completed the giving of commandments binding on all humanity, these seven commandments are referred to as the "Commandments of Noah's Sons" (*Mitzvoth Beney Noach*, מִצְוֹת בְּנֵי נֹחַ).[20]

4:10   These commandments were given so that all humans could partake of God's good by obeying them. It is thus taught that non-Israelites who obey these seven commandments have a portion in the World to Come.[21]

4:11   These commandments were also meant to benefit humanity in this world, serving as the basis of morality and ethics. Thus, the prohibitions against idolatry and blasphemy teach man to worship and respect the Supreme Being, this being the foundation of all ethics. The

17. *Bereshith Rabbah* 16:9; 24:5; *Shemoth Rabbah* 30:6; *BaMidbar Rabbah* 14:24; *Devarim Rabbah* 2:17; *Shir HaShirim Rabbah* 1:16; *Midrash Tehillim* 1:16; *Pesikta* 12 (100b); *Yalkut Shimoni* 1:272, 2:964; *Yad, Melakhim* 9:1; *Kesef Mishneh, Lechem Mishneh, ad loc.*

18. Genesis 1:29; *Sanhedrin* 59b; *Bereshith Rabbah* 34:18; *Etz Yosef* (on *Eyn Yaakov*), *Sanhedrin* 100. Others, however, maintain that Adam was also given this commandment; *Sanhedrin* 56b; *Zohar* 1:35b. While he was allowed to eat flesh, he was not allowed to kill for food, but flesh from a living animal was forbidden even if it was not cut from the animal by man; Rashi, *Sanhedrin* 57a, s.v. *LeMishri*; *Tosafoth, Sanhedrin* 56b, s.v. *Achal*; Rashi on Genesis 1:29; *Mizrachi, Sifethey Chakhamim, ad loc.* Others state that this prohibition was hinted to Adam, although it did not actually apply to him; *Bereshith Rabbah* 16:9. Aso see *Teshuvoth Rashbash* 542; *Asarah Maamaroth, Choker Din* 3:21; *Yad Yehudah ad loc.* 36; *Teshuvoth Beth Shaarim, Yoreh Deah* 110, 113.

19. Genesis 9:3,4; Rashi, *ad loc.* Cf. *Shir HaShirim Rabbah* 1:16; *Pesikta* 12 (100b); *Yad, Melakhim* 9:1; *Ikkarim* 3:15.

20. Cf. *Avodah Zarah* 64b.

21. *Sanhedrin* 105a; *Tosefta, Sanhedrin* 13:1; *Midrash Tehillim* 9:15; *Yad, Teshuvah* 3:5 (end), *Eduth* 11:10; *Melakhim* 8:11; Rambam on *Sanhedrin* 10:2.

prohibitions against murder, incest, adultery, robbery and the perversion of justice serve as the foundations of human morality. Finally, the prohibition against eating flesh from a living animal teaches man kindness toward lower creatures as well as control of his base appetites.[22]

4:12   There were ten generations from Adam to Noah, and throughout this period, mankind experienced a continual moral decline.[23] The world reverted to paganism, and most people forgot the universal commandments.[24] In order to give civilization a new start, God brought the Great Flood, destroying all the descendants of Adam, with the exception of Noah and his family.[25]

4:13   Soon after the Great Flood, however, the world once again reverted to paganism and immorality. With very few exceptions, humanity again forgot God's universal laws.[26] There were exceptions, such as Noah's son, Shem,[27] and his grandson, Eber,[28] but even they did not publicly[29] teach God's law.[30] Again, ten generations passed, with the world's morality constantly deteriorating.[31]

22. Cf. *Moreh Nevukhim* 3:48. See Ramban, *Torath HaShem Temimah*, p. 173.
23. *Avoth* 5:2; *Teshuvoth Rashba* 4:30. See *Zohar* 2:104b; *Nitzutzey Zohar ad loc.* 2; *Tikuney Zohar* 69 (102b, top); *Adir BaMarom* 11b.
24. Cf. *Sanhedrin* 37a (top); *Bereshith Rabbah* 31:6; Rashi on Genesis 6:11; *Yad, Avodath Kokhavim* 1:1.
25. Genesis 6:9 ff. If the generation would have been worthy, they would have been the recipients of the Torah; *Shemoth Rabbah* 30:13; *Maharzav* on *Bereshith Rabbah* 32:5. Also see *Adir BaMarom* 11b.
26. *Yad, Avodath Kokhavim* 1:2.
27. Shem was the ancestor of the Semites. See *Bereshith Rabbah* 63:8; *Tanna DeBei Eliahu Rabbah* 28 (109a), 20 (93b); Rashi on Genesis 25:22.
28. *Seder Olam Rabbah* 1; Rashi on Genesis 10:25. Eber (Ever, עֵבֶר) was the ancestor of the Hebrews (Ivri'im, עִבְרִיִּים). See *Bereshith Rabbah* 42:13.
29. Shem and Eber did, however, maintain academies; see *Bereshith Rabbah* 56:11; *Targum Yonathan* on Genesis 25:22; *Bereshith Rabah* 63:6; *Pirkey Rabbi Eliezer* 32; *Radal ad loc.* 32:29; *Targum Yonathan*, Rashi, on Genesis 25:27; *Bereshith Rabbah* 63:10; *Megillah* 17a; Rashi on Genesis 25:17, 28:9; *Bereshith Rabbah* 67:8; *Yerushalmi, Sanhedrin* 4:7 (22b); *Karban HaEdah ad loc.* (4:8); *Esther Rabbah* 4:6.
30. Cf. Raavad, *Kesef Mishneh*, on *Yad, Avodath Kokhavim* 1:3. They were prophets; *Seder Olam Rabbah* 1; *Kuzari* 1:49 (35a); *Moreh Nevukhim* 2:39.
31. *Avoth* 5:2.

4:14   It was into this pagan atmosphere that a most unique individual was born. From his earliest childhood,[32] Abraham transcended his pagan environment[33] and recognized that the world was governed by one Supreme Being.[34] As one of the greatest geniuses of his time,[35] Abraham was able to use his keen mind to see through the sham and falsehood of the values of his generation, and understand the true purpose of creation.

4:15   Abraham's faith developed and overshadowed everything else in his life, until he was even willing to suffer martyrdom for it.[36] Never in history had an unaided individual made such a complete break with his environment, overcoming all obstacles for the sake of a yet unknown faith.[37]

4:16   When Abraham was 48 years old, a crucial historical event took place. God saw in Abraham a force that could bring all mankind back to Him, if only humanity could be unified. He therefore brought a spirit of unity upon the world, influencing all mankind to act in one accord. However, instead of uniting to serve God, mankind united to build the Tower of Babel.[38]

32. Some say from the age of three; *Nedarim* 32a; *Bereshith Rabbah* 30:8, 64:4, 95:2; *BaMidbar Rabbah* 18:17; *Shir HaShirim Rabbah* 6:1; *Esther Rabbah* 6:5; *Tanchuma, Lekh Lekha* 3; *Zohar* 3:302a; Raavad, *Avodath Kokhavim* 1:3; *Kesef Mishneh; Migdal Oz; Hagahoth Maimonioth* 1, *ibid.*
33. Such as by ridiculing and destroying his father's idols: *Bereshith Rabbah* 38:19; *Tanna DeBei Eliahu Zuta* 25 (57a).
34. *Bereshith Rabbah* 39:1; *BaMidbar Rabbah* 14:7; *Yad Avodath Kokhavim* 1:3; *Beth Elohim, Shaar HaYesodoth* 48.
35. Abraham was thus the world's greatest astronomer; *Bava Bathra* 15a. He was also the leading personage of his time; *Kiddushin* 32b; Ramban on Genesis 26:29, 40:14.
36. As when he was thrown in the fiery furnace by Nimrod for his faith; *Eruvin* 53a; *Pesachim* 118a; *Bereshith Rabbah* 38:19; *Midrash Tehillim* 118:11; *Pirkey Rabbi Eliezer* 26 (61a); *Tanna DeBei Eliahu Zuta* 25 (58a); Rashi on Genesis 11:28, 14:1.
37. Abraham had no teacher, *Bereshith Rabbah* 61:1. However, there is an opinion that he studied under Shem and Eber as a young child; *Sefer HaYashar* (ed. Alter Bergman, Tel Aviv), p. 23.
38. Alshekh on Genesis 11:1. At this time, Abraham was 48 years old, and he had

4:17   Humanity as a whole then lost the opportunity to come under the category of "Israel," the group designed to receive the Torah and fulfill the purpose of creation. Instead, the human race was split up into nations, each with its own language and mission. It was at this time that God decreed that the descendants of Abraham also become a nation, with the special mission of serving God and fulfilling His purpose in creation.[39]

4:18   At the age of seventy[40] Abraham took a voluntary pilgrimage to the Holy Land. After a sojourn in Egypt, where he gained great wealth,[41] he returned to the Holy Land, where he soon became caught up in a great battle that was raging there.[42] After playing a decisive role in this battle, Abraham was blessed by Shem[43] and was taught by him the traditions that had been handed down from the time of Adam.[44] At this time, Abraham took over from Shem the task of being the bearer of these traditions.[45]

already begun spreading God's teachings; see below, note 50. Cf. *Derashoth HaRun* 1.

39 *Derekh HaShem* 2:4:3. It is thus written, "When the Most High gave nations inheritance; when He separated the sons of man; He set up the borders of the nations, according to the number of the children of Israel. For God's portion is His people, Jacob, the lot of His inheritance" (Deuteronomy 32:8,9). See *Sifri;* Alshekh; Bachya; *Or HaChaim; Kli Yekar; ad loc.*

40. According to most sources, this occurred when Abraham was seventy years old, before God told him to leave Ur at the age of seventy-five (below, note 40). See *Seder Olam Rabbah* 1; *Mekhilta* on Exodus 12:40; Ramban; Mizrachi; *Sifethey Chakhamim; ibid.;* Rashi, *Sanhedrin* 92b, s.v. *U'Ta'u; Tosafoth, Shabbath* 10b, s.v. *VeShel, Avodah Zarah* 9a, s.v. *U'Gemirei;* Rosh, *Yevamoth* 6:2. According to this, we must say that the account in Genesis 12:10-15:21 occurred when Abraham was 70 years old, since this is an uninterrupted account. God's second call to Abraham when he was 75 is then described in Genesis 12:1-9. For further discussion, see HaGra on *Seder Olam Rabbah* 1; Abarbanel on Genesis 12:2; *Baaley Tosafoth* on Genesis 12:4.

41. Genesis 12:16, 13:2. See above, note 35.

42. Genesis 14.

43. Genesis 14:19. Malkhizedek is identified with Shem, see *Targum Yonathan,* Rashi, ad loc.; Radak; Ralbag on Joshua 10:1. Cf. Psalms 110:4.

44. *Pirkey Rabbi Eliezer* 8 (18b).

45. *Nedarim* 32b; Ran *ad loc.* s.v. *U'Malki Tzedek.*

4:19   Using the methods taught to him by Shem,[46] Abraham sought to attain true prophecy.[47] Soon, God revealed Himself to Abraham, and promised that his children would eventually grow into a great nation.[48] A while after this, when Abraham was 75, God revealed Himself to him again, and instructed him to leave his homeland permanently and to settle in the Holy Land.[49]

4:20   By this time, Abraham's faith was not only fully developed, but he also had the courage to act on the basis of his convictions.[50] Realizing that one cannot live a truth while allowing others to remain ignorant of it, Abraham became the first one publicly to teach about God and His universal commandments.[51]

4:21   Therefore, unlike the other righteous people of his time, whose children quickly became reabsorbed in the paganism of their time, Abraham was able to transmit his values to his offspring. He was able to establish his teachings among his descendants, until a self-sustaining group of the faithful was firmly established.[52] God thus said, "Abraham shall surely become a great and mighty nation, and all the nations of the earth shall be blessed through him. For I have known him, and I know that he will instruct his children and his

46. *Pesikta Chadata*, in A. Jellnek, *Beth HaMidrash* (Leipzig, 1853) 6:36; quoted in Rabbi Yehudah Barceloni, Commentary on *Sefer Yetzirah*, p. 268; *Sefer Rokeach* (Jerusalem, 1967), p. 19.
47. *Sefer Yetzirah* 6:4; Raavad, *ad loc.*; *Tzioni* on Genesis 12:5; Rabbi Eliezer of Worms on *Sefer Yetzirah* (Przemysl, 1883), p. 1a; Rabbi Moshe Botril on *Sefer Yetzirah* 1:1.
48. Genesis 15.
49. Genesis 12:1-9. See above, note 40.
50. *Bereshith Rabbah* 39:21; *Sanhedrin* 99b; Rashi on Genesis 12:5. Also see Genesis 12:8; *Bereshith Rabbah* 39:24.
51. He was thus the first to refer to God as "Lord" (*Adonoy*), *Berakhoth* 7b. Also see *Sotah* 10b; Maharatz Chajas on *Chagigah* 3a. Cf. *Yalkut Shimoni* 1:766. Also see Ezekiel 33:24.
52. *Yad, Avodath Kokhavim* 1:3. Cf. *Yoma* 28a.

household after him, that they will keep God's way, and maintain righteousness and justice, so that God will be able to grant Abraham everything He promised him" (Genesis 18:18,19).[53]

4:22   Still, Abraham's environment was so corrupt that it even claimed some of his own children and grandchildren. Of his two sons, only Isaac carried on the tradition, while Ishmael reverted to paganism.[54] Similarly, of Isaac's two sons, only Jacob remained true, while Esau soon abandoned God's law. Thus, of all Abraham's children, only Jacob and his family were able to maintain the tradition intact.[55]

4:23   God changed Abraham's name[56] and gave him and his descendants the commandment of circumcision[57] as an everlasting covenant.[58] Abraham was circumcised by Shem,[59] after which Abraham himself circumcised the rest

---

53. *Moreh Nevukhim* 3:24 (end). See *Sanhedrin* 57b.
54. Abraham's sons by Keturah were likewise sent to the East, Genesis 25:6. They kept many of the mystical traditions from Abraham, but also perverted them with idolatrous practices; see *Zohar* 1:100a,b. See *Sanhedrin* 91a; *Beer Sheva ad loc.*; *Zohar* 1:133b, 1:223a; *Gur Aryeh* on Genesis 25:6.
55. Cf. *Nedarim* 31a; *Yad, Nedarim* 9:21; *Yoreh Deah* 217:40; *Teshuvoth Rivash* 31; *Magen Avraham* 591:8; *Turey Zahav* 591:3.
56. God changed his name from Abram (אַבְרָם) to Abraham (אַבְרָהָם); Genesis 17:5 Nehemiah 9:7. This has a numerical value of 248, signifying that he had control over all his limbs; *Nedarim* 32b. It was for *Abraham* (not Abram) that the world was created; *Bereshith Rabbah* 12:8, from Genesis 2:4. Once his name was changed, it was now determined that he was this Abraham (very much as in the case of Israel, see 4:32). It is thus taught that the Patriarchs were created before the world; *Bereshith Rabbah* 1:5. They are also the Divine Chariot (*Merkavah*). *Bereshith Rabbah* 82:7. This is also related to the paradox of God's foreknowledge and human free will, see above, note 2.
57. Genesis 17:9-14. Cf. *Pesikta* 12 (100b); *Shir HaShirim Rabbah* 1:16; *Yad, Melakhim* 9:1.
58. Genesis 17:9. Regarding the meaning of a "covenant" (*Berith*, בְּרִית), see Rashi on Genesis 15:10; *Ikkarim* 4:45. According to many, it was from the time of his circumcision that Abraham had the status of an Israelite; Ramban on Leviticus 24:10; *Perashath Derakhim* 1. Also see *Yeffeh Toar*; Rabbi Yehudah (ben Yosef) Moskato, *Nefutzoth Yehudah* (Venice, 1589); quoted in *MeAm Lo'ez* on Genesis 17:25. See *Nedarim* 31a.
59. *Pirkey Rabbi Eliezer* 29 (24a); *Radal ad loc.* 29:1. Others maintain that Abraham circumcised himself; see *Bereshith Rabbah* 49:2; *Tanchuma, VaYera* 2.

of his household.⁶⁰ This occurred on Yom Kippur, and that day therefore marks the beginning of Israel's covenant with God.⁶¹

4:24   Circumcision was given to Abraham and his offspring so that they would be set aside by an indelible bodily sign, symbolic of their control of their physical passions.⁶² Since it was on the organ of reproduction, it symbolized that the particular distinction given to Abraham would also be passed on to his children.⁶³ It implied that he would have offspring who would have the distinction of having the status of "Israel."⁶⁴

60. Genesis 17:26,27. *Cf.* Radal on *Pirkey Rabbi Eliezer* 29:2. Cf. *Or HaChaim* on Genesis 17:23.
61. *Pirkey Rabbi Eliezer* 29 (64a). Also see *Tosafoth, Rosh HaShanah* 11a, s.v. *Elah; Baaley Tosafoth* on Genesis 17:26. There is, however, another opinion that Abraham was circumcised on Passover, see *Seder Olam Rabbah* 5; Rashi on Genesis 19:3; Ramban on Genesis 17:26; *Chizkuni* on Genesis 17:19.
62. *Moreh Nevukhim* 3:49; *Kuzari* 1:115 (76a); Ramban on Genesis 17:6; *Tur, Yoreh Deah* 260; *Chinukh* 2; Sforno, Abarbanel, on Genesis 17:11.
63. *Kuzari,* Sforno, Abarbanel, *loc. cit.;* Ibn Ezra on Genesis 17:4. Cf. *Shabbath* 108a; *Tanchuma, Lekh Lekha* 18; *Akedath Yitzchak* 18 (130a); *Menorath HaMaor* 3:1:1:2 (80).
64. Circumcision thus made the sexual organ into the "holy sign of the covenant (*oth b'rith kodesh,* אוֹת בְּרִית קוֹדֶשׁ), through which Abraham and his offspring would be able to use the sex act to draw souls from the highest spiritual levels. It is for this reason that circumcision is performed on the eighth day of the child's life; Genesis 17:12, Leviticus 12:3. Since the world is three dimensional, and each dimension implies two directions, the physical world has six directions, north, south, east, west, up, down. It was for this reason that the world was created in six days. The seventh day then represents the central point, which unifies the other six; *Sefer Yetzirah* 4:3. Seven thus represents the perfection of the physical world, which was completed in seven days. Therefore, eight denotes that which transcends the physical. Since circumcision is performed on the eighth day, it gives the man the power to transcend the physical world. Maharal, *Tifereth Yisrael* 2, 17; HaGra on *Sefer Yetzirah* 6:7. Cf. *.VaYikra Rabbah* 27:10; *Derekh Mitzvothekha* 9b. At the beginning of creation, God made a storehouse of souls, to be given to "Israel" and associated with the Torah; *Zohar Chadash* 74d; *Likutey Moharan* 52. Also see *Niddah* 13b; *Chagigah* 12b; *Akedath Yitzchak* 6; *Nishmath Chaim* 2:16. It was with the commandment of circumcision that Abraham was given accesss to these souls.
   Circumcision was given after the seven universal commandments, and was therefore the eighth commandment given to mankind; *Abudarham,* p. 355; Maharsha, *Menachoth* 43b, s.v. *KeSheNizkar.*
   Since circumcision gives one access to the spiritual, it serves to unify God's name; *Zohar* 1:89a. Cf. *Tanchuma, Tzav* 14; *Tikuney Zohar* 21 (87a).

4:25   To some degree, circumcision restored Abraham and his descendants to the status of Adam before his sin.[65] It was because they were circumcised that Abraham's descendants were able to be the recipients of the Torah.[66] Thus, it was through the commandment of circumcision that the purpose of creation could be fulfilled.[67]

4:26   The commandment of circumcision did not apply to the children of Ishmael, since it was given after his birth.[68] Similarly, it did not apply to the children of Esau, since they rejected the distinction and responsibility that went with the covenant.[69] Thus, of all the descendants of Abraham, only the children of Israel are bound by this commandment.[70]

4:27   God tested Abraham in ten different ways to prove his faith.[71] In the last of these tests, He asked Abraham to sacrifice his beloved son, Isaac.[72] After these tests, God gave

65. *Or HaShem* 2:2:6; Abarbanel on Genesis 17:9 (Jerusalem, 1964), p. 224a; *Kli Yekar* on Leviticus 12:3. Through his sin, Adam had lost the mark of circumcision; *Sanhedrin* 38b. Adam had been circumcised when created; *Tanchuma, Noah* 5. Later, when he sinned, the foreskin appeared; *Maaseh Hashem, Maaseh Bereshith* 19 (Warsaw, 1871), p. 58c. This was then restored with the commandment of circumcision; Ibid., *Maaseh Avoth* 14 (90c).

66. *Tanchuma, Mishpatim* 5. In the Grace, we thus say, "For the covenant that You sealed in our flesh, and for the Torah that You gave us;" see *Berakhoth* 48b, 49a; *Abudarham*, p. 322.

67. *Nedarim* 31b. Cf. *Zohar* 3:13b. See above, 4:6.

68. *Sanhedrin* 59b; *Yerushalmi, Nedarim* 3:8 (12a); *Yad, Melakhim* 10:7. Cf. *Zohar* 2:32a. It was especially not given until after Ishmael was born; Alshekh on Genesis 17:1 (Warsaw, 1779), p. 46c.

69. Ibid. According to some authorities, Esau was never circumcised, see *Baaley Tosafoth* on Genesis 25:25; *Oleloth Ephraim* 3:13:399; *Bereshith Rabbah* 63:13. According to others, however, Esau was circumcised, *Sefer HaEshkol* 40 (Halberstadt, 1868), p. 132; *Yalkut Chadash, s.v. Yitzchak* 55.

70. Cf. *Nedarim* 31b. Some maintain that since the children of Keturah (Genesis 25:1-6) were born to Abraham after he received the commandment of circumcision, they were also obliged to keep circumcision; *Sanhedrin* 59b. According to some, this only applied to them; Rashi *ad loc. s.v. Beney;* while others hold that it also applied to their descendants; *Yad, Melakhim* 10:8. Cf. *Mishneh LaMelekh ad loc.; Teshuvoth Shaagath Aryeh* 49; Maharatz Chajas, *Nedarim* 31a, 32a. Since the children of Keturah intermingled with the Arabs, they also circumcise; *Teshuvoth Nodah Be-Yehudah, Tinyana, Evven HaEzer* 42.

71. *Avoth* 5:3; Rambam, Bertenoro *ad loc.; Teshuvoth Rashbash* 456.

72. Genesis 22.

Abraham the distinction that no one other than his descendants would ever have the status of "Israel."[73] God also promised that even if his descendants sinned, they would never be abandoned.[74]

4:28   Of all the Patriarchs, only Jacob was able to lead all his children in the way of God. It was for this reason that he was chosen to be the father of the nation dedicated to serving Him.[75]

4:29   Jacob became worthy of this after he wrestled with an angel and defeated him.[76] This battle took place on a spiritual level, and was perceived by Jacob in a prophetic vision.[77] The "man" with whom he wrestled symbolized all the forces of evil in the world, and hence, the fact that Jacob was victorious showed that he had enough spiritual fortitude to give over to his children the power to ultimately overcome evil.[78]

4:30   In this episode, Jacob was wounded in his thigh.[79] This symbolized the partial victory of evil as well as the persecutions that his children would have to endure as a

---

73. Cf. *Yevamoth* 63a; Rashi on Deuteronomy 29:12. Rabbi Yoshia Pinto (Riph) in *Eyn Yaakov, ad loc.* Also see *Or HaShem* 2:2:6; *Ikkarim* 3:13.
74. Ramban on Genesis 26:6. See Exodus 32:13, Leviticus 26:44; below, note 131. Until then, God had chosen Abraham as an act of charity, but now he deserved it; *Maaseh HaShem, Maaseh Avoth* 22.
75. Cf. *Tanna DeBei Eliahu Rabbah* 27 (107b), from Hosea 9:10; *Kuzari* 1:47 (33b), 1:95 (47b).
76. Genesis 32:26-29.
77. *Moreh Nevukhim* 2:42. *Divrey Shalom* on Genesis 32:26 writes that this occurred while Jacob was in a meditative state. It is thus taught that the dust from their wrestling reached the Throne of Glory, indicating that this involved a very high spiritual plane; *Chulin* 91a; *Rashba* (in *Eyn Yaakov*) *ad loc.*
78. *Tanchuma, VaYishlach* 8; *Zohar* 1:170a. Cf. *Chulin* 91b; *Bereshith Rabbah* 77:2, 78:6. Others, however, write that the "man" with whom Jacob wrestled was the archangel Michael; *Targum Yonathan* on Genesis 32:25; *Yalkut Shimoni* 1:142.
79. Genesis 32:25. Some say that it was his right thigh; *Chulin* 90b, 91a. Others maintain that it was the left thigh; *Raya Mehemna, Zohar* 3:243a; *Pardes Rimonim* 17; *Etz Chaim, Shaar HaYereach* 5. Also see *Likutey Torah HaAri ad loc.* Jacob was struck in the inner part of the thigh (*yerekh*, יָרֵךְ), since this is near the place of procreation; *Bachya, ad loc.*; cf. Exodus 1:5.

dedicated people.[80] Jacob accepted both the responsibility and its consequences, merely asking for a blessing to give his children the power to endure.[81]

4:31   The angel then gave Jacob the name "Israel."[82] This indicated that Jacob and his offspring would be "great before God,"[83] and that they would have power over the highest spiritual forces.[84] It also indicated that Jacob's offspring would survive to carry the banner of God's teachings to all mankind.[85]

4:32   God later reaffirmed that Jacob was indeed Israel.[86] Jacob had become "Israel," the head of the group that God had originally conceived as the recipients of His good.[87] "Israel" was a concept that had existed before creation, but now

80. *Bereshith Rabbah* 77:4; *Zohar* 1:170b; Ramban on Genesis 32:26; *Chinukh* 3.
81. Genesis 32:27. Jacob and his descendants were then given a commandment not to eat the sciatic nerve (*gid ha-nasheh*, גִּיד הַנָּשֶׁה); Genesis 32:33. This commandment was actually given to Jacob; see *Pesikta* 12 (100b); *Shir HaShirim Rabbah* 1:6; *Yad, Melakhim* 9:1; *Lechem Mishneh ad loc.* In *Chulin* 7:6 (100b), this appears to be the opinion of Rabbi Yehudah, disputed by the majority. However, Rambam, *ad loc.*, writes that there is no dispute as to its origin with Jacob, but as to whether the current obligation stems from the commandment to Jacob or from Sinai. According to Rashi, *ad loc. s.v. Omru,* however, the accepted opinion would be that this commandment was not given until Sinai.
    On the simplest level, this was a commandment given so that Jacob's descendants would always remember this key event. It was a dietary law, given to symbolize the self control required for their mission, especially since it would prohibit the choice hind quarters of all animals, unless the nerve was arduously removed; cf. Ralbag *ad loc.* The blow on the thigh represented the partial victory of evil, and since evil now has a grasp on this nerve, it is forbidden; *Zohar* 1:170b; *Or HaChaim* on Genesis 32:33. It is also a constant reminder that the victory of evil can never be complete, since Israel might be wounded, but never destroyed; *Chinukh* 3.
82. Genesis 32:29. Cf. Hosea 12:4.
83. *Targum ad loc.*; *Bereshith Rabbah* 78:6.
84. *Targum Yonathan ad loc.*; *Chulin* 92a. Cf. Hosea 12:5.
85. See above, note 3. Also see Bachya *ad loc.*; *Yerushalmi, Taanith* 2:6 (10b); *Karban HaEdah ad loc.*; Rabbi Avraham ibn Chiya, *Hegion HaNefesh*, end of Chapter 1.
86. Genesis 35:10.
87. Cf. *Tanchuma, MiKetz* 5. Since Jacob now had the status of an Israelite, he could no longer have two sisters for wives, and for this reason Rachel died; Genesis 35:19; Ramban on Leviticus 18:25; *Perashath Derakhim* 1. Benjamin was now born, completing the twelve tribes; Genesis 35:18. Cf. *MeAm Lo'ez* on Exodus 14:22. Jacob was now also promised by God that he would be the recipient of what was promised to Abraham and Isaac; Genesis 35:12.

Jacob and his descendants would be worthy of carrying both the name and the concept that goes with it.[88]

4:33   Even the ancestry of the Patriarchs, however, would not have been enough to mold Israel into a nation capable of adhering to their faith under all conditions.[89] God therefore decreed that they spend 210 years in Egypt.[90] During this time, they would be subject to the harshest persecution and slavery.

4:34   The Egyptian bondage was like a refining furnace,[91] where all the spiritually weaker elements were weeded out,[92] while at the same time, the Israelites grew from a small desert family to a populous nation.[93] The Egyptian bondage would expose the Israelites to one of the greatest civilizations of the time, while at the same time strengthening them and drawing them together.[94]

4:35   In many ways, the Israelites proved themselves worthy of God's choice. Even under the most degrading slavery,

88. See above, 4:2. Now, Jacob was also worthy of being one whose face was on the Throne of Glory; *Bereshith Rabbah* 78:6. Regarding the question as to when the name Israel is used with regard to Jacob, see *Zohar* 1:174a; Bachya on Genesis 47:29. Also see Rabbi David ben Yehudah HaChasid, *Livnath HaSappir* (Jerusalem, 1913), p. 60b.
89. Hence, the Egyptian exile was due to a lack of faith on the part of Abraham; Genesis 15:13; *Targum Yonathan; Baaley Tosafoth, ad loc.; Pirkey Rabbi Eliezer* 48 (113b); *Yalkut Shimoni* 1:77.
90. *Seder Olam Rabbah* 3; *Pirkey Rabbi Eliezer* 48 (114a); *Yalkut Shimoni* 1:77; Rashi on Genesis 15:13, Exodus 12:40; *Megillah* 9a, Rashi *ad loc.* s.v. *U'BheShaar;* Rashbam, *Bava Bathra* 102a, s.v. *Asher.* The 400 years were counted from the birth of Isaac.
91. Deuteronomy 4:20; Jeremiah 11:4, Radak *ad loc.*
92. Such as those who died during the three days of darkness; *Targum Yonathan;* Rashi; on Exodus 10:23; *Shemoth Rabbah* 14:3; *Tana DeBei Eliahu* 7 (60a). It is taught that less than one fifth of the Israelites lived to experience the Exodus; *Mekhilta;* Rashi; on Exodus 13:18; *Yalkut Shimoni* 1:277; *Zohar* 3:108b; Rashi on Ezekiel 20:8; Radak on Ezekiel 20:9.
93. Exodus 1:7, Deuteronomy 10:22.
94. Cf. *Shemoth Rabbah* 1:1; *Tanchuma, Shemoth* 1; *Yalkut Shimoni* 2:950.

they maintained their identity and basic moral values.[95] Out of the crucible of Egypt, Israel thus emerged, refined and ready to become the torchbearers of God and the recipients of His Torah.[96]

4:36   Nevertheless, in many ways, the Israelites did fall into the pagan ways of the Egyptians.[97] In describing the Israelites before the Exodus, God thus said, "They rebelled against Me and would not listen to Me. None of them rejected the detestable things that attracted them, nor did they abandon the idols of Egypt. I would have decided to pour out My anger against them . . . but I acted for the sake of My name. . . For I had given My word that in the sight of the nations I would lead My people out of the land of Egypt" (Ezekiel 20:8,9).[98]

4:37   Ultimately, the Israelites were chosen by God primarily because of the merit of the Patriarchs. It is thus written, "Only in your fathers did God delight, and He loved them and chose their offspring after them, namely you, above all peoples, as it is today" (Deuteronomy 10:15).[99]

95. Thus, they did not change their names or language, and avoided sexual immorality and slander; *Mekhilta* on Exodus 12:6; *Shemoth Rabbah* 1:33; *VaYikra Rabbah* 32:5; *BuMidbar Rabbah* 20:21; *Shir HaShirim Rabbah* 4·24; *Tanchuma, Balak* 16; *Midrash Tehillim* 114·4; *Pesikta* 10 (83b); *Pirkey Rabbi Eliezer* 48 (109b); *Tana DeBei Eliau Rabbah* 10, 23, 24; *Yalkut Shimoni* 1:657. The common expression that the Israelites did not change their "names, language and clothing" is not found in any Midrashic source; cf. Buber on *Pesikta loc. cit.* 10:66.
96. See notes 91, 94. Cf. *Berakhoth* 5a; *Mekhilta* on Exodus 20:20; *Sifri* on Deuteronomy 6:5; *Midrash Tehillim* 94:2; *Yalkut Shimoni* 2:850. The Torah also could not be given until the number of male Israelites had grown to 600,000; *Bachya* on Genesis 46:27; *Derekh HaShem* 2:4:5. See below, 5:10. There also had to be seven purifications before the Torah was given; *Kad HaKemach,* s.v. *Shavuoth, Mitzvoth Lo Taaseh* (in *Kithvey Rabbenu Bachya,* Jerusalem, 1970), p. 412. Also see Ezekiel 16:7,8; Rashi, Radak, ad loc.
97. *Shemoth Rabbah* 21:7; *Yalkut Shimoni* 1:243; *Zohar* 2:170b. See Ramban on Exodus 12:42; Radak on Ezekiel 16:7; *Likutey Moharan* 21:9.
98. See *Mekhilta* on Exodus 12:6.
99. Rambam, *Iggereth Teimon* (Jerusalem, 1961), p. 6. Also see Genesis 12:2, 17:6, 18:18, Deuteronomy 4:37, 26:5.

4:38   It was through the merit of the Patriarchs that the Israelites were led into Egypt, only to be redeemed amid the greatest miracles ever witnessed by humanity. It is thus written, "God did not set His love over you, nor choose you, because you were greater in number than any other nation, for indeed, you were the least populous of all nations. But because God loved you, and because He kept the oath that He made to your fathers, God brought you out with a mighty hand, and redeemed you from the house of bondage" (Deuteronomy 7:7,8).[100]

4:39   The Exodus was a unique event in the annals of history. God revealed Himself to an entire nation, and literally changed the course of both history and nature. It is thus written, "Did God ever venture to take a nation for Himself from another nation, with a challenge, with signs and wonders, as God your Lord did in Egypt before your very eyes? You have had sure proof that God is the Lord, there is none other" (Deuteronomy 4:34).[101] The Exodus not only made Israel uniquely aware of God, but it also showed Him profoundly involved in the affairs of humanity.[102]

4:40   It was the Exodus and the events surrounding it that makes Judaism unique among all other religions. Other faiths began with a single individual who claimed to have a special message and gradually gathered a following. His followers then spread the word and gathered converts, until a new religion was born. Virtually every great world religion follows this pattern.[103]

100. *Iggereth Teimon, loc. cit. Cf.* Genesis 15:13, Exodus 2:24, 6:5, Deuteronomy 4:37.
101. *Moreh Nevukhim* 2:35.
102. See above, 1:9, from Exodus 20:2.
103. Cf. *Kuzari* 1:6. In order to avoid this, the Torah was not given to Abraham, but to his descendants after they had become a nation; Maharal, *Tifereth Yisrael* 18.

4:41   The main exception is Judaism. God gathered an entire nation, three million strong,[104] to the foot of Mount Sinai, and proclaimed His message. Every man, woman and child heard God's voice, proclaiming the Ten Commandments.[105] A permanent bond was thus forged between God and Israel.[106]

4:42   This unique event remained deeply imprinted in the soul of Israel, and throughout history it was something that was not to be forgotten.[107] We are likewise commanded not to forget the Exodus.[108]

4:43   The miraculous deliverance from Egypt defined Israel's unique responsibility to God. God thus said, "For to Me are the children of Israel servants; they are My servants whom I brought out of the land of Egypt; I am God your Lord" (Leviticus 25:55).[109] God likewise declared, "I am God, who brought you out of the land of Egypt; you shall therefore be holy, for I am holy" (Leviticus 11:45).[110] God promised this to Moses before the Exodus, saying, "I will take you to Me as a nation, and I will be to you as a God; you shall know that I am God your Lord, who brought you out from under the burdens of Egypt" (Exodus 6:7).[111]

4:44   Besides the merit of the Patriarchs, the Israelites also had many unique characteristics of their own.[112] God knew that

---

104. See *Targum Yonathan* on Exodus 12:37. There were approximately 600,000 males over twenty years of age; Exodus 12:37.
105. See above, 1:17.
106. *Yad, Yesodey HaTorah* 8:1; *Kuzari* 1:87.
107. From Deuteronomy 4:9,10. See above, 1:21.
108. From Deuteronomy 6:12. See above, 1:19.
109. Cf. *Sifri* on Numbers 15:41, Deuteronomy 11:10; *Kuzari* 1:27 (29a); Ibn Ezra on Exodus 20:1 (end). Also see Deuteronomy 6:22-24, 7:11; *Shemoth Rabbah* 30:5; Rashi on Exodus 21:6.
110. *Sifra*, Rashi, ad loc. Cf. *Bava Metzia* 61b.
111. Ibn Ezra, Ramban, *ad loc.* Cf. 2 Samuel 7:24, Jeremiah 24:7.
112. Cf. *Yevamoth* 79a; Maharal, *Tifereth Yisrael* 1.

among all the nations of the world, only Israel would have the great faith and intrinsic tenacity[113] to adhere to His teachings throughout all the vicissitudes of history.[114] It was as though God had asked all the nations to accept the Torah and had been refused by them.[115] In contrast, Israel's immediate reaction to the offer of the Torah had been, "All that God has spoken, we will do and we will obey" (Exodus 24:7).[116]

4:45   It was therefore primarily because of this ready acceptance of the Torah that Israel was chosen[117] to the exclusion of the rest of mankind.[118] Before the giving of the Ten Commandments, God thus said, "Now therefore, if you will hearken to My voice and keep My covenant, then you will be My own treasure among all nations, for all the earth is Mine. You shall be My kingdom of priests and holy nation" (Exodus 19:5).[119]

4:46   The Israelites were thus totally sanctified to God, and became virtually a separate species.[120] God said, "You shall

---

113. *Betza* 25b; Ramban on Deuteronomy 7:6; *Maaseh HaShem, Maaseh Torah* 12.
114. Nevertheless, other nations can also serve God in truth; see *Kuzari* 4:3 (8a); *Kol Yehudah ad loc.* 3:32 (32a), s.v. *VeKavar;* from Malachi 1:11. Cf. *Tanchuma, Ekev* 2.
115. *Avodah Zarah* 2b; *Mekhilta* on Exodus 20:2; *Sifri, Targum Yonathan,* Rashi, Ramban, on Deuteronomy 33:2; *Shemoth Rabbah* 27:8; *BaMidbar Rabbah* 14:22; *Eikhah Rabbah* 3:3; *Tanchuma, Yithro* 14, *Shoftim* 9, *Zoth HaBerakhah* 4; *Pirkey Rabbi Eliezer* 41 (95b); *Pesikta* 29 (186a); *Yalkut Shimoni* 1:551; *Zohar* 2:3a, 3:192b. This was the last opportunity given to other nations as a whole to gain the status of "Israel;" *Derekh HaShem* 2:4:5. Although only Esau and Ishmael are mentioned in Deuteronomy 33:2, they include all nations; *Nitzotzey Oroth* on *Zohar* 3:227b; *Tikuney Zohar* 22 (64a).
116. *Eikhah Rabbah* 3:3. Cf. *Shabbath* 88a; *VaYikra Rabbah* 2:4; *Teshuvoth Tashbatz* 3:310; Maharal, *Tifereth Yisrael* 29. This, however, was only true of the written Torah, not the Oral Torah, which they had to be forced to accept; *Tanchuma, Noah* 3. Cf. *Tosafoth, Shabbath* 88a, s.v. *Kafa;* Maharal, *Tifereth Yisrael* 32.
117. Cf. *Shemoth Rabbah* 47:4; *Ruth Rabbah* 1:1; *Yalkut Shimoni* 2:760; *Emunoth VeDeyoth* 3:7 (48a).
118. *Derekh HaShem* 2:4:5. Still, gentiles could convert to Judaism; *Ibid.* 2:4:6. See below, 5:15.
119. Cf. *Mekhilta ad loc.* Also see Deuteronomy 7:6.
120. *Kuzari* 1:103 (70a), 5:20 (53b). Therefore, only Israel is called "man," *Bava Metzia*

be holy to Me, for I, God, am holy, and I have set you apart from all other peoples, that you should be Mine" (Leviticus 20:26).[121]

4:47   But being chosen is more of a responsibility than a privilege. Israel has the incessant mission of proclaiming God's teachings to the world.[122] It is thus written, "I, God, have called you in righteousness . . . and have set you up as a covenant of the people, for a light to the nations" (Isaiah 42:6).[123] This does not mean that the Torah should be taught to gentiles,[124] but that they should be informed of the universal commandments.[125]

114b; *Yevamoth* 61a; from Ezekiel 34:31; *Radak ad loc.; Tosefoth Yom Tov, Negaim* 12:1. Also see *Berakhoth* 26a; *Shabbath* 150a; *Yevamoth* 98a; from Ezekiel 23:20; Maharatz Chajas, *Yevamoth* 61a. Cf. *Tosafoth, Avodah Zarah* 3a, s.v. *Kohanim.*

At Mount Sinai the taint of Adam's sin was removed from the Israelites; *Shabbath* 146a; *Avodah Zarah* 22b; *Yevamoth* 103b. If not for the sin of the Golden Calf, they would have even attained immortality; *Avodah Zarah* 5a, from Psalms 82:6. Cf. Maharal, *Tifereth Yisrael* 47.

121. Rashi *ad loc.* Cf. Leviticus 19:2.
122. Cf. *VaYikra Rabbah* 6.5 (end).
123. According to many authorities, this refers to Israel as a whole; Rashi *ad loc.; Midrash Tehillim.* Others maintain that it refers to the Messiah; Targum, Radak, Metzudoth, *ad loc.; Midrash Tehillim* 43:1. Even if it refers to the Messiah, however, he will be acting as a leader and representative of Israel, and thus fulfilling this part of their goal. The Messiah will first perfect Israel, and they in turn will perfect the entire world. Cf. Isaiah 49:6.
124. *Chagigah* 13a; *Tosafoth ad loc.* s.v. *Ain; Sanhedrin* 59a; *Yad, Melakhim* 10:9; *Teshuvoth Rambam* (Jerusalem, 1934) 364; *Beer Sheva, Beer Mayim Chaim* 14. Some say that this only applies to the Oral Torah; *Magen Avraham* 334:17; *Teshuvoth Rabbi Shmuel Abohav* 75; Maharatz Chajas, *Sotah* 32b. If a gentile wishes to become a proselyte, it is permitted to teach him Torah; Maharsha, *Shabbath* 31a, s.v. *Amar Ley; Teshuvoth Rabbi Akiba Eiger* 41; *Teshuvoth Machaneh Chaim* (Pressburg, 1862) 7; *Teshuvoth Ben Yehudah* 50.
125. *Tosafoth, Chagigah* 11a, s.v. *Ain.* Cf. *Sanhedrin* 59a; *Tosafoth, Avodah Zarah* 3a, s.v. *SheAfilu; Igroth HaRambam, Iggereth LeRabbi Chasdai HaLevi* (p. 16). Individuals do not have an obligation to correct a gentile if they see him violating one of the seven commandments; Rashi, *Sanhedrin* 75a, s.v. *Velm.* Still, it is a commendable deed to do so; *Sefer Chasidim* 1124. The Israelite people as a whole, however, do have an obligation to bring the gentiles to observe the seven universal commandments; *Yad, Melakhim* 8:10. This will also be the task of the Messiah; *Yad, Melakhim* 11:4.

4:48   Israel has a mission to bear witness to God's existence. God thus told Israel, "You are My witnesses . . . and My servant whom I have chosen" (Isaiah 43:10).[126] It is taught that Israel is like the heart of humanity, constantly beating and infusing all mankind with faith in God and His teachings.[127]

4:49   This universal message would often be proclaimed even at the price of suffering and persecution. It is taught that Israel is likened to an olive, since just as an olive must be crushed to bring forth oil, so Israel is persecuted so that its light should shine forth.[128] Even the dispersion of Israel among the nations was to teach the world how to serve God.[129] Moreover, the fact that Israel was scattered all over the world would guarantee that they not become extinct by means of their persecutions.[130]

4:50   Because of Israel's unique place in God's plan, the people must constantly be corrected whenever they stray from the true path. God thus said, "Only you have I known of all the families of the earth, therefore I will keep account of all your sins" (Amos 3:2).[131] Still, when God punishes Israel, He only does so as a father punishes his children. It is thus written, "As a man chastises his son, so God your Lord chastises you" (Deuteronomy 8:5).[132]

---

126. Mahari Kara *ad loc.; Ikkarim* 1:2. Cf. Isaiah 43:21, 44:8.
127. *Zohar* 2:221b; *Kuzari* 3:36 (51b), 2:12 (13a). It was in this spirit that Judaism gave rise to Christianity and Islam; *Yad, Melakhim* 11:4 (only in Rome, 1475, and Amsterdam, 1703, editions). See Chapter 1, note 20. A third system, Marxism, which, together with the other two, dominates the world, also stemmed from a Jew. Cf. Rabbi Elchanan Wasserman, *Kovetz Maamarim*, p. 108f.
128. *Shemoth Rabbah* 36:1; *Yalkut Shimoni* 2:289.
129. *Pesachim* 87b; Maharsha *ad loc.* s.v. *Lo;* from Hosea 2:25.
130. *Ibid.* from Judges 5:11, see *Kli Yekar* (47c); *Lev Aaron* (21): *ad loc.;* Rabbi Yehudah Aryeh de Modina, *Midbar Yehudah* (Venice, 1602), *Derush LeNesuin.* Also see *Derashoth HaRan* 1 (Jerusalem, 1974), p. 7.
131. *Avodah Zarah* 4a; *Tana DeBei Eliahu Rabbah* 15 (75b); *Zohar* 2:17b; *Chovoth HaLevavoth, Avodath Elohim* 6, *Yichud HaMaaseh* 5; *Kuzari* 2:44 (53b).
132. *Mekhilta* on Exodus 20:20.

4:51   Nevertheless, God promised that despite all these sufferings, Israel would always continue to exist to fulfill His purpose. He thus said, "The mountains may depart, and the hills may be removed, but My kindness will not depart from you, neither will My covenant of peace be removed" (Isaiah 54:10).[133] He continues, "No weapon that is raised against you shall be successful. Every tongue that shall rise against you in judgment shall be condemned by you. This is the heritage of God's servants, and their reward from Me" (Isaiah 54:17).

4:52   God thus made a covenant with Israel that they would continue to be the bearers of His word for all time. He thus said, "This is My covenant with them . . . My spirit that is with you, and My word that I have placed in your mouth, shall not depart from your mouth, nor from the mouths of your children, nor from the mouths of your children's children . . . now and forever" (Isaiah 59:21).

4:53   Although Israel has been persecuted and degraded throughout history, the nation will ultimately be vindicated. God said, "Although you have been hated and forsaken, so that no man is concerned with you, I will make you an object of eternal pride and never ending joy" (Isaiah 60:15). It is God's promise that Israel will ultimately restore the world to good, and cannot be destroyed as long as the task is not completed. He said, "[Israel] shall not fail nor be crushed until he has rectified the world, for the islands await his teachings" (Isaiah 42:4).[134]

133. See note 74.
134. Cf. *Menachoth* 53b. According to Rashi on Isaiah 42:1 this is speaking about the entire Jewish people. Others, however, state that it is speaking of the Messiah; *Targum Yonathan; Radak ad loc.* See above, note 123.

4:54   Most important, Israel has the role of fulfilling God's purpose in creation.[135] God said to Israel, "I have placed My words in your mouth, and have kept you safe under the shelter of My hand, so that I may plant the heavens and lay the foundations of the earth, and say to Zion, 'You are My people' " (Isaiah 51:16).[136] It is thus taught that God, Israel and the Torah are uniquely linked together.[137] The Torah is like oil in a lamp, and Israel is its wick, causing the light of God to shine forth on all creation.[138]

135. Cf. *Shabbath* 88a; *Avodah Zarah* 3a, 5a; *Tanchuma, Bereshith* 1; from Jeremiah 33:25; Rashi on Genesis 1:1, 1:31.
136. *Zohar* 1:5a; *Tikuney Zohar* 69 (104a, 118a); *Nefesh HaChaim* 1:12. Cf. *Sanhedrin* 99a; *Yerushalmi, Taanith* 4:2 (21a), *Megillah* 3:6 (26a); *Pesikta* 19. (140b); *Tanchuma, Yithro* 14, *Re'eh* 1; *Avoth* 1:2; *Shabbath* 10a.
137. *Zohar* 3:73a, 3:93a; *Nefesh HaChaim* 1:16, note s.v. *Af Al Pi.*
138. *Tikuney Zohar* 21 (60a).

FIVE

THE COMMANDMENTS

5:1   The means through which Israel gains the good for which God created the universe are the commandments.[1] If Adam would have kept his one commandment, then he would have immediately attained this goal.[2] Since he did not, numerous commandments are required.[3]

5:2   It is for this reason that the Torah contains many commandments. It is thus taught, "God wanted to benefit Israel; He therefore gave them Torah and commandments in abundance."[4] The essence of the Torah is its commandments.[5]

5:3   There are basically two types of commandments. In some places the Torah mandates certain action. This is a positive or mandatory commandment (*mitzvath aseh,* מִצְוַת עֲשֵׂה). In other places, the Torah prohibits certain action. This is a negative or prohibitive commandment (*mitzvath lo thaaseh,* מִצְוַת לֹא תַעֲשֶׂה).

1. *Derekh Hashem* 1:2:2, 1:4:5. See above, 3:15; below, 5:45.
2. *Derekh HaShem* 1:3:6.
3. Cf. *Or HaShem* 2:2:5.
4. *Makkoth* 3:16 (23b).
5. Rashi on Genesis 1:1; Mizrachi; Maharal, *Gur Aryeh; ad loc.;* Radak, *Sefer Sherashim,* s.v. *YaRaH* (ירה).

5:4   There is a tradition[6] that God included 613 commandments in the Torah.[7] Of these, 248 are positive, while
365 are negative.[8]

5:5   Many of these commandments, however, deal with the
laws of purity and sacrifice, and were thus only applicable
when the Temple stood in Jerusalem.[9] Therefore, of all the
commandments, only 369 apply today. Of these, 126 are
positive, and 243 are negative.[10]

5:6   Even of these, however, many only pertain to special
cases or circumstances. The total number of commandments
which apply to everyone under all conditions is 270. Of
these, 48 are positive, and 222 are negative.[11]

5:7   All the commandments, including their interpretations
and laws, were given to Moses during the forty days that he

---

6. Ramban on *Sefer HaMitzvoth, Shoresh* 1 (Vilna edition), p. 1a.
7. *Makkoth* 23b; *Mekhilta* on Exodus 20:2; *Sifri* on Deuteronomy 12:23 (Freidman
   edition) 76; *Bereshith Rabbah* 24:5; *Shemoth Rabbah* 33:8; *Shir HaShirim Rabbah*
   1:13; *Pirkey Rabbi Eliezer* 41 (98a); *Pesikta* 12 (101a). Also see *Shabbath* 87a;
   Yevamoth 47b; *Nedarim* 25a; *Shavuoth* 29a; Rashi *ad loc.* s.v. *Shakulah*; Rashi,
   Menachoth 43b, s.v. *Shekulah*; *Tosafoth, Menachoth* 39a, s.v. *Lo*; Rashi on Genesis
   32:5, Numbers 15:39. For a detailed discussion of this number, see Ramban on *Sefer
   HaMitzvoth, Shoresh* 1; *Tashbatz*, introduction to *Zohar HaRakia*; *Sh'nei Luchoth
   HaB'rith*, beginning of *Torah SheBeK'thav* (3:3b). Also see *BaMidbar Rabbah* 13:15,
   18:17.
8. The positive commandments parallel the 248 parts of the body (*Ohaloth* 1:8), while
   the negative commandments parallel the 365 days of the solar year; *Makkoth* 23b.
   They also parallel the 365 major blood vessels, tendons and nerves (collectively
   giddim, גידים) in the human body; *Targum Yonathan* on Genesis 1:27. Also see
   Tanchuma, Ki Thetze 2; *Zohar* 1:170b; *Maarekheth Elohuth* 10 (147a).
9. This does not contradict the principle that the Torah is eternal (below, 5:20), since in
   the Messianic Age all these commandments will be restored; *Yad, Melakhim* 11:1;
   Beth Elohim, Shaar HaYesodoth 50.
10. *Sh'nei Luchoth HaB'rith*, beginning of *Torah SheBeK'thav* (3:1b, in note), quoting
    Megillath Setharim; quoted in *Pri Megadim, introduction to Orach Chaim*; and in
    Letter by author of *Minchath Chinukh* (printed before author's introduction, New
    York 5722), p. iv. Rabbi Yisrael Meir HaCohen, *Sefer Mitzvoth HaKatzar*, lists 77
    positive commandments, and 194 negatives, for a total of 271. The *Sefer Mitzvoth
    Katan (S'mak)* lists 320 commandments that apply today.
11. *Ibid.* In *Sefer HaMitzvoth*, however, at the end of Positive Commandment 248, only
    60 such positive commandments are listed.

spent on Mount Sinai.[12] God thus told Moses, "Come up to Me on the mountain and stay there. I will give you tablets of stone, as well as the Torah and commandments which I have written, so that you may teach them" (Exodus 24:12). Everything was thus given on Sinai.[13]

5:8   There were numerous commandments that had been known at earlier times. The seven universal commandments had been given to Adam and Noah.[14] Later, circumcision was given to Abraham,[15] and a dietary law not to eat the sciatic nerve (*gid ha-nasheh*, גִּיד הַנָּשֶׁה), to Jacob.[16] Jacob's son, Judah, instituted the levirate marriage (*yibum*, יִבּוּם).[17] Detailed laws of marriage and divorce were given to Amram in Egypt.[18]

5:9   The Israelites were also given other laws before they reached Mount Sinai. The rules of the Sabbath were initially given to them when they first received the Manna.[19] Likewise, the laws regarding the honor due one's parents[20]

---

12. According to some, not all details were given at that time; *Sotah* 37b; *Chagigah* 6a; *Zevachim* 115a. Also see *Sifra*, Rashi, Ramban, on Leviticus 25:1; *Sifra* on Leviticus 27:34; *Sefer HaMitzvoth, Shoresh* 1, from *Makkoth* 23b. The forty days are mentioned in Exodus 24:18, 34:28, Deuteronomy 9:9, 9:11, 9:18, 10:10.
13. *Berakhoth* 5a. Cf. *Avoth* 1:1. See below, 9:3.
14. See above, 4:8.
15. Above, 4:23.
16. See Chapter 4, note 81.
17. Genesis 38:8. In *Pesikta* 12 (100b), there is an indication that this was actually given as a commandment; cf. *Yad, Melakhim* 9:1. Other sources, however, indicate that Judah instituted this of his own accord; cf. *Bereshith Rabbah* 85:5; *VaYikra Rabbah* 2:9; Ritva, Maharatz Chajas, *Yevamoth* 5b.
18. *Yad, Melakhim* 9:1. Cf. *Teshuvoth Makom Sh'muel* 23; Maharatz Chajas, *Sotah* 12a. Also see *Mekhilta* on Exodus 18:1 (Freidman edition, Vienna, 1870), p. 57b; *Meir Eyin ad loc.* 28. Compare *Yerushalmi, Kiddushin* 1:1 (2a); *Bereshith Rabbah* 18:8; *Yad, Melakhim* 9:8; *Peney Yehoshua* on *Tosafoth, Kiddushin* 13b, s.v. *LeKulo Alma.*
19. Exodus 16:5,29. It had earlier been given at Marah, see Deuteronomy 5:12, Rashi *ad loc.*; *Sanhedrin* 56b; *Seder Olam Rabbah* 5; *Targum Yonathan, Mekhilta, Yalkut Shimoni* (1:257), Rashi, on Exodus 15:25. Cf. *Pirkey Rabbi Eliezer* 18 (42b); *Tosafoth, Shabbath* 87b, s.v. *Ka'asher; Turey Zahav, Yoreh Deah* 1:0.
20. *Ibid.* In *Mekhilta, loc. cit.*, this is disputed by Rabbi Eliezer HaModai, who substitutes sexual laws. Rashi on Exodus 15:25 substitutes the laws of the Red Heifer (*Parah Adumah*, פָּרָה אֲדֻמָּה, Numbers 19); cf. *Seder Olam Zuta.*

and certain judicial regulations[21] were given at Marah, shortly before the Israelites came to Sinai.[22]

5:10   Nevertheless, the final authority for all the commandments was their revelation at Sinai.[23] As soon as the Israelites entered into this covenant with God, they were only bound by the Torah as revealed by Moses. At this time, they were absolved of all previous commandments.[24] It is for this reason that we do not learn laws from acts done before the revelation at Sinai.[25]

5:11   Therefore, although the Torah embodied earlier laws, and was written over a forty year period, its commandments all became binding at the instant of their acceptance at Sinai.[26] As a religion, therefore, Judaism did not evolve, but came into being at once with the revelation at Sinai.[27]

5:12   The Israelites accepted the Torah through both an oath and a covenant.[28]

5:13   In presenting the Torah to the Israelites, Moses bound them by an oath.[29] This oath was taken by all Israel[30] at

21. *Ibid.* This is a secondary opinion in *Seder Olam Rabbah.*
22. Exodus 15:25. For a discussion of other laws given before Sinai, see *Yevamoth* 5b; *Megillah* 6b; *Teshuvoth Rashbash* 543.
23. Rambam on *Chulin* 7:6; Maharatz Chajas, *Berakhoth* 13a, *Yevamoth* 5b, *Sanhedrin* 56b, *Makkoth* 23b. Cf. *Mishneh LaMelekh* on *Yad, Melakhim* 10:7; *Teshuvoth Makom Sh'muel* 22.
24. Rashi, *Sanhedrin* 59a, s.v. *LeZeh.* Cf. *Sanhedrin* 71b; *Yad, Melakhim* 10:4.
25. *Yerushalmi, Moed Katan* 3:5 (14b); *Tosafoth, Moed Katan* 20a, s.v. *Mah; Bekhor Shor ad loc.; Yad, Avel* 1:1; *Arukh,* s.v. *Shachar;* Maharatz Chajas, *Yoma* 28b, *Taanith* 28a, *Moed Katan* 20a, *Nazir* 15b, *Chullin* 16a; *Torath HaNevi'im* 11.
26. Cf. *Eruvin* 21b; Maharatz Chajas *ad loc.*
27. *Kuzari* 1:81 (49a). Cf. Deuteronomy 27:9.
28. *Tosafoth, Shabbath* 88a, s.v. *Modaah, Akedath Yitzchak* 100. Also see Ezekiel 16:8. Some authorities write that there was a second convenant and oath at the end of the forty years, since the first had been annulled with the making of the Golden Calf; Ramban on Exodus 24:27; Bachya on Deuteronomy 29:9,11. However, from numerous sources, it seems that the oath from Sinai is still binding, see Note 31.
29. *Shevuoth* 29a; *Nedarim* 25a. Also see *Nedarim* 8a; *Nazir* 4a; *Yad, Nedarim* 3:7, *Shevuoth* 11:3; *Sifethey Cohen, Yoreh Deah* 119:22; *Teshuvoth Nodeh BeYehudah, Orach Chaim* 38; *Teshuvoth Shaagath Aryeh* 61; Maharatz Chajas, *Nedarim* 8a, 12a, *Nazir* 4a. Cf. *Teshuvoth Rambam* 170. Also see Nehemiah 10:30.
30. Even if a single Israelite had refused, the Torah would not have been given; *Sefer*

Mount Sinai.[31] It is eternally binding,[32] on all future generations.[33]

5:14   The covenant consisted of three elements.[34] First was circumcision for all males, just before the Exodus.[35] Second was immersion for the entire people just before the revelation at Sinai.[36] Third, they offered sacrifice.[37] It was through this that the Israelites were accepted like proselytes into their new faith. Immediately after this, the Israelites declared, "We will do and obey" (Exodus 24:7).[38]

5:15   Whenever a gentile converts to Judaism, he essentially duplicates this oath and covenant. He must accept upon himself all the commandments, and then, if he is a male,

Chasidim 233, from Exodus 24:3. Also see *Mekhilta* on Exodus 19:11; *Bereshith Rabbah* 87:9; *Sifri* on Numbers 10:36.

31. There is thus the expression regarding the commandments that we are "continually bound by an oath from Mount Sinai" (מֻשְׁבָּע וְעוֹמֵד מֵהַר סִינַי); *Shevuoth* 3:6 (27a), 21b; *Yoma* 73b; *Nedarim* 8a. This oath may have been the statement, "we will do and we will listen" (Exodus 24:7). Hence, in Deuteronomy 29:9, the oath comes after the covenant. Many authorities, however, maintain that the oath was the curse declared on Mount Ebal; Deuteronomy 29:28; Rashi, Ramban, ad loc.; Rashi on Genesis 12:6; *Karban HaEdah, Yerushalmi, Sotah* 2:5 (12a), s.v. *LeAurekha*. Cf. *Shevuoth* 36a; Rashi, *Sanhedrin* 43b, s.v. *B'rith*. Also Rashi, *Pesachim* 38b, s.v. *B'rith; VaYikra Rabbah* 6:5; *BaMidbar Rabbah* 9.54.
32. *Maharsha, Shevuoth* 39a, s.v. *KeSheHishbia; Rashash ibid.* Rabbinical commandments are also binding; *Sifethey Cohen, Yoreh Deah* 119:22. Cf. *Shevuoth* 39a, from Esther 9:27.
33. Although an individual cannot bind his descendants with an oath, a community can; *Mishpat HaCherem, Kol Bo* (end); *Teshuvoth Ramban* 288; *Yoreh Deah* 228:35; *HaGra ad loc.* 228:99. Cf. *Yerushalmi, Nedarim* 3:1 (8b); *Shevuoth* 39a; from Deuteronomy 29:14; *Teshuvoth HaRosh* 5:4; *Teshuvoth Rivash* 399. Also see Esther 9:27; *Bava Bathra* 60b, from Malachi 3:9.
34. *Kerithuth* 9a; *Yad, Issurey Biah* 13:1. The covenant at Sinai is mentioned in Deuteronomy 5:2,3, 28:69.
35. Cf. Exodus 12:48, Joshua 5:5. Also see *Yevamoth* 71b; *Kerithoth* 9a; *Tosafoth ad loc.* s.v. *VeKethiv;* Radal (on *Pirkey Rabbi Eliezer*) 29:1, 29:49; Ramban, Rashba, *Yevamoth* 46a, s.v. *SheKen;* Rambam, *Iggereth HaShmad,* p. 6. Also see Ezekiel 16:6; Rashi, Radak, *ad loc.; Shemoth Rabbah* 17:3; *BaMidbar Rabbah* 14:12; *Shir HaShirim Rabbah* 1:5, 5:2; Rashi on Exodus 12:6; *Yad, Issurey Biyah* 13:2.
36. Exodus 19:14; *Mekhilta,* Ramban, *ad loc.;* Ezekiel 16:9, Radak, Abarbanel, *ad loc.* Cf. *Yevamoth* 46a; *Tosefoth Yom Tov, Pesachim* 8:8; *Yad, Issurey Biyah* 13:3.
37. Exodus 24:5-8. It is specifically called "blood of the covenant" (Exodus 24:8). This took place on the fifth of Sivan, before the giving of the Ten Commandments; Rashi on Exodus 24:1,5. Others, however, dispute this, see Ramban ibid. See note 39.
38. See above, 4:44. This might have been the oath at Sinai; see note 31. See Rashi on 2 Kings 17:35.

undergo circumcision. Both male and female must then immerse in a valid *mikvah* (מִקְוֶה).[39] In this manner, they enter a covenant in the same way that all Israelites did originally.[40]

5:16   It was this oath and covenant that established the special relationship between God and Israel for all time. Moses thus said, "You are standing before God your Lord . . . to enter into the covenant and oath that God your Lord is making with you today. Today, He will thus permanently make you His people, and He will be your God, as He swore to your fathers, Abraham, Isaac and Jacob. It is not with you alone that I am making this covenant and oath, . . . but also with those who are not here this day" (Deuteronomy 29:9-14).[41]

5:17   The Torah and its commandments were given only to Israel. It is thus written, "Moses bound us by the Torah, an inheritance for the community of Jacob" (Deuteronomy 33:4).[42] Similarly, "[God] declared His word to Jacob, His decrees and laws to Israel; He has not done this to any other nation" (Psalms 147:19,20).[43]

5:18   Therefore, no law appearing in the Torah is binding on any people other than Israel. The only exceptions are the universal laws, which are known by tradition to be binding on the entire human race.[44] This is usually indicated by a

39. *Yoreh Deah* 268:2. It must be before a rabbinical court (*beth din,* בֵּית דִּין) of three; Ibid. 268:3. Since the Temple is no longer standing, sacrifice is no longer required; *Kerithoth* 9a; *Yad, Issurey Biyah* 13:5. This is derived from Numbers 15:14, which indicates that converts can be accepted "in all generations," even when the Temple is not standing.
40. *Kerithoth* 9a; *Yad, Issurey Biyah* 13:4.
41. Ramban, *Yalkut* (1:560), *ad loc.; Tanchuma, Netzavim* 3; Maharsha, *Shevuoth* 39a, s.v. *KeSheHishbia.* Also see Deuteronomy 26:18, 27:9, Jeremiah 31:32. Cf. *Yerushalmi, Nedarim* 3:1 (8b); *Yerushalmi, Sotah* 2:5 (12a).
42. *Sifri, Yalkut Shimoni* (1:552), *ad loc.; Sanhedrin* 59a.
43. Ibn Ezra *ad loc.; Chagigah* 13a. Also see *Teshuvoth Chakham Tzvi* 26; *Maharatz Chajas, Bava Metzia* 61a. See Chapter 4, notes 124, 125.
44. Cf. *Kuzari* 3:73 (75b).

special redundancy, where the commandment is repeated especially for gentiles.[45]

5:19   Therefore, there is no case where the law is stricter for gentiles than for a Jew.[46] There are a few exceptions to this general rule, but these are all governed by specific traditions.[47]

5:20   One of the foundations of our faith is the affirmation that the commandments were given for all times.[48] It is thus written, "Things that are revealed to us belong to us and our children *forever*, to keep all the words of this Torah" (Deuteronomy 29:28).[49]

5:21   It is therefore forbidden to add or subtract any commandments from the Torah. It is thus written, "All this word which I command you, you shall be careful to do it. You shall not add to it, nor diminish from it" (Deuteronomy 13:1).[50] It is forbidden even to interpret a commandment so as to add a prohibition not included in the tradition.[51]

45. *Sanhedrin* 59a; *Tosafoth, Avodah Zarah* 5b, s.v. *Menayin, Zevachim* 68b, s.v. *VeSheNimsis, Chulin* 23a, s.v. *Tamuth;* also *Tosafoth, Bava Kama* 55a, s.v. *Le-Minehu.* Cf. *Teshuvoth Rashbash* 543; *Teshuvoth Chakham Tzvi* 26; Rabbi Yeshiah Berlin, *She'elath Shalom* (on *She'iltoth,* Dyhernfurth, 1786) 10; *Maharsha* on *Tosafoth, Chagigah* 2b, s.v. *Lo;* Maharatz Chajas, *Chagigah* 11b, *Bava Kama* 55b, *Bava Metzia* 61b, *Sanhedrin* 56b; *Torath HaNevi'im* 10.
46. *Sanhedrin* 59a. Also see *Sanhedrin* 58b; *Tosafoth, Yevamoth* 34b, s.v. *VeLo.* Also see *Teshuvoth Chatham Sofer, Yoreh Deah* 19; *Pith'chey Teshuvah, Yoreh Deah* 62:1; *Teshuvoth Panim Meiroth* 2:158.
47. *Sanhedrin* 59a; *Tosafoth, ad loc.* s.v. *Leika.*
48. Thirteen Principles of Faith 9. See *Ikkarim* 3:16; *Maharal Tifereth Yisrael* 51. See below 8:3, 8:41.
49. *Yad, Yesodey HaTorah* 9:1.
50. *Yad, Mamrim* 2:9; *Raavad ad loc.; Sefer HaMitzvoth,* Negative Commandments 313, 314; *Sefer Mitzvoth Gadol,* Negative Commandments 364, 365; *Chinukh* 454, 455. Cf. Deuteronomy 4:2. Some authorities, however, maintain that this only applies to the addition of positive commandments, and not negative ones; *Raavad; Chinukh; loc. cit.*
51. *Yad, loc. cit.; Minchath Chinukh* 454. Cf. *Bereshith Rabbah* 7:2; *BaMidbar Rabbah* 18:3; *Koheleth Rabbah* 7:43; *Tanchuma, Chukath* 6; *Pesikta* 4 (35b).

5:22   God gave the Sanhedrin the power to legislate new laws as they were required.[52] These laws are called "rabbinical commandments" (*mitzvoth de-rabanan*, מִצְוֹת דְּרַבָּנָן). When legislating, however, the Sanhedrin had to be most careful to distinguish their legislation from actual Torah laws. There are major differences in strictness between "rabbinical commandments" and commandments of the Torah (*mitzvoth de-oraitha*, מִצְוֹת דְּאוֹרַיְתָא).[53]

5:23   The Ten Commandments served as an introduction to the other commandments. They contain the essence of the entire Torah.[54]

5:24   The Ten Commandments had formed the basis of morality and religion even in the times of the Patriarchs.[55] They contain the main principles necessary for the survival of the Jewish people, both religiously and ethically.[56]

5:25   God gathered the entire Israelite people to the foot of Mount Sinai and publicly declared the Ten Command-

52. See below, 11:24.
53. *Yad, loc. cit.*; Ramban on Deuteronomy 4:2 (end); *Pri Megadim*, Introduction to *Orach Chaim* 1:35; *Amudey Yerushalayim* on *Yerushalmi, Megillah* 1:5 (7a); Maharatz Chajas, *Megillah* 14a. See below, 11:24.
54. Exodus 20:2-14; Deuteronomy 5:6-18. It is taught that the Ten Commandments include all 613; *BaMidbar Rabbah* 13:15; *Shir HaShirim Rabbah* 5:12; *Yerushalmi, Shekalim* 6:1 (25a); *Yalkut Shimoni* 1:368, 1:825; Rashi on Exodus 24:12; *Kuzari* 1:87 (52b). It is likewise taught that the Decalogue contains 613 letters, alluding to all 613 commandments; *BaMidbar Rabbah* 13:15, 18:17; *Bahir* 124. Actually, the Decalogue contains 620 letters, but the last seven, which are the words *asher le-reye-kha* (אֲשֶׁר לְרֵעֶךָ) — "to your neighbor" — are not included, since they contain the very essence of the Torah; Saadia Gaon on *Sefer Yetzirah* (translated from the Arabic by Yosef Kapach, Jerusalem, 1972), p. 48; Rabbi Yehudah Barceloni on *Sefer Yetzirah*, p. 278; *Megalleh Amukoth* 197. See below, note 134. Also see *Sefer Mitzvoth Gadol*, end of Positive Commandments; *Torath HaOlah* 3:33. Cf. Rashash, *Sanhedrin* 21b.
55. Cf. *Yalkut Shimoni* 1:276 (end).
56. Thus, the first five commandments deal primarily with the foundations of our faith, namely the belief in God, the negation of idolatry, respect for God's name, the Sabbath as a commemoration of creation, and honor to parents to insure the survival of tradition. The second five deal with moral necessities, namely, the respect for life, chastity and property, the pursuit of justice, and the subjugation of man's covetous desires; *Ikkarim* 3:26; Maharal, *Tifereth Yisrael* 36.

ments.[57] They were then written on two stone tablets.[58] These tablets were placed in the Holy Ark, which was eventually stored in the Holy of Holies in the Temple.[59]

5:26   It was through the Ten Commandments that the covenant was sealed. It is thus written, "[God] proclaimed to you His covenant, which He commanded you to keep — Ten Commandments — and He wrote them on tablets of stone" (Deuteronomy 4:13).[60]

5:27   In some places, the Tablets were called "tablets of the covenant" (luchoth ha-brith, לוּחוֹת הַבְּרִית).[61] This indicates that they contain the words through which the covenant at

57. See above, 4:41. Although the versions in Exodus 20:2-14 and Deuteronomy 5:6-18 contain somewhat different wording, it is taught that they were both given in a single act of divine speech; *Shevuoth* 10b; *Rosh HaShanah* 27a; *Yerushalmi, Nedarim* 3:2 (9a); *Yerushalmi, Shevuoth* 3:8 (17b); *Mekhilta* (69a), Rashi, on Exodus 20:8; *Sifri* (233) on Deuteronomy 22:11; *Tosafoth, Bava Kama* 54b, s.v. *Behemtekha; Maaseh HaShem, Maaseh Torah* 17; Maharal, *Tifereth Yisrael* 44, 45.
58. Exodus 24:12, 31:18, 32:15, Deuteronomy 4:13, 5:19, 9:9. The first two tablets were broken; Exodus 32:19, Deuteronomy 9:17. A new set were then made by Moses; Exodus 34:1, Deuteronomy 10:2. Ibn Ezra on Exodus 20:2 writes that the Exodus version was written on the first set of tablets, while the Deuteronomy version was written on the second set. This view is supported in *Bava Kama* 55a; cf. Rabbi Yoshia Pinto (Riph, in *Eyn Yaakov* 15); *Peney Yehoshua; ad loc.;* Rabbi Reuven Margolies, *HaMikra VeHaMesorah* 1. In *Shemoth Rabbah* 47:10, however, there is an opinion that both sets contained the exact same wording; cf. Exodus 34:1, Ibn Ezra *ad loc.;* Deuteronomy 10:2,4, Alshekh *ad loc.* Regarding the script on the Tablets, see *Teshuvoth Radbaz* 883 (3:442); below, 7:58. Regarding the pairing of the Ten Commandments, see *Mekhilta* (70b) on Exodus 20:14. For a discussion as to how they were written on the Tablets, see *Yerushalmi, Shekalim* 6:1 (25a); *Mekhilta* (70b) to Exodus 20:14; *Shemoth Rabbah* 47:10; *Targum* on Song of Songs 5:13; *Shir HaShirim Rabbah* 5:12; *Teshuvoth Radbaz* 980 (3:549). For the dimensions of the tablets, see *Bava Bathra* 14a; *Yerushalmi, Shekalim, loc. cit.* For an explanation of how God wrote the Tablets, see Exodus 31:18; *Moreh Nevukhim* 1:46; *Maaseh HaShem, Maaseh Torah* 14; *Avodath HaKodesh* 4:32; *Shiur Komah* 49.
59. Deuteronomy 10:5, Ramban, Bachya, *ad loc.;* 1 Kings 8:9, 2 Chronicles 5:10; *Bava Bathra* 14a; *Yoma* 52b.
60. Cf. *Mekhilta* (71b) on Exodus 20:16; Deuteronomy 5:22. Also see Rambam, *Tosefoth Yom Tov,* on *Tamid* 5:1; *Maharsha, Berakhoth* 11b, s.v. *VaKaru.*
61. Deuteronomy 9:9, 9:11, 9:15. Since the Ark contained the Tablets, it was called the "Ark of the Covenant" (aron ha-b'rith, אֲרוֹן הַבְּרִית); Exodus 25:22, 26:33, 30:6, 30:26, 39:25, 40:3, 40:21, Numbers 4:5, 7:89, Joshua 4:16; see note 63. It appears that to the Israelites who witnessed the revelation at Sinai it was referred to as "Testimony," while to those of the subsequent generations, it was referred to as "Covenant."

Sinai was sealed.⁶² Elsewhere, they are called "tablets of the testimony" (luchoth ha-eduth, לוּחוֹת הָעֵדוּת), since they are permanent, tangible testimony to the existence of this covenant.⁶³ The Tablets thus represented the physical reality of the covenant, the special relationship between God and Israel.⁶⁴

5:28   The reading of the Ten Commandments was originally included in the daily liturgy.⁶⁵ There were, however, heretics who claimed that only these ten were actually given by God.⁶⁶ Because of them, the reading was deleted.⁶⁷ Moreover, it was legislated that they not be read as part of any public service.⁶⁸ Although the Ten Commandments are of cardinal importance, all the commandments were given by God and are essential to Judaism.

5:29   The main significance of the commandments is the fact that they were given by God Himself. They are therefore the

62. There were therefore two tablets, since a covenant (b'rith) consists of two objects; Rabbi Yitzchak Hutner שליט״א, Pachad Yitzchak; cf. Rashi on Genesis 15:10. For the significance of this, see Rashi on Jeremiah 34:18; Ralbag on Genesis 15:10; Ikkarim 4:45; Rashbam on Exodus 24:21; HaGra on Sefer Yetzirah 1:3. Also see Rabbi Yehudah Barceloni on Sefer Yetzirah 1:3, p. 141.
63. Exodus 31:18, 34:29. This is another reason that there were two tablets; in order to testify, two witnesses are needed (Deuteronomy 19:15); Devarim Rabbah 3:16; Midrash HaGadol, Bachya, on Exodus 31:18. Also see Tanchuma, Ki Thisa 16; Shemoth Rabbah 41:7; Bachya on Exodus 25:10.
64. However, this is also true of the Torah as a whole, Yad, Sefer Torah 10:10. The Torah is thus also referred to as the "Book of the Covenant" (sefer ha-b'rith, סֵפֶר הַבְּרִית); Exodus 24:7, 2 Kings 22:11, 23:2, 23:21.
65. Tamid 5:1.
66. Yerushalmi, Berakhoth 1:5 (9b); Rashi, Berakhoth 12a, s.v. Mip'ney; Rambam on Tamid 5:1; Magen Avraham 1:9; Turey Zahav 1:5.
67. Berakhoth 12a; Rambam, Bertenoro, on Tamid 5:1.
68. However, they may be read privately, and this was once a custom; Orach Chaim 1:5 in Halah; Beer Hetiv 1:11; Mishnah Berurah 1:16; Teshuvoth Rashba 184; Teshuvoth Beth Yaakov 155; Chida, Tov Eyin 10 (Husatian, 1904). This also does not preclude chanting the Ten Commandments as part of the regular Torah reading, and indeed, they have a special chant; Rabbi Binyamin Aaron (ben Avraham) Salnik, Mas'ath Binyamin 6 (Cracow, 1633); Chizzkuni on Exodus 20:14; Rabbi Menachem (ben Yehudah) de Lonzano, Or Torah, in Sh'tey Yadoth (Venice, 1618); HaKothev on Eyn Yaakov, Yerushalmi, Shekalim 7; Magen Avraham 494:0; Biur Halakhah 494:1.

only means through which we can approach Him ad fulfill His purpose in creation.[69]

5:30   The commandments make Judaism more than a mere religious philosophy.[70] It is a way of life involving action and observance, rather than a mere confession of faith.[71]

5:31   The commandments should be observed because they were given by God, and not because logic demands it.[72] The commandments themselves define a higher logic, as it is written, "Observe and keep [the commandments], for this is your wisdom and understanding in the sign of the nations" (Deuteronomy 4:6).[73]

5:32   Similarly, the commandments should not be kept because of one's personal tastes, but because of their divine origin. It is thus taught that one should not refrain from eating pork because it disgusts him, but because it is forbidden by God.[74]

5:33   It is likewise prohibited to keep any commandment as a superstitious luck charm.[75] In no case were the commandments given for our own material pleasure.[76]

69. *Kuzari* 1:79 (47a), 1:98 (66b), 2:46 (54b), 3:23 (31b). See above 3:13,14.
70. *Kuzari* 4:13 (30a). Cf. *Avoth* 1:17, *Zohar* 1:17a, 3:118a, 3.230a, 3:278b. See *Teshuvoth Rashbash* 3.
71. *Kuzuri* 1:115 (75b). Cf. *Avoth* 3:15; Bertenoro, *Tosefoth Yom Tov, ad loc.* s.v. *VeHaKol.* See chapter 3, note 85.
72. *Chayay Adam* 68:18. Cf. *Rosh HaShanah* 16a; Maharatz Chajas *ad loc.;* Rambam on *Makkoth* 3:16; *Chovoth HaLevavoth* 3:3.
73. Rashi *ad loc.* Cf. *Sifra* on Leviticus 18:3 (86a); *Moreh Nevukhim* 3:31. See Chapter 2, note 30; Chapter 3, note 52.
74. *Sifra* (93d), *Yalkut Shimoni* (1:626), Rashi, on Leviticus 20:26; Rambam, *Shemonah Perakim* 6; *Reshith Chokhmah,* introduction to *Perek HaMitzvoth* (240c); *Sh'nei Luchoth HaB'rith, Maamar HaSheni* (1:78b). Cf. *Sifri* (28) on Deuteronomy 3:25. The Rambam, *loc. cit.,* writes that this is true only of ritual laws, but not of ethical and moral laws.
75. *Yad, Tefillin* 5:4. Cf. *Avodah Zarah* 11a; *Menachoth* 33b; Rashi, *Pesachim* 4a, s.v. *Chovoth; Hagahoth Maimonioth* on *Yad, Tefillin* 1:11 #7; Maharatz Chajas, *Bava Metzia* 101b.
76. *Rosh HaShanah* 28a; *Nedarim* 16b; *Yad Shofar* 1:6; Ran, *Nedarim* 15b, s.v. *VeHah* (end); *Ibid.* 35b, s.v. *U'Melamdo; Magen Avraham* 233:6; *Sifethey Cohen, Yoreh Deah* 215:2, 221:4; *Mishnah Berurah* 589:12; *Teshuvoth Menachem Azariah of Fano* 31; *Teshuvoth Nodeh BeYehudah, Tinyana, Orach Chaim* 133; *Teshuvoth*

5:34   The commandments can be divided into two categories, decrees (*chukim*, חֻקִּים) and ethical laws (*mishpatim*, מִשְׁפָּטִים).[77]

5:35   The ethical laws are necessary for the preservation of society. As such, they provide the basis for the moral structure of Judaism.[78]

5:36   God's decrees (*chukim*) are commandments for which there is no apparent reason. To some degree, these serve to test our allegiance to God in observing His commandments even when not dictated by logic.[79]

5:37   There is also a third category, midway between the above two, known as "testimonies" (*edoth*, עֵדֹות).[80] These have no moral basis, but are inherently logical insofar as they serve to remind us of important religious truths or key events in our history. Included in this group are the various holidays, as well as such commandments as Tefillin and the Mezuzah. These are the commandments that bear "witness" to the important concepts of Judaism.[81]

5:38   Even where the true reason for a commandment or law is not known, we should strive to understand its benefits and

Shaagath Aryeh 60; *Pri Megadim*, introduction to *Orach Chaim* 4:5; Maharatz Chajas, *Gitten* 55a, *Nedarim* 15b, 16b, 35b.

77. Leviticus 26:46, Deuteronomy 4:1, 4:5, 4:8, 5:1, 5:28, 6:1, 7:11, 11:32, 12:1, 26:16, 2 Kings 17:37, Malachi 3:22, Nehemiah 1:7, 1 Chronicles 19:10, 22:13, 2 Chronicles 33:8. For a discussion of the two categories, see *Yoma* 67b; Maharatz Chajas *ad loc.*; *Sifra* on Leviticus 18:4 (86a); *BaMidbar Rabbah* 19:3 (end); *Pesikta* 4 (38b); *Yalkut Shimoni* 1:577; Rambam, *Shemonah Perakim* 6; *Yad, Meilah* 8:8; *Moreh Nevukhim* 3:26; Rashi on Genesis 26:5, Leviticus 18:4; Ramban on Leviticus 16:8; *Emunoth VeDeyoth* 3:2 (54a); *Kuzari* 2:48 (55a); *Ikkarim* 1:17, 3:28; Radak, *Sefer HaSherashim*, s.v. YaRaH; Bachya, introduction, and commentary on Numbers 15:38 (p. 102); *Beth Elohim, Shaar HaYesodoth* 26, 27; *Reshith Chokhmah*, introduction to *Perek HaMitzvoth* (240c). See below, note 131.
78. *Cf.* Exodus 21:1, Numbers 24:3, Numbers 35:24. See below, 5:61.
79. See Rashi, Ramban, on Numbers 19:1; *BaMidbar Rabbah* 19:4; *Pesikta* 4 (40b).
80. Deuteronomy 4:45, 6:17, 6:20.
81. Ramban on Deuteronomy 6:20; Radak on 1 Kings 2:3; *Sefer Sherashim*, s.v. YaRaH; *Beth Elohim, Shaar HaYesodoth* 26, 27; Maharal, *Tifereth Yisrael* 48.

symbolism.[82] Moreover, even where the basic reason for a commandment is known, we should attempt to understand the logic of its detailed laws.[83]

5:39 Nevertheless, even where an apparent reason for a commandment is known, we cannot depend on the reason to change or restrict any law.[84] This is even true where the reason is specified in the Torah,[85] since there may be other reasons that are not revealed.[86] It is also possible that the laws may involve subtle arguments, not readily ascertained by logic or experience.[87]

5:40 It is likewise forbidden to hold God to any reason that we may attempt to give for His commandments. Thus, for

82. *Yad, Temurah* 4:13, *Teshuvah* 3:4, *Mikvaoth* 11:12; *Moreh Nevukhim* 3:26, 3:31; Ramban on Leviticus 19:19, Deuteronomy 22:6; *Chinukh* 545; Ibn Ezra on Exodus 20:1; *Tosafoth Yom Tov, Berakhoth* 5:3; *Etz Yosef* on *VaYikra Rabbah* 27:10, *Devarim Rabbah* 6:1; Maharatz Chajas, *Sotah* 14a.
83. *Tosafoth, Sotah* 14a, *Chulin* 5a, s.v. *Kedey, Gittin* 49b, s.v. *Rabbi Shimeon;* Maharam *ad loc.; Tosefoth Yom Tov, Sanhedrin* 8:6, 10:5. Cf. *Bava Kama* 79b; *Bava Metzia* 3a; Maharatz Chajas, *Rosh HaShanah* 16a; Ramban, *Milchamoth HaShem, Rosh HaShanah* (Rif, 11a), s.v. *VeOd.* See note 87.
84. *Yerushalmi, Nazir* 7:2 (35a); Maharam de Lanzano, *Shiurey Karban, ad loc.; Shiltey Giborim, Avodah Zarah* (Rif 6a) 1; *Sh'nei Luchoth HaB'rith, Torah SheBeAl Peh, K'lal Derushim VeAgadoth* (3:241a); *Terumath HaDeshen* 108; *Sheyareh Berakhah, Yoreh Deah* 183:1. Actually, Rabbi Shimon does derive laws from logical reason, but this opinion is rejected by the majority; *Bava Metzia* 115a; *Kiddushin* 68b; *Yoma* 42b; *Yevamoth* 23a; *Sotah* 8a; *Gittin* 49b; *Sanhedrin* 16b, 21a; *Menachoth* 2b; Rashi, *Kiddushin* 20b, s.v. *LePhi, Sanhedrin* 112a, s.v. *MiP'ney;* Maharatz Chajas, *Sanhedrin* 70a; *Chinukh* 591; HaGra, *Evven HaEzer* 16:2; *Choshen Mishpat* 97:4; *Turey Zahav ad loc.; Teshuvoth Makom Sh'muel* 32; Rashash, Maharatz Chajas, *Bava Metzia* 115a; *Sedey Chemed, Teth* 14-16 (3:19ff).
85. There is an opinion, however, that Rabbi Shimon's opinion is followed in such a case; *Kesef Mishneh* on *Yad, Issurey Biyah* 12:2. However, this is not the accepted opinion; *Evven HaEzer* 16:1 in *Hagah; Beth Sh'muel, Turey Zahav, ibid.* 16:1; HaGra *ibid.* 16:2.
86. *Sefer HaChinukh* 95. Cf. *Menachoth* 65a,b. Also see *Torath HaShelamim, Yoreh Deah* 183:4; *Kerethei U'Pelethei, Tifereth Yisrael* 183:3; *Darkey Teshuvah* (on *Yoreh Deah*) 183:13.
87. See *Yad, Terefoth* 10:12,13. An example of this is the regeneration of the hymen of a girl under three; *Niddah* 5:4 (44b); *Kethuvoth* 11b. This depends on the lunar calandar, which in turn is designated by the courts. Although this might seem highly illogical, different rules of logic are in effect here; *Yerushalmi, Kethuvoth* 1:2 (4a); *Yerushalmi, Nedarim* 6:8 (23b); *Yerushalmi Sanhedrin* 1:2 (6a); *Maggid Mishneh,* on *Yad, Ishuth* 2:21; *Kol Yehudah* on *Kuzari* 3:41 (50a), s.v. *Lo.*

example, God commanded that when one finds a bird's nest, he must send away the mother before taking the eggs or young.[88] However, it is forbidden to pray that God should have mercy on us just as He has mercy on a bird's nest.[89] Any reason that we might give for a commandment, no matter how logical, falls short of its infinitude of meaning.[90]

5:41   It is for this reason that God did not include the reasons for the commandments in the Torah, and did not reveal them to any mortal in this world other than Moses.[91] Had they been revealed, an imperfect understanding of such reasons and of one's own nature may have lead people to make unwarranted personal exceptions to the commandments.[92]

5:42   We must therefore be equally careful to observe all of God's commandments.[93] To profess to believe in a divinely revealed Torah, and at the same time to choose commandments according to one's own judgment, is to claim to be greater than their Giver.[94]

5:43   God is inherently perfect, and it is therefore obvious that He did not give any of the commandments for His own

---

88. Deuteronomy 22:6.
89. *Berakhoth* 5:3 (33b); *Tosefoth Yom Tov ad loc.*; *Megillah* 4:9 (25a); *Yerushalmi, Berakhoth* 53 (40a); *Yerushalmi, Megillah* 4:10 (33a); *Yalkut Shimoni* 1:930; *Yad, Tefillah* 9:7; *Moreh Nevukhim* 3:48; Ramban on Deuteronomy 22:6; *Chinukh* 545; Maharal, *Tifereth Yisrael* 6; *Etz Yosef* on *VaYikra Rabbah* 27:10, *Devarim Rabbah* 6:1.
90. Ibid. Significantly, the commandment to send away the mother bird also has many Kabbalistic reasons; *Bahir* 104, 105; *Zohar* 1:158a, 1:219a, 2:8b, 2:9a, 2:85b, 2:93a, 3:15b, 3:204b, 3:216a, 3:238b, 3:252b, 3:254a, 3:309a; *Tikuney Zohar* 2a, 3a, 69 (106b); Recanti on Deuteronomy 22:6· Radbaz, *Metzudoth David* 206.
91. *BaMidbar Rabbah* 19:4; *Pesikta* 4 (39a); *Yalkut Shimoni* 1:759. However, they will be known in the World to Come; below, note 129.
92. *Sanhedrin* 21b; *Sefer HaMitzvoth*, Negative Commandment 365. *Moreh Nevukhim* 3:26; Maharatz Chajas, *Shabbath* 12b.
93. Cf. *Avoth* 2:1; *Yerushalmi, Peah* 1:1 (3b, end).
94. *Moreh Nevukhim* 3:31. Cf. *Tanna DeBei Eliahu Rabbah* 26 (104a); Abarbanel, *Nachalath Avoth* on *Avoth* 2:1.

needs.[95] It is thus written, "If you are righteous, what do you give Him? What does He receive from your hand?" (Job 35:7).[96]

5:44   It must therefore be concluded that God gave the commandments for a purely altruistic motive, for the sole good of the recipients.[97] It is thus written, "Keep God's commandments . . . for your own good. Behold, the heavens belong to God your Lord . . . along with the earth and everything in it" (Deuteronomy 10:13,14).[98]

5:45   The commandments were therefore given as a means through which God would be able to fulfill His altruistic purpose in creation,[99] and are all primarily for the benefit of those who observe them.[100] It is thus written, "God commands us to keep all these decrees . . . for our eternal good. It shall be righteousness for us if we observe and keep all this commandment before God our Lord, as He commanded us" (Deuteronomy 6:24,25).[101]

5:46   Since the commandments were given for man's ultimate benefit, they were made difficult enough to present a

---

95. See above, 2:32,33, 3:4.
96. Cf. *Yerushalmi, Nedarim* 9:1 (29a); Ramban on Deuteronomy 22:6; *Chinukh* 545; *Nefesh HaChaim* 2:4; *Shomer Emunim* 2:11 #4. Also see Job 22:3; Psalms 16:2, *Radak ad loc.*
97. It is thus taught that God does not need the commandments, but only gave them to "purify His creatures;" *Bereshith Rabbah* 44:1; *VaYikra Rabbah* 13:3; *Tanchuma, Shemini* 8; *Midrash Tehillim* 18:25; *Yalkut Shimoni* 2:121; *Moreh Nevukhim* 3:26; Ramban, *Chinukh, loc. cit.; Avodath HaKodesh, Chelek HaAvodah* 3; *Sh'nei Luchoth HaB'rith, Shaar HaGadol* (1:48b); Maharal, *Tifereth Yisrael* 7. Cf. *Or HaShem* 2:6:4.
98. Since God owns heaven and earth, He does not need our observance; hence it is for our own good; Rashi, Ramban, *ad loc.; Chinukh* 95.
99. *Derekh HaShem* 1:2:2-4; *Mesilath Yesharim* 1 (3b). See above, 5:1.
100. Cf. *Makkoth* 3:16 (23b); *Shemoth Rabbah* 30:16; *VaYikra Rabbah* 30:12; *Reshith Chokhmah*, Introduction to *Perek HaMitzvoth* (239d).
101. *Moreh Nevukhim* 3:27; Ibn Ezra on Exodus 20:1 (end); Ramban on Deuteronomy 22:6; *Chinukh* 545. Cf. Jeremiah 32:39. The Torah states, "God *commanded us,*" since the significance of the commandments is that they were commanded; above 3:13.

challenge,[102] but not so difficult as to make their observance prohibitively burdensome.[103] God thus said, "This commandment, which I give you this day, is not too hard for you, neither is it far off" (Deuteronomy 30:11).[104]

5:47   In giving the commandments, God was cognizant of the fallibility of man. It is thus taught that "the Torah was not given to ministering angels."[105] The commandments were thus conceived in such a way that man should not find it impossible to observe them. It is taught, "God does not act as a tyrant toward His creatures."[106]

5:48   The most difficult commandments are therefore not those which involve our relationship with God. Rather, they are those which are required to maintain an orderly society. It is not God who makes the commandments difficult, but man's moral weaknesses.[107]

5:49   The main immediate benefit of the commandments is in the spiritual realm; obeying the commandments brings a person closer to God.[108] Each commandment acts as nourishment for the soul,[109] strengthening it,[110] and increasing a person's spiritual fortitude.[111]

102. See above, 3:22,25.
103. *Shemoth Rabbah* 34:1; *Sefer Chasidim* 567, from Job 37:23.
104. Ramban *ad loc.*; *Akedath Yitzchak* 77; *Ikkarim* 4:25.
105. *Berakhoth* 25b; *Yoma* 30a; *Kiddushin* 54a; *Meilah* 14b. Cf. *Shabbath* 89a.
106. *Avodah Zarah* 3a.
107. *Sefer Chasidim* 567. Cf. *Makkoth* 3:15 (23a).
108. *Zohar* 3:31b, 3:86b, 3:128a; *Likutey Amarim (Tanya), Sefer Shel Benonim* 4 (8a); *Nefesh HaChaim* 1:6, note, s.v. *VeYadua.*
109. *Zohar* 1:24a; *Raya Mehemna, Zohar* 3:99b ff.; *Nefesh HaChaim* 2:6; *Anaf Yosef,* on *Eyn Yaakov* (23), *Yoma* 28b. Cf. *Shemoth Rabbah* 30:18; *Tanchuma, Mishpatim* 3; *Koheleth Rabbah* 2:26, 3:16, 5:24, 8:16. Also see Isaiah 3:10; *Raya Mehemna, Zohar* 3:29b, 3:227a (end), 3:244b (end). See Bachya, Introduction, and Introduction to *VaYelekh.*
110. *Sh'nei Luchoth HaB'rith, Beth Chokhmah* (1:26b).
111. Cf. *Yoma* 39a.

5:50   Conversely, sin detracts from one's perfection[112] and separates him from God. It is thus written, "Only your sins have separated you from your God" (Isaiah 59:2).[113]

5:51   Sin is therefore like poison to the soul.[114] The prohibitions of the Torah were given by God so as to protect us from this spiritual poison.[115]

5:52   Just as God created a self-sustaining system of physical law, so He created a self-sustaining system of spiritual law.[116] God conceived creation so that man's good comes, not as a *reward* for his action, but as a *direct result* of his action.[117] It is thus written, "Righteousness guards the one who is upright in his ways, but wickedness overthrows the sinner" (Proverbs 13:6).[118]

5:53   Every human act is therefore reflected spiritually on high.[119] Man's own deeds are thus the means that generate

112. *Derekh HaShem* 1:4:5.
113. Rambam, *Shemonah Perakim* 8; *Reshith Chokhmah, Shaar HaYirah* 7 (22b); *Nefesh HaChaim* 1:18.
114. *Raya Mehemna, Zohar* 3:99b, 3:232a (end); *Tikuney Zohar* 20 (47b); *Nefesh HaChaim* 2:7.
115. *Sh'nei Luchoth HaB'rith, Beth Chokhmah* (1:26b). Cf. *Shabbath* 49a, 130a. Also see *Devarim Rabbah* 8:4; *Reshith Chokhmah,* Introduction to *Perek HaMitzvoth* (239c,d). The prohibitions also protect a person from the effects of Adam's sin; *Or HaShem* 2:2:6. Hence, the "taint of the serpent" is removed by the commandments; see Chapter 4, note 120.
116. *Derekh HaShem* 2:6:1; *Shaarey Gan Eden, Orach Tzadikim* 3:2 (3b). Cf. *Berakhoth* 58a; *Zohar* 1:157a, 1:197a, 3:176b; *Zohar Chadash* 29d; Rabbi Yitzchak Lampranti, *Pachad Yitzchak,* s.v. *Tzarikhav.*
117. Recanti, beginning of *BeChukothai; Avodath HaKodesh, Chelek HaAvodah* 18; *Sh'nei Luchoth HaB'rith, Beth Chokhmah* (1:22a); *Nefesh HaChaim* 1:12. Cf. *Avoth* 4:11; *Nachalath Avoth; Midrash Sh'muel; ad. loc.; Tomer Devorah* 2; *Zohar* 3:307b; *Moreh Nevukhim* 3:17. As a result of these automatic spiritual mechanisms, God does not change when reward or punishment is given; *Amud HaAvodah, Vikuach Shoel U'Meshiv* 174 (48d).
118. Cf. *Yerushalmi, Peah* 1:1 (5b); *Yerushalmi, Kiddushin* 1:9 (23a); *Yerushalmi, Sanhedrin* 10:1 (49a); *Yalkut Shimoni* 2:935. See Proverbs 29:6.
119. "According to the awakening from below, there is an awakening from above;" *Zohar* 1:35a, 1:82b; *Nefesh HaChaim* 1:6. Cf *Yoma* 39a; *Shir HaShirim Rabbah* 6:4; Rashi on Song of Songs 7:2 (end); *Berakhoth* 6a. See above, 3:37,38.

the spiritual closeness that is his ultimate reward.[120]

5:54   On a universal scale, the commandments serve to fulfill God's purpose in creation.[121] They thus enhance God's relationship with His universe.[122]

5:55   Therefore, the commandments lead to the manifestation of God's absolute unity in the universe,[123] even in the physical world.[124]

5:56   Israel thus becomes the means through which God's essence becomes more strongly revealed in the world. It is

120. *Ohev Yisrael (Ekev)* on Deuteronomy 8:3. This is the reason that the physical world is necessary, even though the ultimate purpose is spiritual. The main difference between the physical and spiritual is that the physical is built around a spacial framework. Hence, space exists only in the physical world, and not in the spiritual. Since there is no space in the spiritual world, things that are different cannot be brought together; cf. *Yad, Yesodey HaTorah* 1:7; *Moreh Nevukhim,* Introduction to 3 #16; *Or HaShem* 1:1:16; Commentary on *Yad, Yesodey HaTorah* 2:5; *Amud HaAvodah, Vikuach Shoel U'Meshiv* 99 (26a). In the spiritual domain, two different things can only be brought together when they are bound to the same physical object. God is infinitely higher than man, so it would be impossible for man to attain closeness to God on the spiritual plane. But the commandments are God's will, and as we have seen, God and His will are one; above, 2:40. Therefore, when a person performs a commandment, his soul becomes attached to God's will, and hence to God. The soul is bound to his physical body, which is involved in the commandment, and at the same time, the commandment is bound to God's will. Hence, at the moment that the commandment is being done, the soul is in proximity with God. But there is another principle that a spiritual effect cannot be removed; *Zohar* 1:244b (end), 2:114a; *Etz Chaim, Shaar HaAkudim* 5, 6, *Shaar Oznaim Chotem Peh (Achap)* 3. Therefore, the observance leaves a permanent impression on the soul. This is the "garment of the soul," through which one gains closeness to God; *Sanhedrin* 98a; *Yerushalmi, Kelayim* 9:3 (44a); *Yerushalmi, Kethuvoth* 12:3 (65a); *Koheleth Rabbah* 5:12; *Tanchuma, VaYigash* 8; *Zohar* 1:224a (end); *Pardes Rimonim* 31:5 (end); *Shaarey Kedushah* 1:1 (beginning); *Etz Chaim, Shaar Penimiuth VeChetzoniuth* 4.
121. Cf. *Sh'nei Luchoth HaB'rith, Shaar HaGadol* (1:46 ff). Also see Rabbi Moshe Cordevero (Ramak), *Elemah Rabathai* 1:1:2; *Shomer Emunim* 2:75.
122. *Eikhah Rabbah* 1:35; *Yalkut Shimoni* 1:744; *Zohar* 1:61a, 2:32b, 2:58a, 2:65b; *Sh'nei Luchoth HaB'rith, Shaar HaGadol* (1:47b); *Nefesh HaChaim* 1:3. Cf. *Zohar* 2:155a. This also involves the process described in note 120.
123. *Zohar* 2:85b, 2:118a, 2:162b, 2:165a; *Tikuney Zohar* 70 (131a); *Nefesh HaChaim* 1:6; *Likutey Amarim (Tanya), Sefer Shel Benonim* 4 (8b).
124. See above, 2:39, 3:12. Cf. *Avoth* 3:2; *Berakhoth* 6a.

thus written, "[To] give strength to God is the duty of Israel His pride" (Psalms 68:35).[125]

5:57   Thus, although the average person may not realize it, the commandments serve the highest purpose in God's plan for creation.[126] They are an essential part of the invisible cosmic drama through which this plan is fulfilled.

5:58   Therefore, if a person understands the true spiritual nature of the universe, including the nature of good and evil, he will readily understand the significance of all the commandments. It was in this manner that the Patriarchs understood the Torah before it was given,[127] and to a large measure, observed all its commandments.[128] This is also why the true reasons for all the commandments will be obvious in the World to Come, when all truth will be revealed.[129]

5:59   Although the primary benefit of the commandments lies on the spiritual plane, they also provide a great many mundane benefits.

125. *Zohar* 2:23b; *Nefesh HaChaim* 1:3.
126. Cf. *Berakhoth* 6b.
127. Cf. *Avoth deRabbi Nathan* 33:1; *Bereshith Rabbah* 61:1; 95:2; *BaMidbar Rabbah* 14:7; *Tanchuma, VaYigash* 11; *Midrash Tehillim* 1:13; Ramban on Genesis 26:5; *Nefesh HaChaim* 1:21; *Anaf Yosef* on *Eyn Yaakov* (23), *Yoma* 28b.
128. *Kiddushin* 4:13 (82a); *Yoma* 28b; Maharsha, Maharatz Chajas, *ad loc.*; *Yerushalmi, Kiddushin* 4:12 (48b); *Bereshith Rabbah* 49:6, 64:4, 95:2; *VaYikra Rabbah* 2:9; *Tanchuma, Lekh Lekha* 1, 11, *Behar* 1; *Midrash Tehillim* 1:13; Ramban on Genesis 26:5; *Nefesh HaChaim* 1:21; *Lechem Mishneh* on *Yad, Melakhim* 9:1; *Perashath Derakhim* 3; Maharatz Chajas, *Taanith* 4a. Cf. *Berakhoth* 26b. Some say that they only kept the commandments in the Holy Land; Ramban on Leviticus 18:25; *Teshuvoth Rashba* 94; *Midbar Kedemoth, Yud* 55; *Yad Shlomo* 62a; *Beer Mayim Chaim, Girsa DeYankutha* 29; *Kesef Nivchar*, beginning of *VaYishlach*; *Teshuvoth Radbaz* 2:696; *Sedey Chemed, Alef* 186. Regarding details of circumcision, see *Tosafoth, Yevamoth* 71b, s.v. *Lo*; Maharatz Chajas *ad loc.*; *Zohar* 1:163b; Radal on *Pirkey Rabbi Eliezer* 29:29, note 8. Regarding Noah, see Rashi, *Baaley Tosafoth*, on Genesis 7:2. See above, 5:24; Chapter 4, notes 58, 87.
129. *BaMidbar Rabbah* 19:4; *Pesikta* 4 (39a); *Yalkut Shimoni* 1:759.

5:60   A great number[130] of the commandments deal with man's relationship with his fellow humans,[131] and are necessary for the preservation of a harmonious society.[132] Thus, the basis of the Torah is the maxim, "What is hateful to you, to your neighbor do not do."[133] It is written, "You shall love your neighbor as yourself" (Leviticus 19:18), and it is taught that this is the prime rule of the Torah.[134] It is similarly written, "[The Torah's] ways are ways of pleasantness, and all its paths are peace" (Proverbs 3:17).[135]

5:61   The ritual commandments serve the purpose of sanctifying our lives and bringing us closer to God.[136] They penetrate every nook and cranny of a person's existence,[137] hallowing even the lowliest acts and elevating them to a service to God.[138]

5:62   Thus, the multitude of laws governing even such mundane acts as eating, drinking, dressing and business, sanctify every facet of life, and constantly remind one of his responsibilities toward God.[139]

5:63   Every commandment therefore serves to make us more holy and Godly.[140] Before observing many of the

---

130. Cf. Rashi, *Shabbath* 31a, s.v. *DeAlaich*.
131. The commandments are thus divided into two categories "between man and his fellow" (*beyn adam le-chavero*, בֵּין אָדָם לַחֲבֵרוֹ), and "between man and God" (*beyn adam le-Makom*, בֵּין אָדָם לַמָּקוֹם); *Yoma* 8:9 (85b). Cf. Rambam on *Peah* 1:1; *Zohar* 2:106b; *Birkey Yosef*, *Orach Chaim* 606:1.
132. *Kuzari* 2:48 (55b).
133. *Shabbath* 31a.
134. *Sifra* (89b), Rashi, *ad loc.*; *Yerushalmi, Nedarim* 9:4; *Bereshith Rabbah* 24:8; *Yalkut Shimoni* 1:40, 1:613.
135. Cf. *Yad,* *Shabbath* 2:3. See *Avoth* 3:10.
136. See note 69.
137. Cf. *Menachoth* 43b; *Sifra* on Leviticus 8:16 (42a); *BaMidbar Rabbah* 10:3, 17:7; *Shir HaShirim Rabbah* 6:4; *Tanchuma, Sh'lach* d14, *Ki Thavo* 4.
138. Cf. *Berakhoth* 62a.
139. *Chovoth HaLevavoth* 8:3:21; Ibn Ezra on Deuteronomy 5:18 (end); *Moreh Nevukhim* 3:35:9, 3:44.
140. *Mekhilta* to Exodus 22:30. Cf. Rashi, Ramban, *ibid.*; Ramban on *Sefer HaMitzvoth*, *Shoresh* 4 (41b).

commandments, we therefore recite a blessing including the words, "Who has made us holy through His commandments."[141] God likewise said that, "you should remember and keep all My commandments, and be holy to your God" (Numbers 15:40).[142]

5:64 The many rituals associated with daily life also serve to teach self-discipline.[143] It is thus taught, "When Israel is occupied with the Torah and commandments, they master their desire, and are not mastered by it."[144] It is likewise written, "You shall remember all God's commandments and keep them, and not stray after your heart and after your eyes, by which you are led astray" (Numbers 15:39).[145]

5:65 The commandments also serve to maintain the identity of the Jewish people, keeping them apart from the gentiles. With regard to many laws, God thus states, "I am God your Lord, who has set you apart from the nations" (Leviticus 20:24).[146]

5:66 The many rituals also provide opportunities for communal observance and fellowship. Individuals are thus able to identify with the community at large.[147]

5:67 The commandments also serve to unify the Jewish people by constantly reminding them of their unique history. There is the constant reminder, "That you may remember the day you left Egypt all the days of your life" (Deuteronomy

141. *Nefesh HaChaim* 1:6, note s.v. *VeZeh; Derekh HaShem* 4:9:3.
142. Cf. *Berakhoth* 12b.
143. Rambam, *Shemonah Perakim* 4; *Moreh Nevukhim* 3:35:13. Cf. *Chovoth HaLevavoth* 3:3.
144. *Avodah Zarah* 5b.
145. Cf. *Berakhoth* 12b.
146. *BaMidbar Rabbah* 10:3; *Shir HaShirim Rabbah* 6:4. Cf. *Avodah Zarah* 31b, 36b.
147. *Moreh Nevukhim* 3:42; *Emunoth VeDeyoth* 3:2 (54b). Cf. *Yerushalmi, Chagigah* 3:6 (21a); *Yerushalmi, Bava Kama* 7:7 (33b); Maharatz Chajas, *Niddah* 34a.

16:3).[148] Moreover, remembering our unique history also serves to remind us of our unique responsibilities.

5:68   The commandments also serve in a pedagogic capacity, transmitting God's teachings from one generation to the next.[149] The Torah thus states that the Israelites should recall the commandments, "So that their children who have not known, may hear and learn to fear God our Lord" (Deuteronomy 31:13).[150] It is likewise written, "[God] gave a solemn charge to Jacob, and established a law in Israel, which He commanded our fathers to teach their children, so that it may be known to future generations, to children yet unborn; and these would in turn repeat it to their children" (Psalms 78:5,6). This is of the highest importance, since it is only such constant transmission that can guarantee the continuance of our faith.[151]

5:69   The commandments therefore act as a survival mechanism, enabling Judaism to remain vital, even through the harshest persecutions.[152] Indeed, this is an indication of the divine nature of the commandments. They have kept the Jewish people alive for countless generations, while a single generation's lapse has led to major spiritual and physical debilitation of the Jews.

5:70   The commandments therefore set limits through which a person can fulfill the divine purpose while living in a world that is essentially hostile toward it. Through the command-

---

148. Cf. *Kuzari* 3:10 (12b).
149. *Bereshith Rabbah* 1:1; *Yalkut Shimoni* 2:942.
150. *Cf.* Exodus 12:26, 13:8, 13:14, Leviticus 23:43.
151. *Shir HaShirim Rabbah* 1:24; *Tanchuma, VaYigash* 2; *Midrash Tehillim* 8:4.
152. *Kuzari* 3:10 (12b).

ments, one can be part of the world, and at the same time, dedicated to the spiritual.[153]

5:71 Above and beyond all the meager reasons that we can give for God's commandments, there is an infinitude of depth known only to Him. God thus said, "My thoughts are not your thoughts; your ways are not Mine . . . For as the heavens are higher than the earth, so are My ways higher than your ways, and My thoughts than your thoughts. But the rain and snow descend from heaven, and return not without watering the earth, making it blossom and bear fruit, providing seed to sow and bread to eat, so shall the word that emanates from My mouth not return to Me void, without accomplishing My purpose, and succeeding in furthering My goal for it" (Isaiah 55:8-11).[154]

153. *Derekh HaShem* 1:4:4. Cf. *Berakhoth* 35b; *Avoth* 2:1.
154. *Emunoth VeDeyoth* 3:2 (55a). Cf. *Teshuvoth Rashba* 94.

SIX

INSPIRATION

6:1   Although God created man to live on a physical plane, He did not close off the spiritual completely.[1]

6:2   God arranged creation so that even while in the physical world, man would be able to open a door to the spiritual and experience the Divine. This would constitute the highest perfection that a mortal human can attain.[2]

6:3   God also used this spiritual experience as a means of revealing His will.[3]

6:4   One of the foundations of our faith is the belief that God grants such inspiration and thus reveals His will to mankind.[4]

6:5   Since God created the universe for a purpose, it is inconceivable that He would not communicate this purpose to His creatures.[5]

1. *Derekh HaShem* 3:2:1. See above, 5:71.
2. *Derashoth HaRan* 8 (Jerusalem, 1974), p. 61; Rabbi Yehudah Chayit, *Minchath Yehudah*, on *Maarekheth Elohuth* 10 (Mantua, 1558), p. 144b; *Akedath Yitzchak* 35 (2:11a,b); *Beth Elohim, Shaar HaYesodoth* 19; *Derekh HaShem* 3:2:3. See below, 6:77.
3. *Beth Elohim, Shaar HaYesodoth* 19.
4. *Yad, Yesodey HaTorah* 7:1; Rambam on *Sanhedrin* 10:1, Thirteen Principles of Faith 6.
5. Cf. *Ikkarim* 3:8.

6:6   The only way that man can approach God is by striving to achieve His purpose as revealed by Him.[6]

6:7   Although God has given us the intelligence to understand our responsibilities, we cannot seek Him on our own.[7]

6:8   In case of illness we must seek the advice of an expert physician, since a seemingly logical cure can sometimes kill the patient. Similarly, we must seek God's revelation, since an apparently reasonable morality may actually draw a person away from God.[8]

6:9   Revelation is also a more perfect way to the good life than human intellect, since any rational morality is always debatable.[9] God's revealed will, on the other hand, needs no further arguments to strengthen it.[10]

6:10   Furthermore, God had to reveal His will because the majority of people do not act according to the dictates of pure logic.[11] Man is a complex creature, who is strongly influenced by his environment[12] and material desires.[13] It is written, "A bribe blinds the eyes of the wise and perverts the words of the righteous" (Deuteronomy 16:19).[14] Our desires for recognition and material pleasures can likewise blind our eyes to moral truth.[15] If God had not revealed His will in an

6. *Kuzari* 3:53. See above, 3:14.
7. *Kuzari* 1:98, 3:23. Cf. *Ikkarim* 3:7.
8. *Kuzari* 1:79; *Derashoth HaRan* 8 (p. 61).
9. *Kuzari* 2:49.
10. Rambam, letter to Rabbi Chasdai HaLevi (in *Iggeroth HaRambam*, Warsaw, 1926), p. 13.
11. *Chovoth HaLevavoth* 3:3 #5.
12. *Yad, Deyoth* 6:1.
13. *Chovoth HaLevavoth* 3:3 #6.
14. Cf. *Kethuvoth* 105a.
15. Rabbi Elchanan Wasserman, *Kobetz Maamarim, Maamar al HaEmunah* 6, 7 (Jerusalem, 1963), pp. 13,14. Cf. *Avoth* 4:21.

unambiguous manner, man would be likely to rationalize a morality of convenience, rather than one of sincerity.[16]

6:11   Just as God is unknowable, so is His ultimate purpose. Even if man were to have a high degree of intellectual integrity, his intellect would not be sufficiently perfect to comprehend God's purpose well enough to seek Him.[17]

6:12   Even if pure logic could be used to define general moral principles, it cannot fill in the details through which they must be used to approach God and for man's ultimate good.[18]

6:13   Although logic may define a general morality, only God can reveal the seriousness of various immoral acts.[19]

6:14   Although logic may dictate that certain actions are morally and ethically wrong, reason alone cannot prescribe how to correct wrongs that have already been committed. Therefore, a person who attempts to live by a man-made system of morality is likely to find himself beset by guilt feelings that cannot be resolved. It is only God, Author of all morality, who can reveal the ways of repentance and reconciliation.[20]

6:15   Israel's unique history and relationship to God predicate a unique responsibility, and only God Himself can teach us how to fulfill it.[21] Experience has shown that only by observing God's revealed will has Israel survived.[22]

---

16. This is also a very strong argument against "situation ehtics."
17. *Chovoth HaLevavoth* 3:3 #3.
18. *Ibid.* 3:3 #2; *Emunoth VeDeyoth* 3:3.
19. *Ibid.; Beth Elohim, Shaar HaYesodoth* 19, third reason.
20. Original. *See Avodah Zarah* 17a (end).
21. *Chovoth HaLevavoth* 3:3 #4.
22. See above, 5:69.

6:16   Besides morality, there are many things that cannot be fathomed with human intellect, and can only be known through revelation.[23] These include knowledge of future events, especially the Messianic promise, as well as the rewards in the afterlife.[24] Also revealed are many mysteries that would otherwise be inaccessible to human intellect.[25]

6:17   Inspiration and prophecy are not mere psychological processes in which the human imagination constitutes the main factor. Rather they are conditions in which man becomes the instrument through which God exerts His power.[26] They are experiences that are as real as physical sensation,[27] leaving absolutely no doubt as to their authenticity.[28] True prophets were therefore even willing to sacrifice their lives for the sake of their teachings.[29]

6:18   The lowest[30] level of inspiration is divine guidance that is granted to a person without his knowledge.[31] This was the minimal attainment of all the great Biblical[32] and Talmudical[33] leaders, who were guided by God in all their words

23. *Derekh HaShem* 3:3:1.
24. *Beth Elohim, Shaar HaYesodoth* 19, fifth reason. A prophet would not prophesy about the future when a greater prophet was available; Ramban on Numbers 11:28.
25. Rabbi Moshe Cordevero (Ramak), *Elemah Rabathai, Eyn Kol* 1:16. Cf. *Shomer Emunim* 1:7-13.
26. *Moreh Nevukhim* 3:36; *Or HaShem* 2:4:3; *Ikkarim* 3:8; *Akedath Yitzchak* 19; *Derekh HaShem* 3:3:6.
27. *Derekh HaShem* 3:3:4. Revelation can thus involve all five senses; *Tikuney Zohar Chadash* 120b.
28. Rabbi Moshe de Leon, *Shekel HaKodesh* (London, 1911), p. 19; *Derekh HaShem* 3:3:1, 3:4:1, 3:4:5. Cf. Rabbi Eliezer Rokeach of Worms, *Sodi Razia* (Bilgorey, 1936), p. 50. See below, 6:67.
29. *Moreh Nevukhim* 3:24 (end); *Divrey Shalom* on Genesis 22:1.
30. *Moreh Nevukhim* 2:45, first level. Cf. *Zohar* 3:35a.
31. *Kuzari* 3:32 (38a), 2:14 (14a), 3:65 (67b); *Kol Yehudah ad loc.* This level is frequently referred to as Divine Inspiration (*Ruach HaKodesh*), but this is a misnomer, since true Inspiration is always felt consciously; *Derekh HaShem* 3:3:3.
32. *Tanchuma, VaYechi* 14, from Psalms 25:14. Also see *Sifri* (176) on Deuteronomy 18:18; *Seder Olam Rabbah* 20:21. Such Inspiration also appeared in the Sanhedrin occasionally; *Makkoth* 23b.
33. *Bava Bathra* 12a,b; *Kuzari* 3:65 (71a). For examples, see *Eruvin* 64b; *Tosafoth ad loc.* s.v. *Kiven; Yerushalmi, Shevi'ith* 9:1 (25b); *Yerushalmi, Sotah* 1:4; *Pesikta* 176b;

and deeds. It is thus written, "God's council is with those who fear Him" (Psalms 25:14).[34] Such inspiration also marked the beginning of the careers of the prophets.[35]

6:19 The gift of divine guidance is granted to those who teach Torah publicly, bringing the people closer to God.[36] It is thus written, "This book of the Torah shall not depart from you . . . and you shall observe everything written in it, for then you shall . . . have good success" (Joshua 1:8).[37] Therefore, any Torah leader whose works have been accepted by all Israel is assumed to have been divinely guided.[38]

6:20 This gift is attainable by any person, at any time or place, as long as the person makes himself worthy of it.[39]

6:21 The next degree of revelation[40] is Divine Inspiration (*Ruach HaKodesh*, רוּחַ הַקּוֹדֶשׁ).[41] On this level, a person is consciously aware of God's guidance in his speech or

Raavad on *Yad, Lulav* 8:5; Ramban on *Bava Bathra* 11b; *Akedath Yitzchak* 6; *Teshuvoth Chatham Sofer, Orach Chaim* 208; *Beth Shlomo, Orach Chaim* 2:112. Actually, the Talmud states that *Ruach HaKodesh* ceased to exist after the death of the last prophets, see below, note 258. This is speaking of the level described in 6:21 or 6:27. Some say that although it still existed even after the death of the last prophets, it was very rare, Rabbi Reuven Margolies, introduction to *Sheeloth U'Teshuvoth Min HaShamayim* (Jerusalem, 1957), p. 25.

34. *Bereshith Rabbah* 49:3; *Midrash Tehillim* 25:13.
35. *Moreh Nevukhim* 2:45, First Level. See Abarbanel *ad loc.*, Second Level. To some degree, this was attained through their mystical practices. See *Hekheloth Rabathai* 1,2. See below, 6:23.
36. *Shir HaShirim Rabbah* 1:8 (end), 1:9 (end).
37. *VaYikra Rabbah* 35:6.
38. Rabbi Yisrael ben Shabbathai, the Koznitzer Maggid, *She'erith Yisrael* (Lublin, 1895); Rabbi Mendel of Rimenov, *Menachem Tzion, Netzavim* (Satmar, 1935); *Taamey HaMinhagim* 754 and notes (p. 334). See below, Chapter 12, note 11.
39. *Tana DeBei Eliahu Rabbah* 9 (63a); *Yalkut Shimoni* 2:42; *Shaarey Kedushah* 3:7; *Reshith Chokmah*, Introduction (3a).
40. *Moreh Nevukhim* 2:45, Second Level; Abarbanel *ad loc.* This is also derived from a lower spiritual level than prophecy, *Shiur Komah* 16 (31d); *Shaar Ruach HaKodesh*, *Derush* 1.
41. Psalms 51:13. *Cf.* Isaiah 63:10,11.

actions.⁴² Through such inspiration, a person can be aware of future events,⁴³ as well as other people's thoughts.⁴⁴

6:22   There are ten steps through which one must prepare himself before he can attain Divine Inspiration.⁴⁵ They are:⁴⁶

1. Constant study and observance of the teachings of the Torah (*Torah*, תּוֹרָה).⁴⁷

2. Scrupulous care not to violate a single law (care; *zehiruth*, זְהִירוּת).⁴⁸

3. Constant dilligence to fulfill every commandment (dilligence; *zerizuth*, זְרִיזוּת).⁴⁹

4. Living completely free of sin, in thought⁵⁰ and in deed (cleanliness; *nekiuth*, נְקִיּוּת).⁵¹

---

42. Ramban on Exodus 28:30; Bachya on Deuteronomy 33:8; *Derekh HaShem* 3:3:1, 3:3:3.

43. Bachya on Leviticus 8:8; *Derekh HaShem* 3:3:2.

44. *Eliah Rabbah, Orach Chaim* 101:8; Maharatz Chajas, *Shabbath* 12b, from Megillah 7a. Cf. Rabbi Chaim Vital's introduction to *Etz Chaim* (Tel Aviv, 1960), p. 18. Also see *Hekheloth Rabathai* 1.

45. It is most probably referring to this level of Divine Inspiration; see *Mesilath Yesharim* 26 (end). Also see *Yad, Yesodey Hatorah* 7:1; *Moreh Nevukhim* 2:45, Second Level. However, it is also possible that it is the level in 6:18. Also see Rabbi Yehudah Chayit, *Minchath Yehudah* on *Maarekheth Elohuth* 10 (148b, end).

46. *Avodah Zarah* 20b; *Sotah* 9:14 (but not in Gemara); *Yerushalmi, Shabbath* 1:3 (8b); *Yerushalmi, Shekalim* 3:3 (14b; 9b in *Bavli*); *Shir HaShirim Rabbah* 1:9; *Midrash Mishle* 15 (end); *Yalkut Shimoni* 1:933; *Rif. Avodah Zarah* 6a; *Rosh, Avodah Zarah* 1:20; *Machzor Vitri* 937; *Sefer Chasidim* 16; Rabbi Avraham ibn Daud (Raavad) of Toledo, *HaEmunah HaRama* (Frankfurt am Mein, 1852), p. 74; *Maarekheth Elohuth* 10 (148b); Rabbi Yehudah Chayit, *Minchath Yehudah ad loc.*; *Akedath Yitzchak* 35 (2:14a); *Reshith Chokhmah, Shaar Ahavah* 11 (89d); *Mesilath Yesharim* 1 (end). Each of these steps is explained in detail in *Reshith Chokhmah*, and all of *Mesilath Yesharim* is a commentary on them. Although there are many varient readings, we follow that of *Avodah Zarah* 20b, which is also that of *Mesilath Yesharim*.

47. Rashi, *Avodah Zarah* 20b. This is omitted in *Sotah* 9:15; *Yerushalmi; Shir HaShirim Rabbah*; *loc. cit.* Cf. *VaYikra Rabbah* 35:6. Also see below, 6:24.

48. Rashi *loc. cit.; Mesilath Yesharim* 2-5. *Sefer Chasidim* interchanges 2 and 3, as apparently does Rashi *loc. cit.* However, see Rashi, *Chulin* 107b, s.v. *Lo*. Omitted in same sources as above.

49. Rashi, *loc. cit.; Tosefoth Yom Tov, Sotah* 9:15; *Mesilath Yesharim* 6-9.

50. Ran on Rif *loc. cit.*

51. Rashi *loc. cit.; Mesilath Yesharim* 10-12.

5. Avoiding even the permissible when it may lead to wrong (abstinence; *perishuth*, פְּרִישׁוּת).[52]

6. Purifying oneself of all sin, both past[53] and present (purification; *tohorah*, טָהֳרָה).[54]

7. Dedication to God, far beyond the call of the Law (piety; *chasiduth*, חֲסִידוּת).[55]

8. Absolute negation of the self (humility; *anavah*, עֲנָוָה).[56]

9. Loving God so much[57] as to dread all sin and evil (fear of sin; *yirath chet*, יִרְאַת חֵטְא).[58]

10. Total negation of the worldly (holiness; *kedushah*, קְדוּשָׁה).[59]

6:23   Once a person had completed all these steps, he was then ready to engage in the exercises of meditation (*hithbodeduth*, הִתְבּוֹדְדוּת)[60] that were used to attain inspiration.[61] These exercises would consist of the repetition of divine

---

52. Rashi *loc. cit.; Mesilath Yesharim* 13-15. Omitted in sources cited in note 47. *Sotah* 9:15 and *Sefer Chasidim* interchange 5 and 6.
53. *Karban HaEdah* on *Yerushalmi loc. cit.; Tosefoth Yom Tov loc. cit.*
54. *Mesilath Yesharim* 16,17. Cf. *Yad, Tumath Ochlin* 16:12.
55. Ran *loc. cit.; Mesilath Yesharim* 18-21. Other sources interchange 7 and 10; *Reshith Chokhmah*; Marginal Note of Rabbi Yeshiah Berlin, *Avodah Zarah* 20b.
56. Ran *loc. cit.; Mesilath Yesharim* 22,23. Rif, Rosh, *loc. cit.* interchange 8 and 9. Cf. *Tosafoth, Avodah Zarah* 20b, s.v. *Anavah*; Maharsha *ad loc.*
57. *Tosefoth Yom Tov loc. cit.*
58. Ran *loc. cit.; Mesilath Yesharim* 24,25.
59. *Mesilath Yesharim* 26. Others have this as the seventh level, see note 55.
60. This is the word for meditation, see note 65. For examples, see Hai Gaon, quoted in Rabbi Moshe Botril on *Sefer Yetzirah* 4:2; Rambam, *Iggereth HaMusar* (in *Iggeroth HaRambam*) p. 7; *Moreh Nevukhim* 3:51; Ibn Ezra on Exodus 20:8, Michah 2:1, Psalms 92:5; *Yesod Moreh* 8; Ramban on Deuteronomy 13:2; Rabbi Shem Tov ibn Shaprut, *Pardes Rimonim* on *Bava Metzia* 59a (Sabbioneta, 1554), p. 4a; *Sefer Halkkarim* 2:25 (Warsaw, 1871), p. 90b; *Teshuvoth HaRadbaz* 816, 967 (3:532); *Sefer Cheredim, Teshuvah* 3 (Jerusalem, 1958), pp. 214, 215; *Shiur Komah* 13:3,17; Rabbi Yisrael Baal Shem Tov, *Tzavaath HaRivash* (Kehot, New York, 1975) 8; *Likutim Yekarim* (Jerusalem 1974) 38; Chida, *Avodath HaKodesh, Tziporen Shamir* 51; *Midbar Kedamoth, Heh* 13; *Beiur Halakhah* 571:2, s.v. *Talmid Chokham.*
61. *Yad, Yesodey HaTorah* 7:1; *Teshuvoth Hai Gaon*, quoted in *HaKothev* (on *Eyn Yaakov*), *Chagigah* 14b; *Otzar HaGaonim ibid.*; *Rabenu Chananel ibid.*; *Arukh* s.v. *Avney Shayish Tahor; Teshuvoth Rashba* 854. Some of these techniques are discussed in *Shaarey Kedushah* 3:7,8. See 6:53.

names,[62] as well as the chanting of psalms[63] and prayers.[64] The purpose of these exercises was to totally isolate the mind, both from external stimuli and internal thought, leaving it perfectly clear to receive the divine influx.[65]

6:24   Although these practices were helpful, Divine Inspiration could be attained without them, merely through incessant and fervent study of the Torah.[66] It can also be attained through deep meditation in prayer.[67] Often it comes automatically through a great act of faith,[68] or from the observance of a commandment in utter joy.[69]

6:25   When a person attains Divine Inspiration, he can understand things with a knowledge completely different than anything that he ever experienced previously.[70] He may also gain information about lofty mysteries not accessible to logic alone.[71] He can also reach a level where he is clearly

62. *Derekh HaShem* 3:4:4; *Teshuvoth Rashba* 220. Also see *Tosafoth, Chagigah* 14b, s.v. *Nichnesu, Gittin* 84a, s.v. *Al Menath ShTaali*; Ramban, *Torath HaShem Temimah* (in *Kithvey Ramban*), p. 168; *Shaarey Kedushah* 3:6; *Shaar Ruach HaKodesh* (Tel Aviv, 5723), pp. 74, 108. For specific examples, see *Hekheloth Rabathai* 16:4 (in *Batey Midrashoth*, Jerusalem, 1968); *Merkava Shlemah* (Jerusalem, 1921), p. 4b; *Pardes Rimonim* 21:1.
63. *Shaarey Kedushah*, Introduction.
64. See note 67.
65. The word *hithbodeduth* (הִתְבּוֹדְדוּת) literally means "self isolation." However, besides physical isolation, there is also mental isolation, where through meditation one isolates the mind from all extraneous thought; Rabbi Avraham ben HaRambam, *Kifayat al-Abidin* (translated from the Arabic as *Sefer HaMaspik LeOvdey HaShem*, Jerusalem, 1965), pp. 177ff. The Ralbag similarly speaks of, "the isolation (*hithbodeduth*) of the consciousness from the imagination, or of both of these from the other perceptive mental faculties" (התבודדות השכל מן הדמיון או שניהם מבין שאר הכחות הנפשיות המשיגות); *Milchamoth HaShem* 2:6 (Riva di Trento, 1560), p. 19a. Rabbi Chaim Vital likewise states that "one must seclude himself (*hitboded*) in thought" יתבודד במחשבה *Shaarey Kedushah* 3:8; cf. *Likutim Yekarim* 29, 38. Also see *Shaarey Kedushah* Part Four (British Museum, Manuscript 749), p. 15b.
66. *Shaarey Kedushah* 4:0. Cf. *Tana DeBei Eliahu Rabbah* 2; *Tana DeBei Eliahu Zuta* 1; *Zohar* 3:121, 3:202.
67. *Tur, Orach Chaim* 98; *Shulchan Arukh ibid.* 98:1.
68. *Mekhilta* on Exodus 14:31 (end).
69. *Ibid.*; *Pesikta Rabathai* 3:4 (Warsaw, 1893), p. 20b. Also see below, note 220.
70. *Yad, Yesodey HaTorah* 7:1.
71. *Derekh HaShem* 3:3:2.

aware of otherwise imperceptible spiritual entities and stuctures.[72]

6:26   A person experiencing Divine Inspiration attains an insight far above ordinary people, and thus virtually becomes a different person. The prophet Samuel thus told King Saul, "God's spirit shall descend upon you . . . and you shall be transformed into a different man" (1 Samuel 10:6).[73]

6:27   There are many levels of Divine Inspiration.[74] The highest degree is just below actual prophecy.[75] The only difference is that Divine Inspiration does not involve trance nor vision as does prophecy.[76] It is for this reason that such inspiration is often referred to as a spirit of prophecy (*ruach nevuah*, רוּחַ נְבוּאָה).[77]

6:28   In such a state, a person can speak or write words without being aware of their source.[78] It was in this manner that the third portion of the Bible, the Writings or Hagiographa (*Kethuvim*, כְּתוּבִים) were written.[79] King David

---

72. See *Teshuvath Hai Gaon*, quoted in note 61. This is what is meant by the statement that he is on the level of angels; *Yad, Yesodey HaTorah* 7:1. Also see *Chovoth HaLevavoth* 8:3; *Kuzari* 5:12 (28a); *Teshuvoth HaRambam (P'er HaDor)* 155; *HaEmunah HaRama*, p. 73.

73. *Yad, Yesodey HaTorah* 7:1; Abarbanel on 1 Samuel 10:5.

74. *Derekh HaShem* 3:3:3.

75. *Moreh Nevukhim* 3:45, Second Level; Bachya on Leviticus 8:8. This ceased to exist after the prophets died; see below 6:86.

76. *Moreh Nevukhim, loc. cit.*; Radak, Introduction to Psalms; *Avodath HaKodesh, Chelek Sithrey Torah* 24 (132d).

77. Cf. *Targum Yonathan* to Genesis 41:38, 43:14; *Targum* on 2 Samuel 23:2, 2 Kings 9:26, Isaiah 32:15, 40:13, Psalms 51:13. Cf. *Moreh Nevukhim, loc. cit.* (end).

78. Bachya on Deuteronomy 33:8. Cf. Rabbi Yehudah Chayit, *Minchath Yehudah* on *Maarekheth Elohuth* 10 (143b); *Avodath HaKodesh, Chelek Sithrey Torah* 24 (132c). See next note.

79. See note 76. Also see *Yedayim* 3:5; *Tosefta, Yadayim* 2:6; *Edduyoth* 5:3; *Megillah* 7a. Some sources appear to indicate that such works as Proverbs, Ecclesiastes and Song of Songs were King Solomon's own wisdom; *Beer Sheva, Sotah* 44a; *Maharatz Chajas, Berakhoth* 4a; *Shabbath* 151b, 153a. Other sources, however, indicate that they were written with Divine Inspiration; *Shir HaShirim Rabbah* 1:6-10; *Yalkut Shimoni* 2:953. The meaning is that they were written with inspired wisdom; *Zohar*

thus said, "God's spirit speaks through me, His word is on my tongue" (2 Samuel 23:2).[80] Hence, the Writings are on a lower level of holiness than the Prophets (*Nevi'im*, נְבִיאִים).[81]

6:29   A low level of Divine Inspiration[82] was a *bath kol* (בַּת קוֹל),[83] literally the "daughter of a voice."[84]

6:30   Even after message bearing Divine Inspiration ceased to exist[85] a *bath kol* could deliver a clear, unambiguous message.[86]

3:64a; *Raya Mehemna, Zohar* 3:223a. Also see *Yad, Avoth HaTumah* 9:6; *Chazon Nachum* on *Yadayim* 3:5; *Teshuvoth Mahari Bruno* 66; *Gilyoney HaShas, Megillah* 7a.

80. *Targum*, Rashi, Radak, *ad loc.; Moreh Nevukhim* 2:45, Second Level. Also see *Yalkut Shimoni* 2:165 *ad loc.* Cf. *Shaar Ruach HaKodesh, Derush* 1.

81. *Moreh Nevukhim* 2:45, Second Level. Cf. *Bava Bathra* 14b; *Tosafoth, Bava Bathra* 13b, s.v. *Rabbi Yehudah; Yoreh Deah* 282:19 in *Hagah.*

82. Ramban on Exodus 28:30; *Zohar* 1:138a; *Tikuney Zohar Chadash* 116c. It is like a touch of Divine Inspiration; Rashi, *Yoma* 9b, s.v. *Amar Rabbi Abba; Shir HaShirim Rabbah* 8:11.

83. The word *bath kol* also often denotes an echo; *Shemoth Rabbah* 24:8, 29:9; *Etz Yosef ad loc.* s.v. *Bath Kol*; Rashi on Job 4:16; *Machzor Vitri*, p. 556; *Tosafoth, Sanhedrin* 11a, s.v. *Bath Kol.* Cf. *Shir HaShirim Rabbah* 1:21 (end). Some interpret bath kol as a "measured voice;" *Shita Mekubetzeth* at the end of Rabbi Chaim Benveniste, *Chamra VeChayay* (Livorno, 1802), on *Sanhedrin* 11a, quoting the Rosh; *Sefer HaNetzachon*, quoted in *Etz Yosef* (on *Eyn Yaakov*), *Berakhoth* 3a. Cf. 1 Kings 7:26, Isaiah 5:10, Ezekiel 45:10. See note 96. Also see *Sefer HaTishbi*, s.v. *Bath Kol; Ragley Mebhaser ad loc.* For an extensive discussion of *Bath Kol*, see *Imrey Binah* 6 (in *Kithvey Maharatz Chajas*), p. 937.

84. This is because prophecy is the true voice of God, and this is merely an offspring and echo of prophecy; *Tosafoth Yom Tov, Yevamoth* 16:6; *Avodath HaKodesh, Chelek Sithrey Torah* 24 (133a). For reasons why it is called a *bath kol* and not a *ben kol* (son of a voice), see *Teshuvoth Rabbi Yitzchak Alfasi* (Rif) 1 (Livorno, 1781); Rabbi Yehudah Barceloni on *Sefer Yetzirah*, p. 178; Bachya on Deuteronomy 33:8; *Pardes Rimonim* 33:2, s.v. *Bath Kol.* One reason is because it comes from a feminine spiritual level; *Tikuney Zohar* 30 (74b), 69 (104b); *Avodath HaKodesh, Chelek Sithrey Torah* 24 (132d). Cf. *Yad Ramah, Sanhedrin* 11a; Maharal *ibid.*

85. See below, 6:86. However, the *bath kol* existed even in the time of the Patriarchs and prophets; *Shabbath* 14b, 56b; *Eruvin* 22b; *Yoma* 22b; *Sotah* 10b, 13b; *Sanhedrin* 99b, 102a, 104b; *Makkoth* 23b; *Horioth* 12a; *Kerithoth* 5b; *Targum Yonathan* on Numbers 21:5,6; *Targum* on Song of Songs 2:14, 4:1; *VaYikra Rabbah* 20:2; *Devarim Rabbah* 11:9; *Midrash Shmuel* (on Samuel) 3.

86. *Yoma* 9a; *Sanhedrin* 11a; *Sotah* 48b; *Tosefta, Sotah* 13:4; *Zohar* 1:238a; *Kuzari* 3:11, 3:41, 3:73. For a general discussion, see Reuven Margolies, introduction to *She'eloth U'teshuvoth min HaShamayim, Perek Giluyim* 2 (Jerusalem, 1957), p. 27ff. Use of a *bath kol* was not considered superstition; *Megillah* 33a; *Tosafoth ad loc.* s.v. *Menayin.* It could even occasionally have legal status; *Yevamoth* 16:6 (122a); *Tosefoth Yom Tov ad loc.* See below, Chapter 8, note 70.

6:31   Normally, a *bath kol* was only heard by saints,[87] who were otherwise worthy of prophecy.[88] Nevertheless, when the situation demanded it, it could even be heard by gentiles.[89] In many cases, it was heard by everyone worthy,[90] but in others, it was only heard by a single individual.[91] The *bath kol* was heard until the Sanhedrin ceased to function (around 361 c.d.).[92]

6:32   A *bath kol* is like a voice heard in the mind.[93] Although it sometimes sounds like a voice from heaven,[94] it is a prophetic, rather than a physical voice,[95] and it is only heard by those for whom it is intended.[96] It was a voice often heard by neophytes not yet ready for prophecy.[97] Regarding the

---

87. *Avodath HaKodesh, Chelek Sithrey Torah* 24 (132d).
88. Ramban, *Torath HaShem Temimah* (in *Kithvey Ramban*), pp. 148, 149. Cf. Ramban on Genesis 18:1.
89. *Taanith* 29b. Cf. *Gittin* 56b; *Bava Bathra* 3b. A *bath kol* can be in any language; Rashi, *Sotah* 33a, s.v. Bath Kol.
90. *Berakhoth* 17b, 61b; *Shabbath* 14b, 149b; *Taanith* 25b; *Megillah* 3a, 12a, 29a; *Moed Katan* 9a, 18b; *Kethuvoth* 103b, 104a; *Sotah* 2a, 34a; *Gittin* 57b; *Bava Metzia* 86a; *Bava Bathra* 73b; *Sanhedrin* 39b, 94a, 102a; *Avodah Zarah* 10b, 18a; *Avoth* 6:2; *Chulin* 87a; *Kerithoth* 5b.
91. *Berakhoth* 3a; *Shabbath* 33b, 57b; *Eruvin* 54b; *Yoma* 22b; *Rosh HaShanah* 21b; *Sotah* 10b; *Horioth* 12a.
92. Radal on *Pirkey Rabbi Eliezer* 8:53. Cf. *Pesikta Rabathai* 10:2 (end) *Zohar* 1:238a; Ramban, *Torath HaShem Temimah*, p. 149.
93. Rashi, *Megillah* 32a, s.v. Menayin.
94. *Targum Yonathan* on Numbers 21:6; *Tosafoth, Sanhedrin* 11a, s.v. Bath Kol; *Raziel HaMalakh*, p. 23. Also see *Yevamoth* 16:6 (122a); Rashi *ad loc.* s.v. Al; *Tosefoth Yom Tov ad loc.*; *Mateh Dan (Kuzari Sheni)* 4:298; *Tosefta, Nazir* 1:1. In the city it has the sound of a man, while in the field it sounds like a woman; to be accepted, it must repeat the message; *Megillah* 32a. It is also heard with a voice like a dove; *Berakhoth* 3a; *Avoduth HaKodesh, Chelek Sithrey Torah* 24 (133a). It sounds as if it is echoed on a board; Rabenu Chananel, *Yoma* 9a.
95. *Yoma* 9b; *Pesiktu Rabathai* 160a; *Kuzari* 3:73 (76a); Bachya on Deuteronomy 38:7.
96. *Shita Mekubetzeth* at end of *Chamra VeChayay, Sanhedrin* 11a; Maharatz Chajas *ibid.*; *Sedey Chemed, Beth* 65; *Ibid., P'ath HaSadeh, Beth* 25; Rabbi Yaakov Bachrach, *Ishtadluth im Shadal* 23 (Warsaw, 1896); *Taamey HaMinhagim, Likutim* 45 (p. 508); *Etz Yosef* (in *Eyn Yaakov* 14) on *Sanhedrin* 11a; *Anaf Yosef, Tanchuma, Ki Thisa* 16. Cf. Rashi, *Sotah* 33a, s.v. Bath Kol. Also see Radak on 1 Samuel 3:8, Ezekiel 1:24.
97. Ramban on Exodus 3:2; Ibn Ezra on Exodus 3:4. This appears to indicate that persons who engage in the exercises and meditation necessary for inspiration and prophecy also develop the faculty to hear a *bath kol*.

bath kol it is written, "Your ears shall hear a voice behind you" (Isaiah 30:21).[98]

6:33   A high degree of Divine Inspiration[99] was also involved in consulting the Urim and Thumim (אוּרִים וְתֻמִּים),[100] the oracle associated with the breastplate (*choshen,* חֹשֶׁן) of the High Priest (*cohen godol,* כֹּהֵן גָּדוֹל).[101]

6:34   The Urim and Thumim could only be consulted by a king, the Sanhedrin, or a public official in the interest of the entire community.[102] This oracle was in use until the destruction of the First Temple (420 b.c.e.).[103]

6:35   When the Urim and Thumim would be consulted, the High Priest would have to wear all eight vestments.[104] Both he and the questioner would face the ark.[105] The questioner would then make his inquiry in such a low voice,[106] that no one else but he would hear it.[107]

98. *Megillah* 32a; *Yerushalmi, Shabbath* 6:9 (38b). Cf. *Tosafoth, Yevamoth* 14a, s.v. *Rabbi.*
99. *Yoma* 73b; *Otzar Geonim ad loc.; Moreh Nevukhim* 2:45, Second Level; Ramban on Exodus 28:30; Bachya on Deuteronomy 33:8. See below, note 109.
100. Usually translated, "lightings and perfections," since the message shone forth and was then perfected by the cohen-priest; *Yoma* 73b; *Berakhoth* 4a in marginal note; Ramban on Exodus 28:30. Others write that the word *Thumim* has the connotation of pairing, since this was the inspiration that allowed the cohen-priest to arrange the letters to spell out a message; Bachya on Numbers 28:21.
101. Cf. Exodus 28:30, Leviticus 8:8, Numbers 27:21, Deuteronomy 33:8, 1 Samuel 28:6. The word *choshen* (חֹשֶׁן) comes from the root *chush* (חוש), meaning to "sense" or "detect;" Rabbi Shlomo Pappenheim, *Yerioth Shlomo,* Volume 1 (Dyherenfurth, 1784), p. 19b. Some say that there is a commandment to consult the Urim and Thumim; Ramban on *Sefer HaMitzvoth,* additions to Negative Commandments (49b), s.v. *VeAtah* (end); *Megillath Esther ad loc.* 1.
102. *Yoma* 7:5 (71b); *Yad, K'ley HaMikdash* 10:12.
103. *Sotah* 9:12 (48a); *Yoma* 21b; *Yad, K'ley HaMikdash* 10:10; Rashi on Exodus 28:30. There is another opinion, however, that it could no longer be used after the death of Samuel and David; *Yerushalmi, Sotah* 9:13 (45a,b).
104. *Yoma* 7:5 (71b); *Yad, K'ley HaMikdash* 10:12. For the significance of the eight, see Chapter 4, note 64.
105. *Yoma* 73a; *Yad, K'ley HaMikdash* 10:11. Rashi *ad loc.,* however, maintains that they faced each other; cf. *Kesef Mishneh* on *Yad, loc. cit.* Also see Rambam, Bertenoro, *Tosefoth Yom Tov,* on *Yoma* 7:5.
106. *Ibid.*
107. Cf. *Berakhoth* 31a; *Yad, Tefillah* 5:9; *Orach Chaim* 101:2. Also see *Magen Avraham* 101:3; *Mishnah Berurah* 101:5; from *Zohar* 1:209b (end), that this

6:36   The High Priest would then meditate on the stones of the breastplate until he reached a level of Divine Inspiration.[108] He would then see the breastplate with inspired vision.[109] The letters[110] containing the answer would appear to stand out.[111] With his Divine Inspiration, the High Priest would then be able to combine the letters to spell out the answer.[112]

6:37   Only one question at a time could be asked of the Urim and Thumim. If more than one question were asked, only the first would be answered.[113]

6:38   The Urim and Thumim were necessary even while there were prophets. While a prophet cannot receive a message at will,[114] the Urim and Thumim could be used at any time.[115] Moreover, while an evil decree foretold by a prophet could

---

implies that only the lips should be heard, without the words being heard, even by the worshiper himself. Cf. *Zohar* 2:138b, 2:208b; *Raya Mehemna, Zohar* 3:230b; *Tana DeBei Eliahu Rabbah* 28.

108. *Or HaShem* 3:7:1 (80b).

109. *Yad, K'ley HaMikdash* 10:11. Cf. *Otzar HaGaonim, Yoma* 73a.

110. The breastplate contained the names of the Twelve Tribes; Exodus 28:21. In order to complete all the letters of the alphabet, the names of the Patriarchs (אַבְרָהָם יִצְחָק יַעֲקֹב) and the words *Shiv'tey Yeshurun* (שִׁבְטֵי יְשֻׁרוּן) were added; *Yoma* 73b. Other sources have *Shiv'tey Yah* (שִׁבְטֵי יָהּ), "the Tribes of God," *Yad, K'ley HaMikdash* 10:11; Bertenoro on *Yoma* 7:5; cf. Psalms 122:4; *Bereshith Rabbah* 79:7; Rashi on Numbers 26:5. *Yerushalmi, Yoma* 1:3 (38b), has *Shiv'tey Yisrael* (שִׁבְטֵי יִשְׂרָאֵל), "Tribes of Israel," cf. *Chatham Sofer ad loc.* for discussion. For a discussion as to how these words were arranged on the Breastplate, see *Targum Yonathan; Targum Yerushalmi; Bachya; Chizzkuni;* on Exodus 28:17-20; *Targum Yonathan* on Exodus 39:1-13; *Targum* on Song of Songs 5:14; *BaMidbar Rabbah* 2:7; Tzioni, *BaMidbar* (Lemberg, 1882), p. 58c; *Peliyah (Sefer HaKanah;* Koretz, 1784), p. 32a; *Zohar* 2:230a; *Siddur Rav Saadiah Gaon* (Jerusalem, 1941), p. 271; Ritva, *Yoma* 73b. In all, the Breastplate contained 72 letters; *Raziel HaMalakh*, p. 44; Bachya, Chizzkuni,, on Exodus 28:15,20.

111. *Yoma* 73b; *Yad, K'ley HaMikdash* 10:11; *Zohar* 2:230a.

112. *Ramban* on Exodus 28:30; *Bachya* on Numbers 28:21.

113. *Yoma* 73a; *Yad K'ley HaMikdash* 10:12. In *Yerushalmi, Yoma* 1:3 (38b), this is disputed.

114. See below, 6:75

115. *Or Hashem* 3:7:2. Cf. *Yad K'ley HaMikdash* 10:11. It could also be used by one who was not yet able to attain prophecy; *Or HaShem* 3:7:1. Also see *Yerushalmi, Sanhedrin* 1:3 (7b).

be changed,[116] the message of the Urim and Thumim was irrevokable.[117]

6:39   The next degree of revelation is true prophecy (nevuah, נְבוּאָה).[118] Here the prophet is in such a high meditative state that his mind is totally blank, serving as a clear channel for the divine message.[119] When the prophet then returns to a normal state of consciousness, he is able to relate his message.[120]

6:40   Prophecy is a gift of God that cannot be attained through a person's own efforts.[121] Nevertheless, a very high degree of spiritual and mental preparation, as well as difficult disciplines, is also necessary.[122]

6:41   God only grants the gift of prophecy for the sake of His people.[123] Therefore, even when a person is worthy of prophecy, it cannot be attained unless his generation is also worthy.[124]

6:42   A major source of prophetic inspiration was the Ark of the Covenant, containing the two tablets of the original

116. See below, 8:16.
117. Yoma 73b.
118. *Moreh Nevukhim* 2:45, Third and subsequent levels; Bachya on Deuteronomy 33:8.
119. *Moreh Nevukhim* 2:45 (end), 2:36; Bachya on Leviticus 8:8, Deuteronomy 33:8; *Derekh HaShem* 3:3:4. It was thus unlike Divine Inspiration, above, 6:27.
120. *Kedushath Levi, Lekh Lekha* (Jerusalem, 1958), p. 19. The ability to return with a clear message is an important difference between prophecy and a simple mystical experience. Also see below, note 196.
121. *Yad, Yesodey HaTorah* 7:5; *Moreh Nevukhim* 2:32. Cf. *Ikkarim* 3:8; *Akedath Yitzchak* 35.
122. *Yad Yesodey HaTorah* 7:1. See 6:53.
123. *Mekhilta* (2b) on Exodus 12:1; *Sifra* (115d) to Leviticus 27:34; Rashi on Deuteronomy 2:16; *Ikkarim* 3:12; *Avodath HaKodesh, Chelek Sithrey Torah* 25; *Shiur Komah* 16 (31a); *HaEmunah HaRama*, p. 74; *Sh'nei Luchoth HaB'rith, Mesekhta Taanith* (2:137a). This may be true even if the prophet does not have a message for others; see below 6:77.
124. *Sanhedrin* 11a; *Berakhoth* 57a; *Succoth* 28a; *Bava Bathra* 134a; *Tosefta, Sotah* 13:4; *Pirkey Rabbi Eliezer* 8 (20b); *Avodath deRabbi Nathan* 14:1; *Yalkut Shimoni* 1:261; Rabbi Yaakov Emden, *Migdal Oz, Even Bochen* 3:5.

Torah,[125] which stood in the Holy of Holies (*Kodesh Ha-Kedoshim*, קֹדֶשׁ הַקֳּדָשִׁים) in the Holy Temple. God told Moses, "I will commune with you, and I will speak with you from above the ark-cover from between the two Cherubim, which are on the Ark of Testimony" (Exodus 25:22).[126] What was true of Moses was also true of the other prophets.[127]

6:43   The influence of the Ark only extended as far as the borders of the Holy Land, making it particularly suited for prophecy.[128] Moreover, outside the Holy Land, there are many spiritual barriers that must be penetrated before a vision can be obtained.[129]

6:44   Therefore, since prophecy requires the highest degree of sanctification, it can only be attained in the Land of Israel, which is the Holy Land.[130] It is thus written, "God your Lord will raise up a prophet *in your midst*" (Deuteronomy 18:15). This implies that prophecy would only take place in the

---

125. See above 5:26.
126. Also see Numbers 7:89.
127. *Derashoth HaRan* 8 (p. 128); *Ikkarim* 3:11; *Avodath HaKodesh, Chelek Sithrey Torah* 25. Cf. *Bereshith Rabbah* 70:8. Before the Temple was built and the Ark was in its proper place, prophecy was therefore difficult to attain; see 1 Samuel 3:1. There is evidence that the prophets would meditate on the Cherubim, Abarbanel on 1 Samuel 3:3.

      The Cherubim were seen as the guardians of the spiritual experience, that is, the "Tree of Life;" Genesis 3:24. The Cherubim on the ark therefore represented the spiritual cherubim. It was for this reason that the first angels seen by the prophets were cherubim; Ezekiel 1:5, 10:20; cf. Radak, Abarbanel, on Ezekiel 1:28; *Devarim Rabbah* 7:8. Cf. 1 Samuel 4:4, 2 Samuel 6:2, Psalms 18:11, Targum ad loc. Also see Radak, Abarbanel, on 1 Samuel 10:5.
128. *Ikkarim* 3:11; *Avodath HaKodesh, Chelek Sithrey Torah* 24, 25.
129. *Shaarey Orah* 2 (Warsaw, 1883), p. 31b; *Reshith Chokhmah, Shaar HaYirah* 4 (16c).
130. *Mekhilta* to Exodus 12:1 (1b); *Tanchuma, Bo* 5; *Midrash Tehillim* 132:3 (end); *Yalkut Shimoni* 1:187, 2:336, 2:549, 2:883; Rashi, Radak, on Jonah 1:3; *Zohar* 1:85a, 1:121a, 2:170b; *Emunoth VeDeyoth* 3:5 (end; 57a); *Kuzari* 2:14; Ibn Ezra 3:1; *Teshuvoth Radbaz* 2:842; *HaEmunah HaRama*, p. 74; *Shiur Komah* to (30d); Radal on *Pirkey Rabbi Eliezer* 10:11. This requirement is not mentioned by the Rambam, and some maintain that his position is that this is not an absolute requirement; Rabbi Avraham Abulafia, *Sefer HaCheshek* (Jewish Theological Seminary, Manuscript 1801), p. 32a. Cf. Maharibatz, *Megillah* 15a.

Land of Israel when it is settled by the Israelites.[131] A prophet can therefore only obtain his first revelation in the Holy Land. Once he has attained prophecy in the Holy Land, however, he can later obtain a vision even in other lands,[132] provided that it is absolutely necessary[133] for the sake of Israel.[134] Even in such cases, however, the vision could only be obtained in a secluded place, such as in a valley or near a river, which is not contaminated by the general population.[135]

6:46   Prophecy originally extended to all mankind. Moses, however, prayed that prophecy be restricted to Israel, and God conceded to his request. Moses thus said to God, "You shall go with us, so that we will be distinguished . . . from all the nations on the face of the earth." God said to Moses, "I will also grant you this request" (Exodus 33:16,17).[136]

6:47   Therefore, from the time that the Tabernacle (mishkan, מִשְׁכָּן) in the desert was completed,[137] true prophecy was restricted to Israelites.[138] A gentile could only experience

131. Sifri, Yalkut Shimoni (1:919), Ramban, ad loc. Before the Holy Land was settled by the Israelites, however, prophecy could be attained in all lands; Mekhilta to Exodus 12:1; Midrash Tehillim 132:3. According to some, once Jerusalem had been chosen as the Holy City, prophecy could not be attained elsewhere; Tanchuma, Bo 5. Moreover, once the Temple was built, prophecy could only be attained in its precincts; Tanchuma loc. cit. according to reading of Bachya on Exodus 12:1. This might be one reason that many prophets prophesied in the Lishcath HaGazith (לְשִׁכַּת הַגָּזִית) on the Temple grounds; Rashi, Taanith 16a, s.v. Chad; Targum Sheni on Esther 4:1. See below 6:88.
132. Targum, Rashi, Radak, on Ezekiel 1:3. Cf. Moed Katan 25a; Rashi ad loc. s.v. SheHaya; Kuzari 2:14; HaEmunah HaRama, p. 74. Some say this is also true of the discipline of a prophet; Rashi, Megillah 15a, s.v. BeShlemah.
133. Cf. Zohar 1:149a.
134. Kuzari 2:14; Maharatz Chajas, Moed Katan 25a. This explains why Jonah could not attain prophecy outside the Holy Land, even though he had previously attained it; Jonah was going to warn a gentile city. Cf Zohar 1:85a.
135. Mekhilta on Exodus 12:1; Tanchuma, Bo 5; Yalkut Shimoni 2:366; Shiur Komah 16 (31a).
136. Berakhoth 7b; Bava Bathra 15b; Seder Olam Rabbah 21; HaEmunah HaRama, p. 74. Cf. Shemoth Rabbah 32:3.
137. Exodus 25-28, 40:17.
138. VaYikra Rabbah 1:12; Shir HaShirim Rabbah 2:12.

prophecy when it was for Israel's benefit.[139] Even in such cases, however, the vision would come secretly at night, 'in an ambiguous manner.[140] It would appear far off, as though it were seen through a dull filter.[141] A gentile prophet thus said, "Now a word was brought to me secretly" (Job 4:12).[142]

6:48 There are seven gentile prophets mentioned in the Bible:[143] Balaam,[144] Beor,[145] Job, Eliphaz the Taimonite, Bildad the Shuhite, Zepher the Naamathite,[146] and Elihu ben Berachel the Buzite.[147]

6:49 Normally, prophecy is only granted to individuals of total Israelite lineage.[148] They must be direct descendants of Abraham, as God told him, "I will be a God to you and to your descendants after you" (Genesis 17:7).[149] Moses said, "God your Lord will elevate a prophet from you . . . from

139. *Ibid*. Cf. Maharsha, *Bava Bathra* 15b, but this answers his question.
140. *Esther Rabbah* 7:24.
141. *Bereshith Rabbah* 52:7, 74:5; *VaYikra Rabbah* 1:13; *Yalkut Shimoni* 1:28, 2:896, 2:953. Some say that this was not true prophecy, but Divine Inspiration; *Moreh Nevukhim* 2:45, Second Level.
142. *Ibid.*; Rashi *ad loc.*, and on Exodus 33:17. The traits cited in 6:52 were not necessary for a gentile prophet; *Migdal Oz, Evven Bochen* 3:3.
143. *Bava Bathra* 15b. These were before the Torah was given and prophecy restricted to Israel; *Seder Olam Rabbah* 21. Also see *Yeshuralmi, Sotah* 5:6 (26b).
144. Numbers 22:5. Some say that Balaam learned the methods of prophecy from his work in the occult arts; *BaMidbar Rabbah* 20:6.
145. The father of Balaam; *Tosafoth, Bava Bathra* 15b, s.v. *Balaam*. Some say that Beor was Laban's son; *Zohar* 1:166b. Cf. *Sanhedrin* 105a, *Tanchuma, Balak* 12.
146. Job 2:11. Cf. *Koheleth Rabbah* 7:2. Some say that Eliphaz was Esau's grandson; Genesis 36:12; *Targum Yonathan ad loc.*
147. Job 32:2. However, he may have been an Israelite, *Bava Bathra* 15b; *Tosafoth ad loc.* s.v. *Elihu; Zohar* 2:166a; *Midrash Sekhel Tov* on Genesis 19:21; *Yerushalmi, Sotah* 5:6 (26b, end). In any case, he was a descendant of Abraham; *Targum* on Job 32:2.
148. *Kiddush* 70b, from Jeremiah 30:25; *Tosafoth ad loc., Yevamoth* 47b, *Niddah* 13b, s.v. *Kashim; Kuzari* 1:114 (76b).
149. *BaMidbar Rabbah* 12:4; Rashi, *Sanhedrin* 39b, s.v. *Mipney*. Cf. Ramban on Exodus 19:9.

your brothers, just like me" (Deuteronomy 18:15), that is, of total Israelite ancestry, just like Moses.[150]

6:50   Therefore, prophecy usually is not granted to proselytes. Nonetheless, a proselyte may also be granted the gift of prophecy because of special merit. Thus, the prophet Obadiah, was an Edomite convert, but still became author of one of the books of the Bible.[151] A prophet is therefore accepted because of his qualifications and message, and not because of his ancestry.[152]

6:51   God said to Moses, "I will raise up a prophet for them . . . just like you" (Deuteronomy 18:18). This indicates that to be worthy of prophecy, a person must perfect himself like Moses, above and beyond the ten steps leading to Divine Inspiration.[153]

6:52   It is taught that a prophet must be intelligent, wealthy and strong.[154] These refer to psychological, rather than physical traits. A prophet must be in perfect mental health,[155] with his intellect developed as perfectly as possible for a human being.[156] Besides this, he must also be expert in

150. *Sifri, Yalkut Shimoni* (1:919), Rashi, *ad loc.*; Rambam, *Iggereth Teimon* (in *Iggeroth HaRambam*), p. 20.
151. *Sanhedrin* 39b; Rashi *ad loc.* s.v. *Mipney; VaYikra Rabbah* 18:2; *Tanchuma Tazria* 8; *Yalkut Shimoni* 2:549, 2:562; Rashi, Radak, on Obadiah 1:1; *cf.* Ibn Ezra *ad loc.; Zohar* 1:171a; *Kol Yehudah* (on *Kuzari*) 1:115, s.v. *Ki; Otzar Nechaman ibid.* s.v. *HaEzrachim.* However, Obadiah was a descendant of Abraham, since Edom is from Esau; see note 149.
152. *Iggereth Teimon*, p. 21. Cf. *Moreh Nevukhim* 2:40.
153. Maharsha, *Nedarim* 38b; Rabbi Yoshia Pinto (Riph) *ibid.* (*Eyn Yaakov* 20); *Etz Yosef, Shabbath, Eyn Yaakov* 66. Cf. *Targum Yonathan* on Deuteronomy 18:15, 18:18; *Yad, Yesodey HaTorah* 7:7. See above, note 47.
154. *Shabbath* 92a; *Nedarim* 38a. Some say that this is so that they will be respected when they declare a message: *Derashoth HaRan* 5(p.63), 6(p.79). Hence, these gifts are only needed if the prophecy is for others, but not if it is for their own edification (cf. 6:77); *Ikkarim* 3:10. However, others say that these gifts are needed for the concentration required for meditation; *Shiur Komah* 16 (30d). Cf. *Akedath Yitzchak* 35 (2:11b ff).
155. *Moreh Nevukhim* 2:36. Cf. *Shabbath* 92a.
156. *Ibid.; Nedarim* 38a; *Yad, Yesodey HaTorah* 7:1.

all areas of the Torah.[157] He must have a wealth of spirit, with no desire for additional wealth or gain.[158] Likewise, he must have strength of character, with his passions well balanced, and all his desires aimed toward God.[159]

6:53 A person who attains these qualities is then ready to prepare himself for prophecy. He must focus his entire being toward God,[160] and engage in meditation (*hithbodeduth*, הִתְבּוֹדְדוּת),[161] using methods known to the prophets.[162] It is only in a deep meditative state that he can be worthy of a vision.[163] At the time of prophecy, he is thus on a totally spiritual level.[164]

6:54 An individual seeking prophecy must be careful to keep his motives absolutely pure. The preparations for prophecy are extremely rigorous, and without divine help, they can lead to psychosis and false visions rather than to true

---

157. *Teshuvoth Rashba* 548.
158. *Moreh Nevukhim* 2:36; *Avoth* 4:1; Rambam *ad loc.*; *Shemonah Perakim* 7; *Iggereth Teimon*, p. 31.
159. *Ibid.*
160. *Kuzari* 5:10 (16b); *Derekh HaShem* 3:4.4.
161. See above, notes 60,65.
162. *Yad, Yesodey HaTorah* 7:4; Recanti on *VaYechi* (Levov, 1880), p. 37d; quoted in Rabbi Yehudah Chayit, *Minchath Yehudah* on *Maarekheth Elohuth* 10 (143b); *Or HaShem* 2:4:4 (46a); Rabbi Shimon ben Tzemach Duran (Rashbatz), *Magen Avoth* 2:2 (Livorno, 1785), p. 16a; Abarbanel on 1 Samuel 10:5; *Avodath HaKodesh, Sithrey Torah* 27 (135c,d); *Shiur Komah* 17 (30d), 28 (42c); Bachya on Leviticus 8:8; *Milchamoth HaShem* 2:6; *Shekel HaKodesh*, p.58. Cf. Rabbi Yehudah Chayit, *Minchath Yehudah* on *Maarekheth Elohuth* 8 (96a); Ramban on Deuteronomy 13:2; *Chinukh* 510; Ralbag on 1 Samuel 28:8, 2 Kings 9:1; Ibn Ezra on Isaiah 44:25; Abarbanel on 1 Samuel 10:5, 19:10, 19:18, 28:7, 1 Kings 18:42, 2 Kings 9:11; *Nachalath Avoth* on *Avoth* 1:1, 3:4; *Kav HaYashar* 12; *Shalsheleth HaKabbalah* (Jerusalem, 1962), p. 51; *Divrey Shalom*, *VaYishlack* (Warsaw, 1904), p. 26b,c; Rabbi Menachem Mendel of Vitebsk, *Iggroth HaKodesh* 30; Malbim on Genesis 24:63.
163. *Avodath HaKodesh, Chelek Sithrey Torah* 21 (130a). Prophecy is called serenity (*menuchah*, מְנוּחָה); *Mekhilta* on Exodus 12:1, from Jeremiah 24:3; Rashi, Radak, ad loc.; *Avodath HaKodesh, Chelek Sithrey Torah* 25. Cf. *Kuzari* 4:15 (34b); *Akedath Yitzchak* 15.
164. Cf. *VaYikra Rabbah* 1:1; *BaMidbar Rabbah* 16:1; *Tanchuma, VaYikra* 1, *Sh'lach* 1; *Derekh Eretz Zuta*, end; *Targum* on Judges 2:1; *Moreh Nevukhim* 3:42.

prophecy.[165] Moreover, a neophyte prophet, who has not yet learned to master his gift, can easily misunderstand his revelation.[166]

6:55   Therefore, every individual who desires to attain prophecy must have a master and guide.[167] The function of the master is to teach the neophyte the techniques of prophecy, and help him avoid the pitfalls along the way.[168] Those who sat at the feet of the great prophets and engaged in meditation attempting to attain prophecy were known as the "Sons of the Prophets" (*beney ha-nevi'im*, בְּנֵי הַנְבִיאִים).[169]

6:56   With the exception of Isaiah, every prophet in the Bible received his gift through his predecessors.[170]

6:57   Even after a prophet attains a vision, he still needs a master in order to advance to higher degrees of prophecy.[171] Like every other faculty, prophecy must be nurtured and developed.[172]

6:58   A prophet's first experience may be so negligible that he might not even recognize it as prophecy.[173] The prophecy may consist of a voice indistinguishable from human

165. *Shabbath* 149b; *Sanhedrin* 89a; Maharsha *ad loc.* s.v. *Ruach Navoth; Derekh HaShem* 3:4:9. Cf *Shaarey Kedushah*, Introduction and 3:7.
166. *Derekh HaShem* 3:4:6. Cf Rashi, *Sanhedrin* 89b, s.v. *Melkra.*
167. *Derekh HaShem* 3:4:9.
168. *Ibid.* 3:4:4. Cf. Abarbanel on 1 Samuel 10:5, 19:18.
169. 1 Kings 20:35, 2 Kings 2:3, 2:5, 2:7, 2:15, 4:1, 4:38, 5:22, 6:1, 9:1; *Targum ad loc.*; Radak on 2 Kings 2:3; *Yad, Yesodey HaTorah* 7:5; *Moreh Nevukhim* 2:32; *Derekh HaShem* 3:4:2.
170. *VaYikra Rabbah* 10:2; *Pesikta* 16 (125b). This may have actually been spiritual power to help prophecy, *Ikkarim* 3:11; *Migdal Oz, Evven Bochen* 3:4. Cf. *BaMidbar Rabbah* 18:19; *Mekhilta* on Exodus 12:1. See 1 Samuel 10:5, 10:11, 19:20-24.
171. *Derekh HaShem* 3:4:4.
172. *Ibid.* 3:4:2
173. *Ibid.* 3:4:3. Cf. *Sotah* 12b.

speech,[174] as in the case of Samuel.[175] It is then very much like a *bath kol.*[176]

6:59   A prophet may also begin his career by seeing an angel,[177] as in the case of Moses.[178]

6:60   Although an angel is an incorporeal spiritual being, with no shape or form,[179] God can cause a person to see an angel in a vision.[180] It is thus written, "God opened Balaam's eyes, and he saw the angel" (Numbers 22:31).[181] Often God uses the vision of an angel to prepare a person for prophecy.[182]

6:61   Prophecy itself is often channeled through an angel.[183] A prophet would thus make such a statement as, "I am a prophet like you, and the angel speaks to me" (1 Kings 13:18).[184]

---

174. *Cf.* Megillah 32a.
175. 1 Samuel 3:4 ff. Cf. *Moreh Nevukhim* 2:44; *Derekh HaShem* 3:4:3; Abarbanel on 1 Samuel 3:7.
176. Mahari Kara on 1 Samuel 3:1.
177. Ramban on Exodus 3:2; Ibn Ezra on Exodus 3:4.
178. Exodus 3:2. Cf. *Moreh Nevukhim* 3:45.
179. *Yad, Yesodey HaTorah* 2:3. However, see *Pardes Rimonim* 2:7, 24:11.
180. *Yad, Yesodey HaTorah* 2:4; Ramban to Genesis 18:2. In *Moreh Nevukhim* 2:41, 42, the Rambam writes that all visions of angels are prophetic. The Ramban. *loc.cit.*, however disputes this, and maintains that perceiving an angel is a lower degree experience than true prophecy. Also see Ramban on Numbers 22:31; Raavad on *Sefer Yetzirah*, Introduction (Warsaw, 1884), p. 4c; *Pardes Rimonim* 24:15. Cf. *Shemoth Rabbah* 2:8. Also see Ramban, *Toruth HaShem Temimah* (in Kithvey Ramban), p. 148; Bachya on Numbers 24:14; *Sodi Razia*, p. 8; *Avodath HaKodesh, Chelek Sithrey Torah* 28 (136c).
181. Ramban *ad loc.*
182. *Ibid.* See note 177. Also see *Shemoth Rabbah* 2:9.
183. The Rambam maintains that all prophecy, other than that of Moses was through an angel; *Yad, Yesodey HaTorah* 7:6; *Moreh Nevukhim* 2:34. The Ramban, *loc.cit.*, however, disputes this, and writes that a message through an angel is no prophecy at all. The Midrash states that prophecy can be through an angel, but not necessarily so; *VaYikra Rabbah* 1:9. Cf. *Zohar* 1:149b, 2:234b; *Berakhoth* 55b. Also see Ramban on Numbers 22:23. Cf. note 180.
184. Ramban *loc cit.* A similar phenomenon occurred when Elijah would appear in a vision to instruct people; *Shabbath* 33b, *Kethuvoth* 105b; *Nedarim* 50a; *Gittin* 50a; *Bava Metzia* 59b; *Makkoth* 11a; *Pirkey Rabbi Eliezer* 1; *Tikuney Zohar* 3b. Elijah is considered to move about like an angel; *Berakhoth* 4b; *Targum* on Ecclesiastes 10:20; *Midrash Tehillim* 8:7, Ibn Ezra on Malachi 3:24; *Pardes Rimonim* 24:13. For

6:62   Just as there are many levels of intelligence, there are many degrees of prophecy.[185] God grants a degree of revelation to each prophet according to his spiritual gifts and the needs of the time. It is thus written, "[God] makes a measure for the spirit" (Job 28:25).[186]

6:63   Just as the depth and content of prophecy may vary, so may its quantity. While one prophet may only receive a very short message, another may receive enough to write one or more entire books.[187]

6:64   Prophecy may occur in a wakeful vision or in a prophetic dream. A vision gained while the prophet is awake is a higher degree of prophecy.[188] Similarly, hearing words is a higher level of prophecy than seeing a mere vision. Seeing the speaker is higher than hearing mere words. Having an angel speak is higher than being given a message through the vision of a human. The highest level of prophecy is hearing a voice, and knowing that it is directly from God.[189]

6:65   The human brain is like a receiving mechanism upon which the soul can act.[190] This action, however, usually occurs on the subtlest sub-quantum levels [191] and it is masked by the mind's normal reverie and reaction to

an extensive discussion, see Rabbi Reuven Margolies, Introduction to *She'eloth U'Teshuvoth min HaShamayim*, p. 36 ff.

185. *Yad, Yesodey HaTorah* 7:2; *Derekh HaShem* 3:4:5. Cf. *Zohar* 1:183a, 2:251b.
186. *VaYikra Rabbah* 15:2.
187. *Ibid.*
188. Cf. *Pirkey Rabbi Eliezer* 28. See below, 6:66.
189. *Moreh Nevukhim* 2:45. Some say that the face that the prophet sees is his own; *Shoshan Sodoth* (Koretz; 1784), p. 69; cf. Bachya on Numbers 12:6. Likewise, the voice that the prophet hears is his own; *Ibid.*; cf. Ibn Ezra on Daniel 10:21. It is likewise taught that God spoke "with the voice of Moses;" *Berakhoth* 45a; *Midrash Tehillim* 18:29, 24:11; *BaMidbar Rabbah* 14:21; *Tanchuma, Ki Thisa* 15.
190. *Derekh HaShem* 3:3:1,2. See Rabbi Moshe of Narbonne on *Moreh Nevukhim* 1:46 (Vienna, 1852), p. 5a.
191. See above, 3:23.

external stimuli.[192] When a person's mind is completely relaxed as during sleep, the effects of the soul can sometimes be detected. On rare occasions, these effects may be manifest in normal dreams.[193]

6:66 Through his meditation, the prophet may experience a vision while awake, or in a dream while sleeping.[194] While receiving the vision, the prophet is totally unconscious of his surroundings.[195] However, immediately after the vision is over, he returns to a normal state of consciousness.[196]

6:67 Since the mechanism of prophecy resembles that of a dream, it is often referred to as a prophetic dream.[197] God thus said, "If there will be a prophet among you, I . . . will make Myself known to him in a vision, I will speak with him in a dream" (Numbers 12:6).[198] It is likewise written,

---

192. Rabbi Yitzchak HaYisraeli, *Sefer HaYesodoth* (Drohavitz, 1900), p. 54; *HaEmunah HaRama*, p. 70; *Derekh HaShem* 3:1:5.
193. *Ikkarim* 4:11; *Derekh HaShem* 3:1:6. Cf. *Moreh Nevukhim* 2:36; *Zohar* 1:183a; *Pirkey Rabbi Eliezer* 34. There are techniques known as she'elath chalom (שְׁאֵלַת חֲלוֹם) which is used to enhance this effect; see Ibn Ezra on Exodus 14:19, 28:9; Bachya on Deuteronomy 29:28; Rabbi Yehudah Barceloni on *Sefer Yetzirah*, p. 104; Rabbi Moshe Botril on *Sefer Yetzirah* 4:3; *Taam Zekenim* (Frankfurt am Mein, 1855), pp. 54-56; *B'rith Menuchah* (Warsaw 1889), pp. 49d, 55a; *Raziel HaMalakh* (Amsterdam, 1701), pp. 31c, 40a; *Lekutey HaShas MeHaAri* (1783), p. 29a. For a detailed discussion, see Rabbi Reuven Margolies, introduction to *She'eloth U'Teshuvoth min HaShamayim*, p. 15ff. Also see *Menachoth* 67a; *Bava Metzia* 107b; *Rabenu Chananel*, *Shitah Mekubetzeth, ad loc.*; *Arukh*, s.v. *Davar* 2; *Yerushalmi, Kelayim* 9:3.
194. *Pirkey Rabbi Eliezer* 28 (63a); *Radal ad. loc.* 28:1 #3; *Bereshith Rabbah* 17:6, 44:19; *Yalkut Shimoni* 1:23; *Rambam* on *Sanhedrin* 10:1, Thirteen Principles 7; *Yad, Yesodey HaTorah* 7:2; *Moreh Nevukhim* 2:41; *Abarbanel* on Genesis 21:27; *Derekh Hashem* 3:5:2. The meditations used by the prophet may have been similar to those used to bring about an induced dream (*she'elath chalom*, שְׁאֵלַת חֲלוֹם).
195. *Yad, Yesodey HaTorah* 7:6; *Sifri* on Deuteronomy 34:10; *BaMidbarRabbah* 14:34; *Zohar* 1:171a; *Rashi* on Numbers 24:4; *Derekh HaShem* 3:5:3.
196. *Avodath HaKodesh, Chelek Sithrey Torah* 27 (135c,d); *Shaarey Kedushah* 3:5; *Derekh HaShem* 3:5:3. Cf. Ezekiel 1:28, *Radak ad loc.* See above, note 120.
197. *Bereshith Rabbah* 44:7; *Sifri* on Numbers 12:6; *Avoth de Rabbi Nathan* 34:8; *Moreh Nevukhim* 2:36; *Bachya* on Genesis 28:12; *Abarbanel* on Isaiah 2:1.
198. *Rambam* on *Sanhedrin* 10:1, Principles of Faith 7; *Yad, Yesodey HaTorah* 7:2; *Moreh Nevukhim* 2:41. Cf. *Berakhoth* 55b; *Zohar* 2:234b.

"In a dream, in a vision of the night . . . [God] opens the ears of men" (Job 33:15).¹⁹⁹

6:68   Dreams are therefore spoken of as a touch of prophecy.²⁰⁰ The differences between a dream and a prophetic vision is quantitative rather than qualitative.²⁰¹ Most dreams, however, do not contain true information.²⁰²

6:69   Man's physical nature acts as a barrier, preventing him from experiencing the effects of his soul.²⁰³ Since these barriers are never totally overcome, one can only experience prophecy through one's physical senses, most often by seeing and hearing.²⁰⁴ Moreover, the human mind does not have any faculty to perceive the spiritual directly. Therefore, any vision of the spiritual that a prophet may perceive is seen as reflected in a dull, imperfect mirror.²⁰⁵

199. *Zohar* 1:183a; *Ikkarim* 4:6,11; *Akedath Yitzchak* 69; Radal on *Pirkey Rabbi Eliezer* 28:1.
200. *Berakhoth* 57b; *Bereshith Rabbah* 17:7, 44:19; *Yalkut Shimoni* 1:23; *Zohar* 1:149b, 1:183a, 1:191b, 1:238a, 2:247b, 3:222b, 3:234b; *Tikuney Zohar* 21 (56a).
201. *Moreh Nevukhim* 2:36; *Teshuvoth Ramban* 286.
202. *Berakhoth* 55a,b. Nevertheless, it is customary to fast when one has a particularly distressing dream; *Shabbath* 11a; *Taanith* 12b; *Bereshith Rabbah* 44:14; *Zohar* 3:92a; *Yad Taanith* 1:12; *Orach Chaim* 220; *Teshuvoth Tashbatz* 2:128.
203. Rambam, *Shemonah Perakim* 6; *Shaarey Kedushah* 3:3; *Nefesh HaChaim* 1:18. This is especially true of sin; above 5:50.
204. Prophecy can involve all five senses; *Tikuney Zohar Chadash* 120b on Genesis 18:1; *Shaarey Kidushah* 3:5. It can also involve synesthesia; *Mekhilta*, *Yalkut Shimoni* (300), Rashi on Exodus 20:15. Cf. *Kli Yekar, ibid.* Also see Genesis 27:27; *Moreh Nevukhim* 1:46; Ibn Ezra on Ecclesiastes 11:7.
205. *Yevamoth* 49b; Rashi, Rambam, ad loc.; *Sanhedrin* 97b; *VaYikra Rabbah* 1:14, *Zohar* 1:171a; Rashi, Sforno, to Numbers 12:6; Rambam on Genesis 18:2; *Yad, Yesodey HaTorah* 7:6; Rambam on *Kelim* 30:2; *Ikkarim* 3:17; Bachya on Leviticus 1:1; *Shiur Komah* 16 (32b); *Shekel HaKodesh*, p. 86; *Ikkarim* 3:17; *Derekh HaShem* 3:5:4. This is related to various spiritual forces (*sefiroth*); *Shaar Ruach HaKodesh, Drush* 1 (p. 12); *Etz Chaim, Shaar HaYereach* 2. This is in distinction to Moses, who was able to see perfectly clearly; below, 7:5.
      The word for "mirror" here is in one place vocalized as *ispaklaria* (אִסְפַּקְלַרְיָא); *Targum Yonathan* on Exodus 19:17. However, the Hebrew word for glass (*zechuchith,* וְכוּכִית) is translated into Aramaic as *aspaklara* (אַסְפַּקְלָרָא) *Targum* on Job 28:17; cf. Ibn Ezra *ad loc.* This would indicate that the *ispaklaria* or *aspaklara* was a glass, lens or speculum; and this is the opinion of *Tosefoth Yom Tov* on *Kelim* 30:2. Others, however, interpret it to denote a mirror; Bertenoro; *Tifereth Yisrael;* on *Kelim* 30:2; *Yad Kelim* 12:17. According to one opinion, a "clear glass" is a lens, while an "unclear glass" is a mirror; Rabbi Moshe Chaim Luzzatto, *Adir BaMarom*

6:70   It is for this reason[206] that prophecy is usually expressed symbolically,[207] just as in dreams. God thus said, "I have also spoken to the prophets, and have granted many visions; in the mission of the prophets, I have used symbolisms" (Hosea 12:11).[208] It is for this reason that many prophets,[209] especially neophytes, misunderstood[210] or misinterpreted[211] their prophecy.

6:71   Since its spiritual influx completely overcomes the prophet's physical being, prophecy can be an overwhelming, and even terrifying experience.[212] Regarding Abraham, the Torah states, "Abraham fell into a trance, and a great dark dread fell upon him" (Genesis 15:12). In describing his vision, Daniel likewise said, "I saw this great vision and I became powerless. My appearance was destroyed, and my strength deserted me. I heard the sound of his words, and I fell on the ground in a trance" (Daniel 10:8,9).[213]

6:72   Prophets often describe their visions in terms of whirlwinds, clouds and fire.[214] These denote the mental

(Warsaw, 1886), p. 78a; Cf. Bachya on Numbers 12:6. It may be that *ispaklaria* denotes a mirror, while *aspaklaru* is a lens or glass. See above, note 189.

206. *Zohar* 1:183a; *Tikuney Zohar* 30 (74b, end). Also see *Kedushath Levi*, *Lekh Lekha*, p. 19; above note 120.

207. *Yad*, *Yesodey HaTorah* 7:3; *Moreh Nevukhim* 2:43; *Teshuvoth Radbaz* 816. Cf Genesis 28:12, Jeremiah 1:13, Ezekiel 2:9, Zechariah 4:2, 6:1, Amos 7:7, Daniel 7:1, 8:1.

208. *VaYikra Rabbah* 1:14; *Moreh Nevukhim*, Introduction.

209. It is thus taught that only Moses and Isaiah (and some include Elijah) understood the full content of their prophecy; *Midrash Tehillim* 90:4; *Yalkut Shimoni* 2:841. Also see *Mekhilta* (43b), Rashi, on Exodus 15:17; *Bava Bathra* 119b; *Yad Melakhim* 12:2.

210. *Derekh HaShem* 3:4:6.

211. *Ibid.* 3:4:7.

212. *Ibid.* 3:3:6

213. Rambam on *Sanhedrin* 10:1, Principles of Faith 6; *Yad*, *Yesodey HaTorah* 7:2; *Migdal Oz*, *Evven Bochen* 3:8; Radak, Abarbanel on Ezekiel 1:28. Cf. Genesis 17:3, Joshua 5:14, Isaiah 6:5, Jeremiah 1:6.

214. Exodus 19:18; *Mekhilta*, Rashi, Bachya, *ad loc.*; Deuteronomy 4:10,11, 5:4, 5:19,20, 1 Kings 19:11,12; Ezekiel 1:4, Job 38:1.

states through which the prophet must pass before he can obtain a vision.²¹⁵

6:73 A prophetic vision can only be obtained when one is in a perfect mental state.²¹⁶ It cannot be attained when one is depressed, languid,²¹⁷ or angry.²¹⁸

6:74 Before attaining a vision, a prophet must therefore be in a pleasant joyous mood.²¹⁹ Joy in serving God is conducive to the prophetic influx.²²⁰ It is for this reason that prophets often made use of music in attaining vision.²²¹

6:75 Even with every possible preparation and meditation, no prophet has enough control over his spiritual being to have a vision at will. Although a prophet may be in a state of readiness, a vision can only come when granted by God.²²² However, even when a prophet is not granted a vision under

---

215. Abarbanel on Ezekiel 1:4. Cf. *Zohar* 2:81a, 2:131a, 2:203a, 3:227a; *Pardes Rimonim* 25:7; *Shaarey Orah* 5 (50b); *Shaarey Kedushah* 3:6. These are forces that confuse the mind; *Zohar* 3:123a; *Tikuney Zohar* 11b; *Reshith Chokhmah, Shaar HaYirah* 4 (16c).
216. *Moreh Nevukhim* 2:36.
217. *Shabbath* 30b; *Pesachim* 117a; *Midrash Tehillim* 24:4; *Tikuney Zohar* 21 (56a); Rambam, *Shemonah Perakim* 7; *Yad, Yesodey Hatorah* 7:4; Rosh, *Berakhoth* 5:2; *Ikkarim* 3:10. Cf. *Tosafoth, Bava Bathra* 121a, s.v. *Yom.*
218. *Pesachim* 66b. Cf. *Likutey Amarim (Tanya), Iggereth HaKodesh* 25 (138b).
219. Cf. Radak on 2 Kings 3:15; *Zohar* 2:45a.
220. *Yerushalmi, Sukkah* 5:1 (22b); *Bereshith Rabbah* 70:8; *Yalkut Shimoni* 2:550; *Tosafoth, Sukkah* 50b. s.v. *Chad.* Cf. Rabbi Yehudah Chayit, *Minchath Yehudah* on *Maarekheth Elohuth* 8 (96a), 10 (143b). See above, note 69.
221. 1 Samuel 10:5, 2 Kings 3:15, 1 Chronicles 25:1; *Yad, Yesodey HaTorah* 7:4; *Livnath HaSapir,* quoted in *Avodath HaKodesh, Chelek HaTakhlith* 10; *Moreh Nevukhim* 3:45; Rabbi Shlomo Pappenheim, *Yerioth Shlomo,* Volume 1, p. 76b, Volume 2 (Roedelheim, 1831), p. 22b; *Likutey Moharan* 64:5, from Song of Songs 4:8; Hirsch on Genesis 49:22. Music has the same spiritual source as prophecy; *Zohar* 3:223b; *Zohar Chadash* 26d, 48a; *Likutey Moharan* 3. It has the power to penetrate the barriers that prevent prophecy; *Shaarey Orah* 1 (4a); cf. Isaiah 18:5; Rashi on Exodus 15:2, Isaiah 25:5; Radak, *Sherashim,* s.v. *ZaMaR* (זמר). The music would be stopped before the prophecy would begin; *Shaarey Kedushah,* Part Four (British Museum, Manuscript 749), p. 15b.
222. *Yad, Yesodey HaTorah* 7:4; *Avodath HaKodesh, Shaar Sithrey Torah* 20; *Derekh HaShem* 3:5:6.

such circumstances, he is granted an experience of the Divine.[223]

6:76   The revelation of Moses was not prophecy, but a totally different, higher spiritual experience.[224] Therefore, the 'imitations of other prophets did not apply to him.[225]

6:77   Although revelation is primarily a gift to perfect the prophet himself,[226] there are many instances in which a prophet is sent with a message to others.[227]

6:78   When a prophet is sent with a message for others, he is compelled to reveal it, even against his will.[228] Jeremiah thus said, "If I say, 'I will not make mention of Him, nor speak any more in His name,' then there is a burning fire in my heart, shut up in my bones; I struggle to hold it in, but I cannot" (Jeremiah 20:9).[229]

6:79   During the time of the First Temple, prophecy was very common in Israel. At times there were approximately a million people who had experienced prophecy.[230]

6:80   Similarly, there were occasions when many people at once were granted prophetic[231] experiences of God's presence,[232] as by the Red Sea and at Sinai.[233] It is thus

223. *Beth Elohim, Shaar HeYesodoth* 20.
224. *Moreh Nevukhim* 2:33.
225. See below, 7:5-10.
226. *Derekh HaShem* 3:4:6. See above, note 2. This adequately answers the question raised by Moshe Aaron Shatzkes in *HaMafteach* on *Megillah* 14a (Warsaw, 1866).
227. *Yad, Yesodey HaTorah* 7:7; *Moreh Nevukhim* 2:37; *Ikkarim* 2:12; *Milchamoth HaShem* 2:6; *Beth Elohim, Shaar HaYesodoth* 20.
228. It is forbidden to withhold prophecy; below 8:25.
229. *Moreh Nevukhim* 2:37.
230. *Megillah* 14a; *Shir HaShirim Rabbah* 4:22; *Ruth Rabbah* 1:2. See note 226. Occasionally, a different prophet was sent every day; *Pesikta Rabathai* 34:9. In the future, the names of all will be revealed; *Koheleth Rabbah* 1:30.
231. *Kuzari* 1:87 (52b). The Rambam, however, maintains that this was not true prophecy; *Moreh Nevukhim* 2:32. Cf. *Teshuvoth Rashba* 4:234. See next note.
232. Ramban on Genesis 18:2; *Derashoth HaRan* 5 (p. 81); *Ikkarim* 3:11; *Avodath HaKodesh, Chelek Sithrey Torah* 27, 33; *Derekh HaShem* 3:5:7.
233. *Mekhilta* on Exodus 19:11. But see *Yad, Yesodey HaTorah* 1:9.

taught that a common handmaid experienced a greater revelation at the Red Sea than Ezekiel did in his visions.[234]

6:81 A prophet is usually shown concepts and ideas in symbolic form.[235] Nevertheless, there were many prophecies that were destined to be preserved literally in the Bible.[236] These were revealed to the prophet word for word.[237] A prophet thus said, "[God's] word was in my mouth" (2 Samuel 23:2).[238]

6:82 Every prophet express his prophecy in different language.[239] The language of a prophet's revelation will usually reflect his own style of speech or writing.[240]

6:83 Although many people had the gift of prophecy, the Bible only mentions those who had a message for all generations.[241] There is a tradition that besides Moses and Aaron,[242] there are 48 prophets mentioned in the Bible.[243] [They are listed in Table 6:1, at the end of this chapter.]

6:84 Just as many men experienced prophecy, so did many women.[244] In many cases, they even attained higher degrees

234. Mekhilta (37a), Yalkut Shimoni (1:244), Rashi, on Exodus 15:2; Ramban on Genesis 18:2. Cf. Devarim Rabbah 7:8; Radak ad loc. s.v. Kol; Moreh Nevukhim 3:6.
235. See above, 6:70.
236. Cf. Megillah 7a; Mekhilta (55a) on Exodus 17:14.
237. Kuzari 5:20 (50b); Ramban on Numbers 23:5; Maharal, Tifereth Yisrael 65; Derekh HaShem 3:4:8. This even included minor spelling variations and cantillations; Or HaShem 2:4:1.
238. Sforno on Numbers 22:38. See above, 6:28.
239. Sanhedrin 89a; Ikkarim 3:9 (end). However, compare Isaiah 2:2-4 and Micah 4:1-3. See Abarbanel on Isaiah 2:2.
240. Derekh HaShem 3:4:8.
241. Megillah 14a; Seder Olam Rabbah 21; Shir HaShirim Rabbah 4:22; Ruth Rabbah 1:2; Koheleth Rabbah 1:30. Cf. Ran, Megillah (Rif 4a), s.v. Tanu.
242. HaGra, Megillah 14a, writes that Moses and Aaron are not included among the 48 prophets in Seder Olam 20, cf. HaGra ad loc. However, they are included by Rashi and Rabenu Chananel, Megillah 14a; Halakhoth Gedoloth, Hesped (Venice, 1548), p. 143b.
243. Megillah 14a; HaGra, Seder Olam 20; Halakhoth Gedoloth, loc cit., Zohar 1:125a.
244. There were as many prophetesses as prophets; Shir HaShirim Rabbah 4:22; above 6:79.

of prophecy than did men.[245] There are seven prophetesses mentioned in the Bible:[246] Sarah,[247] Miriam,[248] Deborah,[249] Hannah,[250] Abigail,[251] Hulda,[252] and Esther.[253]

6:85 There is a tradition that whenever a prophet's father is mentioned in the Bible, then the father is also a prophet.[254] There is also a tradition that where a prophet's birthplace is not mentioned, he is a native of Jerusalem.[255]

6:86 Prophecy lasted for 1000 years in Israel,[256] from the time of the Exodus (2448; 1313 b.c.e.) until 40 years after building the Second Temple (3448; 313 b.c.e.).[257] The spirit

245. As in the case of Sarah, *Shemoth Rabbah* 1:1; *VaYikra Rabbah* 29:9; *Tanchuma, Shemoth* 1; Rashi on Genesis 21:2; Bachya on Exodus 15:20. According to some, this was a general rule; Rabbi Yitzchak de-min Acco; *Otzar Chaim* (Guenzberg Collection, Moscow, Manuscript 775), p. 95b, quoting Rabbi Yaakov (ben Yaakov) HaCohen of Segovia, *Shaarey Orah* (actually *Sefer HaOrah*, existant in manuscript; Ambrosiana, Milan 62; Vatican 428; Vienna 258; Schocken Collection, Kabbalah 14).
246. *Megillah* 14a; *Seder Olam Rabbah* 21. Cf. *Asarah Maamaroth, Em Kol Chai* 2:1 (Lemberg, 1858), p. 175a.
247. From Genesis 11:28, 26:11. See note 245.
248. Exodus 15:20.
249. Judges 4:4.
250. From 1 Samuel 2:1. Hannah was Samuel's mother.
251. From 1 Samuel 25:29-34. She later married King David, 1 Samuel 25:42.
252. 2 Kings 22:14. She was a contemporary and relative of Jeremiah, and a descendant of Joshua; *Megillah* 14b.
253. From Esther 5:1.
254. *Megillah* 15a; *VaYikra Rabbah* 6:6; *Yalkut Shimoni* 2:252, 2:385.
255. *Megillah* 15a. Cf. Ramban, *Torath HaAdam* (in Kithvey Ramban) p. 298. See above, note 131.
256. Rav Saadia Goan, *Sefer HaGaluy*, quoted in *Zekher LeRishonim* 5:152; and Binyamin Menasheh Levin, *Iggereth Rav Sherira Goan* (Jerusalem, 1972), p. 5a; Rabbi Avraham ben Chiyyah, *Sefer Halbbur* 3:8; Rav Nissim Gaon, *Mafteach Man'oley HaTalmud*, Introduction (in Vilna Shas, before Berakhoth). *Kuzari* 1:87 (53a) writes that it lasted 900 years, but this was actually the period of time that the Divine Presence was in Israel; cf. *Ibid.* 2:23 (39b). However, *Kol Yehudah ad loc.* writes that it was actually only 890 years. This does not include the 70 years of the Babylonian exile (Jeremiah 25:11), and the 40 years during the time of the Second Temple that prophecy still remained (next note), a total of 110 years. Adding this to the 890 results in 1000 years. Cf. *Avodah Zarah* 10a; Rashi *ad loc.* s.v. *U'Shivkei; Megalleh Amukoth* 228.
257. *Kuzari* 3:39 (46b), 3:65 (67b); Rabbi Avraham ibn Daud, *Sefer HaKabbalah* (Jerusalem, 1971), p. 8. Some authorities dispute this, and maintain that prophecy ceased in 3442; *Tzemach David* 3442; *Seder HaDoroth* 3442.

of prophecy ceased that year when the last of the prophets, Haggai, Zechariah and Malachi, all died[258] in a single month.[259]

6:87   Prophecy is very difficult to attain when the Ark of the Covenant is not in its place in the Holy Temple.[260] Therefore, when the Temple was destroyed and the Ark permanently concealed, prophecy became very difficult.[261]

6:88   Moreover, prophecy can only exist in the Holy Land when it is inhabited by the majority of Israelites in the world.[262] Therefore, when the majority of Israelites refused to return to the Holy Land in the time of Ezra, the land ceased to have its special status with respect to prophecy, and prophecy ceased to exist.[263] However, it will be restored in the Messianic age, when the majority of Israelites once again live in the Holy Land.[264]

258. *Sanhedrin* 11a; *Yoma* 9b; *Sotah* 48b; *Tosefta, Sotah* 13:4; *Shir HaShirim Rabbah* 8:11.
259. Radak on Zechariah 11:14, from Zechariah 11:18.
260. See above, note 127.
261. *Avodath HaKodesh, Chelek Sithrey Torah* 28.
262. See above, 6:44. The words, "in your midst" (Deuteronomy 18:15,18) may denote that the majority of Israelites must be in the Holy Land.
263. *Yoma* 9b; *Kuzari* 2:24 (40a). For the reason that prophecy lasted for 40 years during the Second Temple, see *Kuzari* 3:65 (67b); Abarbanel on Haggai 1:1. Also see *Arkhin* 32b; *Tosafoth, Gittin* 36a. s.v. *BiZ'man* (end); *Yad, Shemitah VeYovel* 10:8,9. Another reason that prophecy ended was because prophets were murdered; *Midrash Tadshe* 20, from Nehemiah 9:26 (*Otzar Midrashim*, p. 485).
264. The Rambam maintains that prophecy will return before the Messiah's coming; *Iggereth Teimon* (in *Iggeroth HaRambam*), p. 30, from Joel 3:1. *Cf.* Abarbanel *ad loc.* Also see Joel 4:1. It appears that prophecy will return after the war of Gog and Magog, Ezekiel 39:29; *Targum*, Abarbanel, ad loc. *Cf. BaMidbar Rabbah* 16:18 (end).

TABLE 6:1

THE PROPHETS OF ISRAEL[1]

1. Assir ben Korach

2. Elkanah ben Korach

3. Aviasaph ben Korach[2]

4. Joshua[3]

5. Pinchas[4]

1. These are enumerated in Rashi, Rabbenu Chananel, *Chidushey HaRan*, on *Megillah* 14a; *Halakhoth Gedoloth, Hilkhoth Hesped* (Venice, 1548), p. 143b; Rabbi Eliahu, Vilna Gaon (HaGra) on *Seder Olam* 20. For further discussion see *Asarah Maamaroth, Em Kol Chai* 2:1 (Lemberg, 1858), p. 176b, 177a; Chida, *Pethach Eynayim*, on *Megillah* 14a.
   Here, we follow the listing of the Gra, *Megillah* 14a and on *Seder Olam* 20. Rashi, Rabbenu Chananel and *Halakhoth Gedoloth* list Moses and Aaron among the 48, but their names are not found in the listing of *Seder Olam*, and they are omitted by the Gra. In general, these are the prophets who lived *after* Moses, since the Talmud states explicitly that the forty-eight prophets did not add to the Torah. For the same reason, although Rashi lists Abraham, Isaac and Jacob, they are omitted in *Seder Olam* and the Gra; cf. *Pethach Eynayim*, loc. cit. Rashi and Rabbenu Chananel also count Solomon, but the Gra omits him, since he is not considered a prophet; *Moreh Nevukhim* 2:45. Moreover, there is a rule that no king was ever a prophet, see below, note 12. However, see *Sotah* 48b, Maharatz Chajas, *Niddah* 30a, *Yoma* 37a. Rashi alos includes Neriah and Machsiah, since they were fathers of prophets (see 6:85, below, notes 34,36), but *Seder Olam* omits them because they were not full prophets. Rabbenu Chananel likewise includes Bilshan, but the Gra omits him since he is identified as Mordecai; below note 37.
2. Exodus 6:24, 1 Chronicles 6:7, 6:22, 9:19. They were the authors of Psalms 42, 44-49, 84, 85, 87, 88. Although Korach died when he rebelled against Moses, his sons were spared; Numbers 26:11. They were prophets in Egypt (see Gra on *Seder Olam*) and in the desert; *Seder Olam* 20. Also see Sanhedrin 110a; *Midrash Tehillim* 1:6, 1:15, 45:2,4, 46:3. See below, 8:73. They are omitted from Rashi's list. See Maharatz Chajas, *Rosh HaShanah* 4a.
3. He was the author of the Book of Joshua. It was also he who received the Torah from Moses; *Avoth* 1:1; cf. Numbers 27:18,22, Deuteronomy 31:14. His ancestry is given in 1 Chronicles 7:20-27. According to Rashi it is: Joseph, Ephraim, Beriah, Rephach, Telach, Taachan, Laadan, Amihud, Elishama, Nun, Joshua. According to the Ralbag it is: Joseph, Ephraim, Rephach, Telach, Taachan, Laadan, Amihud, Elishama, Nun, Joshua. According to the Malbim, it is: Joseph, Ephraim, Shuthelach, Beriah, Taachan, Laadan, Amihud, Elishama, Nun, Joshua. Joshua reached the tenth level of prophecy, the highest next to that of Moses; *Moreh Nevukhim* 2:45.
4. Numbers 26:10, Judges 20:28. He was the grandson of Aaron. Also see *BaMidbar Rabbah* 16:1; *Tanchuma, Sh'lach* 1; *Yalkut Shimoni* 2:40; Rashi, Radak, on Judges 2:1, 6:8. Pinchas received the Torah tradition from Joshua; Introduction to *Yad*.

6. Elkanah ben Yerocham[5]

7. Nathan[6]

8. Gad[7]

9. Asaph ben Berachiah[8]

10. Heman ben Yoel[9]

11. Yeduthun[10]

12. Ethan ben Kishi[11]

There is, however, an opinion that Pinchas is identical with Elijah; below, note 20. According to this, we may substitute his father, Elazar; cf. *Pethach Eynayim; Turey Aven;* on *Megillah* 14a.

5. 1 Samuel 1:1; *Targum ad loc.; Sifri* on Deuteronomy 33:1; *Yalkut Shimoni* 2:91; Rashi, Radak, on 2 Samuel 2:27; Rashi, *Eruvin* 18b, s.v. *Elkana.* He was the husband of Hannah and the father of Samuel (17). He was a descendant of Korach's sons; *Megillah* 14a. His ancestory was: Levi, Kohath, Yitzhar, Korach, Elkana, Tzophai, Nachath, Eliav, Yerocham, Elkana; 1 Chronicles 6:12.

6. 2 Samuel 7:2. A contemporary of Saul and David, he was considered one of the early prophets; *Yerushalmi, Sotah* 9:13. He completed the book of Samuel; *Bava Bathra* 15a; and possibly other books; 1 Chronicles 29:29, 2 Chronicles 9:29; Ralbag, *Metzudoth ad loc.* Cf. 1 Chronicles 2:36, 11:38.

7. 1Samuel 22:5, 2 Samuel 24:11, 1 Chronicles 22:9. He was a contemporary of David, and one of the early prophets; *Yerushalmi, Sotah* 9:13. He also helped finish the Book of Samuel; *Bava Bathra* 15a; cf. 1 Chronicles 29:29. He was a student of Samuel; *Machzor Vitri.* He was killed by an angel; *Tanna DeBei Eliahu Rabbah* 8, from 1 Chronicles 21:16.

8. 1 Chronicles 6:24, 15:17. He was a singer and psalmist in the time of King David, as well as a prophet; 1 Chronicles 25:2; *Targum, Metzudoth ad loc; Tana DeBei Eliahu Rabbah* 30. He was the author of Psalms 50, 73-83. His ancestry is: Levi, Gershom, Yachath, Shimi, Zimah, Ethan, Adayah, Zerach, Ethni, Malkiah, Asayah, Michael, Shima, Berachiah, Asaf; 1 Chronicles 6:24. Cf. *VaYikra Rabbah* 16:1. He is omitted by Rashi, but included in *Seder Olam* and in *Halakhoth Gedoloth.*

9. He is called a prophet; 1 Chronicles 25:5. He was the author of Psalm 88 (but Rashi and Radak attributes this to Heman ben Zerach ben Judah; cf. 1 Chronicles 2:6; see below, note 11). He was a grandson of Samuel; Samuel, Yoel, Heman; 1 Chronicles 6:18; Rabbenu Gershom, *Bava Bathra* 15a; see above, note 5. Omitted by Rashi; see note 8.

10. He was a prophet and seer; 1 Chronicles 25:3, 2 Chronicles 35:15. He was the possible author of Psalms 39, 62, 71; see below, Chapter 8, note 69. Omitted by Rashi, see note 8.

11. Omitted by Rashi and Rabbenu Chananel, but added by Gra in *Seder Olam.* A contemporary of David; 1 Chronicles 15:17. His ancestory was: Levi, Merari, Mushi, Machli, Shemer, Bani,, Amtzi, Chilkiya, Amatziah. Chashaviah, Malukh, Avidi, Kishi, Ethan; 1 Chronicles 6:29-32. He may have been the author of Psalm 89. However, Rashi, Ibn Ezra, Radak, identify him as Ethan ben Zerach, a grandson of Judah; 1 Chronicles 2:6; cf. Targum *ad loc.* He was the brother of Heman ben

13. David[12]

14. Achiya the Shilonite[13]

15. Samuel[14]

16. Shemaiah[15]

17. Iddo[16]

18. Azariah ben Oded[17]

19. Chanani the Seer[18]

Zerach. According to the Targum, all five sons of Judah's son Zerach (Genesis 38:30) were prophets, and could be included in this list. Indeed, in *Seder Olam* 20, there is a mention of the sons of Zerach (זרח), but the Gra ammends this to read Korach (קרח). According to the Gra, only those after Moses are included. Zerach's sons are also omitted in all lists.

12. Cf. *Sotah* 48a; *Yoma* 53b; *Succah* 52a; *Yerushalmi, Sotah* 9:13. There is an opinion, however, that no one was ever both a prophet and king simultaneously; *Zohar* 2:154a. Cf. *Moreh Nevukhim* 2:45.

13. 1 Kings 11:29. He was alive during the time of the Exodus; *Bava Bathra* 121b; Introduction to *Yad*. He was also a Levite, *Bava Bathra loc. cit.*; Rashi *ad loc.* s.v. *Achiah*, identifies him with *Achiay* in 1 Chronicles 26:20. He also wrote a book; 2 Chronicles 9:29. Also see *Bereshith Rabbah* 35:2; Ibn Ezra on Genesis 46:23.

14. He was the author of the book that goes by his name, *Sh'muel* in Hebrew. See 1 Samuel 3:1, 3:20. He was the son of Elkana, above, note 5. He was also a student of Eli. See *Zohar* 2:154a.

15. 1 Kings 12:22; *Targum ad loc.*; 2 Chronicles 11:2, 12:7, 12:15. He lived in the time of Rechovoam; *Seder Olam*. He is identified with Shemayahu in 2 Chronicles 11:2; Rashi on 2 Chronicles 12:15. Together with Iddo (17), he wrote a book; 2 Chronicles 12:15. Omitted by Rashi.

16. He wrote a *midrash* about Aviya; 2 Chronicles 13:22; and the chronicle of Rechovoam together with Shemaiah (16); 2 Chronicles 12:15. Cf. 2 Chronicles 9:29; *Targum ad loc.* He was the anonymous prophet mentioned in 1 Kings 13:1; *Seder Olam* 20; *Sanhedrin* 89b, Rashi, *Sanhedrin* 104a, s.v. *U'Mashrey*; cf. *Zohar* 2:64a, *Teshuvoth Rashba* 11. According to one opinion, he was the grandfather of Zechariah; *Radak* on Zechariah 1:1. He was also the son of the Shunamite woman visited by Elisha; 2 Kings 4:8; *Yalkut Shimoni* (2:228); Radak; *ad loc.* from *Pirkey Rabbi Eliezer* 33. This Shunamite woman was also the sister of Avishag the Shunamite; 1 Kings 1:3. Hence, Iddo was Avishag's nephew. Moreover, the prophet Habakkuk (29) was also a son of the Shunamite woman; *Zohar* 1:7b. Hence, he was at least a half brother of Iddo; *Zera Berakh*, Part 1, *Kedoshim*. In *Pirkey Rabbi Eliezer* itself (75a), however, the reading is that the Shunamite woman was Iddo's *wife*. See *Radal ad loc.* 33:29.

17. 2 Chronicles 15:1; *Targum ad loc.* He was in the time of King Asa. He was the son of Oded (40); *Radak* on 2 Chronicles 15:8; cf. *Ralbag ibid.* See *Moreh Nevukhim* 2:45, Second Level.

18. 2 Chronicles 16:7. He was in the time of King Asa. Cf. 1 Chronicles 25:4, Nehemiah 1:2, 12:36. Omitted by Rashi, but added by *Asarah Maamaroth, Em Kol Chai* 2:1 (177a); *HaGra* on *Megillah* 14a.

20. Yehu ben Chanani[19]

21. Elijah[20]

22. Michaiah ben Yimla[21]

23. Obadiah[22]

24. Elisha[23]

25. Eliezer ben Dodavahu[24]

26. Jonah ben Amittai[25]

19. 1 Kings 16:1, 16:7, 16:12; 2 Chronicles 19:2, 20:34. He lived in the time of Kings Baasha, Elah, Asa, and Yehoshaphat. He was the son of Chanani the Seer (19); 2 Chronicles 19:2. He wrote a book that was apparently included in Kings; 2 Chronicles 20:34.
20. 1 Kings 17:1, Malachi 3:23, 2 Chronicles 21:12. Some authorities identify him with Pinchas (5); *Targum Yonathan* on Numbers 25:10; *Pirkey Rabbi Eliezer* 47; *Zohar* 3:214a, 3:215a; Rashi on Joshua 2:4; Rashi, *Bava Metzia* 114b, s.v. *Lav*; Maharatz Chajas, *Sotah* 13a. However, others state that Elijah is from the tribe of Gad; *Bereshith Rabbah* 99:11. Elijah came from Gilead (1 Kings 17:1), and Gilead is a city of Gad (Joshua 13:25); *Bereshith Rabbah* 71:9; *Midrash Tehillim* 90:3. Others state that Elijah was from the tribe of Benjamin; *Bereshith Rabbah* 71:9; *Tanna DeBei Eliahu Rabbah* 18 (86b), from 1 Chronicles 8:27; Mahari Kara on 1 Samuel 2:30. Also see *Tanna DeBei Eliahu Zuta* 15 (22a); Rashi, Ralbag, on 1 Kings 17:1.
21. 1 King 22:8, 22:13, 2 Chronicles 18:7. He lived in the time of Kings Ahab and Yehoshaphat, and a contemporary of Yehu ben Chanani (20). He was also the anonymous prophet who made the statements in 1 Kings 20:13, 20:22, 20:28, 20:35; *Seder Olam Rabbah* 21; *Sanhedrin* 89b. He was a student of Elijah; *Pirkey Rabenu HaKodesh* 3, in *Sefer HaLikutim* (Jerusalem, 1899).
22. The author of the book that goes by his name; see Radak on Obadiah 1:1. He was the overseer of King Ahab's house; 1 Kings 18:3; *Shemoth Rabbah* 31:4; *Sanhedrin* 39b. He was a contemporary (and student) of Elijah, and he hid the other prophets; 1 Kings 18:4. He was the husband of the woman for whom Elisha performed the miracle of the oil; 2 Kings 4:1; Targum, Rashi, Radak, *ad loc.*; *Zohar Chadash* 82b. He was an Edomite proselyte; above, 6:50.
23. Elisha ben Shaphat of the plain (avel) of Mecholah was anointed by Elijah at the same time as King Yehu; 1 King 19:16. He was a prophet for sixty years; *BaMidbar Rabbah* 14:18. *Cf.* 1 Chronicles 27:29; 1 Samuel 18:19, 2 Samuel 21:8.
24. 2 Chronicles 20:37. There is an indication that it was he who brought the "letter from Elijah;" 2 Chronicles 21:12; *Seder Olam* 20. This was seven years after Elijah's death; *Seder Olam* 17.
25. He was the author of the book that goes by his name; Radak, Ibn Ezra, Abarbanel, on Jonah 1:1. Also see 2 Kings 14:25; Radak *ad loc.* He lived in the time of King Yehu. He was the son of the widow in Tzarephath whom Elijah resurrected; 1 Kings 17:9-24; *Bereshith Rabbah* 98:11; *Pirkey Rabbi Eliezer* 33 (74b); Radal *ad loc.* 33:10; *Zohar* 2:197a; Abarbanel on Jonah 1:1. His mother was from the tribe of Asher, while his father was from Zebulun; he first received prophecy at the Sukkoth celebration; *Yerushalmi, Sukkah* 5:1 (22b). Jonah and Elisha were the prophets sent to King Yoash; 2 Chronicles 24:19; *Seder Olam* 20 in HaGra.

27. Zechariah ben Yehoyada[26]

28. Amotz[27]

29. Habakkuk[28]

30. Zephaniah ben Cushi[29]

31. Jeremiah[30]

26. Zechariah, son of Yehoyada the Cohen-priest; 2 Chronicles 24:20. His father, Yehoyada, was High Priest and leader of the Sanhedrin in the time of King Yoash; 2 Kings 11:4, Jeremiah 29:26. The wife of Yehoyada and mother of Zechariah was the daughter of King Yehoram and sister of his son, King Achazia; 2 Chronicles 22:11. Hence, Zechariah was a grand-uncle of King Yoash. After rendering his prophecy, he was stoned by the people at the instigation of the king; 2 Chronicles 24:21. His blood in the Temple was a constant blot on the record of the Israelites; *Gittin* 57b; Rashi *ad loc. s.v. Shel Zechariah* (top); *Koheleth Rabbah* 3:16, 10:4. His death was one reason that prophecy later ceased; *Midrash Tadshe* 20 (in *Otzer Midrashim*, p. 485), from Nehemiah 9:26. Regarding Yehoyada, cf. *Zevachim* 103a; *Seder Olam* 18. Zechariah is omitted by Rashi. Some say that he did not reach a level of true prophecy; *Moreh Nevukhim* 2:45, Second Level. He was head of the Sanhedrin in his time; Introduction to *Yad*.
27. The father of Isaiah (32); Isaiah 1:1; *Megillah* 15a. He was the anonymous prophet mentioned in 2 Chronicles 25:7, 25:15; *Radak ad loc.; Seder Olam* 21; Rashi *Megillah* 14a. He was the brother of King Amatzia, son of King Yoash; *Megillah* 10b; *Sotah* 10b. Therefore, his ancestry was: David, Solomon, Rechovoam, Aviyah, Asa, Yehoshaphat, Yoram, Achazia, Yoash, Amatzia and Amotz; 1 Chronicles 3:10-12. See *Pethach Eynayim, Megillah* 14a.
28. The author of the book that goes by his name. He was the son of the Shunamite woman who was resurrected by Elishah. He was also possibly the brother (or son) of the prophet Iddo (17); see above, note 16. Alternatively, he might have been a brother of the prophet Oded (40); see below, note 39. He was a contemporary of Joel and Nachum, in the time of Menasheh; *Seder Olam* 21; Rashi on Joel 1:1; Radak on Habakkuk 1:1. See Abarbanel *ibid.*
29. Author of the book that goes by his name, Tzephaniah ben Cushi ben Gedaliah ben Amariya ben Hezekiah in time of Yoshia; Zephaniah 1:1. He was a contemporary of Jeremiah; Jeremiah would preach in the streets, while he would preach in the synagogues; *Pesikta Rabathai* 27:2; Radak on Zephaniah 1:1. Some say that the Hezekiah who was his great-great-grandfather was King Hezekiah; Ibn Ezra on Zephaniah 1:1; cf. Abarbanel *ibid.* Acccording to this, his ancestry was: David, Solomon, Rechovoam, Aviya, Asa, Yehoshaphat, Yoram, Achaziah, Yoash, Amatzia, Azariah, Yotham, Achaz, Hezekiah, Amariya, Gedaliah, Cushi, Tzephaniah; *Cf.* 1 Chronicles 3:10 ff. Ibn Ezra writes that Amariah was the brother of Menasheh ben Hezekiah.
30. Author of the book that goes by his name. Jeremiah ben Chilkiah the cohen-priest in Anothoth in Benjamin. He was also the author of the Books of Kings and Lamentations; *Bava Bathra* 15a. Some say that he was the son of the Chilkiah who found the Torah; 2 Kings 22:4; Radak, Abarbanel on Jeremiah 1:1; cf. *Bereshith Rabbah* 64:5. According to this, his ancestry was: Aaron, Elazar, Pinchas, Avishua, Buki, Uzi, Zerachia, Meraioth, Azariah, Amariah, Achituv, Tzaduk, Shallum, Chilkiah, Jeremiah; 1 Chronicles 5:30-33, 37-39; Ezra 7:1. He was also a descendant of Joshua and Rachav; *Megillah* 14b (end).

32. Isaiah[31]

33. Ezekiel[32]

34. Daniel[33]

35. Barukh ben Neriah[34]

36. Uriah ben Shamaiah[35]

37. Seriah ben Neriah[36]

31. The author of the book that goes by his name. Also see 2 Kings 19:2, 20:1, 2 Chronicles 35:25. He was the son of Amotz, see above, note 27. He prophesied during the reign of four kings: Uzziah, Yotham, Achaz, Hezekiah; Isaiah 1:1. He was one of the four prophets in that time; *Pesachim* 87a. He was killed by Menasseh; *Yevamoth* 49b. He reached the seventh level of prophecy; *Moreh Nevukhim* 2:45. He was a student of Amos (42) and leader of the Sanhedrin in his time; Introduction to *Yad*.

32. Ezekiel ben Buzi, Ezekiel 1:3. He was the author of the book that goes by his name. He lived during the Babylonian exile. Some say that Buzi was Jeremiah, and hence Ezekiel was Jeremiah's son; Radak, Abarbanel, on Jeremiah 1:3, quoting *Targum Yerushalmi*. He was thus also a descendant of Joshua and Rachav; *Pesikta* 13 (115b); *Yalkut Shimoni* 1:771. Also see Job 32:3; *Zohar* 2:166a; *Midrash Sekhel Tov* on Genesis 22:21.

33. Daniel 1:6. He lived during the Babylonian Exile. Some say that he was a descendant of Hezekiah; Radak on 2 Kings 20:18; Rasag, Malbim, on Daniel 1:6; cf. *Megillah* 15a. Rashi, however, omits him, since there is a teaching that he was not a prophet; *Megillah* 3a. However, Rashi himself states that this merely means that he had no message for the general populace; Rashi, *Megillah* 3a, s.v. *Delhu*; cf. *Turey Aven ad loc.*; *Pethach Eynahim, Megillah* 14a. Also see *Sanhedrin* 94a; Maharsha *ad loc.*; *Moreh Nevukhim* 2:45, Second Level. Others write that he was not a prophet because his vision came through an angel; Ramban on Genesis 18:2; see above, Chapter 16, note 183; 180.

34. Barukh ben Neriah ben Machseya; Jeremiah 32:12. He was a descendant of Joshua and Rachav; *Megillah* 14b. Ezra the Scribe was his disciple; *Megillah* 16b. He was not a disciple of Jeremiah. He was possibly the brother of Seriah. who was also the son of Neriah ben Machseya; Jeremiah 51:59; see below, note 36. See *Megillah* 15a; Rashi *ad loc.* s.v. *BeShlemah*; Rabbi Yaakov Emden (Maharibatz) *ad loc.* See *Mekhilta* (2b) on Exodus 12:1; above 6:45; Targum on 2 Chronicles 35:25.

35. Uriah ben Shamaya of Kiryath HaYearim; Jeremiah 26:20. He was killed by Yehoiakim, Jeremiah 26:23. He lived in the time of Yoshia; *Halakhoth Gedoloth*. He was possibly the son of Shamaya (16).

36. Seriah ben Neriah ben Machsiah; Jeremiah 51:59. Both Rashi and *Halakhoth Gedoloth* have Seriah ben Machsiah, skipping a generation; also see Rashi, *Megillah* 15a, s.v. *BeShlema*. In *Megillah* 15a, however, the reading is Seriah ben Maasiah (מעשיה), which both the Gra and Rashash amend to read Machsiah (מחסיה). Rabenu Chananel, however, lists Azariah ben Machsiah, a name that is not found in scripture at all. However, Azariah and Seriah are identical, as we see by comparing Ezra 2:2 and Nehemiah 7:7; cf. *Megillah* 15b, Rashi *ad loc.* s.v. *Melkra*. Moreover, there is a reference to Seriah ben Maasiah ben Ananiah of Benjamin; Nehemiah 3:23. Hence, the reading in *Megillah* 15a, Seriah ben Maasiah, can be justified. Seriah, however, was a cohen-priest; *Megillah* 14b.

38. Mordecai[37]

39. Yachaziel ben Zechariah[38]

40. Oded[39]

41. Hosea ben Beeri[41]

42. Amos[41]

43. Micah the Morashtite[42]

44. Joel ben Pethuel[43]

45. Nahum[44]

37. Esther 2:5. Named alongside with Mordecai is Bilshan; Ezra 2:2, Nehemiah 7:7. According to most opinions, Bilshan is a surname of Mordecai, and not a separate individual; *Megillah* 15a; Ibn Ezra, Metzudoth, Malbim, on Ezra 2:2. Rabbenu Chananel, however, appears to list Bilshan separately. Some identify Mordecai with Malachi (48); *Megillah* 15a.
38. Yechaziel ben Zecharayahu ben Benaya ben Yeiyel ben Matanya HaLevi, of the sons of Asaf; 2 Chronicles 20:14. The Matanya mentioned as Yechaziel's great-great-grandfather may be Nethania son of Asaf; 1 Chronicles 25:2. Also see 2 Chronicles 29:13. He is omitted by Rabbenu Chananel. See *Moreh Nevukhim* 2:45, Second Level.
39. 2 Chronicles 28:9. Some say that he was the father of Azarlah ben Oded; Radak on 2 Chronicles 15:8; see above note 17. Some say that Oded (not Iddo) was the son of the Shunamite woman; Radal on *Pirkei Rabbi Eliezer* 33:29; see above, note 16. Omitted by Rabbenu Chananel. See *Asarah Maumaroth, Em Kol Chai* 2:1 (177a).
40. Hoseah ben Beeri, author of the book by that name. He lived in the time of King Uzziah, Yotham, Achaz, Hezekiah; Hosea 1:1. He was a disciple of Zechariah ben Yehoyada (27); Introduction to *Yad*. Beeri is identified with Beerah of Reuben in 1 Chronicles 5:6; *Bereishith Rabbah* 84:19; *Pesikta* 25 (149b). His ancestry was therefore: Reuben, ?, Yoel, Shemayah, Gog, Shimei, Michah, Reaiah, Baal, Beerah, Hoseah; 1 Chronicles 5:4-6.
41. Author of the book of that name. He was a disciple of Hosea; Introduction to *Yad*. Some say that he was of the tribe of Asher; *Yuchsin*; Abarbanel on Amos 1:1. He lived in the time of Uziah and Yeroam. He was very wealthy; *Nedarim* 38a. Cf. *Sukkah* 52a.
42. Author of the book by that name. He was of the tribe of Judah, and is mentioned in Jeremiah 26:18; Ibn Ezra, Radak, Abarbanel on Micah 1:1. He was the head of the Sanhedrin and a student of Isaiah; Introduction to *Yad*.
43. Author of the book by that name. Yoel ben Pethuel; Joel 1:1. He was in the time of Menasseh. Some authorities identify Pethuel with Samuel (15); *BaMidbar Rabbah* 10:5; Rashi on Joel 1:1; but see Ibn Ezra *ibid*. He was the head of the Sanhedrin and a student of Micah; Introduction to *Yad*.
44. Nachum of Alkosh, author of the book by that name; Nahum 1:1. He was in the time of Menassah. He was head of the Sanhedrin and a disciple of Joel; Introduction to *Yad*.

46. Haggai[45]

47. Zechariah[46]

48. Malachi[47]

45. Author of the book by that name. Prophesied in the second year of Darius; Haggai 1:1. Also see Ezra 5:1, 6:14; *Targum Sheni* on Esther 4:1.

46. Author of the book by that name. Zechariah ben Berakhiah ben Ido, who prophesied in the second year of Darius; Zechariah 1:1. Some say that he was the grandson of Iddo (17); Radak, Abarbanel on Zechariah 1:1. See *Megillah* 23a, from Nehemiah 8:4. Also see *Moreh Nevukhim* 2:45, Third Level.

47. Author of the book by that name. Some say that he was a separate individual; *Megillah* 15a. However, others identify him with Ezra; *Targum*, Radak, Ibn Ezra, on Malachi 1:1. This may be the accepted opinion; *Tosafoth, Yevamoth* 86b, s.v. *Mipney*; Maharatz Chajas *ad loc.* Others identify him with Mordecai; *Megillah* 15a.

SEVEN

THE TORAH

7:1   The Torah is the foundation of Judaism. Without it, Judaism cannot exist.

7:2   God revealed the Torah through Moses. It is thus written, "Moses commanded us the Torah, an inheritance to the congregation of Jacob" (Deuteronomy 33:4).[1]

7:3   It is a foundation of our faith to believe that Moses was the greatest of all prophets, both past and future. It is thus written, "There has not arisen a prophet in Israel like Moses, whom God knew face to face" (Deuteronomy 34:10).[2]

7:4   The revelation of Moses was unique. It differed from all other prophecy both quantitatively and qualitatively.[3] Moreover, Moses was the first prophet with a message for others.[4]

---

1. *Moreh Nevukhim* 2:39; *Ikkarim* 3:12; *Beth Elohim, Shaar HaYesodoth* 21. Cf. *Avoth* 1:1; *Asarah Maamaroth, Choker Din* 4:6 (118a).
2. Thirteen Principles of Faith 7. Moses was even greater in this respect than the Messiah; *Yad, Teshuvah* 9:2.
3. *Bereshith Rabbah* 76:1; *Zohar* 1:171a; *Yad, Yesodey HaTorah* 7:6; *Or HaShem* 2:4:3, 3:6:1; *Ikkarim* 3:17; *Or HaChaim* on Numbers 12:6; *Derekh HaShem* 3:5:1. See above, 6:76.
4. *Moreh Nevukhim* 1:42.

7:5   Moses was therefore born with the capacity for great spiritual accomplishment.⁵ Regarding his birth it is written, "[His mother] saw that he was good" (Exodus 2:2).⁶

7:6   Moses made use of his inherent spiritual gifts to negate himself completely before God. It is thus written, "The man Moses was very humble, more so than any man on the face of the earth" (Numbers 12:3).⁷

7:7   Since Moses' personality was completely nonexistent before God,⁸ his physical nature⁹ no longer acted as a barrier between him and God.¹⁰ Moses' revelation was therefore of a direct nature, as it is taught, "All prophets saw through a dull glass, but Moses saw through a clear brilliant glass."¹¹

7:8   Therefore, unlike other prophets, Moses received his revelation clearly, not masked by symbolism. God thus said, "I speak to [Moses] mouth to mouth, manifestly, and not in allegory" (Numbers 12:8).¹²

7:9   Unlike other prophets, Moses would receive his revelation while wide awake and in full command of his senses. God thus said, "When [I] God speak through one of you . . . I will speak with him in a dream. Not so My servant Moses . . ." (Numbers 12:6).¹³

---

5. *Zohar* 1:120b, 3:138b, 3:187b, 3:289b. Cf. *Likutey Amarim (Tanya), Sefer Shel Benonim* 14 (20a). From the time of his birth, the Divine Presence never left Moses; *Zohar* 2:12a, 2:21a.
6. *Sotah* 12a; *Shemoth Rabbah* 1:24; *Zohar* 2:12a, 2:19a, 2:54a.
7. Cf. *Ramban; Or HaChaim; ad loc.*
8. *Chulin* 89a, from Exodus 16:8; *Nefesh HaChaim* 3:13.
9. See above, 6:69.
10. *Shaarey Kedushah* 3:5; *Nefesh HaChaim* 3:13. Cf. *Tikuney Zohar* 26 (70b).
11. See Chapter 6, note 205. Also see *Avodath HaKodesh, Chelek Sithrey Torah* 22; *Shiur Komah* 14; *Bachya* on Exodus 3:5 (end). Cf. *Zohar* 3:155b; *Shaarey Orah* 3 (33a); *Bachya* on Numbers 12:6; *Ikkarim* 3:8.
12. Rambam on *Sanhedrin* 10:1, Thirteen Principles 7; *Yad, Yesodey HaTorah* 7:6; *Or HaShem* 3:6:2; *Shiur Komah* 16 (31a); *Derekh HaShem* 3:5:5. See above, 6:70.
13. *Ibid.; Zohar* 1:171a. Also see *Kedushath Levi, Lekh Lekha* on Genesis 15:1 (p. 19). See above, 6:39.

7:10   Unlike other prophets, Moses did not experience God's revelation as an overwhelming occurrence. It is thus written, "God spoke to Moses face to face, as a man speaks to his friend" (Exodus 33:11).[14]

7:11   Unlike other prophets, Moses was always in a potential state of prophecy.[15] He could therefore receive God's revelation at will.[16] It is thus written, "When Moses went into the Tent of Meeting (*Ohel Moed*, אֹהֶל מוֹעֵד), he heard the Voice speaking to him . . ." (Numbers 7:89).[17] When asked an opinion, Moses was able to answer, "Stand by, and let me hear what instructions God gives regarding you" (Numbers 8:9).[18] Moses was able to receive revelation from God at any time and in any place.[19]

7:12   Unlike other prophets, whose revelation was limited, Moses had access to all the gates of wisdom.[20] God had thus promised him, "I will make all My benefits pass before you" (Exodus 34:19).[21] God likewise said, "[Moses] is trusted in all My house" (Numbers 12:7).[22]

---

14. See note 12. See above, 6:71.

15. Cf. *Shabbath* 87a; *Pirkey Rabbi Eliezer* 46 (109b), from Deuteronomy 5:27.

16. See note 12. Cf. *Shemoth Rabbah* 2:12; Rashi on Deuteronomy 34:10. See above, 6:75.

17. *BaMidbar Rabbah* 14:34. There, however, it is only the opinion of Rabbi Shimon, and it is disputed. One reason for his entering the Tabernacle was to be in close proximity to the Ark; *Ikkarim* 3:11; *Avodath HaKodesh, Chelek Sithrey Torah* 24; Above, 6:42.

18. *Sifri*, Rashi, ad loc. Cf. Numbers 27:5.

19. *Nefesh HaChaim* 3:14; from *Shemoth Rabbah* 2:9; *BaMidbar Rabbah* 12:4.

20. That is, 49 gates; *Rosh HaShanah* 21b; *Nedarim* 35a; *Zohar* 1:260b (top), 2:115a 3:280a (end); *Tikuney Zohar* 7b, 22 (68a), 32 (76b, top); *Shiur Komah* 13:8; *Toledoth Yaakov Yosef, Devarim* (Koretz, 1780), p. 166c,d.

21. Ramban *ad loc.*; *Derekh HaShem* 3:5:6.

22. *Shiur Komah* 16; *Derekh HaShem* loc. cit. Cf. *Shaarey Kedushah* 3:6.

7:13   Moses was therefore the master of all the prophets.[23] All other prophecies are alluded to in the Torah.[24] God even revealed to Moses many future speculations and discussions surrounding the Torah.[25]

7:14   It is a foundation of our faith that the entire Torah, both written and oral, was revealed to Moses by God.[26]

7:15   Moses performed greater miracles than any other prophet.[27] Still, it is not because of miracles that we believe his revelation, but because God Himself bore witness that Moses was the bearer of His word. God thus told Moses, "I will come to you in a thick cloud, so that the people will hear when I speak with you, and they will believe in you forever" (Exodus 19:9). The authority of the Torah does not come from any miracle, but from God Himself.[28]

7:16   It is a foundation of our faith to believe in the eternal authority of the Torah.[29] It is thus written, "Things that are revealed belong to us and to our children forever" (Deuteronomy 29:38).[30]

---

23. *VaYikra Rabbah* 1:3; Rambam on *Sanhedrin* 10:1, Principle 7; *Shiur Komah* 16 (31c). Cf. *Ikkarim* 3:11; *Avodath HaKodesh, Chelek Sithrey Torah* 23 (132a). Also see Rashi, *Megillah* 15a, s.v. *BeShlema.*
24. *Taanith* 9a; *Shemoth Rabbah* 28:4, 42:7; *Tanchuma, Yithro* 11; *Zohar* 3:121a; *Tikuney Zohar Chadash* 105a. Cf. Maharatz Chajas, *Bava Kama* 93a.
25. *Megillah* 19b; *Berakhoth* 5a; *Yerushalmi, Peah* 2:4 (13a); *Shemoth Rabbah* 47:1, *VaYikra Rabbah* 22:1. Cf. *Megillath Esther* on *Sefer HaMitzvoth, Soresh* 1:16 (9a); *Tosefoth Yom Tov,* Introduction. Also see *Yerushalmi, Megillah* 4:1 (28a); *Yerushalmi, Chagigah* 1:8 (7b); *Likutey Amarim (Tanya), Kuntres Acharon* (159b).
26. Thirteen Principles of Faith 8. See below, 7:18 ff.
27. *Moreh Nevukhim* 2:35, from Deuteronomy 34:11; *Or HaShem* 3:6:2. It is for this reason that the Rambam, *Moreh Nevukhim loc. cit.* plays down the miracle of Joshua making the sun stand still. However, there is evidence that a similar miracle occurred for Moses; *Taanith* 20a; *Avodath Zarah* 25a.
28. Ibn Ezra, Ramban on Exodus 19:9; *Yad, Yesodey HaTorah* 8:1; *Kuzari* 1:87 (52a); *Chinukh,* Introduction; *Migdal Oz, Evven Bochen* 4:1,2. Cf. *Mekhilta* (62b), Rashi, on Exodus 19:4.
29. Thirteen Principles of Faith 9. See above, 5:20.
30. Cf. *Emunoth VeDeyoth* 3:9.

7:17 Just as God Himself does not change, so the Torah which is His eternal testimony to Israel, cannot be changed.[31] Moses thus said, "You shall not add to the word which I command you, nor shall you subtract from it; you must keep the commandments of *God your Lord*, which I command you" (Deuteronomy 4:2).[32] Therefore, no commandment of the Torah can ever be abrogated or changed.[33]

7:18 The Torah scrolls that we have today are exactly the same as the Torah given to Moses by God.[34]

7:19 The Torah consists of five books:[35]

Genesis	*Bereshith*	בְּרֵאשִׁית
Exodus	*Shemoth*	שְׁמוֹת
Leviticus	*VaYikra*	וַיִּקְרָא
Numbers	*BaMidbar*	בְּמִדְבָּר
Deuteronomy	*Devarim*	דְּבָרִים

7:20 It is a foundation of our faith that every word of the Torah was dictated to Moses by God.[36]

7:21 A person who denies the divine origin of even a single word or variant spelling[37] or reading[38] in the Torah is considered a nonbeliever[39] who has no portion in the World to Come.[40] Concerning such a person, it is written, "Because

---

31. *HaEmunah HaRamah* 5:2 (p. 75); *Ikkarim* 3:13,14. See above, 2:29.
32. Ramban *ad loc.* Also see Deuteronomy 13:1.
33. *Yad, Yesodey HaTorah* 9:1. Cf. *Tanna DeBei Eliahu Rabbah* 15 (74b), from Leviticus 16:34.
34. See below, 7:43.
35. For the reason for this number, see *Beth Elohim, Shaar HaYesodoth* 32 (95b). Cf. *Zohar* 3:228a; *Baal HaTurim* on Numbers 15:38.
36. Thirteen Principles of Faith 8.
37. *Sanhedrin* 99a; Rashi *ad loc.* s.v. *Dikduk Zeh*. Cf. *Nedarim* 37b. See below, 7:63.
38. Rabbenu Menoach (ben Yaakov) of Narbonne, *Sefer HaMenuchah*; quoted in *Kesef Mishneh* on *Yad, Tefillah* 12:6.
39. *Sanhedrin* 99a; *Yerushalmi, Sanhedrin* 10:1 (49b); *Yad, Teshuvah* 3:8.
40. *Sanhedrin* 10:1 (90a).

he has despised God's word . . . his soul shall be utterly cut off; his sin shall remain upon him" (Numbers 15:31).[41]

7:22   The entire Torah was therefore written by Moses as dictated by God. This included all the happenings recorded in it from the time of creation.[42]

7:23   Balaam was a prophet, and his prophecies are contained in the Torah. Nevertheless, they were written by Moses as dictated by God.[43]

7:24   Although the Book of Deuteronomy is written as the testimony of Moses, every word in it was written at the express commandment of God. God dictated the book as if Moses himself were addressing the people.[44]

7:25   There is a controversy regarding the last eight verses of Deuteronomy (34:5-12) which deal with Moses' death. Some authorities maintain that they were written by Moses

41. *Sanhedrin* 99a; *Yerushalmi, loc. cit.* Cf. *Shavuoth* 13a.
42. *Sefer Chasidim* 1016; Ramban, Introduction to Torah; *Torath HaShem Temimah* (in *Kithvey Ramban*), p. 145; Bachya on Deuteronomy 33:4; *Beth Elohim, Shaar HaYesodoth* 25 (72c). Also see Rashi, Ramban, on Genesis 1:1. Earlier stories might have been recorded in writing, but not in their final form; *Shemoth Rabbah* 5:18, 5:22; *Midrash Tehillim* 119:35; *Torah Sh'lemah, Seder Kethivath HaTorah* 5 (19:356).
43. *Bava Bathra* 14b; Rashi *ad loc.* s.v. *U'Pharshath Balaam; Yad Ramah,* Ritva, *ad loc.;* Tzioni, *Balak* (66b); *Sh'nei Luchoth HaB'rith, Torah SheBeKethav, Balak* (3:163a); *Torah Sh'lemah* 19:363. Similarly, all conversations recorded in the Torah were revealed to Moses in the precise language in which they should be written in the Torah. One must say that if a person's conversations were recorded in the Torah, then God directed precisely what he would say; cf. *Beth Elohim, Shaar HaYesodoth* 32 (94c).
44. Cf. Deuteronomy 1:3; *Megillah* 31b; Rashi, *Tosafoth, ad loc.* s.v. *Moshe;* Ran (on Rif 11a) *ad loc.* s.v. *Halalu;* Ramban on Leviticus 26:16, Deuteronomy 1:1, 5:12; Ibn Ezra on Exodus 20:1; *Chinukh,* Introduction to Deuteronomy (before Commandment 414); Abarbanel, Introduction to Deuteronomy; *Or HaChaim* on Deuteronomy 1:1, 5:19; Ralbag, *Kli Chemdah,* Mizrachi, *Toledoth Yitzchak, Ohel Yaakov,* on Deuteronomy 1:1; *Teshuvoth Rabbi Eliezer ben Nathan* (HaRaavan) 34 (in *Evven HaEzer,* Prague, 1610); *Teshuvoth Rashbash* 21; *Teshuvoth Radbaz* 6:2143; *Teshuvoth Maharsham* 3:290; *Midbar Kedamoth, Tav* 19; Rabbi Yaakov Emden (Maharibatz) on Sanhedrin 99a; *Mishnah Berurah* 428:18; *Torah Sh'lemah* 19:333ff. God spoke from Moses' throat; *Zohar* 3:232a; *Nefesh HaChaim* 3:14. Also see *Zohar* 3:7a, 3:261a, 3:265a (end); *Shaarey Zohar* on Shabbath 87a.

himself at God's dictation.[45] Others maintain that these verses were written by Joshua.[46]

7:26   Just before the revelation at Sinai[47] Moses wrote everything that had transpired up until that point. It is thus written, "Moses wrote all of God's words" (Exodus 24:4).[48] Before completing the covenant,[49] he read this part of the Torah. It is written, "[Moses] took the Book of the covenant, and read it so that the people would hear. They said, 'All that God has spoken, we will do and we will listen' " (Exodus 24:7).[50]

7:27   After this, God would call Moses to the Tent of Meeting (*Ohel Moed,* אֹהֶל מוֹעֵד) to dictate the Torah to him. God would call Moses, and Moses would acknowledge that he was ready.[51]

45. Rabbi Shimon, *Bava Bathra* 15a; *Menachoth* 30a. Cf. Ran, *Megillah* (Rif 12a), s.v. *Hakafoth;* *Hagahoth Maimonioth Tefillah* 13:6 #4; *Mishnah Berurah* 428:21.
    Some write that Moses wrote these verses while weeping, while others maintain that he wrote them with tears rather than ink; Ritva (in *Eyn Yaakov* 25); Maharsha, *ad loc.* s.v. *Amar Lo;* Mizrachi, *Gur Aryeh, Toledoth Yitzchak,* on Deuteronomy 34:5. Some interpret the word dema (דְּמַע) here to mean that Moses wrote these verses with different letter combinations; Rabbi Eliahu, the Vilna Gaon, *Kol Eliahu, VeZoth HaBerakhah* 133; Rabbi Gerson Pieston, *Avodath HaGershoni* (Vilna, 1885) on Deuteronomy 34:5; Rabbi Avraham (ben Yisrael) of Zitomer, *Geulath Yisrael* (Ostrog, 1821), *Pithgamin Kadishin; Sefer Baal Shem Tov, VeZoth HaBerakhah* 4. Cf. *Beth Elohim, Shaar HaYesodoth, Asarah Maamaroth, Choker Din* 13 (52b); above, Chapter 3, note 10. See *Chidushey HaGriz* 3:234.
46. *Bava Bathra* 14b; Rabbi Yehudah or Rabbi Nechemiah, *Bava Bathra* 15a. Also see *Makkoth* 11a; Rashi, Abarbanel, on Deuteronomy 34:5, Joshua 24:26.
47. Rashi on Exodus 24:1. The Ramban, ibid., however, disputes this and maintains that this occurred after the giving of the Ten Commandments.
48. Rashi *ad loc.; Beth Elohim, Shaar HaYesodoth* 25 (72c). Cf. Ramban, Introduction to Torah.
49. See above, 5:14.
50. Above 4:44, 5:14. Also see Rashi *ad loc.;* Ramban on Deuteronomy 31:2,4; *Torah Shlemah* 19:331. There is actually a controversy whether Moses read the Torah, or only certain commandments; *Mekhilta* (63b) on Exodus 19:10; *Yalkut Shimoni* 1:279.
51. *Sifra* (3c), Rashi, Ramban, on Leviticus 1:1; *BaMidbar Rabbah* 14:35; *Thirty Two Middoth of Rabbi Eliezer ben Rabbi Yosi* 8. Cf. *Yoma* 4b.

7:28   God would dictate each passage of the Torah to Moses, and Moses would repeat it aloud.[52] He would then write it down.[53]

7:29   God would dictate a paragraph to Moses, and then give him a break in order to consider it.[54] These breaks are preserved in the Torah in the form of spacings, dividing the text into paragraphs (*parshioth*, פָּרְשִׁיוֹת).[55]

7:30   Moses would transcribe each of these portions as a small scroll. Shortly before his death, he combined all these portions to form the Torah that we have today.[56] According to another opinion, however, with the exception of certain portions that were needed earlier,[57] the entire Torah was preserved orally until just before Moses' death when he wrote it all down at once.[58]

7:31   Since parts of the Torah were not assembled until many years after they were given, they are not always in chrono-

52. *Tosafoth, Menachoth* 30a, s.v. *U'Moshe; Ran, Megillah* (Rif 12a), s.v. *Hakafoth.*
53. *Bava Bathra* 15a; *Menachoth* 30a; *Toledoth Yitzchak,* Abarbanel, on Deuteronomy 34:5.
54. *Sifra* on Leviticus 1:1 (3c), 1:10 (7c); Rashi on Leviticus 1:1.
55. There are two types of paragraph breaks, the "open" one (*pethuchah,* פְּתוּחָה), and the "closed" one (*sethumah,* סְתוּמָה); *Shabbath* 103b; *Sofrim* 1:14; *Yad, Sefer Torah* 7:11, 8:1-4; *Yoreh Deah* 275. These were the places where Moses interrupted; *Berakhoth* 12b. See below, note 146.
56. Rabbi Yochanan, *Gittin* 60a. *Beth Elohim, Shaar HaYesodoth* 25 (73c,d). Some say that this is the accepted opinion; Rosh, *Gittin* 5:20, quoting Rif. Bachya on Genesis 24:22 derives this from Deuteronomy 28:69.
57. *Gittin* 60a,b; Rashi *ad loc.* s.v. *Ei Nami.* Among these are the portions dictated when the Tabernacle was erected: Leviticus 10:8-11, 16, 21:1-24, Numbers 5:1-4, 8:1-4, 8:5-26, 9:9-14, 19. There was no obligation to keep any commandment until it was written down; *Beth Elohim, Shaar HaYesodoth* 25 (72c,d).
58. Rabbi Shimon ben Lakish, *Gittin* 60a, according to Rashi *ad loc.* s.v. *Chathumah.* Also see Rashba *ibid.; Iyun Yaakov* (on *Eyn Yaakov*), *Eruvin* 21b. However, *Tosafoth, Gittin* 60a, s.v. *Torah,* questions this on the basis of Rashi on Exodus 24:4,7 (see above 7:24), and writes that the Torah was originally transcribed in its final order. The only portions not included were those which were not given in their proper place; these were preserved orally and then inserted in their place. However, there is actually a controversy as to whether or not Moses originally wrote any part of the Torah, see note 50. This may be related to the controversy here. Also see Ibn Ezra, Ramban, Abarbanel, on Leviticus 25:1; Maharatz Chajas, *Yoma* 75a; *Teshuvoth Radbaz* 5:2143; *Torah Sh'lemah* 19:345.

logical order.[59] However, wherever chronological order is
ignored, there is something to be learned from the ordering
in the Torah.[60] According to some authorities, laws can even
be derived from the ordering of the paragraphs in the
Torah.[61] With regard to the book of Deuteronomy, which
was written all at once, this is a unanimous opinion.[62]

7:32   The entire Torah was given to Moses during two
intervals. The first part was given during the year after the
Exodus.[63] The rest was given shortly before Israel crossed
the Jordan at the end of the forty years in the desert.[64]
Between these two periods, there was a hiatus of 38 years,
during which no portion of the Torah was given.[65]

59. *Pesachim* 6b; *Yerushalmi, Shekalim* 6:1; *Yerushalmi, Sotah* 5:3 (end); *Mekhilta* (40b), *Ramban,* on Exodus 15:9; *Koheleth Rabbah* 1:31; *Yalkut Shimoni* 1:249, 2:264; *Rashi* on Genesis 6:3, 18:3, Exodus 4:20; *Ibn Ezra, Ramban* on Numbers 16:1; *Zohar* 3:148a; *Tikuney Zohar* 16a (top); *Pachad Yitzchak,* s.v. *Ain* (1:60a); *Torah Sh'lemah* 19:351.
60. *Bachya,* Introduction (p. 10); *Sh'nei Luchoth HaB'rith, Torah SheB'al Peh, Alef* (3:228b). See *Midrash Tehillim* 3:2; *Yalkut Shimoni* 2:624; *Shevil Emunah* (on *Emunoth VeDeyoth*) Introduction 6:17.
61. *Berakhoth* 10a; *Pesachim* 22a; *Yevamoth* 4a.
62. *Berakhoth* 21b; *Yevamoth* 4a; *Maharatz Chajas ad. loc.; Torah Sh'lemah* 19:339.
63. Until after the sending of the spies; Numbers 13, 14. Cf. Leviticus 27:34. The only event mentioned after the spies is the rebellion of Korach; Numbers 16. This, according to some, occurred before the spies; *Ibn Ezra* on Numbers 16:1. Others, however, maintain that it occurred immediately afterward; *Ibn Ezra, ibid.* Cf. *Rashbam, Bava Bathra* 12b, s.v. *Lo; Rashi, Taanith* 30b. s.v. *Lo.*
64. Cf. Numbers 35:1, 36:13. The first revelation came to Moses after the death of Miriam; cf. *Ibn Ezra* on Numbers 20:1, 6. This was after all the generation of the Exodus had died; *Rashi* on Numbers 20:1; see note 65. Perhaps Miriam's death was the atonement that restored prophecy to Moses; cf. *Moed Katan* 28a.
    The times that the Torah was given are then: Genesis and Exodus, between the revelation at Sinai (6 Sivan, 2448) and the time the Tabernacle was completed (1 Nissan, 2449). The 8 portions mentioned above in note 57 were given on 1 Nissan, 2449. The book of Leviticus was given during the rest of Nissan, 2449. The first part of Numbers, until 18 was given before 8 Av, 2449 (Numbers 19 was one of the eight portions given on 1 Nissan, 2449, above, note 57). The rest of Numbers was given between 15 Av, 2487 and 1 Teveth, 2488. (Cf. *Ramban* on Numbers 28:2). Deuteronomy was given between 1 Teveth 2488 and 7 Adar 2488 (when Moses died). *Beth Elohim, Shaar HaYesodoth* 32.
65. *Taanith* 30b; *Bava Bathra* 121a (end); *Tosufoth ad loc.* s.v. *Yom; Mekhilta* on Exodus 12:1 (2a); *Sifra* on Leviticus 1:1 (4b); *Yerushalmi Taanith* 3:4 (15a); *Shir HaShirim Rabbah* 2:27; *Yalkut Shimoni* 1:809; *Rashi* on Deuteronomy 2:16; *Teshuvoth Radbaz* 6:2143.

7:33   God always dictated the Torah, as well as other books of the Bible, in the language used by the people at the time.[66]

7:34   Before his death, Moses wrote thirteen Torah scrolls. Twelve of these were given to the twelve tribes. The thirteenth was placed in the Ark of the Covenant.[67] This was eventually deposited in the Holy of Holies in the Temple.[68]

7:35   This last Torah was the standard by which all other scrolls were judged. It was occasionally removed from the Ark for this purpose.[69]

7:36   There were times that this Torah was almost lost. A number of Israelite kings had attempted to uproot or change the teachings of the Torah. Thus, during the reign of Achaz (3183-3199; 578-562 b.c.e.) many Torah scrolls were destroyed.[70] Because of this, the cohen-priests hid the Torah written by Moses in order to safeguard it.[71]

7:37   Later during the reign of Manasseh (3228-3283; 533-478 b.c.e.), efforts to destroy the Torah were so successful that

66. See above, 6:82; below, note 186. For discussion of the language in general, see *Beth Elohim, Shaar HaYesodoth* 32. Since language depends on environment, one would expect that a radical change occurred in the language of the Israelites during their forty years in the desert, when their environment changed from that of abject slavery in Egypt, to nationhood in a hostile wilderness, constantly witnessing God's miracles. It is therefore not surprising if different linguistic styles are found in the Torah.

67. *Devarim Rabbah* 9:4; *Midrash Tehillim* 90:3; *Pesikta* 31 (197a); *Yalkut Shimoni* 1:550; *Tosafoth, Menachoth* 30a, s.v. *MiKan*; Rambam Introduction to Mishneh; Introduction to *Yad*; Ramban on Deuteronomy 31:24; Mordecai, *Pesachim*, Chapter 10; Rosh, *Pesachim* 10:13; *Or Zerua* 2:89 (24b); *Beth Chadash, Orach Chaim* 292.

68. *Bava Bathra* 14a. There are, however, some authorities who dispute this opinion, maintaining that the Torah was placed in a second ark, which was kept just outside the Holy of Holies; *Yerushalmi, Shekalim* 6:1 (24b); *Yerushalmi, Sotah* 8:3 (35a); *Yalkut Shimoni* 2:101. Also see, Rashi, Ibn Ezra on Exodus 25:16; Ramban on Deuteronomy 10:5; Rashi, Sforno on Deuteronomy 31:26; Radak on 1 Samuel 4:4, 1 Kings 8:9; Ralbag on 1 Kings 8:9; *Kuzari* 2:28 (48a). See below, notes 93, 136.

69. *Tosafoth, Bava Bathra* 14a, s.v. *SheLo*; Rabbi Yosef Rosen of Rogetchov, *Tzafanath Paaneach* on Deuteronomy 17:18, 31:9.

70. *Yerushalmi, Sanhedrin* 10:2; *Esther Rabbah* 0:11; *Ruth Rabbah* 0:7; Rashi on 2 Kings 22:8.

71. Abarbanel, *Metzudoth David*, on 2 Kings 22:8.

the existence of the Torah written by Moses had to be concealed from all but a dedicated few.[72] It was only later, during the reign of Yoshia (in 3303; 458 b.c.e.) that this Torah was found hidden in the Temple. It is thus written, "Chilkiah the cohen-priest found the book of God's Torah, [written] in Moses' hand" (2 Chronicles 34:14).[73] King Yoshia used this as an occasion to rededicate the people to the observance of the Torah.[74]

7:38   When Jerusalem was in danger of invasion, King Yoshia hid the Ark containing the original Torah and the Tablets of the Ten Commandments.[75] It was concealed in a catacomb that had been prepared by King Solomon when he had first built the Temple.[76] It is still there today.[77]

7:39   During the Babylonian exile (3338-3408; 423-353 b.c.e.), there was a decline in knowledge of the Torah. Intermarriage made headway,[78] and many people forgot the Torah and its commandments.[79] When Ezra and Nehemiah returned to the Holy Land, they restored the Torah to its original place.[80] Ezra also wrote a letter perfect Torah scroll to be used as a standard.[81]

72. Radak on 2 Kings 22:8. Cf. *Sanhedrin* 63b 103b. Manasseh had also killed Isaiah; *Yevamoth* 49b.
73. Cf. 2 Kings 22:8; Malbim *ad loc.* Also see *Ikkarim* 3:22.
74. 2 Kings 23:3, 2 Chronicles 34:31.
75. *Yoma* 52b; *Horioth* 12a; *Kerithoth* 5b; *Tosefta, Yoma* 2:13; *Tosefta, Sotah* 13:2; *Yerushalmi, Shekalim* 6:1; *Seder Olam Rabbah* 24; *Yalkut Shimoni* 2:247; *Yad, Beth HaBechirah* 4:1; *Kuzari* 3:39 (48b). However, there is also an opinion that the Ark was carried off to Babylonia; *Yoma* 53b.
76. *Yad, loc cit.*; Radak, Ralbag, on 2 Chronicles 35:3. The Ralbag writes that there is allusion to this chamber in the Book of Kings.
77. *Shekalim* 6:2. There is a question as to whether it was hidden under the Holy of Holies, or under the Chamber of the Woodshed; *Yoma* 54a.
78. Cf. Ezra 9, 10.
79. Cf. Nehemiah 8:14; *Kuzari* 3:63 (67a); *Ikkarim* 3:22; *Chudushey HaRan, Sanhedrin* 21b.
80. Nehemiah 8:1, 9:14, 10:30. Cf. *Sukkah* 20a.
81. See below, note 100. It is taught that Ezra deserved to be the one to give the Torah. *Sanhedrin* 21b. Ezra was therefore the scribe *par excellence*; cf. Ezra 7:11, 7:12, 7:21, Nehemiah 8:4, 8:5, 8:9, 8:13, 12:26, 12:36; see below, note 107. Also see note 139.

7:40   It is a positive commandment for every Jew to write a
Torah or have one written for him. It is thus written, "Now
write this song for yourselves" (Deuteronomy 31:9).[82] Since
it is forbidden to write portions of the Torah separately,[83] this commandment is an injunction to write the
entire Torah.[84]

7:41   In order to fulfill this commandment, one must write a
letter perfect Torah. If the Torah contains the slightest error,
even in a variant spelling,[85] it is not valid for the fulfillment
of this commandment,[86] although in some cases it may still
be publicly read in the synagogue.[87] Therefore, the most
scrupulous care was taken to copy the Torah, letter for
letter.[88]

7:42   Moreover, every Israelite king was also commanded to
write a second Torah, which was always to accompany
him.[89] It is thus written, "When [the king] sits on the throne

82. *Sanhedrin* 21b; *Yad, Sefer Torah* 7:1; *Sefer HaMitzvoth*, Positive Commandment
18; *Sefer Mitzvoth Gadol*, Positive Commandment 24; *Chinukh* 613; *Yoreh Deah*
270:1; *Chayay Adam* 31:49; *Kitzur Shulchan Arukh* 28:1.
83. *Yoma* 37b; *Gittin* 60a; *Yoreh Deah* 283:2. However, see *Yad, Sefer Torah* 7:14;
Teshuvoth Shaagath Aryeh 49; Maharatz Chajas, *Nedarim* 38b; *Teshuvoth
Chatham Sofer, Yoreh Deah* 254.
84. *Yad, Sefer Torah* 7:1.
85. Some say that this applies to every variant spelling; *Teshuvoth Shaggath Aryeh* 36;
quoted in *Pith'chey Teshuvah, Yoreh Deah* 270:10. Others, however, maintain that
it only applies to variant spellings that contain a lesson; *Minchath Chinukh* 613.
Also see *Teshuvoth Chatham Sofer, Yoreh Deah* 254; Rabbi Menachem Epstein,
Shaarey Torah (Vilna, 1910) on *Sanhedrin* 21b.
86. *Yad, Sefer Torah* 7:11, from *Menachoth* 30a; cf. *Tosafoth Menachoth* 30a, s.v.
Avel, 32b., s.v. *Kathva*; Ran, *Megillah* (Rif 5b), s.v. *VeKathav*. The same law also
applies to Tefillin and Mezuzoth; *Yad, Tefillin* 1:2; *Orach Chaim* 32:20; Rosh,
Hilchoth Tefillin, quoting *Shimusha Rabbah* (123b).
87. Ran, *Megillah* (Rif 5b), s.v. *VeKathav*; HaGra, *Orach Chaim* 142:1, 143:4. Cf.
Maharal, *Tifereth Yisrael* 67.
88. *Eruvim* 12b.
89. In *Sanhedrin* 21b, the text states that it was worn as an amulet. However,
Maharshal *ad loc.* omits this reading and it also omitted in *Yad*, quoted in note 90.
Cf. *Chidushey HaRan*, Rashash, *Sanhedrin* 21b; *Margolioth HaYam ibid.*; *Kessef
Mishneh, Sefer Torah* 7:2; *Lechem Mishneh, Melakhim* 3:1. Some authorities
question how a Torah scroll could be made small enough to be worn as an amulet,
but I personally have seen a perfectly written Torah scroll only two inches high.

of his kingdom, he shall write a copy of this Torah . . . It shall be with him, and he shall read from it, all the days of his life" (Deuteronomy 17:18,19).[90]

7:43 During the time of the first Temple, it was the practice[91] of the Sanhedrin[92] to correct the king's Torah from the Torah written by Moses[93] which was kept in the Temple.[94] After the death of the king, these highly accurate Torah scrolls were kept by the Sanhedrin.[95]

7:44 A Torah was likewise kept in the Second Temple[96] which was read at the great assembly on Yom Kippur[97] and at the Public Reading every seven years.[98] This Torah was also used as a standard to correct all other Torah scrolls.[99] Some say that this was the Torah written by Ezra.[100]

7:45 Throughout all generations, great care was taken to preserve the Torah exactly as it was given by Moses. The scribe is thus given the advice, "Be careful with your task,

90. *Sanhedrin* 2:4 (21b); *Yad, Sefer Torah* 7:2, *Melakhim* 3:1; *Sefer HaMitzvoth,* Positive Commandment 17; *Sefer Mitzvoth Gadol,* Positive Commandment 25; *Chinukh* 503.
91. This was not actually required by law; *Sheyarey Karban* on *Yerushalmi, Sanhedrin* 2:6 (13a).
92. *Yerushalmi, Sanhedrin* 2:6 (13a); *Tosefta, Sanhedrin* 4:4; *Yad, Melakhim* 3:1.
93. Rashi, *Bava Bathra* 14b, s.v. *Sefer.* Rashi also writes there that this Torah was publicly read. See above, 7:34. Also see next note.
94. *Yerushalmi, Sanhedrin* 2:6 (13a); *Yad, Melakhim* 3:1. Some say that the Torah scroll that was in the Holy of Holies was not used after the Temple was built; Rabbi Yosef Rosen, *Tzafanath Paaneach* on Deuteronomy 17:18. However, there were also other Torah scrolls written by Moses; above, 7:32. Also see note 68. According to *Tzafanath Paaneach,* after the Temple was built, the king's scrolls were copied from those written by previous kings, which were kept by the Sanhedrin in the *Lish'cath HaGazith.*
95. *Tosefta, Sanhedrin* 4:4; *Tzafanath Paaneach* on Deuteronomy 17:18, 31:9.
96. *Moed Katan* 3:4 (18b); *Kelim* 15:6, Rambam, Rash, *ad loc.; Yad, Yom Tov* 7:13.
97. Bertenoro, *ibid.* Cf. *Yoma* 7:1 (68b); *Sota* 7:7 (40b); *Yad, Avodath Yom HaKippurim* 3:8 ff.
98. Rashi, *Bava Bathra* 14b. s.v. *Sefer.* Cf. Deuteronomy 31:10-13; *Sotah* 7:8; *Yad, Chagigah* 3:1. This reading took place on the first day of Sukkoth, in the last year of the *Shemitah* cycle.
99. Rashi, *Moed Katan* 18b. s.v. *Afilu.*
100. *Ibid.;* Rash, *Kelim* 15:6. See *Torah Shlemah,* Exodus 24:29; *Dikdukey Sofrim, Moed Katan* 18b.

for it is sacred work; if you add or subtract a single letter, you will destroy everything."[101]

7:46   Since every Torah must be letter perfect, it must be carefully copied from another scroll. It is forbidden to write a single letter without copying it from another Torah.[102]

7:47   Moreover, the scribe must repeat every word out loud before writing it down, so as to insure accuracy in copying.[103] This was the custom among the prophets, as we find, "He pronounced all these words for me with his mouth, and I wrote them with ink in the book" (Jeremiah 36:18).[104]

7:48   If a Torah or other sacred writings are incorrectly written, it is forbidden to keep them for more than thirty days, lest they be used or copied. After this period, they must be either corrected or hidden. It is thus written, "Do not let wrong remain in your tents" (Job 11:14).[105]

7:49   Originally,[106] the Torah and other scripture were so carefully preserved that every letter, word, and sentence was counted.[107] Traditions still exist based on this knowledge.[108]

101. *Eruvin* 12b; *Sotah* 20a.
102. *Megillah* 18b; *Menachoth* 32b; *Yerushalmi, Megillah* 4:1 (28b); *Yad, Tefillin* 1:12; *Yoreh Deah* 274:2. Cf. *Orach Chaim* 691:2 in *Hagah*; *HaGra ad loc.*
103. *Tosafoth, Menachoth* 30a, s.v. *U'Moshe*; *Mordecai, Halakhoth Ketanoth* 957; *Sefer Chasidim* 284; *Yoreh Deah* 274:2. Cf. *Orach Chaim* 691:2 in *Hagah*; *HaGra ad loc.*; *Magen Avraham* 32:42, 691:4; *Mishnah Berurah* 32:136. See above, note 52.
104. *Menachoth* 30a.
105. *Kethuboth* 19b; *Rashi ad loc.* s.v. *Sefer*; *Yad, Sefer Torah* 7:12, *Hagahoth Maimonioth ad loc.*; *Yoreh Deah* 279:1.
106. *Rashi, Kiddushin* 39a, s.v. *Nikrau*, states the scribes referred to here are those mentioned in 1 Chronicles 2:55. Other sources, however, state that they existed well into the Tamudic times; *Teshuvoth Shaagath Aryeh* 36.
107. *Kiddushin* 30a; *Rashi, Shabbath* 49b, s.v. *Lo; Kuzari* 3:31 (36b); *Ikkarim* 3:22; Maharal, *Tifereth Yisrael* 67.
108. There is thus a tradition that the Vav (ו) of the word gachon (גחון) in Leviticus 11:42 is the middle letter of the Torah. *Kiddushin* 30a; *Sofrim* 9:2. The middle word of the Torah is *derash derash* (דרש דרש) in Leviticus 10:6. The middle sentence of the Torah is Leviticus 13:33. *Kiddushin ibid.* Other sources, however, state that

7:50   However, after the Babylonian exile, it became impossible to find precise Torah scrolls, and several questions arose regarding the exact reading of the Torah and other scripture. Therefore, when the Great Assembly fixed the Bible canon under the leadership of Ezra,[109] they also restored the exact readings of the scriptures.[110]

Leviticus 8:15 is the middle sentence; *Sofrim* 9:3; *Kisey Rachamim; Nachalath Yaakov;* ad loc. See below, note 145.

The precise number of letters in our present Torah scrolls is 304,805; see Rabbi Reuven Margolies, *HaMikra VeHamesorah* 12 (Jerusalem, 1964), p. 41; Note in Rabbi Manashe ben Yisrael, the *Conciliator* (Hermon: New York, 1972), Part 1, p. 250 (where the number of each letter is also given). The number of letters in the Torah, however, is not given in the original source; *Othioth Rasag,* quoted there; see Rabbi Eliahu Bekhor, *Mesoreth HaMesoreth* (Venice 1538); Rabbi Yosef Shlomo Rofeh of Candia, *Nov'loth Chakhmah* (Basil, 1631); *Teshuvoth HaGaonim* (Prague, 1590), end; *Othioth DeRav Saadia* (Dyherenfurth, 1821); Rabbi Asher Anshel Worms, *Seyag LaTorah* (Frankfort am Main, (1726), p. 12b; Rabbi Yosef Furst, *Otzar Lashon HaKodesh (Concordantiae)* (Leipzig, 1840), p. 1379f; *Otzar Yisrael,* s.v. *Othioth* 1:221.

Regarding this number, also see Rabbi Menachem Azariah of Fano, *Maamar HaNefesh* 3:5; *Teshuvoth Chavath Yair* 235; Rabbi Avraham Azzulai, *Chesed LeAvraham* 2:11; Rabbi Tzvi Hirsh Horowitz, *Ispaleria HaMeira* on *Zohar, Shemini* (Furth 1771), p. 69b.

There are, however, other traditions. Some say that the number of letters in the Torah is 400,945; Rabbi Aaron (ben Moshe) ben Asher, *Dikdukey HaTaamim* (Leipzig, 1878), p. 55; Rabbi Avraham (ben Yaakov) Bick; *Ohel Moed, Ohel David* (Munkatch, 1898), p. 22a; *Otzar HaGaonim* on *Kiddushin* 30a. Other traditions state that there are 310,674 letters in the Torah; *Midrash Talpioth,* s.v. *Othioth* (Lublin, 1923), p. 29b.

There is, however, a tradition that there are 600,000 letters in the Torah, paralleling the number of Israelites who left Egypt (Exodus 12:37); *Zohar Chadash* 74d; *Megalleh Amukoth* 186. For attempts to reconcile this with the known number, see *Mishnath Chakhamim, Hilkhoth Stam* (Zitomir, 1868); Chida, *Midbar Kedamoth,* Yod 6; Rabbi Shneur Zalman of Liadi, *Likutey Torah, BeHar* (43d); *Peney Yehoshua* on *Kiddushin* 30a; Rabbi Alexander Sender Margolius of Sananov, *Torath HaRaam* (Rabbi Eliahu Mizrach) 20 (Lvov, 1897); Rabbi Shlomo Algazi, *Shema Shlomo,* Introduction (Amsterdam, 1710); Rabbi Avraham (ben Tzvi) Jaffe, *Mishnath Avraham,* Introduction (Zitomir, 1868); Rabbi Yehuda ben Avraham) Koryat, *Meor VeShemesh* (Livorno, 1819), p. 13b (end); *Atereth Rosh* (in Vilna *Eyn Yaakov), Kiddushin* 30a; *Chatham Sofer,* end of *Chidushim* on *Chulin* (Munkatch, 1899), p. 72b; Rabbi Pesach Finfer, *Mesorath HaTorah VeHaNevi'im* (Vilna, 1906); *HaMikra VeHaMesorah* 12.

There is also a question regarding the Vav of *Gachon* (see above), since its number in the Torah is 157,236, while the middle of the Torah is 152,403. For discussion, see *Mishnath Avraham, Sefer Torah;* Rabbi Eliahu Posek, *Piskey Eliahu* 3:1 (Saeni, 1926); Rabbi Yaakov Shor, *Mishnath Rabbi Yaakov* 4:3 (Pieterkov 1930); *HaMikra VeHaMesorah* 12 (p. 44).

109. See below, 8:61.
110. See above, notes 81, 100.

7:51   There were, however, a number of places where the precise reading could not be determined.[111] In such cases, the words or letters in question were stigmatized by placing dots above them.[112] There are ten such places in the Torah.[113]

7:52   There is a tradition that where the dotted letters constituted the majority of a word, they were added for a reason. Therefore, in such a case, the dotted letters are to be studied separately to ascertain this reason. Conversely, where the dotted letters constitute the minority of the word, they were found in the original manuscripts, but there existed a reason that they be deleted. In such a case, the word is interpreted as if the dotted letters were absent.[114]

7:53   During the last days of the Temple, further questions arose regarding the precise readings of the Torah. It was found that the three Torah scrolls which were kept in the Temple as standards had slightly variant readings.[115] It was

111. There may have been a question if this was a place where a word is read but not written (cf. 7:63); see *Ben Avraham* on *Avoth DeRabbi Nathan* 3:44. Cf. *Maharal, Tifereth Yisrael* 66.

112. *Avoth DeRabbi Nathan* 34:4; *Binyan Yehoshua ad loc.; Sofrim* 6:3; *Kissey Rachamim ad loc.; BaMidbar Rabbah* 3:13; *Etz Yoseph ad loc.; Arukh,* s.v. *Nakad; Machzor Vitri,* p. 685; *Piskey Tosafoth, Menachoth* 231; *Derishah, Yoreh Deah* 274:2 (end); *Turey Zahav, Yoreh Deah* 274:7; *Birkey Yosef, Yoreh Deah* 274:5; *Teshuvah MeAhavah* 3:391 (end). Also see *Radak,* Introduction to Joshua (end). The dots over the letters have the effect of partially deleting the letters; *Ikkarim* 3:22 (end). There was a tradition to place such dots in such a case; *Bachya* on Genesis 11:32.

113. *Sofrim* 6:3. The following cases are found in the Torah: Genesis 16:5 on the Yod of *u'bhene-kha* (וּבֵינֶיךָ), Genesis 18:9 on the Alef Yod Vav of *elav* (אֵלָיו), Genesis 19:33 on the Vav of *u'bhe-komah* (וּבְקֻמָהּ), Genesis 33:4 on *ve-yishak-ehu* (וַיִּשָׁקֵהוּ), Genesis 37:12 on *eth* (אֵת), Numbers 3:39 on *veAharon* (וְאַהֲרֹן), Numbers 9:10 on the Heh of *rechokah* (רְחֹקָה), Numbers 21:30 on the Resh of *asher* (אֲשֶׁר), Numbers 29:15 on the Vav of *ve-eseron* (וְעִשָּׂרֹן), Deuteronomy 28:28 on *lanu u-le-vanenu* (לָנוּ וּלְבָנֵינוּ).

114. *Yerushalmi, Pesachim* 9:2 (64b); *Bereshith Rabbah* 48:17, 78:12; *Yalkut Shimoni* 1:82; *Rashi* on Genesis 18:9; *Sifethey Chakhamim ad loc.; Tosafoth, Bava Metzia* 87a, *Nazir* 23a, s.v. *Lama; Nimukey Yosef, Bava Metzia* (Rif 52a), s.v. *VeOmrim, Maharsha, Horioth* 10b, s.v. *Lama; Chizzkuni* on Genesis 16:5.

115. In Exodus 24:5, whether the reading should be *na'arey* (נַעֲרֵי) or *zatutey* (זָאטוּטֵי) (cf. *Torah Temimah ad loc.*); in Deuteronomy 33:27, if the reading should be *me'on* (מְעֹן) or *me'onah* (מְעֹנָה); and in eleven places enumerated in *Avoth Rabbi Nathan* 34:4, if the reading should be *he* (הִיא) or *hu* (הוּא).

decided that the reading which was found to be the same in any two of the three scrolls would be the accepted reading.[116] This was no different than in all other cases of law, where the majority is followed.[117]

7:54   Because of the many persecutions that took place in the century following the destruction of the second Temple, it became difficult to obtain exact copies of the Torah. Many variant spellings became forgotten, especially where their reason was not known.[118] However, where the reason for a variant was known, it was carefully preserved.[119] Similarly, since there is no punctuation in the Torah scroll,[120] questions regarding the precise sentence structure of the Torah also arose during this period.[121]

7:55   Because of this, there are cases where a reading in scripture may disagree with that found in the Talmud.[122] In

---

116. *Yerushalmi, Taanith* 4:2 (20b); *Sofrim* 6:4; *Sifri* (356) on Deuteronomy 33:27; *Yalkut Shimoni* 2:964; Meiri, introduction to *Kiryath Sefer.* There is evidence that this occurred after the Torah was translated into Greek (*Megillah* 9a); *Torah Temimah* on Exodus 24:5. Some sources, however, state that this was done by Ezra, Rashi on 1 Chronicles 8:29 *Sodi Razia,* quoted in *Yalkut Reuveni* on Exodus 4:2 (14a). Also see *Nachal Eshkol* on *Sefer HaEshkol* (Halberstadt, 1868), *Hilkhoth Seder HaSedarim* 20, p. 61, note 15; *Torah Sh'lemah* 19:376.

117. Rashi on 1 Chronicles 8:26 (34a); *Kuzari* 3:26 (34a); *Teshuvoth Ramban* (Rashba) 232; *Teshuvoth Rivash* 284. See below, 11:17, 12:33.

118. *Kiddushin* 30a. See Maharal, *Tifereth Yisrael* 65; *HaMikra VeHaMesorah* 4. This is one reason why we do not observe the commandment to write a personal Torah scroll today; *Shaagath Aryeh* 36; quoted in *Pithchey Teshuvah, Yoreh Deah* 270:10; cf. *Teshuvoth Chatham Sofer, Orach Chaim* 52. Cf. Meiri, *Kiddushin* 30b.

119. *Minchath Chinukh* 365. Cf. Rashi, *Berakhoth* 56a, s.v. *Vav;* Ibn Ezra on Exodus 20:1 *Avi Ezra ad loc.* note 1; Maharal, *Tifereth Yisrael* 67.

120. Cf. *Orach Chaim* 32:32 in *Hagah; Magen Avraham* 32:45; *Mishnah Berurah* 32:146; *Yoreh Deah* 274:7 in *Hagah; Sifethey Cohen* 274:6. See below, 7:59.

121. *Kiddushin* 30a. Cf *Yoma* 52a (end); *Yerushalmi, Avodah Zarah* 2:7 (15a); *Yad Malachi* 278. In *Kiddushin* loc. cit., the number of verses is given as 5888. The number in our present reading, however, is 5845; *Dikdukey HaTaamim,* p. 55. See Rabbi Avraham Harkavi, *Zikhron LeRishonim, Teshuvoth HaGaonim* 3 (Berlin, 1887); *Beth Nakoth Halakhoth* (Frankfurt am Mein, 1882), p. 48; *HaMikra VeHaMesorah* 10. Cf. *Yalkut Shimoni* 1:855; Marginal note on *Berakhoth* 7a.

122. Cf. Rashi, *Shabbath* 55a, s.v. *VeHa;* Maharatz Chajas *ad loc.; Tosafoth, ibid.* s.v. *Mavirin; Minchath Shai* on 1 Samuel 2:24; *Tosafoth, Shabbath* 128a. s.v. *VeNathan, Eruvin* 2a, s.v. *DeK'thiv, Pesachim* 117a, s.v. *SheOmdin, Megillah* 3a, s.v. *VeYalin, Ibid.* 22a, s.v. *Ain; Berakhoth* 61a, s.v. *Eleh,* Maharshal, Maharsha, *ad loc.;* Rashi, *Zevachim* 118b, s.v. *VeLo,* 119b, s.v. *VaYehi; Tosafoth ibid.;*

the case of the Torah, these differences are usually restricted to minor variant spellings and readings.[123] In other parts of the Bible, however, more marked variations are found.[124]

7:56   In the centuries following the writing of the Talmud (around 750 c.e.) the masters of the Masorah followed the footsteps of the earlier manuscript correctors[125] and undertook to prepare a perfect text of the Bible.[126] The text that is followed today is largely based on the work of the Masorite, Aaron (ben Moseh) ben Asher (around 950 c.e.) who prepared an extremely accurate manuscript.[127]

7:57   The Masorites would only correct the scriptures on the basis of existent manuscripts, where they followed the reading found in the majority of the best texts available.[128] However, it was forbidden to correct any manuscript on the basis of argument and logic alone.[129]

Yerushalmi, Sotah 1:8 (7b), Tzion Yerushalayim ad loc.; Meiri, Kiddushin 30a; Teshuvoth Rashba 1:10; Radak on Judges 16:31; Minchath Shai on Isaiah 36:12, Psalms 49:13, Ecclesiastes 8:10; Maharatz Chajas, Moed Katan 5a; Gilyon HaShas, Shabbath 55b; Teshuvoth Radbaz 4:1172; Nefesh Chayah, Orach Chaim 143; HaMikra VeHaMesorah 2, 13. These differences, however, may have been deliberate, cf. Yerushalmi, Megillah 3:2 (24b).
123. Minchath Chinukh 613. Cf. Tosafoth, Niddah 33a. s.v. VeHaNoseh; Rashi, Sanhedrin 4a, s.v. Karnoth. Also see Tosafoth, Sanhedrin 4b, Zevachim 37b, s.v. LeTotafoth.
124. Cf. Yad Malachi 283.
125. Cf. Kethuboth 106a.
126. Dikdukey HaTaamim 69.
127. Cf. Yad, Sefer Torah 8:4. This pentateuch, the Kether Torah was preserved in Allepo, and still exists. There were some very minor variants between the readings of Ben Asher and Ben Naphtali, and they are enumerated in Rabbi Pesach Finfer, Mesorath HaTorah VeHaNevi'im (Vilna, 1906); Rabbi Yosef Furst, Otzar Lashon HaKodesh (Concordantiae) (Leipzig, 1840), p. 1371 ff. Also see Teshuvoth Ramban 232; Teshuvoth Rivash 284. There are also questions regarding the doubling of the Resh (ר); see Sefer Yetzirah 4:1; Saadia Gaon ad loc. pp. 79, 115, 116; Rabbi Donash ibn Tamim ad loc. (London, 1902), p. 21; Rabbi Yehudah Barceloni ad loc. p. 231; Radak, Mikhlol (Lyck, 1842), p. 81b; Dikdukey HaTaamim 4; Rabbi Profait Duran (Ephodi), Ma'aseh Ephod 31 (Vienna, 1865), p. 171; Rabbi Yonah ben Janach, Sefer HaRikmah 2 (Frankfurt am Mein, 1856).
128. See above 7:51.
129. Sefer HaEshkol, Hilkhoth Seder HaSedarim 20 (p. 62, top); Teshuvoth Ramban 232; Meiri, Introduction to Kiryat Sefer; Yoreh Deah 279:1 in Hagah; HaGra ad loc. 279:2; Pith'chey Teshuvah ad loc. 279:3. Cf. Kuzari 3:28 (35a); Rabbenu Yonah on Avoth 3:13, s.v. Mesoroth; Rashash ad loc.

7:58   Although the "Old Hebrew" script[130] was commonly used in ancient Israel, the original Torah scrolls, as well as the Tablets of the Ten Commandments,[131] were written in the same Ashurith script used for Torah scrolls today.[132] According to other opinions, however, the Ashurith script was forgotten during the Babylonian exile, and the common Old Hebrew script was used for Torah scrolls, until the Ashurith script was restored by Ezra.[133] A third opinion is that the Torah and Tablets[134] were originally given in the Old Hebrew script, and the Ashurith script was introduced by Ezra.[135]

130. Cf. Hai Gaon, Rambam, Bertenoro, on *Yadayim* 4:5. For an example, see Rabbi Yaakov Emden, *Migdal Oz, Beth Midoth, Aliyath HaK'thav* 4 (Warsaw, 1886), p. 117a.

131. The letters final Mem (ם) and Samekh (ס) thus stood in the Tablets miraculously; *Megillah* 2b (end); *Shabbath* 104a. Also see *Chidushey HaRan, Sanhedrin* 21b; Maharal, *Tifereth Yisrael* 64.

132. Rabbi Elazar HaModai, *Sanhedrin* 21b; *Tosefta, Sanhedrin* 4:5; *Yerushalmi, Megillah* 4:5 (10a). Some maintain that this is the accepted opinion; Rabbenu Chananel and *Yad Ramah, Sanhedrin* loc. cit.; Maharal, *Tifereth Yisrael* 64; *Teshuvoth Chavath Yair* 106. This also seems to be the opinion in *Yadayim* 4:5, Rambam, Rash *ad loc.; Yad, Avoth HaTumah* 9:7; *Megillah* 2:3 (17a). Also see *Zekher LeRishonim, Teshuvoth HaGaonim* 358; *Teshuvoth Muharam Alshakar* 274. It is only these letters that have the crowns (tagin) given at Sinai; *Menachoth* 29b; Tifereth Yisrael, loc. cit. Reasons are also given for the shapes of the letters; *Menachoth* 29b. See *Chidushey HaGriz* 3:234.

133. Rabbi Yehudah HaNasi, *Sanhedrin* 22a. cf. *Zevachim* 62a. This is why there was a question as to which of the paired letters should be placed at the end of the word; *Shabbath* 104a; *Megillah* 3a; Rivta and *HaKothev* (on *Eyn Yaakov*) ad loc. Cf. *Yerushalmi, Megillah* 1:9 (12b); *Bereshith Rabbah* 1:15.

134. According to this, the Eyin (ע) would be miraculous; *Yerushalmi, Megillah* 1:9 (10b); *Maharsha, Sanhedrin* 21b, s.v. *BeTechilah.* This would appear to contradict Maharal, *Tifereth Yisrael* 64; *Chasdey David* on *Tosefta, Sanhedrin*, 4:5. However, see *Teshuvoth Radbaz* 883 (3:442);Rabbi Yaakov Emden, *Migdal Oz* 117a. Also see *Or Zarua* 1:552; *Teshuvoth Tashbatz* 1:51; *Pachad Yitzchak*, s.v. *Sefer* (p. 141a).

135. Mar Ukva, Rabbi Yosi, *Sanhedrin* 21b; *Tosefta, Yerushalmi,* loc. cit. Cf. Rashi, *Zevachim* 62a, s.v. *SheTikathav*, who appears to accept this opinion. Also see *Ikkarim* 3:16,19. There may have been a tradition from Moses to change the writing in commemoration of the redemption from Babylon; *Ikkarim* 3:22. Some say that Torah scrolls written in this old script were used for study, and not for synagogue reading; *Teshuvoth Rambam* 5 (Jerusalem, 1934); *Teshuvoth Maharam Alshakar* 274; *Migdal Oz* 116b; *HaMikra VeHaMesorah* 9; *Margolioth HaYam, Sanhedrin* 21b. Cf. Rabbi Yosef Rosen, *Tzafanuth Paaneach* on Deuteronomy 31:9. See *Yoreh Deah* 284:2 in *Hagah; Teshuvoth Radbaz* 4:45 (1118); *Beth Yosef Evven HaEzer* 126 (beginning); Rosh, *Megillah* 2:2 (end). For further discussion, see *Teshuvoth Radbaz* 3:549 (980); Rabbi Yaakov Sapir, *Evven Sapir*, Part 2 (Mayence, 1874), p.

7:59   The original Torah scrolls were written without vowels,[136] just as they are written today.[137] However, just as the exact text of the Torah was given to Moses, so were the precise readings.[138] These were preserved orally until they were finally put in writing.[139]

7:60   It is for this reason that every word must be correctly pronounced when the Torah is read.[140] There is a great deal of significance in the vowel signs used in the Torah.[141]

15; Rabbi Yaakov Bachrach, *Sefer HaYachas* (Warsaw, 1854); *Idem, Ishtadluth Im Shadal* (Warsaw, 1896).

136. Teshuvoth Hai Gaon, in *Torathan shel Rishonim* 3 (p. 40); *Machzor Vitri* 120; *Kuzari* 3:30 (35b); *Teshuvoth Radbaz* 3:643. Cf. *Bava Bathra* 21b (top); *Teshuvoth Rivash* 284. Some maintain that the thirteenth Torah written by Moses and stored in the Ark (7:32) was written with vowels and accents; Rabbi Yosef Rosen, *Tzafanath Paaneach* on Deuteronomy 31:9; Rabbi Yaakov Bachrach, *Ishtadluth im Shadel* 55 (p. 77). This may be supported by *Bahir* 115, which speaks of the "vowels in the Torah of Moses."

137. *Sofrim* 3:7; *Yoreh Deah* 174:7.

138. *Nedarim* 37b; *Tosafoth, Ran, ad loc.* s.v. *Mikra; Yerushalmi, Megillah* 4:1 (28b); *Maharal, Tifereth Yisrael* 66, *Migdal Oz* 117b. See above, note 38.

139. Some say that the first books of the Torah with vowels and accents were written in the time of Ezra: Rabbi Gedaliah ibn Yacha. *Shalsheleth HaKabbalah* (Jerusalem, 1962), p. 47; Rabbi Yaakov Culi, *MeAm Lo'ez,* Introduction (translated from Ladino, Jerusalem, 1967), p. 10. There is, however, evidence that vocalized texts existed from even earlier; *Yalkut Reuveni* on Exodus 4:2. Other sources state that vocalized texts were not written until post Talmudic times; Rabbi Eliahu Bachor, *Mesoreth HaMesoreth;* Rabbi Profait Duran (Ephodi), *Maaseh Ephod* 7. Some sources state that the names of the vowels are also very ancient; see *Shaarey Zohar, Nedarim* 37b. Other sources indicate a more recent origin; Rabbi Yaakov Emden, *Matpechoth Sefarim* (Lvov, 1871), p. 23. Cf. *Tifereth Yisrael* 66. Also see *Tikuney Zohar* 69 (107a); *Nefesh Chayah* 187 (end). Some also attribute an ancient origin to the form of the vowels; *Tikuney Zohar* 4b; *Shemonah Shaarim, Shaar Ruach HaKodesh, Yichud* 3 (Tel Aviv, 1963), p. 112. Their forms are also related to the head motions used in various meditations; *Pardes Rimonim* 21:1. For general discussion, see *Kol Yehudah* on *Kuzari* 3:31 (37a); Rabbi Masud Gozlan, *Sefer HaSamdar* (Livorno, 1876); *Sefer HaYachas* 3:15,49; *Ishtadluth im Shadel,* p. 159. Also see Rabbi Ephraim Zalman Margolius, *Shaarey Ephraim* 3:14. Rashi includes vowel points in *Piskey Taamim* (פִּסְקֵי טְעָמִים) regarding which there is a dispute in the Talmud; Rashi, *Nedarim* 37a, s.v. *U'Rabbi Yochanan.*

140. *Yad, Tefillah* 12:6; *Rosh, Megillah* 3:6; *Orach Chaim* 142:1 in *Hagah;* HaGra *ad loc.*

141. *Bahir* 115; *Zohar* 1:15a, *Tikuney Zohar* 5 (20b), 69 (108a, end); *Zohar Chadash* 73b; *Bachya* on Genesis 18:2; Rabbi Shimon ben Tzemach Duran, *Magen Avoth* (Livorno, 1785), p. 54b (end); *Maharal, Tifereth Yisrael* 66; *Nefesh HaChaim* 2:16. Cf. *Teshuvoth Nodeh BeYehudah, Orach Chaim* 2.

7:61   Nevertheless, the written word is pre-eminent. When it contradicts the traditional pronunciation,[142] we always interpret according to the written word.[143]

7:62   Similarly, the Torah was never written with punctuation,[144] although its sentence structure was revealed to Moses and transmitted orally.[145] Since there is a reason for the Torah's sentence structure, when reading scripture, one should complete an entire sentence, and not just read part of it.[146]

7:63   Likewise, the notes used in chanting the Torah were originally taught to Moses.[147] Similar notes were also used by the prophets,[148] but they were chanted with a somewhat different melody.[149] One should therefore be extremely careful to use the correct chant when reading the Torah.[150] Although we do not always follow the accents in

142. *Tosafoth, Succoth* 6b, s.v. *U'Rabbi*, 32a, s.v. *Kapoth, Pesachim* 36a, s.v. *Oni, Sanhedrin* 4a, s.v. *Kulhu, Zevachim* 40a, s.v. *Lo; Sh'nei Luchoth HaB'rith, Torah SheB'al Peh, Alef* (3:229b).
143. *Teshuvoth Ramban* 238; *Turey Zahav, Yoreh Deah* 274:6. See *Sanhedrin* 4a; *Kiddushin* 18b; *Sukkah* 5b; *Pesachim* 86b; *Bekhoroth* 34a; *Kerithoth* 17b; *Makkoth* 7b.
144. *Kuzari* 3:31 (36b), *Sofrim* 3:7; *Teshuvoth Ramban* 238; *Teshuvoth Rivash* 186; *Beth Yosef, Yoreh Deah* 274 (221a); *Yoreh Deah* 274:7, *Turey Zahav* 274:7.
145. See above, 7:52.
146. *Taanith* 27b; *Rashi ad loc.* s.v. *Paskuk; Megillah* 22a; *Zohar* 2:206b; *Tosafoth, Sukkah* 38a, s.v. *Hu;* Ibn Ezra on *Esther* 9:27; *Magen Avraham* 282:0, 422:5; *Chayay Adam* 5:2, *Nishmath Adam ad loc.* 2; *Teshuvoth Tifereth Tzvi* 14; *Pachad Yitzchak*, s.v. *Pasuk* (41b). Some sources indicate that this refers to splitting a paragraph rather than a sentence; *Berakhoth* 12b.
147. *Megillah* 3a; *Chagigah* 6a; *Nedarim* 37b; *Yerushalmi, Megillah* 4:1 (28b); *Bereshith Rabbah* 36:8; *Sefer Chasidim* 302; *Teshuvoth Chatham Sofer* 6:86 s.v. *Avel.* Some sources, however, maintain that the chant was legislated (*me-de-rabanan*); Cf. *Nedarim* 37a; *Tosafoth ad loc.* s.v. *S'khar Pissuk; Ran ad loc.* s.v. *U'Rabbi Yochanan.* Also see Rambam, Bertenoro on *Nedarim* 4:3; *Teshuvoth Radbaz* 1020 (3:594). Cf. *Eruvin* 21b.
148. *Dikdukey HaTaamim* 16. Cf. *Kuzari* 3:31,32.
149. *Sefer Chasidim* 302; *Tosafoth, Bava Bathra* 14b, s.v. *BePeronioth.*
150. *Orach Chaim* 142:1 in *Hagah.* See *Megillah* 32a; *Sofrim* 3:11; *Shir HaShirim Rabbah* 4:23.

interpreting scripture,[151] the notes have a very deep significance.[152]

7:64   There are passages which are traditionally counted as "rectifications of the scribes" (tikun sofrim, תִּקּוּן סוֹפְרִים).[153] In the Torah, these can only be interpreted as interpretations of the scribes,[154] since even a prophet cannot add a single letter to the Torah.[155] However, in other books of the Bible, where the majority of these emendations occur, they may actually be changes introduced by the Great Assembly when they fixed the Bible canon.[156]

7:65   Similarly, Moses was taught[157] that certain words in the Torah should be written and not read,[158] read but not written,[159] or read differently than they are written.[160] Since they understood the reasons for this, the Great Assembly occasionally used similar devices when they had to change or correct a reading in the other books of the Bible.[161]

7:66   Because the Torah reveals God's will to man, it was given letter by letter to avoid any misinterpretation.[162] Therefore,

151. Radak on Hosea 12:12. Cf. Tosafoth, Chagigah 6b, s.v. LePesikey; Maharsha ad loc. Also see Rashi, Megillah 12a, s.v. Kobel.
152. Zohar 1:24b; Tikuney Zohar Chadash 105a, 109c; Zohar Chadash 57d, 58c, 84a; Nefesh HaChaim 2:16.
153. Mekhilta (39b) on Exodus 15:7; Shemoth Rabbah 13:2; Tanchuma, BeShalach 16; Etz Yosef ad loc.
154. Dikdukey Taamim 57; Rashba, quoted in Sh'nei Luchoth HaB'rith, Torah SheB'al Peh, Tav (3:239a); Teshuvoth Radbaz 3:594 (1020); Minchath Shai to Numbers 12:14, Zechariah 2:12; Etz Yosef, loc cit.; Matnath Kehunah on Bereshith Rabbah 49:12. Some say that this is a literary stylism; Ikkarim 3:22. Also see Nedarim 37b; Arukh, s.v. Atar (עטר); Maharal, Tifereth Yisrael 66.
155. Cf. Rambam, Introduction to Mishneh. See below, 8:31.
156. Matnath Kehunah on Bereshit Rabbah 49:12.
157. Nedarim 37b; Yerushalmi, Megillah 4:1 (28b); Bereshith Rabbah 36:8. Cf. Kuzari 3:27,28; Teshuvoth Radbaz 3:594 (1020).
158. Sofrim 6:9.
159. Sofrim 6:8.
160. Sofrim 9:8.
161. Sefer Chasidim 1016; Radak, Introduction to Joshua (end); Abarbanel. Introduction to Jeremiah; Kol Yehudah on Kuzari 3:31 (36b).
162. Mekhilta (94b) on Exodus 22:19. See above, 7:19.

even the most seemingly trivial passages and variations[163] in the Torah can teach many lessons to the person who is willing to explore its depths.[164]

7:67 Although the Torah can be read by the simplest individual, one must delve beneath its surface meaning if one is to discover its true treasures. We thus find that "Ezra set his heart to delve into God's Torah" (Ezra 7:10). It is similarly taught, "If you seek it as silver, and search for it as for hidden treasures, then you shall . . . find the knowledge of God" (Proverbs 2:4).[165]

7:68 Since the Torah is a finite book expressing the will of an infinite God,[166] many lessons must be derivable from each passage.[167]

7:69 The Torah can be understood according to its simple meaning, or according to more complex exegesis. Besides this, many allusions and mysteries can be found when one probes beneath its surface.[168]

7:70 Even the seemingly simple narratives in the Torah contain many secret meanings and lessons.[169] If they were

163. Cf. *Eruvin* 21b; *Menachoth* 29b; Bertenoro, *Avoth* 3:13, s.v *Mesoroth, Zohar* 3:213b.
164. Cf. *Sanhedrin* 99b; Rambam on *Sanhedrin* 10:1, Principle 8; *Moreh Nevukhim* 3:50; *Sefer Chasidim* 1015; Bachya on Leviticus 1:7.
165. Ralbag *ad loc.; Shir HaShirim Rabbah* 1:9, *Emunoth VeDeyoth* 5:8.
166. Cf. *BaMidbar Rabbah* 19:3; *Shir HaShirim Rabbah* 1:11; *Tanchuma, Chukath* 6; *Pesikta* 4 (34b); *Yalkut Shimoni* 2:173; from 1 Kings 5:12; *cf.* Rashi, Radak, *ad loc.*
167. *Shabbath* 88b; *Sanhedrin* 34a; *Yerushalmi, Sanhedrin* 4:2 (21b); *Midrash Tehillim* 12:4; *Zohar* 2:99a (end). Cf. *BaMidbar Rabbah* 19:2.
168. In Hebrew, these four methods are known as p'shat (פְּשָׁט), remez (רֶמֶז), drash (דְּרָשׁ) and sod (סוֹד), collectively known by their initial letters, which spell out *pardes* (פַּרְדֵּ"ס); *Shemonah Shaarim, Shaar HaMitzvoth, VeEthChanan* (Tel Aviv, 1962), p. 79; Alshekh on Job 28:16; Rabbi Meir Poppers, *Or Tzadikim* 22:18; cf. Rabbi Moshe de Leon (Munich, Manuscript 22), p. 128b. Also see *Zohar* 3:110a; *Tikuney Zohar Chadash* 102d. Also see *Chagigah* 14b; *Shir HaShirim Rabbah* 1:28; *Zohar* 1:26b, 2:99a,b.
169. Rambam, *Torath HaShem Temimah* (in Kithvey Ramban), p. 144; Bachya on Genesis 5:28, Introduction to *VaYakhel; Beth Elohim, Shaar HaYesodoth* 30; *Zohar* 2:55b (end), 2:98b, 3:79b, 3:174b.

mere stories, they could have been written by the hand of man, rather than through the highest forms of inspiration.[170]

7:71   Therefore, a person who seeks to explore the true depths of the Torah finds himself on a road that has no end. It is thus written, "Its measure is longer than the earth, and broader than the sea" (Job 11:9).[171]

7:72   The key to understanding the Torah is the oral tradition handed down from the time of Moses and embodied in the Talmud and Midrash.[172] However, even these traditions must be carefully studied, since they were often handed down word for word.[173]

7:73   There are, however, many cases where even the original meaning and wisdom behind these traditions have been forgotten.[174] This was predicted by the prophet: "The wisdom of the wise shall perish" (Isaiah 29:14).[175] Since these traditions may be as difficult to understand as scripture itself, one may occasionally depart from them in interpreting the Torah, as long as no question of law is involved.[176] However, where question of Torah law is involved, the Talmudic traditions must be followed at all times.[177]

---

170. "We could write better stories ourselves;" *Zohar* 1:115a. *Cf.* Rashi, Ramban, on Genesis 1:1.
171. *Pesikta* 12 (107a); *Yalkut Shimoni* 1:273.
172. Ramban on Genesis 1:1; Rabbi Moshe Chaim Luzzatto, *Maamar al HaAgadoth.*
173. *Cf. Edduyoth* 1:3; *Berakhoth* 47a; *Bekhoroth* 5a; *Kuzari* 3:73 (78a).
174. *Kuzari* 3:63 (66b), 4:29 (71b); *Moreh Nevukhim* 3:14. *Cf. Yerushalmi, Peah* 2:4 (13a); *Yad, Melakhim* 12:2.
175. *Moreh Nevukhim* 2:11.
176. *Or HaChaim* on Genesis 1:1, s.v. *VeHaGam.*
177. *Tosafoth, Chulin* 88a, s.v. *U'Rabbi*; Rabbi Yosef Colon, *Teshuvoth Maharik* 139; *Beth Chadash, Choshen Mishpat* 389; Rabbi Shmuel Daniel, *Zaken Sh'muel* (Izmir, 1756); *Yad Malachi* 144.

7:74 · The Torah must be studied as a whole, since one ambiguous passage may be clarified by another.[178] One must be careful to take an overall view, and not interpret any scripture out of context.[179]

7:75 There are times when the Torah speaks in allegory and metaphor.[180] There are four conditions under which there is a tradition that the Torah is not to be taken according to its literal meaning:[181]

1. Where the plain meaning is rejected by common experience.
2. Where it is repudiated by obvious logic.[182]
3. Where it is contradicted by obvious scripture.
4. Where it is opposed by clear Talmudic tradition.[183]

7:76 Where none of these conditions hold, the scripture must be taken literally, and not rejected on the basis of mere prejudice.[184] In such a case, even when a passage is also interpreted allegorically, the literal meaning must still be retained.[185]

---

178. *BaMidbar Rabbah* 19:17; *Tanchuma, Chukath* 23. Cf. *Yerushalmi, Rosh HaShanah* 3:5 (17a); *Tosafoth, Kerithoth* 14a, s.v. *Elah; Sedey Chemed, P'ath HaSadeh, Dalet* 24 (2:134).
179. Rambam, *Iggereth Teimon* (in *Iggeroth HaRambam*), p. 19. Cf. *Berakhoth* 10a; Rashi *ad loc.* s.v. *Shapil.*
180. *Mreh Nevukhim,* Introduction, from Hosea 12:11.
181. *Emunoth VeDeyoth* 7:2 (83a).
182. As in the cases of anthropomorphisms; *Moreh Nevukhim* 2:25. See above, 2:23.
183. Cf. *Minchath Chinukh* 232:4; and *Zohar* 3:85a; *Minchath Pittim, Orach Chaim* 156; *Makor Chesed* on *Sefer Chasidim* 673:1.
184. *Emunoth VeDeyoth* 7:2.
185. *Shabbath* 63a; *Yevamoth* 11b, 24a; *Teshuvoth Rashbam* 415; Rashbam to Genesis 1:1, Ramban on *Sefer HaMitzvoth, Shoresh* 2 (19b); Maharatz Chajas, *Shabbath* 63a, *Megillah* 13a, *Yevamoth* 79a; *HaMikra VeHaMesorah* 16. It is for this reason that the Torah is called a "witness;" *Ikkarim* 3:21.

7:77   The Torah always speaks in the language of man.[186] God worded the Torah so that it would be accessible to all people for all times.[187]

7:78   The most frequently used names in the Bible are the Tetragrammaton (YHVH, יהוה), and *Elohim* (אֱלֹהִים). Each of these has special significance.

7:79   The name *Elohim* represents God as Ruler of creation, and thus, the same word is used for judges and angels.[188] The name *Elohim* is therefore interpreted to indicate that God is the "master of all power."[189] This also indicates that God's primary relationship with the universe is to oversee all the forces of creation and providence.[190] When the name *Elohim* is used in God's relationships with man, it indicates that He is acting in justice, according to laws as strict as those of nature.[191]

7:80   The Tetragrammaton (YHVH, יהוה) is used as a proper name of God,[192] denoting Him as the ultimate Source of all existence,[193] high above the universe and its laws. The

186. *Berakhoth* 31a; *Yevamoth* 71a; *Ketuvoth* 67b; *Gittin* 41b; *Nedarim* 3a; *Kiddushin* 17b; *Bava Metzia* 31b; *Sanhedrin* 64b, 85b, 90b; *Makkoth* 12a; *Avodah Zarah* 27a; *Zevachim* 108b; *Kerithoth* 11a; *Niddah* 32b, 44a; *Sifra* on Leviticus 20:2 (91b); *Yad, Yesodey HaTorah* 1:12.
187. Cf. *Moreh Nevukhim* 2:29; *Zohar* 2:15b.
188. *Moreh Nevukhim* 1:2, 2:6; *Kuzari* 4:1 (2b); *Ibn Ezra* on Genesis 1:1, Exodus 3:15, 33:21; *Ramban* on Exodus 3:13.
189. *Tur, Orach Chaim* 5; *Orach Chaim* 5:1. Cf. *Saadia Gaon* on *Sefer Yetzirah*, p. 43.
190. *Likutey Amarim (Tanya)*, *Shaar HaYichud VeHaEmunah* 6 (80a); *Nefesh HaChaim* 1:2.
191. *Mekhilta* on Exodus 15:2 (35a); *Yalkut Shimoni* 1:242; *Sifra* on Leviticus 18:2 (85c); *Bereshith Rabbah* 73:2, 12:15; *Midrash Tehillim* 47:2; *Pesikta* 22 (151b); *Yalkut Shimoni* 1:645, 1:782, 2:754; *Rokeach* 200; *Pesikta* 22 (149a), 24 (164a); *Yalkut Shimoni* 2:532; *Rashi* on Genesis 1:1, Hosea 14:2.
192. Cf. *Emunoth VeDeyoth* 2:3 (45b); *Moreh Nevukhim* 1:61; *Kuzari* 2:2 (7a), 4:1 (4b); *Ibn Ezra* on Exodus 3:15, 33:21. See above, Chapter 2, Note 65. This is the reason that only the Tetragrammaton was used in the case of the sacrifices; *Sifra* on Leviticus 1:2 (4c). Also see *Yad, Yesodey HaTorah* 6:2; *Avodath Kokhavim* 2:7.
193. *Likutey Amarim (Tanya)*, *Shaar HaYichud VeHaEmunah* 4 (79a); *Nefesh HaChaim* 2:2 (end); cf. *Moreh Nevukhim* 1:61. This is a "complete name" used by a "complete word;" *Bereshith Rabbah* 13:3; *Kuzari* 4:15 (33a).

Tetragrammaton is therefore interpreted to mean that God "was, is and will be,"[194] indicating that He is outside the realm of space, time and all other attributes of nature.[195] Therefore, when the Tetragrammaton is used in relation to man, it indicates that God is acting in mercy,[196] transcending all the rules of providence.

7:81   Since the Torah was written dictated by God, there are many instances where it speaks about things that took place after it was written.[197] The Torah likewise contains other information that could only have been obtained prophetically.[198]

7:82   There are instances where the Torah appears to contain self contradictions. However, with careful study, one can always find another passage[199] or an oral tradition that reconciles all contradictions.[200]

7:83   God wrote the Torah in a complex manner so that it would be a never ending source of inspiration and study. Just as new scientific concepts are derived from apparent contradictions in nature, so can knowledge of God's purpose

194. Rabbi Eliezer of Garmiza (short version) on *Sefer Yetzirah* 1:1; *Tur, Orach Chaim* 5; *Orach Chaim* 5:1; HaGra *ad loc.*; *Sh'nei Luchoth HaB'rith, Beth HaShem* (1:40b), *Mesekhta Shevuoth,* s v. *Shem* (2.100a). Cf. Rashbam on Exodus 3:15, where the *atbash* (אתב"ש) code is deciphered to read, "He calls Himself *Ehyeh* (אהיה), 'I will be,' and we call Him 'He will be' with a Vav (ו) in the place of the [second] Yod (י), as we find, *Ki mah hoveh la-adam* (כִּי מָה הֹוֶה לָאָדָם) (Ecclesiastes 2:22)."
195. *Likutey Amarim (Tanya), Shuar HaYichud VeHaEmunah* 7 (82a). Cf. *Kuzari* 2:2 (7a). See above, 2:18.
196. See note 191. Also see *Turey Zahav, Orach Chaim* 621:2; *Pri Megadim ad loc.* Cf. Ramban on Deuteronomy 3:24.
197. *Kesuvoth* 10b; *Tosafoth ad loc.* s.v. *VeTana; Bereshith Rabbah* 16:2; Rashi on Genesis 2:14; Ibn Ezra on Genesis 12:6; 36:31, Deuteronomy 1:2, Introduction to Psalms.
198. Cf. *Chulin* 60b, 59b, Maharatz Chajas *ad loc.; Bekhoroth* 5a.
199. *Sifra,* Introduction, Thirteen Principles of Rabbi Yishmael 13; *Mekhilta* on Exodus 12:5 (4b).
200. Rabbi Menasheh ben Yisrael, *Conciliator* (Hermon: New York, 1972). The entire book deals with the reconciliation of such passages. Cf. *Shem HaGedolim Maarekheth Sefarim, Nun* 48.

and law be derived from the apparent self contradictions in the Torah. If the Torah were written as simply as other literature, it would hardly be the object of intensive study, much less lifelong devotion.[201]

7:84   The values of the Torah occasionally may not correspond to those of contemporary society, or they may seem irrelevant to our times. However, while contemporary values are of human origin and transient, those of the Torah are divine and eternal. It is taught that when King Solomon, the greatest genius of all time, considered certain commandments irrelevant, God said, "A thousand like Solomon will pass away, but not a single jot of the Torah will be changed."[202]

7:85   Every glory and wonder, and all deep mysteries are hidden in the Torah and sealed in its treasuries.[203] There is no branch of wisdom, natural or divine, that is not contained in its depths.[204] The Psalmist therefore prayed, "Open my eyes, so that I may behold wondrous things out of Your Torah" (Psalms 119:18).[205]

7:86   The divine origin of the Torah is manifest by its incongruity with the age of its birth, its original, unborrowed, solitary greatness, and the suddenness with which it burst forth in an age of violence and superstition, shining forth on the world like a beacon of truth.[206]

7:87   For over three thousand years, the Torah has been kept by the Jewish people, not so much because of the miracles

201. *Moreh Nevukhim,* Introduction (end).
202. *Yerushalmi, Sanhedrin* 2:6 (13a); *Shemoth Rabbah* 6:1; *VaYikra Rabbah* 9:2; *Shir HaShirim Rabbah* 5:8. Cf. Bachya on Genesis 2:7 (p. 65).
203. Ramban, Introduction to Torah. Cf. Maharal, *Tifereth Yisrael* 68.
204. Cf. *Avoth* 5:22; Rabbenu Yonah *ad loc. Menorath HaMaor* 2:1:2:1 (33).
205. *Chovoth HaLevavoth, Shaar Avodath Elohim* 3; Ramban, Introduction to Torah; *Zohar* 1:131b, 1:132a, 1:135a, 1:145b, 3:152a.
206. Cf. *Kuzari* 1:81 (49a).

which accompanied its revelation, but because it embraces the depths and heights of human nature, fulfilling a need that God knows to exist in man. The Torah is therefore intrinsically perfect, and requires no further external evidence for the truths it teaches. The Psalmist thus said, "God's Torah is perfect, it restores the soul" (Psalms 19:8).[207]

207. Ibn Ezra *ad loc.*

EIGHT

THE PROPHETS

8:1   We are commanded to heed the words of a true prophet. It is thus written, "God your Lord will raise up a prophet from among your people ... you shall heed him" (Deuteronomy 18:15).[1]

8:2   One must heed a prophet whether he speaks in God's name or issues an order based on his own judgment.[2]

8:3   One who defies[3] a prophet who speaks in God's name[4] is worthy of death. God thus said, "Whoever does not hearken to My word, which [the prophet] will speak in My name, I Myself will call him to account" (Deuteronomy 18:19).[5]

---

1. *Yad, Yesodey HaTorah* 7:7; *Sefer HaMitzvoth,* Positive Commandment 172; *Sefer Mitzvoth Gadol,* Positive Commandment 6; *Chinukh* 516.
2. *Minchath Chinukh* 516. Cf. *Tosafoth, Sanhedrin* 89b, s.v. *Eliahu.*
3. Rashi, *Sanhedrin* 89a, s.v. *HaMevasser.* Other sources, however, appear to maintain that this is even true if one merely violates a prophet's order, even if he does not directly defy him; *Yad, Yesodey Hatorah* 9:2; *Sefer Mitzvoth Gadol, loc. cit.* Rambam on Sanhedrin 11:5 appears to agree with Rashi, but in *Sefer HaMitzvoth loc. cit.,* he reads "violates" rather than "defies" in the Mishneh. The question is raised that if merely violating a prophet's command is punishable by death, then this should be true of any Biblical commandment, which is certainly not the case; *Minchath Chinukh loc. cit.* See below, note 63.
4. But not when he speaks on his own; *Minchath Chinukh loc. cit.*
5. *Sanhedrin* 11:5 (89a); *Yad, Yesodey HaTorah* 9:2.

8:4   When a prophet is first sent to deliver a public message, he is given a sign to demonstrate that he is bearing a message from God.[6]

8:5   The mere fact that an individual produces a sign, however, is not in itself proof that he is a prophet. Before a person can be accepted as a prophet, he must be known to surpass everyone in his generation, in Torah knowledge, piety and preparation for prophecy. God thus said to Moses, "I will raise up a prophet from among your brothers, just like you" (Deuteronomy 18:18). Hence, a true prophet must be outstanding in wisdom and piety, just as Moses was.[7] If such a person then produces a sign, we are required to believe that his prophecy is from God.[8]

8:6   The sign that God grants a prophet is often a miraculous suspension of the laws of nature.[9] God might also show the prophet himself a miracle in order to strengthen his confidence in his mission.[10]

8:7   The laws of nature are not violated unless the miracle is announced and interpreted by a prophet.[11] At all other times, the laws of nature are immutable and unchanging.[12]

8:8   As Author of the laws of nature, God is likewise Author of any exceptions that take place when He brings about a miracle.[13] It would be inconsistent to believe in God as the

6. *Sanhedrin* 89b; *Yerushalmi, Sanhedrin* 11:6 (57a).
7. Cf. *Targum Yonathan*, Ramban, on Deuteronomy 18:15; Rashi on Deuteronomy 18:22.
8. *Yad, Yesodey HaTorah* 7:7. Cf. Rashi on Deuteronomy 4:34.
9. *Emunoth VeDeyoth* 3:4 (55b); *Or HaShem* 2:4:2; Ramban on Deuteronomy 13:3, 18:21. Cf. Exodus 4:5. Also see *Iggereth Techiyath HaMethim* (in *Iggeroth HaRambam*), p. 22.
10. *Emunoth VeDeyoth* 3:5 (56a).
11. *Ibid.* 3:4 (55b).
12. Cf. *Avodah Zarah* 54b; *Midrash Ne'elam, Zohar* 1:138b; *Moreh Nevukhim* 2:28,29.
13. *Bereshith Rabbah* 5:4; *Shemoth Rabbah* 21:6; *Zohar* 2:49a, 2:56a, 2:170b; Rambam, Meiri, *Midrash Sh'muel, Tosefoth Yom Tov*, on *Avoth* 5:6; *Moreh Nevukhim* 2:29; *Kuzari* 3:73 (78a); Bachya on Exodus 14:27, *Avoth* 5:8; *Derekh HaShem* 2:5:6. Also

omnipotent Creator of the universe, and hold Him to be incapable of miracles.[14] The very quantum nature of matter that God built into the universe implies a sufficient degree of acausality in the laws of nature to allow for exceptions to these laws.[15]

8:9   Science does not contradict, or even concern itself with miracles. Science deals with the laws of nature, while miracles are, by definition, exceptions to these laws. Any disbelief in miracles is thus not scientific, but is based on arbitrary prejudices in conformity to popular styles of thought.[16] Such a disbelief can reduce a person's concept of God to a mere abstract philosophical idea, abolishing the obligation to serve and obey Him.

8:10   Since a miracle violates an otherwise immutable law of nature, its effects can only be temporary.[17]

8:11   God never does anything that might destroy a person's free will. Therefore, He does not allow miracles to occur under any condition where they would force a person to believe in Him.[18] Therefore, a miracle can only occur for people whose faith is so strong that it would not be affected by the suspension of natural law.[19]

see *Pirkey Rabbi Eliezer* 19 (44a); *Targum Yonathan* on Numbers 22:28; *Koheleth Rabbah* 3:17; *Yalkut Shimoni* 2:21. The condition that God made with creation may have been precisely the acausality which permits miracles.

14. *Moreh Nevukhim* 2:25; *Or HaShem* 2:3:1. Cf. Genesis 18:14, Numbers 11:23. See above, 2:13.

15. See note 13. Also see above, 3:23, 6:65.

16. See Chapter 6, note 15.

17. *Moreh Nevukhim* 2:29; *Iggereth Techiyath HaMethim* (in *Iggeroth HaRambam*) p. 23, from Exodus 14:23. Cf. *Bereshith Rabbah* 5:4.

18. Rabbi Yitzchak ben Latif, *Shaar HaShumayim* 1:22 (Munich, Manuscript 45), quoted in *Menorath HaMaor*, end of 3 (237); *Tosefoth Yom Tov, Avodah Zarah* 4:7. See Chapter 3, note 45. However, see *Torath HaShem Temimah* (in *Kithvey Ramban*) p. 150.

19. Cf. *Berakhoth* 4b, 20a; *Sotah* 37a, *Sanhedrin* 94b; *Mekhilta* on Exodus 14:22 (31a); *Reshith Chokhmah, Shaar HaAhavah* 8 (80a).

8:12   A public miracle can only take place in the presence of a prophet.[20] When a prophet stretches forth his hand or makes another sign, he is not causing the miracle to occur, but is merely giving a sign that he has prophetic knowledge that the miracle is about to take place.[21] The death of the last prophets marked the end of public miracles.[22]

8:13   The sign provided by a prophet does not necessarily have to be a miraculous violation of the laws of nature. It is sufficient for a prophet to verify his mission by accurately predicting a future event. It is thus written, "You may ask yourselves, 'How can we know the word was not spoken by God?' If the prophet speaks in God's name but his word does not come true, then that word was not spoken by God; the prophet has declared it falsely" (Deuteronomy 18:21,22).[23] From this, the converse can also be learned; a prophecy that does come true is authentic.[24]

8:14   Therefore, if a person who is worthy of prophecy accurately predicts a future event, he is assumed to be a true prophet. However, if even the most minor detail of his prophecy fails to occur as predicted, then his prophecy is definitely false.[25]

8:15   This, however, is only true if the prophet predicts something good or neutral. In being tested, a prophet therefore will predict something good, since if such a prophecy is truly from God, then it is irrevocable.[26] It is thus

20. See above, 8:7.
21. *Moreh Nevukhim* 2:29; *Tosefoth Yom Tov, Avoth* 5:6. Cf. *Tosafoth Sanhedrin* 89b, s.v. *Eliahu, Yevamoth* 90b, s.v. *VeLiGemor.*
22. The last such miracle was Purim, *Yoma* 29a, from Psalms 22:1. The fact that Chanukah occurred after prophecy had ended was what made it particularly special.
23. Rashi, Ramban, *ad loc.*
24. *Yad, Yesodey HaTorah* 10:1; *Or HaShem* 2:4:2. Cf. *Sotah* 12b.
25. *Yad, loc cit.*
26. *Shabbath* 55a; Maharatz Chajas *ad loc.; Eikhah Rabbah* 2:4; *Tanchuma, VaYereh* 13.

written, "When a prophet predicts peace, and his prophecy comes true, then it shall be known that God has sent that prophet" (Jeremiah 28:9).[27]

8:16   A prophet is never tested through a prediction of evil.[28] It is always possible for such evil to be averted by repentance and prayer.[29]

8:17   Sin can also prevent a good promise from coming true.[30] However, this only occurs when the promise is made to an individual.[31] When a prophet is being tested, if he is a true prophet, then any good prediction he makes must come true.[32]

8:18   Although it is possible that a prophet's prediction may be a lucky guess, we are still commanded to accept him as a prophet and obey him if he is otherwise worthy of prophecy. We obey a prophet, not because we have no doubt of the veracity of his word, but because we are commanded to heed him if certain conditions are fulfilled. This is similar to the commandment that a court of law must believe the testimony of two witnesses, even though they have no actual proof that their testimony is true.[33]

8:19   In all such cases, we can act only on the basis of what we can see. It is thus written, "Secret things are for God our

27. *Yad, Yesodey HaTorah* 10:4 (end). Cf. *Tanchuma, VaYereh* 13; *Yalkut Shimoni* 2:308.
28. *Yerushalmi, Sanhedrin* 11:5 (56b); *Tanchuma, VaYereh* 13; Rashi, Mahari Kara, Radak on Jeremiah 28:7.
29. *Yad, Yesodey HaTorah* 10:4. Cf. Jonah 3:10, 2 Kings 20:1-6; Yoma 73b; Radal on *Pirkey Rabbi Eliezer* 10:4.
30. *Berakhoth* 4a; *Midrash Tehillim* 27:7; *Yalkut Shimoni* 1:131, 2:168, 2:706.
31. Maharsha and *Tzion LeNefesh Chayah* on *Berakhoth* 4a; Rambam, Introduction to Mishneh; *Akedath Yitzchak* 96 (63b). Cf. *Bereshith Rabbah* 77:2.
32. *Or HaShem* 2:4:2; *Lechem Mishneh* on *Yad, Yesodey HaTorah* 10:4.
33. *Yad, Yesodey HaTorah* 7:7. A prophet and his sign are considered as two witnesses; therefore, some authorities maintain that two prophets can attest to each other's veracity without any other sign; *Yerushalmi, Sanhedrin* 11:6 (57b); *Yeffeh Mareh ad loc.*

Lord, but revealed things are for us and our children forever, to observe all the words of this Torah" (Deuteronomy 29:28).[34]

8:20   When a prophet provides a sign to individuals, he must only be accepted by those who witness the sign.[35]

8:21   However, for a prophet to be accepted by all Israel, he must produce a sign before the Sanhedrin and be tested by them.[36]

8:22   If a prophet is examined a number[37] of times and all his predictions are found to come true, it is assumed that he is a true prophet, and he is heeded without any further sign.[38] It is thus written, "Samuel grew and God was with him, letting none of his words go unfulfilled. Then all Israel . . . knew that Samuel had been established as a prophet of God" (1 Samuel 3:18,19).[39]

8:23   If an established prophet testifies that another is a true prophet, the latter is accepted without any further test. Moses thus testified regarding Joshua, and Joshua was accepted by all Israel as a prophet before providing any sign or miracle.[40]

8:24   Once an individual is established as a prophet, he must be accepted and obeyed without any further tests. As long as

34. *Yad, Yesodey HaTorah* 7:7.
35. *Emunoth VeDeyoth* 3:4 (55b).
36. Hai Gaon, in *Teshuvoth HaGaonim (Shaarey Teshuvah)* 14. Cf. *Aggadath Bereshith* 14:4; *Yalkut Shimoni* 2:385; *Torah Temimah* on Genesis 22:2 (#5). Prophets therefore prophesied before the Sanhedrin, who recorded their words; *Targum Sheni*, Esther 4:1; see below, note 148. Moses thus began by presenting himself before the elders of Israel; Exodus 3:16, 4:29; *Mekhilta* (11a), Ramban, on Exodus 12:21. Elijah will likewise present himself before the Sanhedrin; *Eruvin* 43b; Ritva (in *Eyn Yaakov) ad loc.; Urim VeThumim* 1:2 (end).
37. Some say that he must be tested three times; *Turey Aven* on *Yad, Yesodey HaTorah* 10:2, from *Yevamoth* 64b. Moses was thus given three signs; Exodus 4:9.
38. *Sanhedrin* 89b; *Sifri* (175), Rashi, on Deuteronomy 18:22.
39. Ralbag *ad loc.; Yad, Yesodey HaTorah* 10:2; *Ikkarim* 3:8.
40. *Yad, Yesodey HaTorah* 10:5. Cf. *Yerushalmi, Sanhedrin* 11:6 (57b).

he remains worthy of prophecy, it is forbidden to suspect him of being fraudulent. It is forbidden unduly to test a prophet. The Torah thus states, "You shall not test God your Lord as you tried Him at Marah" (Deuteronomy 6:16). It was at Marah that the Israelites questioned Moses' authority as a prophet, asking, "Is God among us or not?" (Exodus 17:7).[41]

8:25   A prophet is forbidden to disregard his own prophecy, the same as every other person. Similarly, it is forbidden[42] for a prophet to withhold a public message entrusted to him by God. If a prophet does either, he is worthy of death.[43]

8:26   It is forbidden to prophesy falsely. This is included in the commandment, "You shall not bear false witness" (Exodus 20:13).[44]

8:27   An individual who falsely claims to have received a message from God is worthy of capital punishment. The same is true even if he repeats another's true prophecy as if it were his own. God thus said, "If a prophet speaks without authority in My name, when I have not commanded him to speak . . . that prophet shall die" (Deuteronomy 18:20).[45]

8:28   A person cannot be judged as a false prophet unless he is otherwise worthy of prophecy.[46] However, one should not

---

41. *Yad, Yesodey HaTorah* 10:5; *Sefer HaMitzvoth*, Negative Commandment 64; *Chinukh* 424.
42. Some say that it is punishable, but not forbidden if the prophet is willing to accept punishment. For discussion, see *Minchath Chinukh* 516. Cf. *Mekhilta* (2a) on Exodus 12:1; *Abarbanel* on Jonah 1:3; *Teshuvoth Rashba* 11; *Teshuvoth Radbaz* 842.
43. *Sanhedrin* 11:5 (89a); *Yad, Yesodey HaTorah* 9:3.
44. *Yerushalmi, Sanhedrin* 11:6 (57a); *P'nei Moshe ad loc.* See, however, *Karban HaEdah* and *Sheyarey Karban ad loc.* who have a different reading. Others derive the prohibition from the commandment, "You shall not lie" (Leviticus 19:11); *Sefer Mitzvoth Gadol*, Negative Commandment 34; *Minchath Chinukh* 317.
45. *Sanhedrin* 11:6 (89a); *Yad, Avodath Kokhavim* 5:7,8; *Sefer HaMitzvoth*, Negative Commandment 27; *Sefer Mitzvoth Gadol*, Negative Commandment 34; *Chinukh* 317.
46. *Minchath Chinukh* 317.

claim to have received a message from God, even as a jest, since it resembles false prophecy.[47]

8:29   The authority of every prophet is derived only from the Torah.[48] Therefore, no prophet can contradict a single word of the Torah, even if he produces a sign or wonder.[49]

8:30   Therefore, if a prophet attempts to contradict the Torah in any way, he is not believed, even if he performs the greatest miracles. God has warned that such signs may occur in order to test our loyalty to His teachings.[50] Any prophet who contradicts the Torah in any way is assumed to be a false prophet, and is judged accordingly.[51]

8:31   It is only in the Torah that we find divinely inspired authority binding for all times. With the completion of the Torah, such authority ceased, and no new law or commandment can be introduced prophetically. It is thus written, *"These are the commandments that God commanded Moses for the children of Israel on Mount Sinai"* (Leviticus 27:34). The revelation at Sinai had the power to impose commandments, but no other revelation can.[52]

47. *Sefer Yereyim* 241 (34); *Hagahoth Maimonioth* on Yad, *Avodath Kokhavim* 5:8 #1; Maharshal on *Sefer Mitzvoth Gadol*, Negative Commandment 34; *Minchath Chinukh* 517 (end); Radal on *Pirkey Rabbi Eliezer* 15:1; *Torath HaNevi'im, Horah Shaah* 1 (in *Kithvey Maharatz Chajas*, Jerusalem, 1958), p. 17.
48. Cf. *Mekhilta* (63b), Rashi, on Exodus 19:9.
49. *Yad, Yesodey HaTorah* 8:2. See above, 8:18.
50. Deuteronomy 13:4; Rashi *ad'loc.* See below, 8:47.
51. *Yad, Yesodey HaTorah* 18:3; Rambam, Introduction to Mishnah; *Emunoth VeDeyoth* 3:8.
52. *Targum Yonathan, Sifra* (115d), Bachya, *ad loc.*; *Shabbath* 104a; *Yoma* 80a; *Megillah* 2b; *Yerushalmi, Megillah* 1:5 (7a); *Ruth Rabbah* 4:7. This interpretation is attributed to Elazar and the prophet Samuel; *Cf.* Numbers 36:13. Although God dictated other parts of the Torah after Sinai (above, 7:25), the commandments themselves were given at Sinai; *Zevachim* 115b; Malbim on Leviticus 25:1. The oath and covenant were also made at Sinai for all the commandments; above, 5:12-16.

8:32   For a long period, however, the prophets were the guardians of the Oral Law (*Torah SheB'Al Peh*, תּוֹרָה שֶׁבְּעַל פֶּה).[53] Many laws found in their writings are hence based on traditions from Sinai.[54] Therefore, any law found in the Bible, whether in the Prophets (*Nevi'im*, נְבִיאִים) or the Writings (*Kethuvim*, כְּתוּבִים), is called a law from "words of tradition" (*divrey kabbalah*, דִּבְרֵי קַבָּלָה).[55] Such laws are binding as a law found in the Torah.[56]

8:33   Similarly, the prophets had traditions that at certain given times or under certain conditions, particular laws should be introduced.[57] In no case, however, did they introduce a law based on prophecy alone.[58]

8:34   Many prophets either headed the Sanhedrin or served as members.[59] In this capacity, they had the right to interpret laws and initiate legislation, just as any other sage.[60]

---

53. *Avoth* 1:1; *Avoth DeRabbi Nathan* 1:3; *Machzor Vitri*, Introduction to *Avoth*; Introduction to *Yad*.
54. Cf. *Taanith* 17b; *Moed Katan* 5a; *Yoma* 71b; *Sanhedrin* 22b; *Zevachim* 18b; Rashi, *Yoma* 35b, s.v. *Mesevey*; *Tosafoth, Yevamoth* 71b, s.v. *Lo, Avodah Zarah* 42a, s.v. *Tenehu*; Ramban on *Sefer HaMitzvoth, Shoresh* 2 (27b). This apparently also answers the question raised in Maharatz Chajas, *Shevuoth* 15a; cf. *Yad, Maasey Karbanoth* 2:14,15. Also see *Tosafoth, Bekhoroth* 58a, s.v. *MiPi*.
55. *Rosh HaShanah* 7a, 19a; *Bava Kama* 3b; *Chulin* 137a; *Niddah* 23a; Rashi, *Bava Kama* 2b, s.v. *Divrey Kabbalah; Machzor Vitri* on *Avoth* 1:1; Maharatz Chajas, *Taanith* 15a; *Torath HaNevi'im, Divrey Nevi'im Divrey Kabbalah*, pp. 137ff. Also see Rashi, *Taanith* 15a, s.v. *U'Kabbalah, Chulin* 137a, s.v. *Torah; Teshuvoth Chavath Yair* 9, 50; *Sedey Chemed, P'ath HaSadeh, Dalet* 25 (2:135).
56. *Rosh HaShanah* 19a; Ramban on *Sefer HaMitzvoth, Shoresh* 2 (27b); *Beth Yosef, Orach Chaim* 686; *Teshuvoth Radbaz* on *Leshanoth HaRambam* 86 (1459); *Pri Megadim*, Introduction 1:18; Maharatz Chajas, *Shabbath* 83b; *Torath HaNeviim*, p. 140. Such rules are even spoken as Torah laws; *Bekhoroth* 59a; *Eruvin* 58a, Maharatz Chajas *ad loc*. It is for this reason that hints for prophetic laws are sought in the Torah; Maharatz Chajas, *Yoma* 38b.
57. Ibn Ezra on Exodus 12:1; *Sh'nei Luchoth HaB'rith, Torah SheB'Al Peh, Tav*, s.v. *K'lal Rabanan* (3:240b). Cf. *Megillah* 14a; *Turey Aven*, Maharatz Chajas, *ad loc.*; *Yerushalmi, Megillah* 1:5 (7a); *Ruth Rabbah* 4:7. Also see *Teshuvoth Beth Ephraim, Orach Chaim* 64:66; Mizrachi on *Sefer Mitzvoth Gadol*, Laws of Megillah.
58. *Torath HaNevi'im, Divrey Nevi'im* 8, p. 144.
59. Cf. *Megillah* 17b; *Yad*, Introduction.
60. Cf. *Shabbath* 14b; *Sukkah* 44a; *Bava Kama* 82a; *Tosafoth, Bava Bathra* 147a, s.v. *Menayin*; Ramban on *Sefer HaMitzvoth, Shoresh* 2 (27b). See below, 8:38.

8:35   Although the logic or need for a law might be revealed prophetically, the law itself can only be legislated by the Sanhedrin.[61] Such a law is then binding because of the authority of the Sanhedrin[62] and not because of the authority of the prophet. The commandment to obey the word of a prophet does not give him the authority to impose permanently binding laws.[63]

8:36   A prophet, however, had the authority to impose a new law temporarily.[64] Such a decree might then be enacted as a permanent law by the Sanhedrin.[65] Nonetheless, all such laws are no different from any other rabbinical law.[66]

8:37   In giving the Torah to Israel, God established a means of authority based on human judgment and reason. It is thus written, "The commandment that I command you today . . . is not in heaven" (Deuteronomy 30:11,12). Laws are to be decided by human intellect, and not by heavenly authority.[67]

---

61. Rashash, *Megillah* 14a; cf. *Kuzari* 3:41 (50a). This may answer the question of Rashash and Maharatz Chajas on Rashi, *Sukkah* 44a, s.v. *VeYasdam*. The forgotten laws may have been restored prophetically, but they were established by the Sanhedrin. See *Torah Temimah* on Leviticus 27:34 (#216).

62. See below, 11:9, 11:24.

63. See above, note 3.

64. See below, 8:44.

65. Rash, Bertenoro, on *Yedayim* 4:3, s.v. *Maaseh*; Rashash, *Megillah* 14a.

66. Ramban on *Sefer HaMitzvoth,,* *Shoresh* 2 (27b); *Mishneh LaMelekh* on *Yad, Megillah* 1:11. See above, note 56. Thus, if a law is known to a prophet from tradition, it can be a Torah law, just as other laws known from the Oral Tradition (*halakhah le-Moshe mi-Sinai*, הֲלָכָה לְמשֶׁה מִסִּינַי). If it is legislated, on the other hand, it is no different than any other rabbinical law. Cf. *Torath HaNevi'im, Divrey Nevi'im* 7, pp. 162ff.

67. *Bava Metzia* 59b; *Temurah* 16a; *Devarim Rabbah* 8:6; Rashi, *Shabbath* 108a, s.v. *Mai*; *Yad, Yesodey HaTorah* 9:1.

8:38   Therefore, no question of Torah law can be decided on the basis of prophecy,[68] Divine Inspiration,[69] heavenly voices,[70] the Urim and Thumim,[71] dreams,[72] or any other supernatural phenomenon.[73] Where a question of law is concerned, a prophet is no better[74] and no worse[75] than any other sage.[76]

8:39   Many secret things were revealed to prophets.[77] Therefore, a prophet can always decide in a question of fact or circumstance, even when such a decision may be used in a question of Torah law.[78] Hence, a heavenly voice can verify

68. However, there are indications that Elijah will decide questions of Torah law; cf. Rashi, *Chulin* 36a, s.v. *LeOlam*. Likewise, some say that the etymology of the word *teku* (תֵּיקוּ) is an acrostic of *Tishbi ye-taretz kushioth ve-ibayoth* (תִּשְׁבִּי יְתָרֵץ קוּשְׁיוֹת וְאִיבַּעְיוֹת), "The Tishbite (Elijah) will answer difficulties and questions;" *Sh'nei Luchoth HaB'rith, Torah SheB'Al Peh, Tav* (3:239a). However, the decisions that he will make will be made rationally rather than prophetically; *Torath HaNevi'im* 2, p. 17ff. See note 76.
69. Cf. Maharatz Chajas, *Sotah* 4b.
70. *Berakhoth* 42; *Eruvin* 7a; *Pesachim* 114a; *Bava Metzia* 59b; *Chulin* 44a; *Yevamoth* 14a; *Tosafoth ad loc.* s.v. *Rabbi*. See note 79.
71. Rashi, *Eruvin* 45b, s.v. *Harey*.
72. The logic behind a law, however, can be revealed in a dream; Rabbi Reuven Margolies, Introduction to *She'eloth U'Teshuvoth Min HaShamayim* 2 (p. 6ff). Cf. *Hagahoth Ashri, Avodah Zaruh* 2:41, s.v. *Rashbam; Tashbatz Katan* 352; *Teshuvoth Tashbatz* 2:159 (end).
73. Cf. *Kesef Mishneh, Tumath Tzaraath* 2:9; Maharatz Chajas, *Bava Metzia* 84b; *Torath HaNevi'im*, pp. 12, 17, 20.
74. Rambam, Introduction to Mishneh. Cf. *Chulin* 124a.
75. Maharatz Chajas, *Berakhoth* 3a, *Bava Metzia* 114a. Cf. *Menachoth* 42a; *Bekhoroth* 22a.
76. However, the logic can be revealed prophetically, and such logic can be used to decide law where no other course is available; Chida, *Shem HaGedolim Yod* 224; *Devash LePhi, Nun* 12; Rabbi Reuven Margolies, Introduction to *She'eloth U'Teshuvoth Min HaShamayim* 1; Rabbi Aaron Marcus, Introduction to *Keseth HaSofer* on *She'eloth U'Teshuvoth Min HaShamayim* (Tel Aviv, 1957).
77. Cf. 1 Samuel 9:6 ff.
78. *Yevamoth* 41b; *Shabbath* 108a; *Tosafoth, Yevamoth* 99b, s.v. *VeAin; Mishneh LaMelekh* on *Yad, Ishuth* 9:6 (end). Also see *Chulin* 5a; Maharatz Chajas *ad loc.*; *Pesachim* 34a; *Teshuvoth Beth Yaakov* 129. However, if a law has been legislated because of a question of fact, a prophet cannot violate it merely because he knows the truth and to him there is no question; *Yevamoth* 41b.

that a sage is greater in wisdom and Torah knowledge, even though this will imply that his opinion must be followed in cases of law.[79]

8:40   In some cases, a monetary case can be settled prophetically.[80] This is because the manner of judgment is entirely up to the litigants.[81]

8:41   In general, however, God has promised that He will never send a prophet to add, subtract, or change any commandment in the Torah. He will also never grant a prophetic vision to interpret a law differently than set forth in tradition, or to render a decision in Torah law. Therefore, any prophet who claims to do any of these things must be assumed to be a false prophet, and is judged accordingly.[82]

8:42   The prophet said in God's name, "Behold, in days to come, I will make a new covenant with the house of Israel" (Jeremiah 31:31). This is not speaking of a new testament or law, but to a renewal of devotion to the teachings of the Torah. The prophet thus concludes in God's name, "But this is the covenant that I will make with the house of Israel . . . I will place My Torah within them, and I will write it in their hearts" (Jeremiah 31:33).[83]

79. Or Sameach on Yad, Yesodey HaTorah 9:4. Cf. Tosafoth, Bava Metzia 59b, s.v. Lo, Yevamoth 14a, s.v. Rabbi.
80. Tosafoth, Niddah 50a, s.v. Kol, Bava Kama 15a, s.v. Asher; Maharatz Chajas ad loc., and on Bava Metzia 84b. Some say, however, that Deborah was a special instance; Beer HaGolah, Choshen Mishpat 7:10. See Reuven Margolies, Introduction to She'eloth U'Teshuvoth Min HaShamayim, page 4, note 10.
81. Sanhedrin 3:2 (24a); Yad, Sanhedrin 7:2; Choshen Mishpat 22:1.
82. Yad, Yesodey HaTorah 9:1,4; cf. Sanhedrin 90a; Tosefta, Sanhedrin 14:4. The founder of Christianity sought to abrogate such important commandments as the Sabbath, the dietary laws, and the laws of divorce, as well as to add numerous commandments to the Torah. It was primarily for this reason that the Jewish people refused to accept him as a prophet or a man of God, despite his miracles. Regarding such teachings, it is written, "He will speak words against the Most High, and he will wear down the saints of the Most High, attempting to change the seasons and the Law" (Daniel 7:25); Iggereth Teimon (in Iggeroth HaRambam), p. 10.
83. Radak, Abarbanel, ad loc.; Emunoth VeDeyoth 3:8 (60a).

8:43   The main message of all the prophets was that we keep the commandments as presented in the Torah.[84] God's last words to His prophets were, "Remember the Torah of Moses My servant, which I commanded him at Horeb (Sinai) for all Israel, decrees and laws" (Malachi 3:22).[85]

8:44   Although a prophet cannot permanently abrogate any law or commandment of the Torah, he can do so temporarily in a specific instance, or for a given time.[86] Regarding a prophet, the Torah states, "you must listen to him" (Deuteronomy 18:15), and this is true even if he gives instructions to violate a commandment temporarily.[87] In such a case, however, the prophet must have a logical reason for suspending a law of the Torah.[88]

8:45   Therefore, for example, if a prophet gives instructions to violate a single Sabbath for a specific reason, he must be obeyed. But if he claims to have received a revelation that the Sabbath is no longer to be kept at all, he is repealing a Torah law and is definitely a false prophet.[89]

8:46   The laws associated with idolatry, however, cannot be abrogated even for an instant. Therefore, if a prophet gives instructions to worship a false god in any manner, or to

84. *Beth Elohim, Shaar HaYesodoth* 24. See Joshua 1:7,8, 8:32, 8:34, 23:6, 24:26, 1 Kings 2:3, 2 Kings 10:31, 14:6, 17:13, 17:34, 17:37, Isaiah 1:10, 5:24, 30:9, Jeremiah 8:8, Hosea 4:6, Amos 2:4, Malachi 3:22, Psalms 1:2, 18:8, 37:31, 119:1, Daniel 9:11, 9:13, Ezra 3:2, 7:6, 7:10, Nehemiah 8:2-14, 10:30-37, 1 Chronicles 16:40, 22:12, 2 Chronicles 1:21, 17:9, 23:18, 25:4, 31:3, 31:21, 35:26, 30:16.
85. *Yad, Yesodey HaTorah* 9:2. Cf. *Devarim Rabbah* 8:6.
86. Cf. *Sanhedrin* 90a; *Lechem Mishneh* on *Yad, Yesodey HaTorah* 9:1. Also see *Yerushalmi, Taanith* 2:8 (11a); *Yerushalmi, Megillah* 1:11 (16b); *BaMidbar Rabbah* 22:6; *Yad, Maasey Karbanoth* 2:14,15.
87. *Yevamoth* 90b; *Yad, Yesodey HaTorah* 9:3.
88. *Tosafoth, Sanhedrin* 89b, s.v. *Eliahu, Yevamoth* 90b, s.v. *VeLiG'mor*. However, other sources give a different answer; *Tosafoth Yeshenim,* ibid. See *Torath HaNevi'im, Horah Shaah* 3, p. 23ff. For the prophet himself, however, no reason is needed; *Ibid.* 4, p. 29ff.
89. Cf. *Yad, Yesodey HaTorah* 9:3.

accept any mediator between God and man, even for a single instance, he is not obeyed. This is true even if he tries to use the greatest wonders and miracles to verify his prophecy.[90]

8:47   Although God may allow such a false prophet to perform miracles, He is merely testing us. It is thus written, "If there shall arise among you a prophet or a prophetic dreamer, and he produces for you a sign or miracle, saying 'Let us follow another god and worship him.' . . . Even if the sign or miracle that he predicted comes true, do not heed the words of that prophet or prophetic dreamer. God your Lord is merely testing you, to see if you really love God your Lord with all your heart and with all your soul" (Deuteronomy 13:2-4).[91]

8:48   A prophet who attempts to lead any people to idolatry is guilty of a capital offense. The Torah thus continues, "That prophet or prophetic dreamer shall be put to death; he has uttered falsehood against God your Lord" (Deuteronomy 13:6).[92]

8:49   It is forbidden to prophesy in the name of any false deity or idol. This is included in the commandment, "You shall not mention the name of other gods" (Exodus 23:13).[93]

8:50   A prophet who claims to be sent by any power or deity other than God, even to uphold the Torah, is guilty of a

90. *Sanhedrin* 90a; *Yad, Yesodey HaTorah* 9:5.
91. Rashi, Ibn Ezra, Ramban, *ad loc.*
92. See note 90. Also see *Sanhedrin* 7:10 (67a); *Yad, Avodath Kokhavim* 5:1; *Lechem Mishnah ad loc.; Minchath Chinukh* 518.
93. *Yad, Avodath Kokhavim* 5:6; *Sefer HaMitzvoth,* Negative Commandment 26; *Sefer Mitzvoth Gadol,* Negative Commandment 32; *Chinukh* 518. See Rabbi Yehudah Rosanes, *Derekh Mitzvothekha* (on *Sefer HaMitzvoth*), Part 2, #1 (at end of Vilna edition of Sefer HaMitzvoth).

capital offense.94 It is thus written "The prophet who speaks in the name of other gods, that prophet shall die" (Deuteronomy 18:20).95

8:51   It is forbidden to dispute with such a prophet, or even ask him for a sign. If he produces a sign on his own, it is forbidden to believe it or even pay any attention to it. It is thus written, "You shall not heed the words of such a prophet" (Deuteronomy 13:4).96

8:52   The most usual reason that God sends a prophet is to admonish the people to keep the Torah.99 A prophet may also reveal God's will regarding questions not involving Torah law, such as waging a war or building a city.100

8:53   There are some prerogatives which are reserved for a prophet alone. Thus, only a prophet, together with the Sanhedrin,101 a king, and the Urim and Thumim,102 can add to the area sanctified for Jerusalem or the Temple.103 They were thus needed for the building of the first Temple.104

94. However, if the prophet says to worship God, he is innocent; Ramban on Deuteronomy 18:20.
95. *Sifri, Rashi, ad loc.; Sanhedrin* 11:6 (89a); *Yad, Avodath Kokhavim* 5:6.
96. Sforno *ad loc.; Yad, Avodath Kokhavim* 5:7; *Sefer HaMitzvoth*, Negative Commandment 28; *Sefer Mitzvoth Gadol*, Negative Commandment 33; *Chinukh* 456. Others, however, count this as another warning against idolatry, and not as a separate commandment; Ramban on *Sefer HaMitzvoth*, Negative Commandment 28; *Minchath Chinukh* 456; *Mishnath Chakhamim* 29.
99. Cf. *Pesikta* 13 (112a); *Yalkut Shimoni* 1:919, 2:256, 2:999; Abarbanel, Introduction to Jeremiah. See note 84.
100. *Yad, Yesodey HaTorah* 9:2; Rambam, Introduction to Mishnah.
101. *Sanhedrin* 1:5 (2a); *Yad, Sanhedrin* 5:1.
102. Some write that a voluntary war (*milkhemeth reshuth,* מִלְחָמָת רְשׁוּת) requires the permission of the Urim and Thumim, as well as the Sanhedrin; *Tosafoth, Shevuoth* 15a, s.v. *SheAin;* cf. *Berakhoth* 3a, *Sanhedrin* 16a. Others, however, require only the Sanhedrin; *Yad, Melakhim* 2:2.
103. *Shevuoth* 2:2 (14a); *Yad, Beth HaBechirah* 6:11, from Exodus 25:8,9. See *Tosafoth, Shevuoth* 15a, s.v. *SheAin.*
104. Cf. *Sifri, Yalkut Shimoni* (869), Ramban, on Deuteronomy 12:5, from 2 Samuel 24:18.

Once the area was sanctified, however, the Temple could be built without them.[105]

8:54   Similarly, only a prophet, together with the Sanhedrin,[106] can appoint a king over Israel, where the king will have all the prerogatives prescribed by the Torah.[107] The Torah thus states, "You shall appoint a king over you, whom God your Lord shall choose" (Deuteronomy 17:15). This indicates that a king must be designated prophetically.[108] This is one reason why the Messiah, who will reign as a king over Israel, will be preceded by the prophet Elijah.[109]

8:55   Although many words of prophecy were spoken and written, only those required for all future generations were recorded in the Bible.[110]

8:56   Besides this, the writings of other prophets were also preserved for a time.[111] Some of these were preserved mainly to be consulted by kings.[112] Since these did not contain any message for the populace at large, they were not preserved.[113] This decision was made by the Great Assembly.[114]

---

105. *Shevuoth* 16a; *Yad, Beth HaBechirah* 6:16.
106. *Tosefta, Sanhedrin* 3:2; *Yad, Sanhedrin* 5:1.
107. See Rabbi Yehudah Gershoni (Gerodner), *Mishpat HaMelukhah* on *Yad, Melakhim* 1:3 (New York, 1950).
108. *Sifri, Ramban,* ad loc.; *Yad Melakhim* 1:3. Some say that a king can also be chosen through the Urim and Thumim; Ramban, *loc. cit.*
109. Malachi 3:23; *Eruvin* 43b; *Yad, Melakhim* 12:2; *Teshuvoth Chatham Sofer* 6:98.
110. *Megillah* 14a. See Chapter 6, note 241.
111. Rashi on 2 Chronicles 12:15; Radak, Abarbanel, on 1 Kings 11:41. Also see 2 Chronicles 9:29, 13:22, 20:34, 24:17, 33:19. Besides these, there were also written chronicles of the kings of Judah and Israel; Abarbanel, Introduction to Kings; cf. 1 Kings 14:29, 15:7, 15:23, 15:31, 16:5, 16:27, 16:29, 22:39, 22:46, 2 Kings 1:18, 8:23, 10:34, 12:20, 13:8, 13:8, 13:12, 14:15, 14:28, 15:6, 15:11, 15:21, 15:31, 15:36 16:19, 20:20, 21:17, 21:25, 23:28, 24:5; 1 Chronicles 9:1, 2 Chronicles 16:11, 25:26, 27:7, 28:26, 35:27, 36:8.
112. Radak on 2 Chronicles 13:22; Ralbag on 2 Chronicles 24:27. Such books were called a *midrash* (מִדְרָשׁ). Cf. *Shekalim* 6:6.
113. Ibn Ezra on Esther 9:32; Ralbag on 2 Chronicles 24:27; *Metzudoth* on 1 Chronicles 9:29.
114. *Sefer Chasidim* 1016. See below, 8:61.

8:57   The Bible is therefore a collection of all inspired writings that God meant to be read and studied for all times.[115] It contains all prophecies that have a message for all future generations. It also includes important historical events, which were recorded prophetically,[116] so that they would teach a lesson for all times.[117]

8:58   The Bible is divided into three major parts: The Torah (תּוֹרָה), the Prophets (*Nevi'im*, נְבִיאִים), and the Writings or Hagiographa (*Kethuvim*, כְּתוּבִים).[118] It is often referred to as the *Tenakh* (תָּנָ"ךְ), an abbreviation of these three words.

8:59   The Torah was dictated to Moses by God. The Prophets were revealed prophetically, as their name suggests. The Writings were written through Divine Inspiration, without prophetic vision.[119]

8:60   The Bible consists of 24 books.[120] Of these, five are in the Torah, eight in the Prophets, and eleven in the Writings.

8:61   The Bible was set in its final form by the Great Assembly (*Kenesseth HaGedolah*, כְּנֶסֶת הַגְּדוֹלָה), under the guidance of Ezra,[121] shortly before prophecy ceased to exist.[122] The Great

115. Cf. *Midrash Tehillim* 1:8 (5a); *Yalkut Shimoni* 2:613, 2:678, from Psalms 19:15; *Sefer Chasidim* 1015.
116. Cf. *VaYikra Rabbah* 34:9.
117. Abarbanel, Introduction to Joshua, Samuel.
118. Cf. *Shabbath* 88a; *Rosh HaShanah* 32a; *Tosefta, Rosh HaShanah* 2:10; *Megillah* 21b, 31a, *Taanith* 31a; *Moed Katan* 21a; *Kiddushin* 49a; *Makkoth* 10b; *Sanhedrin* 90b; 101a; *Bekhoroth* 50a; *VaYikra Rabbah* 16:4; *Devarim Rabbah* 8:3; *Tanchuma, Yithro* 10; *Pesikta* 12 (105a).
119. Cf. *Moreh Nevukhim* 2:45, Second Level; above, 6:28. Cf. *Megillah* 7a; *Tosefta, Yadayim* 2:6. Also see *Maaseh Ephod*, Introduction; Abarbanel, Introduction to Joshua. See *Chidushey HaGriz* 3:235.
120. Cf. *Taanith* 8a; *Targum* on Song of Songs 5:10; *BaMidbar Rabbah* 14:14 (end).
121. Ibn Ezra on Esther 9:27, quoted in *Beth Yosef, Orach Chaim* 690.
122. *Sefer Chasidim* 1016; Rashi, *Bava Bathra* 15a, s.v. *Kathvu*.

Assembly consisted of 120 elders,[123] including the last of the prophets,[124] under the leadership of Ezra.[125]

8:62   The Bible is now a closed canon, to which nothing can be added or subtracted.[126] It is thus written, "Every word of God is true . . . you shall not add to His words" (Proverbs 30:5,6).[127]

8:63   The Torah consists of five books. They were all written by Moses as dictated by God.[128]

8:64   The Prophets consist of eight books. They are:[129]

1. Joshua	*Yeshoshua*	יְהוֹשֻׁעַ
2. Judges	*Shoftim*	שׁוֹפְטִים
3. Samuel (1&2)	*Shmuel*	שְׁמוּאֵל
4. Kings (1&2)	*Melakhim*	מְלָכִים
5. Isaiah[130]	*Yishiahu*	יְשַׁעְיָהוּ
6. Jeremiah	*Yirmiahu*	יִרְמְיָהוּ
7. Ezekiel	*Yechezkel*	יְחֶזְקֵאל
8. The Twelve	*Trey Asar*	תְּרֵי עָשָׂר

123. *Megillah* 17b; Bertenoro on *Avoth* 1:1. For the significance of this number, see *Sanhedrin* 1:6 (2b), 17b. However, only 85 members were in the Great Assembly when it included Esther in the Biblical canon; *Yerushalmi, Megillah* 1:5 (6b). *Cf.* Nehemiah 10:2-28; Malbim ad loc.; *Yerushalmi, Chagigah* 3:8 (22a).
124. Cf. *Targum* on Song of Songs 7:3; Rashi, Bertenoro on *Avoth* 1:1; Rashi, *Bava Bathra* 15a, s.v. *Anshey.* See Ezra 2:2, Nehemiah 7:7.
125. Some say that this was the Sanhedrin led by Ezra; *Yad,* Introduction. See below, Chapter 10, note 9.
126. *BaMidbar Rabbah* 14:14 (end); Maharatz Chajas, *Megillah* 7a Cf. *Tosefta, Yadayim* 2:5.
127. *Sefer Chasidim* 1016. Cf. *Koheleth Rabbah* 12:13.
128. See above, 7:20.
129. *Bava Bathra* 14b; *Yad, Sefer Torah* 7:15; *Yoreh Deah* 283:5.
130. In *Bava Bathra* 14b, however, Isaiah is after Jeremiah and Ezekiel. Current editions of the Bible, nevertheless, have Isaiah first, and the first editions of the Hebrew Bible were printed this way. See Radak, introduction to Jeremiah; Rabbi Eliahu Bachur, *Mesoreth HaMesoreth* (Venice, 1538), p. 19; Abarbanel, Introduction to Isaiah.

8:65   The twelve minor prophets are:

1.	Hosea	*Hoshea*	הוֹשֵׁעַ
2.	Joel	*Yoel*	יוֹאֵל
3.	Amos	*Amos*	עָמוֹס
4.	Obadiah	*Ovadiah*	עוֹבַדְיָה
5.	Jonah	*Yonah*	יוֹנָה
6.	Micah	*Mikhah*	מִיכָה
7.	Nahum	*Nachum*	נַחוּם
8.	Habakkuk	*Chabakkuk*	חֲבַקּוּק
9.	Zephaniah	*Tzephaniah*	צְפַנְיָה
10.	Haggai	*Chaggai*	חַגַּי
11.	Zechariah	*Zekhariah*	זְכַרְיָה
12.	Malachi	*Malachi*	מַלְאָכִי or מַלְאָכִי

8:66   The Writings consist of eleven books:[131]

1.	Psalms[132]	*Tehillim*	תְּהִלִּים
2.	Proverbs[133]	*Mishley*	מִשְׁלֵי
3.	Job	*Iyyov*	אִיּוֹב
4.	Song of Songs[134]	*Shir HaShirim*	שִׁיר הַשִּׁירִים
5.	Ruth[135]	*Ruth*	רוּת
6.	Lamentations	*Eikhah*	אֵיכָה
7.	Ecclesiastes	*Koheleth*	קֹהֶלֶת

---

131. See note 129. The order given there, however, is Ruth, Psalms, Job, Proverbs, Ecclesiastes, Song of Songs, Lamentations, Daniel, Esther, Ezra (Nehemiah), Chronicles. In general, the order there is chronological. The order given in our text is that found in all printed editions. It is found in the earliest printed editions of the Hebrew Bible; Soncino, 1488; Naples, 1491-93; Brescia, 1492-94; Venice, 1517; Venice, 1524-25.
132. In *Bava Bathra* 14b, Ruth is first, since she was before David, the author of the Psalms.
133. In *Bava Bathra* 14b, Job precedes Proverbs. This is because the author of Job was Moses, and it should be the first book, but we do not begin with tragedy. Moreover, this might follow the opinion that Job was in the time of the Queen of Sheba; Rashi *ad loc.*
134. In *Bava Bathra* 14b, Ecclesiastes is before Song of Songs. This is because Song of Songs was written in Solomon's old age; Rashi *ad loc.* See below, note 175.
135. In *Bava Bathra*, Ruth is first. See below, note 180.

8. Esther[136]	*Esther*	אֶסְתֵּר
9. Daniel	*Daniel*	דָּנִיֵּאל
10. Ezra and	*Ezra*	עֶזְרָא
Nehemiah	*Nechemiah*	נְחֶמְיָה
11. Chronicles (1&2)	*Divrey HaYamim*	דִּבְרֵי הַיָּמִים

8:67   The Book of Joshua was written by Joshua.[137] However, the verses which tell of Joshua's death (Joshua 23:20-32), as well as the death of Elazar (Joshua 24:33) were written by Pinchas.[138]

8:68   The Book of Judges was written by the prophet Samuel.[139]

8:69   The first part of the Book of Samuel until his death (1 Samuel 25:1) was written by Samuel.[140] The rest of 1 Samuel and all of 2 Samuel were written by the prophets Gad and Nathan.[141] It is thus written, "The acts of David . . . are written in the words of Samuel the seer, the words of Nathan the prophet, and the words of Gad the seer" (1 Chronicles 29:29).[142]

136. In *Bava Bathra*, Esther is after Daniel, following the chronological order. In printed editions, however, the five Megilloth are presented in the order in which they are read on the festivals.

> Song of Songs—Passover
> Ruth—Shavuoth
> Lamentations—Tisha B'Av
> Ecclesiastes—Shemini Azereth
> Esther—Purim

137. *Bava Bathra* 14b. Some say that it was redacted by Samuel; Abarbanel, Introduction to Joshua. Also see Abarbanel on Joshua 24:26.
138. *Bava Bathra* 15a. We interpret the Talmud's second answer that it was written by Pinchas as a rejection of the first answer, that the portion after Joshua's death was written by Elazar. One reason for this is because Elazar is not counted among the prophets whose words were preserved; see Table 6:1. Some sources, however, do count Elazar in this list; *Turey Aven*, Maharatz Chajas, *Megillah* 14a.
139. *Bava Bathra* 14b. Cf. Radak on Judges 21:25.
140. *Bava Bathra* 14b; Radak on 1 Samuel 9:9. Some say that it was redacted by Jeremiah; Abarbanel, Introduction to Joshua. Also see Abarbanel on 1 Samuel 9:9.
141. *Bava Bathra* 15a. See Table 6:1, notes 6,7. Although majority was written by Gad and Nathan, it is named after Samuel; Abarbanel, Introduction to Samuel.
142. Cf. Ralbag *ad loc.* Others write that they wrote separate books that were later lost; *Metzudoth David ad loc.* Also see Rashi *ad loc.* See above, note 111.

8:70   The two books of Kings were written by the prophet Jeremiah.[143] Some of this included material that had been written by earlier prophets.[144]

8:71   The book of Isaiah was written by the school of King Hezekiah.[145] It was customary for the prophets to write down their prophecies shortly before their death[146] just as Moses had done.[147] However, their public prophecies were declared before the Sanhedrin and recorded by them.[148] Since Isaiah was murdered by King Menasseh,[149] he did not have a chance to set his prophecies in writing.[150] This was later done by the Sanhedrin which had been established by King Hezekiah, and which functioned for many years after his death.[151]

8:72   The book of Jeremiah was written by Jeremiah.[152] It was completed by the Great Assembly.[153]

---

143. *Bava Bathra* 15a; cf. *Tosafoth ad loc.* s.v. *Yirmiahu.* But see Abarbanel, Introduction to Samuel (Jerusalem, 1955), p. 162.
144. *Cf.* 2 Chronicles 35:25; Abarbanel on 1 Kings 11:41; Introduction to Kings (p. 428).
145. *Bava Bathra* 15a. See below, note 178. Regarding questions of authorship, see Ibn Ezra on Isaiah 40:1.
146. Rashi, *Bava Bathra* 15a, s.v. *Kathvu.*
147. Deuteronomy 31:9; see above, 7:32. Also see Joshua 24:26; *Tanchuma, Tetzaveh* 9.
148. See above, note 36. The Sanhedrin had recording scribes; *Yad, Sanhedrin* 1:2; *Sanhedrin* 17b.
149. *Yevamoth* 49b.
150. Rashi, *Bava Bathra* 15a, s.v. *Kathvu.*
151. *Tosafoth, Bava Bathra* 15a, s.v. *Chizkiahu.* Cf. Abarbanel, Introduction to Joshua, p. 10.
152. *Bava Bathra* 15a.
153. Abarbanel on Jeremiah 51:64. Some authorities ask how Jeremiah could have completed his book, since scripture cannot be written outside the Holy Land, and Jeremiah was exiled to Egypt (Jeremiah 43:7), and did not return; *Tosafoth, Bava Bathra* 15a, s.v. *Perush HaKuntres.* Some say that the last chapters were written by Barukh ben Neriah; Rabbi Yaakov Emden (Maharibatz) *ad loc.*; Table 6:1, note 34. However, Barukh accompanied Jeremiah to Egypt (Jeremiah 43:7), and died in exile; *Koheleth Rabbah* 12:8; quoted in Rashi on Ecclesiastes 12:6; *Shir HaShirim Rabbah* 5:4; quoted in Rashi, *Megillah* 16b, s.v. *SheKol.* The one who completed the final chapters may have been Seriah, Jeremiah 51:50-61; Table 6:1, note 36. Seriah did return with Ezra; Ezra 2:2. Other sources seem to indicate that Jeremiah did return to the Holy Land; Rashi on Jeremiah 44:14. Other sources state that he

8:73   Although under certain conditions prophecy could be received in other lands,[154] no prophecy or other scripture could be published outside the Holy Land.[155] Therefore, since Ezekiel lived outside the Holy Land, he did not publish his prophecies. They were preserved by the Sanhedrin and finally published by the Great Assembly.[156]

8:74   The Twelve Minor Prophets (Hosea, Joel, Obadiah, Jonah, Micah, Nahum, Habakkuk, Zephaniah, Haggai, Zechariah, and Malachi) were first published in a single scroll by the Great Assembly.[157] Each of these books was so small that they would have been lost if published separately.[158]

8:75   King David published the Psalms.[159] A number, however, had been transmitted from earlier generations.[160] There is a tradition that the Psalms were published by ten elders:[161]

went from Egypt to Babylon; *Seder Olam* 26. He would have then passed through the Holy Land.

154. Above, 6:45.
155. Rashi, *Bava Bathra* 15a, s.v. *Kathvu Yechezkel.*
156. *Ibid.* It could have been written, as in the case of Esther (below, 8:80), but not published as scripture. There was a question as to whether Ezekiel should be included in the canon; *Shabbath* 13b; *Chagigah* 13a; *Menachoth* 45a.
157. Rashi, *Bava Bathra* 15a, s.v. *Kathvu Yechezkel.*
158. *Ibid.* Cf. *Bava Bathra* 14b.
159. *Bava Bathra* 14b; *Pesachim* 117a; Rashi on Psalms 72:20. Regarding Psalm 137, which speaks of the exile, some say that it was written prophetically; *Gittin* 57b; *Midrash Tehillim* 137:1; *Yalkut Shimoni* 2:883. Others, however, maintain that it was written during the exile; Ibn Ezra, Introduction to Psalms, and on Psalm 137:1. It may have been written by Ezra; see note 163.
160. Cf. *Shir HaShirim Rabbah* 4:3; *Koheleth Rabbah* 7:39; *Midrash Tehillim* 1:6. For a discussion whether the Psalms were written prophetically, see Ibn Ezra, Introduction to Psalms; *Moreh Nevukhim* 2:45, Second Level.
161. *Bava Bathra* 14b; Radak, Introduction to Psalms. Although the Talmud does not count David himself among the ten, other sources include him; *Shir HaShirim Rabbah* 4:3; *Koheleth Rabbah* 7:39; *Midrash Tehillim* 1:6; Rashi on Psalms 1:1. The same sources also count Solomon as the author of Psalm 72; cf Targum on Psalm 72:1; *Tosafoth, Bava Bathra* 15a, s.v. *VeAl.* Other sources, however, state that this psalm was written by David for Solomon; Rashi, Ibn Ezra, Radak, on Psalms 72:1; cf. *Tosafoth, loc. cit.* Also see Malbim on Psalms 72:20.

1. Adam	Psalms 92[162]
2. Malchi-tzedek[163]	Psalms 110[164]
3. Abraham	Psalms 89[165]
4. Moses	Psalms 90-100[166]
5. Heman[167]	Psalms 88[168]
6. Yeduthun[169]	Psalms 39,62,77
7. Asaph[170]	Psalms 50,73-83
8. Assir ben Korach[171]	Psalms 42,49,78,84,85,88
9. Elkanah ben Korach	Same
10. Aviassaph ben Korach	Same

162. Rabbenu Gershom, *Bava Bathra* 14b; cf. *Targum* on Psalm 92:1; *Koheleth Rabbah* 1:3; *Yalkut Shimoni* 2:843; *Zohar* 2:138a; Radak, Introduction to Psalms. However, this is also among the Psalms written by Moses; see note 166; *Sefer Chasidim* 355, 356. This may be the reason that Rashi does not count this as the Psalm written by Adam, but substitutes Psalm 139:16; cf. *Sanhedrin* 38b. There is an opinion, however, that Psalm 92 was written by Adam, forgotten, and then restored prophetically by Moses; *Bereshith Rabbah* 22:28; *Pirkey Rabbi Eliezer* 19(44a). Other sources omit Psalm 92 from the list of Psalms written by Moses; *Pesikta* 31 (198a).

163. Malchi-tzedek is omitted in *Shir HaShirim Rabbah* 4:3; *Koheleth Rabbah* 7:39. In his place, Ezra is listed among the ten. A number of commentators write that this is an error, and substitute Malchi-tzedek; *Yeffeh Kol*; Radal; *Etz Yosef*; ad loc. However, Ezra may have been the author of Psalm 137; see above, note 159.

164. Cf. Psalm 110:4; Ibn Ezra, Radak, on Psalms 110:1.

165. Cf. *Targum*, Rashi, Radak, on Psalms 89:1.

166. *Midrash Tehillim* 90:3, *Yalkut Shimoni* 1:990; *Pesikta* 31 (198a). However, the *Pesikta* omits Psalm 92 and substitutes Psalm 33; see above, note 162.

167. Omitted in *Midrash Tehillim* 1:6; Rashi on Psalms 1:1. The Heman of 1 Kings 5:11 is identified with Moses, but the Talmud states that a second Heman wrote Psalm 88; *Bava Bathra* 15a. It is possible, however, that the *Midrash Tehillim* disputes this answer and omits Heman, considering him identical with Moses. Heman is included in the lists of *Shir HaShirim Rabbah* 4:3; *Koheleth Rabbah* 7:39. See Table 6:1, note 9.

168. See Rashi, Radak, Ibn Ezra, on Psalms 88:1.

169. Rav counts him as the prophetic singer (see Table 6:1, note 10); *Shir HaShirim Rabbah* 4:3; *Koheleth Rabbah* 7:39; *Midrash Tehillim* 1:6. This opinion is shared by the Talmud, *Bava Bathra* 14b; *Targum* on Psalms 39:1, 62:1, 77:1; Rashi, Ibn Ezra on Psalms 39:1; Ibn Ezra, Radak on Psalms 62:1. Rabbi Yochanan, however, holds that *Yeduthun* is a common noun referring to judgment; cf. Rashi on Psalms 1:1, 77:1; Hirsch on Psalms 39:1. Other sources indicate that the *yeduthun* (ידותן) is a musical instrument; Rashi on Psalms 62:1; *Metzudath Tzion* on Psalms 39:1.

170. Rabbi Yochanan identifies Asaph with Aviassaph ben Korach, while Rav counts him as a separate individual; *Shir HaShirim Rabbah* 4:3; *Koheleth Rabbah* 7:39. Cf. Rashi, *Bava Bathra* 15a, s.v. *Lashon Acher*; *Tosafoth ibid*. s.v. *VeAl*. See Table 6:1, notes 2, 8.

171. Rabbi Yochanan counts the three sons of Korach separately, while Rav counts them as a single individual; *Shir HaShirim Rabbah* 4:3; *Koheleth Rabbah* 7:39. See Table 6:1, note 2.

8:76   The books of Proverbs,[172] Ecclesiastes,[173] and Song of Songs[174] were written by King Solomon in the order given.[175] However, toward the end of his life, he was too busy with affairs of state to publish them.[176] This was therefore done by the School of King Hezekiah.[177] It is thus written, "These are the proverbs of Solomon, which the men of King Hezekiah of Judah copied out" (Proverbs 25:1).[178]

8:77   The Book of Job was written by Moses.[179]

8:78   The Book of Ruth was written by the prophet Samuel.[180]

8:79   The Book of Lamentations was written by Jeremiah.[181]

172. For the question as to whether it is included in the canon, see *Avoth DeRabbi Nathan* 1:4.
173. For question regarding inclusion in canon, see next note. Also see *Shabbath* 30b, *VaYikra Rabbah* 28:1, *Koheleth Rabbah* 1:4; *Pesikta* 8 (68b); *Moreh Nevukhim* 2:28.
174. For question of inclusion in canon, see *Edduyoth* 5:3; *Yadayim* 3:5; *Tosefta, Yadayim* 2:5; *Avoth deRabbi Nathan* 1:4; *Megillah* 7a; *Shir HaShirim Rabbah* 1:11. See above, Chapter 6, note 79.
175. Cf. Rashi, *Bava Bathra* 14b, s.v. *Shir*, that Solomon wrote the Song of Songs in his old age. Some sources question this, since there is a dispute, in which Rabbi Chiya Rabba gives the order of composition as Proverbs, Song of Songs, Ecclesiastes, and Rabbi Yochanan gives it as Song of Songs, Proverbs, Ecclesiastes. The opinion of Rashi, followed here, however, is that of Rabbi Simon, *Shir Hashirim Rabbah* 1:10.
176. Maharsha on *Tosafoth, Bava Bathra* 15a, s.v. *Yirmiahu.* It was also not published immediately, because the sages wanted time to deliberate on it; *Avoth deRabbi Nathan* 1:4; Rashi on *Avoth* 1:1;
177. *Bava Bathra* 15a. Cf. *Chasdey David* on *Tosefta, Yadayim* 2:14.
178. Rashi, Ibn Ezra, *Metzudoth David*, HaGra, *ad loc.*; Rashi, *Bava Bathra* 15a, s.v. *Mishley.* Also see *Sanhedrin* 101b; Rashi *ad loc.* s.v. *Gam.*
179. *Bava Bathra* 14b. It may be that Moses wrote the book of Job to comfort the Israelites in Egypt. This may explain why it is in the Writings rather than the Prophets; cf. *Moreh Nevukhim* 2:45 Second Level; Rabbi Yosef (ben Abba Mari) Kaspi, *Amudey Kesef ad loc.* (Franfurt am Mein, 1848). Moses might have written Job before he attained full prophecy. This, however, is only according to the opinions that Job lived before or contemporary to Moses. Ohters, however, maintain that Job was later; *Bava Bathra* 15a,b; *Yerushalmi Sotah* 5:6 (26a). According to those opinions, Job was most probably published by the Great Assembly. Also see Rashi, *Bava Bathra* 14b, s.v. *Ruth*, which seems to indicate that the accepted opinions is that Job was in the time of the Queen of Sheba. Some authorities state that the style of Job indicates that it was written in a language other than Hebrew and then translated. Ibn Ezra on Job 2:11. Others, however, state that the original language of the dialogue was Hebrew; *Kuzari* 2:68 (79b).
180. *Bava Bathra* 14b. For discussion as to why it is in the Writings, and not in the Prophets or in the Book of Judges, see Abarbanel, Introduction to Joshua (p. 9). Also see Abarbanel on *Moreh Nevukhim* 2:45.
181. *Bava Bathra* 15a; Targum, Rashi, on Lamentations 1:1. This was the scroll written

8:80   The Book of Esther was originally written by Mordecai as a letter to the various Jewish communities, informing them of the miracle.[182] However, there was a question as to whether or not this letter should be included in the Bible.[183] Even after it was decided to include it,[184] it could not be published outside the Holy Land.[185] Therefore, it was eventually published by the Great Assembly.[186]

8:81   The prophecies of Daniel occurred outside the Holy Land in Babylonia, and therefore could not be published immediately.[187] Hence, the Book of Daniel was published by the Great Assembly.[188]

8:82   The Books of Ezra and Nehemiah[189] were written by Ezra.[190]

by Barukh, dictated by Jeremiah; *Moed Katan* 26a; *Yalkut Shimoni* 2:324; Rashi, Mahari Kara, on Jeremiah 36:23; Radak, Abarbanel, on Jeremiah 36:2. For discussion of why it was included in the Writings and not in the Prophets, see Abarbanel, Introduction to Joshua (p. 10). Cf. 2 Chronicles 35:25.

182. Esther 9:20, Rashi *ad loc.* Cf. Esther 9:29.
183. *Megillah* 7a. Cf. *Yerushalmi, Megillah* 1:5 (7a). There was later also a question regarding its inclusion in the canon; *Megillah* 7a; *Magen Avraham* 147:1.
184. Rashi, Malbim, on Esther 9.32 (but see Ibn Ezra *ibid.*). Cf. *Megillah* 19b.
185. See above, note 155.
186. *Bava Bathra* 15a. From here we see that the expression "written" in the Talmud sometimes denotes authorship, but at other times denotes publication.
187. Rashi, *Bava Bathra* 15a, s..v. *Kathvu*. For the reason that Daniel is included among the Writings and not among the Prophets, see *Moreh Nevukhim* 2:45, Second Level; Abarbanel *ad loc.* Also see Table 6:1, note 33. Cf. *M'ayney HaYeshua*.
188. *Bava Bathra* 15a.
189. Although the book itself is called "the words of Nehemiah" Nehemiah 1:1, Rashi, Malbim *ad loc.* For the reason why Nehemiah is attributed to Ezra, see *Sanhedrin* 93b; *Sefer Chasidim* 482. We also see that Nehemiah is counted as the second book of Ezra rather than a separate book in *Bava Bathra* 14b. In many places there are quotations from Nehemiah attributed to Ezra; cf. *Sukkah* 37a, Rashi on Deuteronomy 32:25; Rashi, *Berakhoth* 53b, s.v. *BeMashma, Pesachim* 2a, s.v. *Tzeth, Betza* 15b, s.v. *Akhlu*, 27b, s.v. *Ain, Megillah* 3a, s.v. *VaYikra, Sukkah* 12a, s.v. *Te'u, Sotah* 39a, s.v. *U'VePathcho*, 40b, s.v. *Kumi, Bava Bathra* 25a, s.v. *LeAvothenu, Sanhedrin* 103b, s.v. *VeNechemiah, Shevuoth* 15a, s.v. *VeA'Amuda, Makkoth* 23b, s.v. *VeHavothi; Tosafoth, Yevamoth* 86b, s.v. *Mipney*; Ramban on Numbers 15:22; *Zohar* 1:160b. See *Gilyon HaShas, Sukkah* 12a; *Makor Chesed* on *Sefer Chasidim* 482:4; *Netzutzey Or* on *Bava Bathra* 15a. Also see Maharshal, *Bava Bathra* 15a.
190. *Bava Bathra* 15a. Since Ezra was the head of the Great Assembly, the fact that this is attributed to him personally and not to the Great Assembly would seem to indicate

8:83   The first Book of Chronicles and the second book up to 2 Chronicles 21:2 was written by Ezra.[191] The rest of the book was completed by Nehemiah.[192]

8:84   Other books, such as those of the Apocrypha, also contain wisdom, but they were not written with Divine Inspiration, and are therefore not included in the Bible.[193] However, when the necessity arises, they may be studied to obtain information.[194]

8:85   Although the Bible was originally given only to the Jewish people, it is now accepted by a large portion of humanity, and it forms the cornerstone of western civilization.[195] Through ways that we cannot understand, God is thus using the Bible to bring the entire world to the truth.[196]

that he published this individually. However, like all other holy scripture, it was included in the canon by the Great Assembly. It can be said, however, that it was published somewhat before the canon was closed. Moreover, while the other books written by the Great Assembly were a group effort, this was written by a single individual.

191. Rabenu Chananel, quoted in *Tosafoth, Bava Bathra* 15a, s.v. *Ad*. This verse may have been selected because it mentions Azariah, which hints at Ezra. Other sources, however, indicate that he wrote as far as his own lineage; Rashi, Rabbenu Gershom, Maharshal, *Bava Bathra* 15a. This would mean that Ezra wrote up to 1 Chronicles 5:40, where his father, Seriah, is mentioned; see Ezra 7:1. The Talmud writes that this was written before Ezra journeyed to the Holy Land. There is then a question as to how it could have been written outside the Holy Land; Rashash, *Bava Bathra* 15a. However, it may have been written in Babylonia, but published in the Holy Land; see above, note 186.

192. *Bava Bathra* 15a. For a discussion of earlier writings included in this book, see Radak, Introduction to Chronicles; above, note 111. For discussion as to why information in Chronicles is not included in the Book of Samuel and Kings, see Abarbanel, Introduction to Samuel (p. 163); Introduction to Kings (p. 428). For reason why not included in Prophets, see Abarbanel, Introduction to Joshua (pp. 9, 11).

193. *Sanhedrin* 10:1 (90a), 100b; *Yerushalmi, Sanhedrin* 10:1 (50a); *Tosefta, Yadayim* 2:5; *BaMidbar Rabbah* 14:14 (end); *Pesikta Rabathai* 3:2; Hai Gaon on *Yadayim* 4:6; Rabbi Reuven Margolies, *Yesod HaMishnah VeArikhathah* 1 (Tel Aviv, 1956), p. 5; Maharatz Chajas, *Bava Kama* 92b. Also see Josephus, *Contra Apion* 1:8.

194. Ritva (in *Eyn Yaakov*), *Bava Bathra* 98a; *Nimukey Yosef, Bava Bathra* (Rif 48b); *Koheleth Rabbah* 12:13; *Etz Yosef*, Radal, *ad loc*.

195. Cf. *Chulin* 92b (top).

196. *Yad, Melakhim* 11:4 (only in Rome, 1475, and Amsterdam, 1703, editions), quoted in *Torath HaShem Temimah* (in *Kithvey Ramban*), p. 144.

NINE

THE TRADITION

9:1   It is a foundation of our faith to believe that God gave Moses an oral explanation of the Torah along with the written text.[1]

9:2   This oral tradition is now essentially preserved in the Talmud and Midrashim.[2]

9:3   We thus speak of two Torahs.[3] There is the written Torah (*Torah SheBiKethav*, תּוֹרָה שֶׁבִּכְתָב), and the Oral Torah (*Torah SheB'Al Peh*, תּוֹרָה שֶׁבְּעַל פֶּה). Both are alluded to in God's statement to Moses, "Come up to Me to the mountain, and I will give you ... the Torah and the commandments" (Exodus 24:12).[4]

9:4   In many instances, the Torah refers to details not included in the written text, thus alluding to an oral tradition. Thus, the Torah states, "You shall slaughter your cattle ... as I have commanded you" (Deuteronomy 12:21),

1. Thirteen Principles of Faith 8.
2. Cf. *Yerushalmi, Peah* 2:4 (13a); *Yerushalmi Chagigah* 1:8 (7a); Rabbi Sh'muel HaNaggid, *Mavo HaTalmud; Shenoth Eliahu* (long) on *Peah* 2:6. Cf. *Kerithoth* 13b; *Koheleth Rabbah* 1:28.
3. *Sifra* (112c), Rashi, on Leviticus 26:46; *Sifri* (251) on Deuteronomy 33:10; *Shemoth Rabbah* 1:16, *Beth Elohim, Shaar HaYesodoth* 16; *Sh'nei Luchoth HaB'rith, Mesekhta Shevuoth,* s.v. *Maalath* (2:108b). Cf. Daniel 9:10.
4. *Berakhoth* 5a; *Yad,* Introduction; *Rabbenu Yonah, Avoth* 1:1, s.v. *Moshe.*

implying an oral commandment concerning ritual slaughter (*shechitah*, שְׁחִיטָה).[5] Similarly, such commandments as Tefillin[6] and Tzitzith[7] are found in the Torah, but no details are given, and they are assumed to be in the Oral Torah.[8] Although keeping the Sabbath is one of the Ten Commandments, no details are given as to how it should be kept, and these are also in the unwritten tradition.[9] God thus said, "You shall keep the Sabbath holy, as I have commanded your fathers" (Jeremiah 17:22).

9:5   Just as we depend on tradition for the accepted text, vocalization, and translation of the Torah, so must we depend on tradition for its interpretation.[10]

9:6   The written Torah cannot be understood without the oral tradition. Hence, if anything, the Oral Torah is the more important of the two.[11]

9:7   Since the written Torah must appear largely defective unless supplemented by the oral tradition, a denial of the Oral Torah necessarily leads to the denial of the divine origin of the written text as well. Therefore, one who does not believe in any part of the Oral Torah is considered a nonbeliever in all respects.[12]

9:8   The Oral Torah was originally meant to be transmitted by word of mouth.[13] It was transmitted from master to

5. *Sifri*, Rashi, *ad loc.*; *Chulin* 28a; *Yoma* 75b; *Yad, Shechitah* 1:4; *Tanna DeBei Eliahu* 15 (74a).
6. Deuteronomy 6:8.
7. Numbers 15:38.
8. *VaYikra Rabbah* 22:1; *Koheleth Rabbah* 5:7. Cf. *Sanhedrin* 88b.
9. *Chagigah* 1:8 (10a). Cf. *Mekhilta* on Exodus 35:1 (104b); *Shabbath* 97b (top); *Yerushalmi, Shabbath* 7:2 (44a).
10. *Kuzari* 3:35 (39a); Raavad on *Sifra*, Introduction (la). Cf. *Shabbath* 31a.
11. Bachya, *Kad HaKemach*, s.v. *Torah* (Jerusalem, 1970), p. 422. Cf. *Bava Metzia* 33a.
12. *Sanhedrin* 99a; *Yad, Teshuva* 3:8, *Mamrim* 3:1,2; Rabbenu Yonah on *Avoth* 2:14; Maharal, *Tifereth Yisrael* 68, 69. Cf. *Beur Halakhah, Orach Chaim* 39:4.
13. *Gittin* 60b; *Temurah* 14b; *Yerushalmi, Megillah* 4:1 (28a); Rashi on Exodus 34:27;

student in such a manner that if the student had any question, he would be able to ask, and thus avoid ambiguity.[14] A written text, on the other hand, no matter how perfect, is always subject to misinterpretation.[15]

9:9   Furthermore, the Oral Torah was meant to cover the infinitude of cases which would arise in the course of time. It could never have been written in its entirety. It is thus written, "Of making many books there is no end" (Ecclesiastes 12:12).[16] God therefore gave Moses a set of rules through which the Torah could be applied to every possible case.[17]

9:10   If the entire Torah would have been given in writing, everyone would be able to interpret it as he desired. This would lead to division and discord among people who followed the Torah in different ways. The Oral Torah, on the other hand, would require a central authority to preserve it, thus assuring the unity of Israel.[18]

9:11   Since many non-Jews also accept the Bible as sacred, the Oral Torah is the main thing that distinguishes Judaism and makes it unique. The Oral Torah could therefore not be written until the gentiles had adopted their own religion based on the Bible. God thus said, "If I would have written

Rashi, *Gittin* 60a, s.v. *VeHah*; Ran, *Gittin* (Rif 27b), s.v. *VeHah*; *Iggereth Rav Sherira Gaon* (Levin ed. Jerusalem, 1972), pp. 71, 72. Also see *Teshuvoth HaGaonim* (Shaarey Teshuvah) 187; Rabbi Shalom Albak, *Mishpachath Sofrim* (Warsaw, 1902), Introduction, pp. 13,14; *Sedey Chemed, P'ath HaSadeh, Dalet* 22 (2:134).

14. Cf. *Chagigah* 11b.

15. Rambam, Introduction to Mishnah, *Hagah*, s.v. *U'MiYemoth*; *Moreh Nevukhim* 1:71, Ritva, *Gittin* 60b; *Ikkarim* 3:23; *Sh'nei Luchoth HaB'rith, Torah SheB'Al Peh, Daleth* (3:231a); *Halikhoth Olam*, Introduction.

16. *Eruvin* 21b; *BaMidbar Rabbah* 14:12; *Ikkarim* 3:23; Maharsha, *Gittin* 60a, s.v. *VeHah*; Maharal, *Tifereth Yisrael* 68; *Gur Aryeh* on Exodus 34:27.

17. *Shemoth Rabbah* 41:6; *Tanchuma, Ki Thisa* 16.

18. *Moreh Nevukhim* 1:71, Maharal, *Tifereth Yisrael* 69. See below 10:1, 11:8.

the majority of My Torah, [Israel] would be counted the same as strangers" (Hosea 8:12).[19]

9:12 The Oral Torah is therefore the basis of God's covenant with Israel.[20] It is even more dear to God than the written Torah.[21]

9:13 The Oral Torah is the means through which we devote our lives to God and His teachings.[22]

9:14 God revealed all the details of how the commandments should be observed while Moses was on Mount Sinai.[23]

9:15 God also revealed to Moses many interpretations and laws that would not be used until much later.[24] These, however, were not taught to the people at large.[25]

9:16 There is a tradition that God taught Moses the written Torah by day and the Oral Torah by night.[26]

19. *Yerushalmi, Peah* 2:4 (13a); *Yerushalmi, Chagigah* 1:8 (7b); *Shemoth Rabbah* 47:1; *BaMidbar Rabbah* 14:22; *Tanchuma, Ki Thisa* 34; *Pesikta Rabathai* 5:1; *Sefer Mitzvoth Gadol*, Introduction; Bachya on Exodus 34:23; Maharal, *Tifereth Yisrael* 68. Also see *Tosafoth, Gittin 60b, s.v. A'temohi; P'nei Moshe, Yerushalmi, Peah* 2:4 (13a), s.v. *Rabbi Abin.*
20. *Gittin* 60b; *Tanchuma, Noah* 3; *Yerushalmi, loc. cit.;* Bachya, Maharal, *loc. cit.; Derashoth HaRan* 7 (p. 115). Cf. *Teshuvoth HaGaonim (Shaarey Teshuvah)* 62. Some say that the covenant was that the Oral Torah would never be forgotten; *Tanchuma, Noah* 3; *Otzar HaGaonim* on *Gittin* 60b (pp. 135, 136, 137); from Isaiah 59:21. Cf. *Tanchuma, Tazria* 9.
21. *Yerushalmi, Peah, Chagigah, loc cit.; Yerushalmi, Megillah* 4:1 (28a); *BaMidbar Rabbah* 14:12; *Shir HaShirim Rabbah* 1:18.
22. *Tanna DeBei Eliahu Zuta* 2 (4a).
23. *Sifra* (105a), Rashi, Bachya, Malbim, on Leviticus 25:1; Rambam, Introduction to Mishnah. Cf. *Chagigah* 6a; *Sota* 37b; *Zevachim* 115b.
24. *Berakhoth* 5a; *Megillah* 19b; *Shevuoth* 39a; *Yerushalmi, Peah* 2:4 (13a); *Yerushalmi, Chagigah* 1:8 (7b); *Yerushalmi, Megillah* 4:1 (28a); *Shemoth Rabbah* 47:1; *VaYikra Rabbah* 22:1; *Koheleth Rabbah* 1:29, 5:7; *Tanna DeBei Eliahu Zuta* 6 (11a); *Kuzari* 3:38 (47a).
25. *Megillath Esther* on *Sefer HaMitzvoth, Shoresh* 1 (p. 9a); *Tosefoth Yom Tov*, Introduction to Mishnah.
26. From Psalms 19:3. *Pirkey Rabbi Eliezer* 46 (109b); *Shemoth Rabbah* 47:13; *Tanchuma, Ki Thisa* 36; *Midrash Tehillim* 19:7; *Yalkut Shimoni* 2:672; Maharal, *Tifereth Yisrael* 68; Recanti, *Yithro* (97c).

9:17   Although the Israelites accepted the written Torah voluntarily, they had to be forced to accept the Oral Torah.[27]

9:18   Moses taught the Oral Torah to Aaron, his sons, and the Elders, in that order.[28] It is thus written, "Moses called Aaron, his sons, and the Elders of Israel" (Leviticus 9:1).[29] The laws were then taught to all the people and reviewed, until each person had gone over them four times.[30]

9:19   Before his death, Moses again reviewed the Oral Torah and clarified any ambiguous points. It is thus written, "Moses took upon himself to expound this Torah" (Deuteronomy 1:5).[31]

9:20   Besides receiving many explanations and details of laws, Moses also received hermeneutic rules for deriving laws from the Torah[32] and for interpreting it.[33] In many cases, he was also given the cases in which these rules could be applied.[34] Although the study of these rules was originally a central part of the tradition, their details were gradually

27. *Tanchuma, Noah* 3; *Bachya* on Exodus 19:8; *Baal HaTurim* (long), *Gur Aryeh*, on Exodus 19:17. Cf. *Tosafoth, Shabbath* 88a, s.v. *Kafah*.
28. *Eruvin* 54b; Rambam, Introduction to Mishnah. Cf. *Avoth* 1:1; Exodus 24:1, *Yalkut Shimoni* 1:520 (end). The elders were the members of the Sanhedrin, and as such, were the guardians of the Oral Torah. See below, note 53.
29. *Sifra* (43c) *ad loc.*
30. *Eruvin* 54b.
31. *Sifri ad loc.; Yalkut Shimoni* 1:801. He explained the Torah from 1 Shevat until 6 Adar, a day before his death; *Seder Olam Rabbah* 10.
32. Such as the Thirteen Rules of Rabbi Yishmael; *Sifra*, Introduction (1a). There are also the Seven Rules of Hillel; *Sifra*, Introduction (3a); *Avoth deRabbi Nathan* 37:10; *Tosefta, Sanhedrin* 7:5 (end). Cf. *Shevuoth* 26a.
33. Such as the Thirty Two Rules of Rabbi Eliezer ben Rabbi Yosi HaGelili (printed in Talmud after *Berakhoth*). See Rabbi Shimshon (benYitzchak) of Chinon, *Sefer Kerithoth* 3 (Warsaw, 1885), p. 14b; *Sh'nei Luchoth HaB'rith, Torah SheB'al Peh, K'lal Middoth* (3:207a); Maharatz Chajas, *Mavo HaTalmud* 19. Cf. *Chulin* 89a.
34. Such as in the case of *Gezerah Shava* (גְּזֵרָה שָׁוָה); *Pesachim* 66a; *Niddah* 19b; Ramban on *Sefer HaMitzvoth, Shoresh* 2 (22a); *Nimukey Yosef, Bava Kama* (Rif 30a), s.v. *Yerushalmi*; Maharatz Chajas, *Bava Metzia* 32a; *Yad Malachi* 34. Regarding the other rules, see Rashi, *Sukkah* 31a, s.v. *Lo Makshinin; Tosafoth*, *ibid.* s.v. *U'Rabbi*; also Rashi, *Gittin* 41b, s.v. *DeKulo Alma.* Also see *Pachad Yitzchak*, s.v. *Gezerah Shava* (23b); *Maley HaRo'im*. Beginning of Part 2 (Warsaw, 1880), p. 134a; Rabbi Reuven Margolies, *Yesod HaMishnah* (Tel Aviv, 1956), p. 41.

forgotten when persecutions destroyed the great academies.[35]

9:21 Laws and details involving common everyday occurrences were transmitted directly by Moses. However, laws involving infrequently occurring special cases were given in such a way as to be derivable from scripture by hermeneutic rules. Otherwise, there would be danger that they would be forgotten.[36]

9:22 Laws which Moses taught directly are referred to as "Laws to Moses from Sinai" (halakhoth le-Moshe mi-Sinai, הֲלָכוֹת לְמשֶׁה מִסִּינַי). These laws were carefully preserved from generation to generation, and for this reason one never finds a dispute concerning them.[37]

9:23 However, in the case of laws derived from hermeneutic rules or logic, occasional disputes can be found.[38] These include all the debates in the Talmud. The sages thus had the rule, "If it is a law, it must be accepted, but if it is derived it can be debated."[39]

9:24 The laws received directly and those derived by hermeneutic rules are equivalent in scope and importance, and are approximately equal in number.[40]

35. *Kuzari* 3:73 (75a). The prophets could derive rules from every letter, while the later sages, only from every word; Rabbi Meir Aldabi, *Sheveiley Emunah* 8 (Warsaw, 1887), p. 80b; cf. *Menachoth* 29b.
36. *Tosafoth, Eruvin* 21b, s.v. *Mipney;* Maharatz Chajas *ad loc.; Teshuvoth Chavath Yair* 192; *Teshuvoth Chut HaShani* 53. Some laws were so well known that they were not even included in the Mishnah; Rambam on *Menachoth* 4:1.
37. Rambam, Introduction to Mishnah; *Tosafoth, Yevamoth* 77b, s.v. *Halakhah; Ikkarim* 3:23; *Sh'nei Luchoth HaBrith, Torah SheB'al Peh,* s.v. *K'lal Halakhah* (3:246b); *Menorath HaMaor* 2:7:1:1; *Tosefoth Yom Tov, Sukkah* 4:9, *Sotah* 2:2; *Teshuvoth Chavath Yair* 192; Maharatz Chajas, *Chulin* 72a, *Niddah* 15a; *Idem., Torath HaNevi'im* 4 (in *Kol Kithvey Maharatz Chajas,* Jerusalem, 1958), p. 115.
38. See below, 11:22.
39. *Yevamoth* 8:3 (76b); *Kerithoth* 3:8 (16b); *Sifra* (16c) on Leviticus 4:1, Rambam, Introduction to Mishnah. However, see *Tosafoth, Yevamoth* 77b, s.v. *Halakhah: Yavin Shemua* 27a.
40. *Gittin* 60b; *Yerushalmi, Peah* 2:4 (13a); *Yerushalmi, Chagigah* 1:8 (7b); *Derashoth HaRan* 7 (p. 115); *Beer Sheva* on *Horayoth* 4a, s.v. *Avel* (Warsaw, 1890), p. 8a;

9:25   Both laws received orally and those derived by hermeneutic rules have the same status as laws written in the Torah, and are counted as Torah commandments (*mitzvoth de-Oraitha*, מִצְוֹת דְּאוֹרַיְיתָא).⁴¹ It is only with regard to oaths that they are in any way differentiated from laws that are actually written in the Torah.⁴²

9:26   All laws which were derived from scripture or logic were formally accepted by the Sanhedrin. They then became part of the Oral Torah and were transmitted from generation to generation.⁴³

9:27   All the laws received by Moses were transmitted orally from generation to generation and needed no further proof or derivation from scripture.⁴⁴ In some cases, however, a scriptural⁴⁵ or logical⁴⁶ basis was provided for even such laws, so that they be remembered better.⁴⁷ This was especially true in the case of laws that were not common knowledge.⁴⁸

9:28   Many oral laws were incorporated into the Bible in the works of the prophets.⁴⁹

Yeffeh Mareh on *Yerushalmi, Peah* 2:4; Maharatz Chajas, *Mavo HaTalmud* 3 (p. 289).
41. Ramban on *Sefer HuMitzvoth, Shoresh* 2; *Teshuvoth Rivash* 163; *Teshuvoth Tashbatz* 1:66; *Teshuvoth Chavath Yair* 192; *Teshuvoth Shaagath Aryeh* 29; Maharatz Chajas, *Nazir* 29a.
42. Ran, *Nedarim* 8a, s.v. *Hah, Shevuoth* (Rif 10a), s.v. *Malkin; Yoreh Deah* 239:6; *Sifethey Cohen, Yoreh Deah* 236:3. Cf. *Tosafoth, Shevuoth* 23b, s.v. *DeMukey.*
43. Rambam, Introduction to Mishnah; *Yad*, Introduction.
44. Rambam, Introduction to Mishnah. Cf. *Yad, Chovel U'Mazik* 1:6.
45. Rambam, Introduction to Mishnah; from *Berakhoth* 41b; *Sukkah* 6a; *Tosafoth ad loc.* s.v. *Eleh; Sukkah* 28a. Also see Rashi, *Sanhedrin* 81b, s.v. *Hekhi; Teshuvoth Chavath Yair* 192; Rabbi Shimon Dweck, *Re'ach HaSadeh, Teshuvah* 12 (Constantinople, 1738), p. 70a; *Yad Malachi* 202, 227, 546; *Sh'nei Luchoth HaB'rith, Torah SheB'al Peh, Alef*, s.v. *Al Tikrey* (3:229b); Maharatz Chajas *Nedarim* 39b, *Bava Kamu* 84a, *Chulin* 61a.
46. Cf. *Yad, Tumath Meth* 2:2; Maharatz Chajes, *Sotah* 5a.
47. *Moreh Nevukhim* 3:43; *Kuzari* 3:73 (75a); Ramban on Genesis 12:11, Leviticus 14:43; *Menorath HaMaor*, Introduction.
48. Cf. *Yerushalmi, Eruvin* 10:1 (59a); *Yad Malachi* 34.
49. See above, 8:32.

9:29   God also gave Moses many rules regarding how and under what conditions to enact new laws.[50] Therefore, details of rabbinical laws are sometimes said to have originated from Sinai.[51]

9:30   All laws legislated by the Sanhedrin eventually became part of the oral tradition which was transmitted from generation to generation.[52]

9:31   The Oral Torah was handed down by word of mouth from Moses to Joshua, then to the Elders,[53] the Prophets, and the Great Assembly.[54] The Great Assembly was the Sanhedrin led by Ezra, at the beginning of the time of the second Temple, which undertook to enact legislation that would make Judaism viable in the diaspora.[55]

50. Ibn Ezra on Exodus 12:1; *Beth Elohim, Shaar HaYesodoth* 38; *Sh'nei Luchoth HaB'rith, Torah SheB'al Peh,* s.v. *K'lal Rabanan* (3:240b); Rabbi Moshe Chaim Luzzatto, *Maamar HaIkkarim, BeInyan Torah SheB'al Peh.* Cf. *Megillah* 14a; *Turey Aven,* Maharatz Chajas ad loc.; *Yerushalmi, Megillah* 1:5 (7a); *Ruth Rabbah* 4:7, *Zohar* 2:191b; Rashi, *Taanith* 28b, s.v. *Minhag; Beth Ephraim, Orach Chaim* 64:66; Mizrachi on *Sefer Mitzvoth Gadol,* Laws of Megillah (Constantinople, 1526); Maharatz Chajas, *Megillah* 19b, *Shevuoth* 39a. Also see *Taana DeBei Eliahu Rabbah* 15 (74a); Maharal, *Beer HaGolah* 1, s.v. *HaSheni* (Zolkiev, 1848), p. 4a; Maharsha, *Sanhedrin* 21b, s.v. *BeTechilah.* Cf. Ramban on *Sefer HaMitzvoth, Shoresh* 3 (38a).
51. Maharshal on *Tosafoth, Eruvin* 5b, s.v. *ShePeratzto.* This also answers the question of Rosh, *Mikvaoth* 1:7, Rash, Bertenoro, *Tosefoth Yom Tov, Yadayim* 4:3, s.v. *Halakhah; Kesef Mishneh, Matnoth Aniyim* 6:5; *Turey Aven,* Maharatz Chajas, *Chagigah* 3b. Similarly, the expression "In truth they said" (be-emeth amru, בְּאֶמֶת אָמְרוּ), denotes a law from Sinai (halakhah le-Moshe me-Sinai); *Yerushalmi Kelayim* 2:1 (6b); *Yerushalmi, Terumoth* 2:1 (9a); *Yerushalmi, Shabbath* 1:3 (8b), 10:4 (63a); Rashi, *Nazir* 42b, s.v. *BeEmeth.* Nevertheless, this expression is also applied to rabbinical laws; Rash, Bertenoro, *Terumoth* 2:1; *Tosefoth Yom Tov, Bava Metzia* 4:11; *Teshuvoth Rashbash* 593; Mabit, *Kiryat Sefer* on *Yad, Shabbath* 3 (end); *Teshuvoth Chavath Yair* 192 (Frankfurt am Mein, 1699), p. 179a; *Yad Malachi* 326; *Gilyon HaShas* on *Yerushalmi, Kelim, Shabbath, loc. cit.* Also see *Shabbath* 92b; *Bava Metzia* 60a; Shmuel HaNaggid, *Mavo HaTalmud,* s.v. *Stam; Yesod HaMishnah,* pp. 40,41.
52. Rambam, Introduction to Mishnah; *Yad,* Introduction.
53. See Joshua 24:31, Judges 2:7; *Avoth deRabbi Nathan* 1:3; *Nachalath Avoth,* Introduction; *Midrash Shmuel* on *Avoth* 1:1, quoting Rabbi Matathyahu HaYitzhari (p. 5a).
54. *Avoth* 1:1.
55. They thus fixed the Bible canon; above, 8:56. They also ordained the various standard prayers and services; *Berakhoth* 33a; *Megillah* 17b; *Yad, Tefillah* 1:4.

9:32   The Great Assembly codified much of the Oral Torah in a form that could be memorized by the students.[56] This codification was known as the *Mishnah* (מִשְׁנָה).[57] One reason for this name was that it was meant to be reviewed (*shanah*, שנה) over and over until memorized.[58] The word also denoted that the Mishnah was secondary (*sheni*, שֵׁנִי) to the written Torah.[59]

9:33   It was required that the oral tradition be handed down word for word, exactly as it had been taught.[60] The sages who taught this first Mishnah were known as *Tannaim* (תַּנָּאִים), *Tanna* (תַּנָּא) in the singular.[61] This word comes from the Aramaic word *tanna* (תנא) equivalent to the Hebrew *shanah* (שנה), meaning "to repeat."[62]

9:34   Although the Oral Torah was meant to be transmitted by word of mouth, it was permissible to keep personal records.[63] Therefore, many individuals would write down

---

56. Saadia Gaon, *Sefer HaGaluy*, quoted in Rabbi Avraham Harkavi, *Zikhron LeRishonim*, Part 4 (St. Petersberg, 1892), p. 194; and in Rabbi Binyamin Menashe Levin, Introduction to *Iggereth Rav Sherira Gaon*, p. 5a. Also see Meiri, Introduction to *Avoth*, s.v. *VeNashuv* (Jerusalem, 1964), p. 21; Maharatz Chajas, *Mavo HaTalmud* 33; *Doroth HaRishonim* 1:3:14 (102b), 1:3:17. Cf. *Shabbath* 132b; *Yerushalmi, Shekalim* 5:1 (21a). However, see *Teshuvoth HaGaonim* 1 (Lyck, 1864); *Iggereth Rav Sherira Gaon*, pp. 5, 17. Where a source is not given for legislation, it is also from Ezra; *Machzor Vitri, Seder MeKabley HaTorah* (Berlin, 1889), p. 481, note 90; *Sefer Kerithoth, Yemoth Olam* 1:19.
57. There is a question as to whether the word is pronounced *Mishnah* (מִשְׁנָה) or *Mishneh* (מִשְׁנֶה); see *Arukh HaShalem*, s.v. *Mishnah*.
58. *Arukh*, s.v. *Mishnah*. See *Avoth* 3:7,8; *Taanith* 8a.
59. *Arukh* loc. cit.; Bachya on Exodus 34:43. Cf. *Kiddushin* 49a (end).
60. *Edduyoth* 1:3; *Berakhoth* 47a; *Bekhoroth* 5a; *Iggereth Rav Sherira Gaon*, p. 19.
61. See *Nazir* 53a; *Chulin* 137b; *Bekhoroth* 58a. Also see *Shabbath* 123b; *Rosh HaShanah* 19b; *Yevamoth* 16a; *Kiddushin* 43a. Cf. *Kuzari* 3:65 (68a).
62. *Sefer HaTishbi*, s.v. *Tana; Kitzur Keleley HaShas*, on *Mavo HaTalmud*, s.v. *Mishnah*. Cf. *Kiddushin* 49b (top). They were distinguished from the sages of the Gemara who were known as *Amoraim* (אֲמוֹרָאִים), *Amora* (אֲמוֹרָא) in the singular. The *Amoraim* could neither add nor subtract from the Mishnah, only speak (*amar*, אמר) and interpret the Mishnah.
63. *Yesod HaMishnah*. p. 6, note 4, p. 39. Cf. *Tosafoth, Temurah* 14b, s.v. *Devarim; Piskey Tosafoth, Menachoth* 77; *Orach Chaim* 49:1. See above, 9:8.

personal notes of what was taught in the academies.[64] This was especially true of teachings that were not often reviewed.[65] Many also added marginal notes to the Biblical scrolls which they used to study.[66]

9:35   Similarly, the heads of the academies would keep written notes in order to preserve the traditions accurately.[67] However, since none of these notes was published, they were known as "hidden scrolls" (*megilloth setharim*, מְגִילּוֹת סְתָרִים).[68]

9:36   During the generations following the Great Assembly, the Mishnah developed into a program of study for the students to memorize.[69] This was expanded by new legislation and case law.[70] This was known as the "first Mishnah" (*Mishnah Rishonah*, מִשְׁנָה רִאשׁוֹנָה).[71]

9:37   As controversies began to develop, variations in the Mishnahs of the various masters began to appear.[72] At the same time, the order of the Mishnah was improved,

64. Rambam, Introduction to Mishnah; *Yad*, Introduction; cf. *Yevamoth* 49a; *Sanhedrin* 57b; *Menachoth* 70a; *Chulin* 60b; *Yerushalmi, Berakhoth* 9:5 (68a); Maharatz Chajas, *Shabbath* 6b.
65. Rashi, *Shabbath* 6b, s.v. *Megillath*.
66. Maharatz Chajas, *Sotah* 20a; from *Bereshith Rabbah* 9:5; *Yerushalmi, Taanith* 1:1 (3a). See *Sefer Chasidim* 282. Also see *Eruvin* 21b, 54b; *Sh'nei Luchoth HaB'rith, Torah SheB'al Peh, Daleth*, s.v. *Devarim* (3:231a); *Halikhoth Olam*, Introduction.
67. *Yad*, Introduction.
68. Rashi, *Shabbath* 6b, *Bava Metzia* 92a, s.v. *Megillath*.
69. We thus find that earlier sages often discuss the meaning of an expression in a Mishnah. Such disputes were even found between Beth Hillel and Beth Shamai: *Shevi'ith* 8:3; *Chagigah* 1:1; *Yevamoth* 3:1; *Kiddushin* 1:1; *Nedarim* 3:1; *Chulin* 11:1,2; *Temurah* 1:4; *Kelim* 2:6, 14:2; *Ohaloth* 2:3. Also see *Peah* 4:5; *Pesachim* 5:6; *Ohaloth* 14:2,3. See *Doroth HaRishonim* 1:3:15, 1:3:18.
70. *Kethuboth* 5:3. See *Doroth HaRishonim* 1:3:16.
71. *Sanhedrin* 3:4 (27b); *Edduyoth* 7:2; *Gittin* 5:6 (55b); *Nazir* 6:1 (34b); Maharatz Chajas, *Yoma* 53b. Also see Rashi, *Sanhedrin* 33a, s.v. *To'eh*; Rabbi Chaim Benveneste, *Chamra VeChayay ad loc.* (Livorno, 1802); Rashi *Bekhoroth* 28b, s.v. *VeTepuk*.
72. *Iggereth Rav Sherira Gaon*, p. 18; *Sheveiley Emunah* 8 (79b).

especially by Rabbi Akiba (1-121 c.e.).[73] Certain parts of the Mishnah were placed in almost their present form.[74]

9:38 At this time, however, no part of the Oral Torah had been published. The only exception were such minor works as the Scroll of Fasts (*Megillath Taanith*, מְגִילַת תַּעֲנִית).[75]

9:39 The final and most precise redaction of the Mishnah was made by Rabbi Yehudah the Prince (רַבִּי יְהוּדָה הַנָּשִׂיא).[76]This is the Mishnah that we have today, as part of the Talmud.[77] The work was completed in 3948 (188 c.e.).[78]

73. Cf. *Avoth deRabbi Nathan* 18:1; *Gittin* 67a; Rashi ad loc. s.v. *Otzar*; *Tosefta, Zuvim* 1:2. A Mishnah of Rabbi Akiba is mentioned in *Sanhedrin* 3:4 (27b); *Tosefta, Maaser Sheni* 2:13; *Shir HaShirim Rabbah* 8:1; *Koheleth Rabbah* 6:2. Cf. *Sanhedrin* 86a; *Iggereth Rav Sherira Gaon*, p. 27; *Yesod HaMishnah*, p. 63.

74. Thus, earlier authorship is ascribed to certain portions of the Mishnah; see *Iggereth Rav Sherira Gaon*, p. 24,25. See *Yoma* 14b regarding *Tamid*; *Yoma* 16b regarding *Middoth*; *Eruvin* 79a regarding *Oholoth* and *Eruvin*; *Kinnim* 3:6, *Zevach:m* 67b, *Avoth* 3:19 regarding *Kinnim*; *Horioth* 13b regarding *Uktzin*. *Kelim* 30:4 also indicates that it had earlier authorship. Also see *Pesachim* 1:1, 9:6; *Yoma* 8:2; *Meila* 4:3; *Niddah* 1:3; *Tohoroth* 2:2; *Zavim* 5:1; *Tevul Yom* 4:6. See *Sefer Kerithoth*, *Lashon Limudim* 2:58 (29a); *Sh'nei Luchoth HaB'rith, Torah SheB'al Peh*, s.v. *Kathav* (3:217a); *Teshuvoth Chakham Tzvi* 10; *Maharatz Chajas, Bava Kama* 6b; *Yesod HaMishnah*, p. 17.

75. *Frunin* 62b; Rashi, *Shabbath* 13b, s.v. *Megillath*, *Taanith* 12a, s.v. *Batlu*, 15b, s.v. *Megillath*; *Maharatz Chajas, Megillah* 7a; *Yesode HaMishnah*, p. 20. *Megillath Taanith* was first printed in Amsterdam, 1659. Other works, such as *Pirkey Rabbi Eliezer* may have been also authored before the Mishnah, but they were not published for the populace at large; see above, 9:35. Moreover, the strictures against putting aggadah in writing were not as strict as those against halakhah; *Gittin* 60a,b; *Temurah* 14a. See Radal, Introduction to *Pirkey Rabbi Eliezer*, p. 12a. If works such as the *Zohar, Bahir*, and *Hekhaloth* were put in writing before the Mishnah, they were also not published for the populace at large. See Rabbi David Luria (Radal), *Kadmuth Sefer HaZohar* 5:1 (New York, 1951), p. 82ff; Rabbi Yerocham Leiner of Radzin, *Maamar Zohar HaRakia* 2 (New York, 1951), p. 123ff. Some say that the Zohar was written down after the time of the Mishnah by Rabbi Abba, a disciple of Rabbi Shimon bar Yochai; *Kadmuth Sefer HaZohar* 5:2 (p. 84ff).

76. *Bava Metzia* 86a (top); *Yevamoth* 64b.

77. Rambam, Introduction to Mishnah; *Yad*, Introduction; Rashi, *Sanhedrin* 33a, s..v. *VeAfilu*; *Iggereth Rav Sherira Gaon*, p. 7.

78. According to tradition, this was 1500 years after the Exodus, and 500 years after the cessation of prophecy; see Rav Saadia Gaon, Rav Nissim Gaon, quoted above, Chapter 6, note 256. Also see Rabbi Avraham ibn Daud (Raavad), Sefer HaKabbalah (Jerusalem, 1971), p 16; Rabbi Yitzchak (ben Yisrael) of Toledo, *Yesod Olam* 18 (Berlin, 1848), p. 34a; Rabbi Menachem ben Zerach, *Tzedah LaDerekh*, Introduction (Feraro, 1554). It was not published, however, until 30 years later, in 3978 (218 c.e.); *Iggereth Rav Sherira Gaon*, Rabbi Nissim Gaon, Introduction to *Mafteach Menoley HaTalmud* (Vienna, 1847, and in Vilna Shas); *Kuzari* 3:67 (72b). See *Tzemach*

9:40   The Mishnah consists of six orders, comprising 63 tracts.[79] (See table 9:1).

9:41   In compiling his work, Rabbi Yehudah made use of the earlier Mishnah, condensing it and deciding among various disputed questions.[80] The sages of his time all concurred with his decisions and ratified his edition.[81] However, even rejected opinions were included in the text, so that they be recognized as such and not revived in later generations.[82]

9:42   There is a question as to when the Mishnah was put in writing. Some authorities maintain that Rabbi Yehudah himself published it.[83] According to others, however, it was preserved orally until several generations later.[84]

David, Seder HaDoroth, 3978. It is known that Rabbi Yehudah the Prince was born on 24 Iyyar, 3881 (April 25, 121 c.e.), the same day as Emperor Marcus Aurelius Antoninus; Menorath HaMaor 3:1:2:2 (83). Hence, he would have been almost a hundred years old when the Mishnah was published.

79. Shabbath 129a; Midrash Tehillim 19:14; cf. BaMidbar Rabbah 13:15; Teshuvoth HaGeonim, Shaarey Teshuvah 20.

80. Iggereth Rav Sherira Gaon pp. 24, 26, 27; Teshuvoth Rivash 417; Sefer Kerithoth, Lashon Limudim 2:58; Note on Rambam, Introduction to Mishnah; Sh'nei Luchoth HaB'rith, Torah SheB'al Peh, s.v. Kathav (3:217a); Kitzur Kelelay HaMishnah (on Mavo HaTalmud, in Vilna Shas), s.v. Kathav; Teshuvoth Chakham Tzvi 10; Maharatz Chajas, Sanhedrin 33a; Mavo HaTalmud 33. Such expressions as, "The first Mishnah did not move from its place" (משנה ראשונה לא זה ממקומה) are thus found; Yevamoth 30a; Kiddushin 25a; Avodah Zarah 35b; Shevuoth 4a; Chullin 32b, 116b. Similarly, Rabbi Yehudah the Prince occasionally wrote a Mishnah without analyzing it; Yerushalmi, Maaser Sheni 5:1 (28a); Maharatz Chajas, Bava Kama 94b. Cf. Rashi, Bava Metzia 33b, s.v. BiY'mey.

81. Maharatz Chajas, Mavo HaTalmud 14 (p. 310). He had gathered all the sages together, Rav Nissim Gaon, Introduction to Mafteach Manoley HaTalmud; Sefer Mitzvoth Gadol, Negative Commandments, Introduction; cf. Yerushalmi, Eruvin 1:6 (9a). Some say that the Mishnah was not ratified by the Sanhedrin; Yesod HaMishnah, p. 36.

82. Edduyoth 1:6; Tosefta, Edduyoth 1:2; Sh'muel HaNaggid, Mavo HaTalmud; Iggereth Rav Sherira Gaon, p. 30; Yesod HaMishnah, p. 35.

83. Rambam, Introduction to Mishnah; Yad, Introduction; Sh'muel HaNaggid, Mavo HaTalmud; Rav Nissim Gaon, Mafteach Menoley HaTalmud, Introduction; Kuzari 3:67 (73a); Iggereth Rav Sherira Gaon, pp. 2, 9, 12; Teshuvoth Chavath Yair 94; Pachad Yitzchak, s.v. Mishnah (219a); Yesod HaMishnah, p. 59.

84. Rashi, Shabbath 3b, s.v. Megillath Eruvin 62b, s.v. KeGon, Bava Metzia 33a, s.v. VeAina, 85a, s.v. U'Mathnitha, Sukkah 28b, s.v. Marki, Taanith 12b, DeKetani; Tosafoth, Megillah 32a, s.v. VeHaShoneh; Sefer Mitzvoth Gadol (Venice, 1547), Introduction (3a), Negative Commandent 65 (16c); Teshuvoth Tashbatz 1:73, 2:53; Rabbi Yaakov Chagiz, Techilath Chokhmah, Hakdama BeDarkey HaMishnah

9:43   There was a tradition that if there was danger that the Oral Torah be forgotten, it could be put in writing.[85] It is thus written, "It is a time to work for God, make void His Torah" (Psalms 119:126).[86] This also implies that when there is danger of the Torah becoming voided and forgotten, it is a time to work for God and remedy the situation.[87]

9:44   In any case, no part of the Oral Torah could be put into writing until the gentiles had adapted the Bible into a religion of their own. The Oral Torah would then be excluded by them and thus remain uniquely Jewish.[88]

9:45   Since the tradition required that the Oral Torah be written under certain conditions, the commandment to write a Torah scroll[89] now also includes an obligation to write or purchase books of Mishnah and Talmud containing the Oral Torah.[90]

9:46   Besides the Mishnah, other volumes were compiled by the students of Rabbi Yehudah during this period. These included the *Tosefta* (תּוֹסֶפְתָּא) which follows the order of the Mishnah, as well as the *Mekhilta* (מְכִילְתָּא), a commentary on Exodus, the *Sifra* (סִפְרָא) on Leviticus, and the *Sifri* (סִפְרִי) on Numbers and Deuteronomy.[91] Works from outside Rabbi

(Warsaw, 1895), p. 38a; Maharatz Chajas, *Taanith* 12b, *Sukkah* 50b, *Bava Metzia* 85b.

85. Rashi, *Gittin* 60b, s.v. *Devarim*; Ritva, *Gittin* 60b; Ran, *Megillah* (Rif 14a), s.v. *Amar Ley*; Perishah, *Orach Chaim* 49:1; *Sheveiley Emunah* 8 (80a).

86. Cf. *Gittin* 60a; *Temurah* 14b; *Yoma* 69a; *Menachoth* 99b; Rashi, *Kerithoth* 8a, s.v. *Maon*; Bachya on Exodus 19:8.

87. *Berakhoth* 9:5 (54a), 66a. But see Rashi, *Gittin* 60a, s.v. *Eth*, *Temurah* 14b, s.v. *Eth*. The very covenant that forbade the publication of the Oral Torah also guaranteed that it would not be forgotten; above, note 20.

88. *Sefer Mitzvoth Gadol*, Introduction (2c). See above, 9:11.

89. See above, 7:38.

90. Rosh, *Halakhoth Ketanoth, Sefer Torah* 1; *Yoreh Deah* 270:2; commentaries ad loc., *Margolioth HaYam, Sanhedrin* 21b #30.

91. The *Tosefta* was written by Rabbi Chiya and Rabbi Hoshia, while the *Mekhilta, Sifra* and *Sifri* were written by Rav; *Yad*, Introduction; Sh'muel HaNaggid, *Mavo HaTalmud; Iggereth Rav Sherira Gaon*, pp. 33,34,42. See *Sanhedrin* 86a.

Yehudah's school went by the name of *Baraitha* (בָּרַיְיתָא).[92] Not too long after this, the Jerusalem Talmud (*Talmud Yerushalmi*, תַּלְמוּד יְרוּשַׁלְמִי) was compiled by Rabbi Yochanan.[93]

9:47   In ancient times, the practice was for students first to memorize the basics of the Oral Torah, and then carefully to analyze their studies.[94] During the period preceding Rabbi Yehudah, the memorized laws developed into the Mishnah, while the analysis developed into a second discipline known as the *Gemara* (גְּמָרָא).[95] After the Mishnah was compiled, these discussions continued, becoming very important in clarifying the Mishnah.

9:48   The Gemara developed orally for some three hundred years following the redaction of the Mishnah. Finally, when it came into danger of being forgotten and lost, Rav Ashi (352-427 c.e.),[96] together with his school in Babylonia undertook to collect all these discussions and set them in order.[97] Rav Ashi spent most of his life on this project together with his colleague Ravina.[98] After his death, his son, Mar bar Rav Ashi (Tavyomi) continued the work along with Meremar.[99] The Babylonian Talmud (*Talmud Bavli*,

---

92. From the word bar (בַּר) meaning "outside." See *Iggereth Rav Sherira Gaon*, pp. 34,42; *Yesod HaMishnah*, p. 20. Cf. *Yevamoth* 42b; *Kiddushin* 51a.

93. *Yad*, Introduction; Sh'muel HaNaggid, *Mavo HaTalmud*; Maharatz Chajas, *Nazir* 20b, *Bava Kama* 60a. Rabbi Yochanan had assumed leadership of the academy in the Holy Land in 3990 (230 c.e.), and died in 4039 (279 c.d.); *Seder HaDoroth*.

94. *Shabbath* 63a.

95. Rashi, *Niddah* 7b, s.v. *Ha*; *Yad*, *Talmud Torah* 1:11. Cf. *Avoth* 5:21; *Bava Metzia* 33b; Maharatz Chajas, *Sotah* 20a. The word Gemara comes from the root *gamar* (גמר) meaning both to study and to finish. Also see *Targum* on Job 22:22.

96. Cf. *Sefer Mitzvoth Gadol*, Introduction (3a). Cf. *Gittin* 59a.

97. *Yad*, Introduction; Rashi, *Bava Metzia* 86a, s.v. *Sof*.

98. Cf. Rashbam, *Bava Bathra* 157b, s.v. *Mahadurah*.

99. *Yad*, Introduction; Rav Nissim Gaon, *Mafteach Manoley HaTalmud*, Introduction; *Sefer HaKabbalah*, p. 19.

תַּלְמוּד בַּבְלִי)[100] as it is called, was published in the year 4265 (505 c.e.).[101]

9:49   The Babylonian Talmud was completed on 37 of the 63 tracts of the Mishnah (see Table 9:1). Its main purpose was to clarify the Mishnah, establish which opinions are binding, provide derivations for the laws, discuss later legislation, and provide homilies and stories to enhance the discussions.[102]

9:50   There were a total of forty generations, comprising 1817 years, from Moses until the final redaction of the Talmud (see Table 9:2).[103]

9:51   The Babylonian Talmud was accepted by all Israel as the final binding authority in all questions of religion and law.[104] All subsequent codifications of Torah law are binding only insofar as they are based on the Talmud.[105] To oppose even a single teaching of the Talmud is to oppose God and His Torah.[106]

100. Cf. *Sanhedrin* 24a; *Yoreh Deah* 246:4 in *Hagah*. Cf. Rashi, *Chagigah* 10a, s.v. *Afilu*; Ritva (in *Eyn Yaakov*) ibid., *Yoma* 57a; *Sheveiley Emunah* 8 (81b); *Sh'nei Luchoth HaB'rith, Beth Chokhmah* (1:24b).
101. *Sefer HaKabbalah*, p. 19; *Yesod Olam* 4:18 (34b); *Kitzur Kelalley HaMishnah* on *Mavo HaTalmud*, s.v. *Kathav*. This was the final redaction of the Talmud in the time of the Savoraim. However, the main work was completed in 4259 (499 c.e.). Rav Nissim Gaon, *Mafteach Menoley HaTalmud*, thus writes that it was completed in 811 of *Shetaroth*, that is 811 + 3448 = 4259. Cf. *Seder HaDoroth* 4260.
102. Rambam, Introduction to Mishnah. The Babylonian Talmud contains some 2,500,000 words.
103. *Yad*, Introduction. See *BaMidbar Rabbah* 13:15.
104. Rif, *Eruvin* 35b. Also see *Sifethey Cohen, Yoreh Deah* 145:1; *Beer Yaakov, Yoreh Deah* 145:1.
105. *Yad*, Introduction; Rashbam, *Bava Bathra* 130b, s.v. *Ad*. See below, 11:20, 12:10.
106. Rav Sherira Gaon, quoted in Rabbi Chaim Modai, *Shaarey Tzedek*, Introduction (Salonika, 1792).

TABLE 9:1 — THE TALMUD

Tractate		Chapters	Bavli	Folios Yerushalmi (Vilna)
I. ZERA'IM	SEEDS			
1. *Berakhoth*	Blessings	9	64	68
2. *Pe'ah*	Corner [of fields]	8	-	37
3. *Demai*	Dubious [tithings]	7	-	34
4. *Kilayim*	Diverse [plantings]	9	-	44
5. *Shevi'ith*	Sabbatical Year	10	-	31
6. *Terumoth*	Priestly Offerings	11	-	59
7. *Ma'aseroth*	Tithes	5	-	26
8. *Ma'aser Sheni*	Second Tithe	5	-	33
9. *Challah*	Dough Offering	4	-	28
10. *Orlah*	Uncircumcision [of trees]	3	-	20
11. *Bikkurim*	First Fruits	4	-	13
Total		74	64	393
II. MO'ED	SEASON			
12. *Shabbath*	Sabbath	24	157	92
13. *Eruvin*	Blendings [of boundaries]	10	105	65
14. *Pesachim*	Passovers	10	121	71
15. *Shekalim*	Shekels	8	-	33
16. *Yoma*	Day [of Atonement]	8	88	42
17. *Sukkah*	Hut	5	56	26
18. *Betza*	Egg [on Festival]	5	40	22
19. *Rosh HaShanah*	New Year	4	35	22
20. *Taanith*	Fast	4	31	26
21. *Megillah*	Scroll [of Esther]	4	32	34
22. *Moed Katan*	Intermediate Festival	3	29	19
23. *Chagigah*	Festival Offering	3	27	22
Total		88	721	474
III. NASHIM	WOMEN			
24. *Yevamoth*	Levirate Marriages	16	122	85
25. *Kethuboth*	Marriage Contracts	13	112	72
26. *Nedarim*	Vows	11	91	40
27. *Nazir*	Nazirite	9	66	47
28. *Sotah*	Suspected Adultress	9	49	47
29. *Gittin*	Divorces	9	90	54
30. *Kiddushin*	Marriages	4	82	48
Total		71	612	353

		Chapters	Bavli	Yerushalmi
IV. *NEZIKIN*	DAMAGES			
31. *Bava Kama*	First Gate [of Damages]	10	119	44
32. *Bava Metzia*	Middle Gate	10	119	37
33. *Bava Bathra*	Final Gate	10	176	34
34. *Sanhedrin*	Supreme Council	11	113	57
35. *Makkoth*	Floggings	3	24	9
36. *Shevu'oth*	Oaths	8	49	44
37. *Eduyyoth*	Testimonies	8	-	-
38. *Avodah Zarah*	Idolatry	5	76	37
39. *Avoth*	Fathers [ethics]	5	-	-
40. *Horayoth*	Rulings]	3	14	19
Total		74	690	281
V. *KEDOSHIM*	SACRED THINGS			
41. *Zevachim*	[Animal] Sacrifices	14	120	-
42. *Menuchoth*	[Meal] Offerings	13	110	-
43. *Chullin*	Unhallowed [Slaughter]	12	142	-
44. *Bekhoroth*	Firstlings	9	61	-
45. *Arakhin*	Estimations	9	34	-
46. *Temurah*	Substitution Offering	7	34	-
47. *Kerithoth*	Excisions	6	28	-
48. *Me'ilah*	Misappropriation	6	22	-
49. *Tamid*	Continual [Offering]	7	9	-
50. *Middoth*	Measurements [of Temple]	5	-	-
51. *Kinnim*	Bird Nests [offerings]	3	-	-
Total		91	560	0
VI. *TOHOROTH*	PURITIES			
52. *Kelim*	Vessels	30	-	-
53. *Oholoth*	Tents	18	-	
54. *Nega'im*	Leprous Signs	14	-	-
55. *Parah*	[Red] Heifer	12	-	-
56. *Tohoroth*	Purities	10	-	-
57. *Mikva'oth*	Immersion Pools	10	-	-
58. *Niddah*	Menstruant	10	73	13
59. *Makh'shrim*	Predisposers [to impurity]	6	-	-
60. *Zavim*	Discharges	8	-	-
61. *Tevul Yom*	Immersion by Day	4	-	-
62. *Yadayim*	Hands	4	-	-
63. *Uktzin*	Stalks	3	-	-
Total		129	73	14
TOTAL FOR TALMUD		527	2720	1514

TABLE 9.2 - THE CHAIN OF TRADITION

1. Moses
2. Joshua[1]

ELDERS

3. Pinchas and Elders[2]
4. Eli[3]
5. Samuel[4]
6. David[5]

PROPHETS

7. Achiyah[6]
8. Elijah[7]
9. Elisha[8]
10. Yehoyada the Priest[9]
11. Zechariah ben Yehoyada[10]
12. Hosea[11]
13. Amos[12]
14. Isaiah[13]
15. Micah[14]
16. Joel[15]
17. Nahum[16]

1. *Avoth* 1:1; *Yad*, Introduction (from which this entire list is taken).
2. *Ibid.* Cf. Joshua 24:31; Judges 20:28; Radak ad loc.
3. 1 Samuel 4:18.
4. See Table 6:1, note 14.
5. *Ibid.* note 12.
6. *Ibid.* note 13.
7. *Ibid.* note 20.
8. *Ibid.* note 23.
9. *Ibid.* note 26. See 2 Kings 11, 2 Chronicles 23.
10. *Ibid.* note 26.
11. *Ibid.* note 40.
12. *Ibid.* note 41.
13. *Ibid.* note 31.
14. *Ibid.* note 42.
15. *Ibid.* note 43.
16. *Ibid.* note 44.

18. Habakkuk[17]
19. Zephaniah[18]
20. Jeremiah[19]
21. Barukh ben Neriah[20]

THE GREAT ASSEMBLY

22. Ezra[21] and the Great Assembly, consisting of 120 Elders,[22] including Haggai, Zechariah, Daniel, Chananiah, Mishael, Azariah,[23] Nehemiah, Mordecai Zarubabel.
23. Shimon the Saint[24]

TANA'IM

24. Antigonos of Sokho[25]
25. Yosé ben Yoezera, Yosé ben Yochanan[26]
26. Yehoshua ben Perachiah, Nittai the Arbelite[27]
27. Yehudah ben Tabbai, Shimon ben Shetach[28]
28. Shemiah and Avtalion[29]
29. Hillel and Shamai[30]
30. Rabban Shimon ben Hillel,[31] Rabban Yochanan ben Zakkai[32]

---

17. *Ibid.* note 28.
18. *Ibid.* note 29.
19. *Ibid.* note 30.
20. *Ibid.* note 34.
21. *Ibid.* note 47.
22. See above, 8:61.
23. See Table 6:1, note 36.
24. *Avoth* 1:2.
25. *Avoth* 1:3.
26. *Avoth* 1:4.
27. *Avoth* 1:6.
28. *Avoth* 1:8.
29. *Avoth* 1:10.
30. *Avoth* 1:12; *Yoma* 35a; *Pesachim* 66b.
31. *Shabbath* 15a.
32. *Avoth* 2:8.

31. Rabban Gamliel the Elder,[33] along with Rabbi Eliezer ben Hyrcanus, Rabbi Yehoshua ben Chananiah, Rabbi Shimon ben Nethanel, Rabbi Elazar ben Arakh.[34]

32. Rabban Shimon ben Gamliel I, along with Rabbi Akiba, Rabbi Tarfon, Rabbi Shimon ben Elazar, Rabbi Yochanan ben Nuri.[35]

33. Rabbi Gamliel II, with Rabbi Meir, Rabbi Yishmael, Rabbi Yehudah, Rabbi Yosé, Rabbi Shimon bar Yochai, Rabbi Nechemiah, Rabbi Elazar ben Shamua, Rabbi Yochanan HaSandlar, Shimon ben Azzai, Rabbi Chanania ben Teradion, Rabbi Yosé HaGelelili, Rabbi Shimon ben Eliezer.

34. Rabbi Shimon ben Gamliel II

35. Rabbi Yehudah the Prince (*The Mishnah*), with Rabbi Efes, Rabbi Chanina bar Chama, Rabbi Chiya, Rabbi Yanai, Bar Kapara, Rabbi Hoshia.

AMARAIM

36. Rav (Abba Arikha), Shmuel, Rabbi Yochanan (*Jerusalem Talmud*).

37. Rav Huna, Rav Yehudah, Rav Nachman, Rav Kahana, Rabba bar bar Channa, Rav Ami, Rav Asi, Rav Dimi, Rav Avin.

38. Rabbah, Rav Yoseph, Rav Chisda, Rabba bar Rav Huna.

39. Abaya, Rava

40. Rav Ashi, Ravina (*Babylonian Talmud*).

33. *Shabbath* 15a.
34. From Rabban Yochanan ben Zakkai, *Avoth* 2:8.
35. All subsequent listings are from *Yad*, Introduction.

TEN

THE SANHEDRIN

10:1 The Sanhedrin (סַנְהֶדְרִין)[1] was the supreme council of Israel. As long as it stood, it was the supreme court and legislative body in all matters of Torah law. As such, the Sanhedrin was entrusted with keeping and interpreting the Oral Torah.[2]

10:2 It is a positive commandment to set up courts to interpret and decide questions of Torah law. It is thus written, "You shall appoint judges and officers in all your gates, which God is giving you" (Deuteronomy 16:18).[3]

10:3 The commandment includes the communal responsibility to appoint a duly ordained[4] Sanhedrin.[5] This precedes the establishment of other courts.[6]

---

1. From the Greek word συνεδρια denoting a council; *Arukh.* Cf. *Targum* on Psalms 107:32. It comes from the two Greek words *syn* συν, "together," and *hedra* εδρια, "seats;" i.e. where a council sits together; *Sefer HaTishbi.* It was also known as the "Great Court" (*Beth Din HaGadol,* בֵּית דִּין הַגָּדוֹל).
2. *Yad, Mamrim* 1:1.
3. *Sanhedrin* 16b; *Sifri* (144) on Deuteronomy 16:18; *Yad, Sanhedrin* 1:1; *Sefer HaMitzvoth,* Positive Commandment 176; *Sefer Mitzvoth Gadol,* Positive Commandment 97; *Chinukh* 491.
4. Some say that since ordination no longer exists, this commandment no longer applies; *Ramban* on Deuteronomy 16:18; cf. *Sefer Meirath Eynayim* (Sema) 1:1.
5. Rashi, *Sanhedrin* 16b, s.v. *Echad;* cf. *Tosafoth, ibid.*
6. *Yad, Sanhedrin* 1:3.

10:4   The Sanhedrin consisted of 71 judges. God thus commanded Moses, "Gather to Me seventy men of the elders of Israel . . . and bring them to the Tent of Meeting, so that they should stand there with you" (Numbers 11:16). This was the first Sanhedrin. Counting Moses himself, it consisted of 71 members.[7]

10:5   Since the membership of the Sanhedrin is fixed by the Torah, its number cannot be changed.[8]

10:6   Nevertheless, it was permitted to allow outside sages to enter into the deliberations of the Sanhedrin without voting privileges. Cases are therefore sometimes found in which a greater number participate in a decision.[9]

10:7   The Sanhedrin could not render judgment unless its entire membership was present.[10] If a member was absent, however, a temporary substitute could be appointed.[11]

10:8   The leading sage of the Sanhedrin was appointed as its head, taking the place of Moses in the first Sanhedrin.[12] His official title was "Head of the Sitting" (*Rosh HaYeshiva*,

7. *Sanhedrin* 1:6 (2a); *Yad, Sanhedrin* 1:3. Cf. *VaYikra Rabbah* 33:2; *Eikha Rabbah* 0:24. The word "elders" (*zekenim*, זְקֵנִים) in the Torah usually denotes the Sanhedrin; *Sotah* 45a. Also see Exodus 24:1; *Rosh HaShanah* 25a; *Margalioth HaYam* on *Sanhedrin* 2a 46. See Ezekiel 8:11, Radak ad loc.
8. *Sanhedrin* 42a; *Yad, Sanhedrin* 9:3, *Mamrim* 2:2; cf. *Beer Sheva* on *Horioth* 3b, s.v. *Meah* (p. 6a). See *Choshen Mishpat* 18:2.
9. *Urim VeThumim, Thumim* 18:3, from *Sanhedrin* 5:4 (40a), cf. *Tosefoth Yom Tov ad loc.*; *Yad, Sanhedrin* 10:8. Cf. *Megillah* 17b; *Zevachim* 1:3 (11b); *Yadayim* 3:5, 4:2; *Horioth* 3b; *Maharatz Chajas ad loc.*; *Mishneh LaMelekh* on *Yad, Sanhedrin* 9:3; *Rashash, Sanhedrin* 16b; *Chasdey David* on *Tosefta, Sanhedrin* 7:3, s.v. *Ain Mosifin*. Regarding the Great Assembly, see above, 8:61. Also see *Yesod HaMishnah*, p. 38; *Margolioth HaYam, Sanhedrin* 13b 5.
10. *Horioth* 30; *Tosafoth, Sanhedrin* 16b, s.v. *Echad*.
11. Cf. *Rashi, Horioth* 4b, s.v. *O; Yad, Shegagoth* 13:1; *Lechem Mishneh ad loc.* s.v. *VeLo*. A decision was rendered in the absence of two regular members; *Horioth* 13b.
12. *Yad, Sanhedrin* 1:3; *Tosafoth, Sanhedrin* 16b, s.v. *Echad*. Cf. *Horioth* 13b; *Chagigah* 2:2 (16b); *Bertenoro, Tosefoth Yom Tov*, on *Avoth* 1:4.

רֹאשׁ הַיְשִׁיבָה).[13] Later, however, he was referred to as the "President" (*Nasi*, נָשִׂיא).[14]

10:9   Any judgment issued by the Sanhedrin in the absence of the *Nasi* was invalid.[15]

10:10   The second ranking sage of the Sanhedrin was appointed as assistant to the *Nasi*. He was known as the "Master of the Court" (*Av Beth Din*, אַב בֵּית דִּין).[16] Both he and the *Nasi* were voting members of the Sanhedrin.[17]

10:11   The Sanhedrin would sit in a semicircle, so that all its members would be able to see each other.[18] They would also have an equal view of all witnesses testifying.[19]

10:12   Out of respect for the *Nasi*, the *Av Beth Din* would sit at the extreme right. He would be followed by the *Nasi*, and then by the rest of the Sanhedrin in order of their capability.[20]

13. *Berakhoth* 57a; *Yad, Sanhedrin* 1:3. He was also called the *mufla* (מוּפְלָא); Rambam on *Horioth* 1:4; *Tifereth Yisrael, Sanhedrin* 1:6 44; *Margolioth HaYam, Sanhedrin* 3b 11.
14. *Taanith* 2:1; *Pesachim* 66a; above, note 12. Also see below, note 16.
15. *Horioth* 4b; *Yad, Shegagoth* 13:1. the *Nasi* could be impeached, however; see *Berakhoth* 27b; *Yerushalmi, Berakhoth* 4:1 (32b).
16. See note 12. Some say that the post of *Av Beth Din* originated with Yosi ben Yochanan (*Avoth* 1:4); Rashash, *Sanhedrin* 16b. However, there is ample evidence that the post existed earlier; see *Moed Katan* 26a; *Melekheth Sh'lomah, Maaser Sheni* 5:15; *Peney Moshe* on *Yerushalmi, Maaser Sheni* 5:5 (37b); *Sheyarey Karban* on *Yerushalmi, Sotah* 9:11 (44b); *Sefer HaYuchsin* 1, s.v. *Shemaya* (Jerusalem, 1962), p. 9a.
17. This is obvious from *Yad, Sanhedrin* 1:3. Others, however, maintain that the *Av Beth Din* was not a voting member of the Sanhedrin; *Tosafoth, Sanhedrin* 3b, s.v. *Rabbi Yehudah*, 16b, s.v. *Echad, Sukkah* 51b, s.v. *VeHayu*; Rashi, *Horioth* 4b, s.v. *O*; Rashash, *Sanhedrin* 3b. This explains why 72 members are occasionally found; *Zevachim* 1:3 (11b); *Yedayim* 3:5, 4:2; *Megillah* 7a; Rashash, *Sanhedrin* 16b; *Tifereth Yisrael* on *Sanhedrin* 1:6 44; *Margolioth HaYam*, *Sanhedrin* 3b, 11. There may have been cases where neither were voting members, see below, notes 44, 49.
18. *Sanhedrin* 4:3 (36b); *Eikhah Rabbah* 0:23; Rashi, *Chulin* 5a, s.v. *SheHayu*. Others say that the reason was so that the *Nasi* and *Av Beth Din* would see all the other members; *Yad, Sanhedrin* 1:3.
19. Rashi, *Sanhedrin* 36b, s.v. *KeChatzi*. See *Margolioth HaYam* 36b 21.
20. *Yad, Sanhedrin* 1:3. This is the opinion of Rabbi Tzadok; *Tosefta, Sanhedrin* 8:1. See *Margolioth HaYam* 19b 1, 36b 20. Others, however, follow the first opinion in

10:13   Every member of the Sanhedrin had to be distinguished in Torah knowledge, wisdom, humility, fear of God, indifference to monetary gain, love of truth, love of fellow man, and good reputation.[21] It is thus written, "You shall provide out of all the people, able men, who fear God, men of truth, disdaining unjust gain, and place them over [the people]" (Exodus 18:21).[22] It is likewise written, "Take from each of your tribes, wise men, with understanding and full of knowledge, and I will make them your leaders" (Deuteronomy 1:13).[23]

10:14   Since the Sanhedrin had to be competent to render judgment in all cases that came before it, all its members had to be expert in all areas of the Torah.[24] They also had to have enough knowledge of science and mathematics to be able to adapt Torah law to all possible problems.[25]

10:15   Members of the Sanhedrin likewise had to have knowledge of other religions, as well as the teachings of idolatry and the occult arts, so as to be able to render judgment in cases involving these matters.[26] For this reason, even studies which were normally discouraged or forbidden, were permitted to members of the Sanhedrin when these studies were required for judgment.[27]

the Tosefta, that the Nasi and Av Beth Din sat in the center; Sefer Mitzvoth Gadol, Positive Commandment 97 (186b). Cf. Yerushalmi, Sanhedrin 1:4 (8b).

21. Yad, Sanhedrin 2:7; Choshen Mishpat 7:11. Cf. Sanhedrin 88b; Yerushalmi, Sanhedrin 1:4 (8b); Tosefta, Chagigah 2:4; Sifri (92) on Numbers 11:16.

22. These were for the original Sanhedrin of Moses; Exodus 24:1, Sifri, loc cit.; Rosh HaShanah 25a.

23. Devarim Rabbah 1:7; Yad, Sanhedrin 2:7; HaGra, Choshen Mishpat 7:43.

24. Yad, Sanhedrin 2:1; Sefer Chasidim 309. Also see Yad, Sanhedrin 1:5.

25. Yad, Sanhedrin 2:1; Kuzari 2:64 (71a). See Rabbi Moshe Cohen (Ramakh), quoted in Kesef Mishneh on Yad, loc cit.

26. Sanhedrin 17a; Menachoth 65a.

27. Sanhedrin 68a; Shabbath 75a; Tosafoth, Menachoth 65a, s.v. Baaley; Sefer Mitzvoth Gadol, Positive Commandment 97 (186c). Cf. Avodah Zarah 18a, 43b; Rosh HaShanah 24b.

10:16   The Sanhedrin was required to hear all testimony directly, and not through an interpreter.[28] It is therefore preferable[29] that its members be familiar with all the languages spoken by Jews around the world.[30]

10:17   When a foreign language is used in testimony, the Sanhedrin must have at least two members who speak that language to examine the witnesses.[31] There must also be a third member who understands the language.[32] These three members then constitute a minor court (*beth din*, בֵּית דִּין) of three, who can report the testimony to the entire body.[33] Once testimony has been accepted by a minor court, it is no longer considered second hand testimony.[34]

10:18   In order that the Sanhedrin command the utmost respect,[35] its members must be of good appearance,[36] and

---

28. *Makkoth* 1:9 (6b); cf. *Tosefoth Yom Tov ad loc.; Yad, Sanhedrin* 21:8; *Choshen Mishpat* 17:6, 28:6; *Pith'chey Teshuvah ad loc.* 28:19; *Teshuvoth Tashbatz* 1:160 (end).

29. But not absolutely necessary; *Meiri, Sanhedrin* 17a; *Margolioth HaYam* 17a 32. There are qualifications that are preferable for the Sanhedrin, but they are not always necessary; *Kesef Mishneh, Lechem Mishneh* on *Yad, Sanhedrin* 2:6; *Sifri, Rashi,* on Deuteronomy 1:15. It appears that the absence of linguistic ability does not invalidate the Sanhedrin; *Horioth* 1:4 (4b).

30. *Yad, Sanhedrin* 2:6. There are, however, indications that members of the Sanhedrin must know 70 languages; *Sanhedrin* 17a; *Menachoth* 65a; *Targum, Rashi,* on Esther 2:22; cf. *Shekalim* 5:1; *Tifereth Yisrael ad loc.* 6. Other authorities, however, write that this is an exaggeration; *Kesef Mishneh* on *Yad, Sanhedrin* 2:6.

31. Cf. *Ran, Makkoth* (Rif 3a), s.v. *Davar Acher; Tosefoth Yom Tov, Makkoth* 1:9; *Sefer Meirath Eynayim* (Sema) 28:34.

32. *Sanhedrin* 17b; *Rashi ad loc.* s.v. *Shenayim; Tosefta, Sanhedrin* 8:1; *Tosafoth, Menachoth* 65a, s.v. *VeYode'im.* Although Rashi indicates that members of the Sanhedrin must know all seventy languages, the reasoning given would indicate that it is not an absolute necessity. The entire issue is interpreted differently in *Yad, Sanhedrin* 1:5.

33. *Maharsha, Sanhedrin* 17b; *Teshuvoth Radbaz* 335.

34. *Rashi, Sanhedrin* 17a, s.v. *MiPi.* See *Sanhedrin* 4:5 (37a); *Yad, Edoth* 17:1; *Choshen Mishpat* 28:8. Some authorities, however, dispute this; *Ramban* on Deuteronomy 17:6. See *Eleh HaMishpatim* on *Makkoth* 5a; *Margolioth HaYam* 17a 33. There are sources which maintain that all members must understand seventy languages; *Yerushalmi, Shekalim* 5:1; *Rabbenu Yonah, Sanhedrin* 16a (in Sam Chaim; Livorno, 1806); *Margolioth HaYam* 17b 3.

35. *Rashi, Sanhedrin* 17a, s.v. *Baaley.*

36. *Sanhedrin* 17a, *Menachoth* 65a; *Yad, Sanhedrin* 2:6.

free of bodily defect.[37] Therefore, a person who is blind, even in one eye, cannot be a member of the Sanhedrin.[38]

10:19   Similarly, the members of the Sanhedrin must command respect as mature individuals. Therefore, it is preferable that each member be at least forty years old,[39] unless he is incomparable in wisdom and universally respected.[40] Similarly, it is preferable that the head of the Sanhedrin be at least fifty years old.[41] Under no condition should a person under eighteen be appointed to the Sanhedrin.[42]

10:20   A person who is very old may not sit on the Sanhedrin, since he is apt to be too severe. The same is true of a man who is sterile, or even childless.[43] A Sanhedrin containing any such member is not validly constituted.[44] Therefore, if a member becomes very old or sexually maimed, he must be replaced.[45]

37. *Sanhedrin* 36b; *Yevamoth* 101a; *Yad, Sanhedrin* 2:6. Cf. *Teshuvoth Chatham Sofer, Orach Chaim* 12; *Margolioth HaYam* 36b 19.
38. *Yevamoth* 101a; *Yad, Sanhedrin* 2:9, 4:10; *Radbaz ad loc.* Also see *Sanhedrin* 34b; *Niddah* 49b; *Choshen Mishpat* 7:2; *Ketzoth HaChoshen; Nethivoth HaMishpat; ad loc.; Yad, Tumath Tzaraath* 9:5.
39. *Avodah Zarah* 19b; *Rashi ad loc.* s.v. *Ad; Sotah* 22b; *Yoreh Deah* 242:31 in *Hagah*. Other sources, however, write that they must have studied for forty years; *Tosafoth, Sotah* 22b, s.v. *VeAd;* cf. *Sifethey Cohen, Yoreh Deah* 242:49. Also see *Avoth* 5:21; *Avodah Zarah* 5b; *Teshuvoth Shevuth Yaakov* 1:140. Cf. *Rashi, Sanhedrin* 86b, s.v. *Nimtza.*
40. *Ibid.; Tosafoth, Sotah* 22b, s.v. *VeShavim; Sifethey Cohen, Yoreh Deah* 242:50.
41. *Chagigah* 14a; *Maharatz Chajas ad loc.* Cf. *Berakhoth* 28a.
42. Cf. *Shabbath* 56b; *Choshen Mishpat* 7:3. Rabbi Elazar ben Azariah was thus appointed as head of the Sanhedrin at the age of eighteen; *Berakhoth* 28a. Some sources, however, state that one must be at least twenty to judge cases involving capital punishment. *Yerushalmi, Sanhedrin* 4:7 (23a); *Peney Moshe, Amudey Yerushalayim, ad loc.;* according to reading in *Tur, Choshen Mishpat* 7; *HaGra, Choshen Mishpat* 7:13.
43. *Sanhedrin* 36b; *Tosefta, Sanhedrin* 7:3; *Yerushalmi, Sanhedrin* 4:7 (23a); *Yad, Sanhedrin* 2:3; *Teshuvoth Rashba* 6:191. As to what is considered "very old," see *Margolioth HaYam* 17a 30.
44. *Horioth* 1:4 (4b); *Rambam, Bertenoro; Tosefoth Yom Tov, ad loc.; Yad, Shegagoth* 13:1. There are indications, however, that sages such as Hillel, Rabbi Yochanan ben Zakkai, and Rabbi Akiba served on the Sanhedrin at a very advanced age. See *Margolioth HaYam, loc cit.* Also see above, note 17.
45. *Rashi (Rivan), Horioth* 4b, s.v. *O SheLo; Rabbenu Yonah, Sanhedrin* 36b; *Teshuvoth Rashba* 6:191; *Teshuvoth Shevuth Yaakov* 1:29; *Teshuvoth Chaim*

10:21 It is preferable that the members of the Sanhedrin be chosen from people of unbroken descent, as in the case of all positions of authority.[46] It is required, however, that all members of the Sanhedrin be of Jewish parentage. Therefore, the son of a proselyte[47] must have at least one[48] parent[49] who is Jewish by birth.[50] A Sanhedrin that has even a single proselyte as a member is invalidly constituted.[51]

10:22 Every member of the Sanhedrin must be of unblemished family,[52] as was the first Sanhedrin under Moses.[53] Therefore a bastard (*mamzer*, מַמְזֵר, i.e., the son of an adulterous or incestuous union) is ineligible for membership[54] and renders a Sanhedrin invalid.[55]

Shaul 89; *Teshuvoth Chazon Nachum* 53; *Tzion Yerushalayim*, on *Yerushalmi, Sanhedrin* 4:7 (23a). Some dispute this; *Meiri, Sanhedrin* 36b.

46. *Yad, Melakhim* 1:4; *Sefer Meirath Eynayim (Sema)* 7:1; Rabbi Akiba Eiger, *Yoreh Deah* 269:11. Cf. *Berakhoth* 27b.
47. However, the son of a Jewish mother and non-Jewish father is eligible; Rabbi Akiba Eiger, *Choshen Mishpat* 7:1; *Minchath Chinukh* 498.
48. But if both parents are proselytes, one is not eligible; Maharshal on *Tosafoth, Yevamoth* 102a, s.v. *LeInyan; Birkey Yosef, Choshen Mishpat* 7:1; Rabbi Aaron (ben Yosef) Sasoon, *Torath Emeth* 66 (Venice, 1626); *Pith'chey Teshuvah, Choshen Mishpat* 7:1. However, see Maharsha on *Tosafoth, Yevamoth* 102a, s.v. *LeInyan; Tosafoth, Kethuvoth* 44b, s.v. *VeAima, Sanhedrin* 36b, s.v. *Chad.* Also see *Kesef Mishneh* on *Yad, Sanhedrin* 2:9.
49. This is true whether it is the mother or father; *Tosafoth, Yevamoth* 102a, s.v. *LeInyan; Choshen Mishpat* 7:1; *Minchath Chinukh* 498; from *Kiddushin* 76b. Cf. *Kesef Mishneh* on *Yad, Melakhim* 1:4. Although Shemaya and Avtalyon were proselytes, they served as the heads of the Sanhedrin; *Chagigah* 2:2 (16a,b); see *Magen Avoth*; Maharal, *Derekh Chaim; Tosefoth Yom Tov*; Rashash; on *Avoth* 1:10; *Baaley Tosafoth* (Riva) on Mishpatim, quoted in *Margolioth HaYam* 36b 5; *Urim VeTehumim, Thumim* 7:1, *Birkhey Yosef, Choshen Mishpat* 7:1; *Kenesseth HaGedolah, Choshen Mishpat* 2; *Teshuvoth Noda BeYehudah, Choshen Mishpat* 2; *Teshuvoth Noda BeYehudah, Tinyena, Yoreh Deah* 182 (end); Maharatz Chajas, *Berakhoth* 19a; Rabbi Tzvi Hirsch (ben Chaim) Ohrbach, *Divrey Torah* 7:1 (Warsaw, 1881); *Margolioth HaYam* 36b 13 (end). Regarding King David, who was a descendant of Ruth, see *Beth Hillel, Yoreh Deah* 269:11. Cf. Rav Nissim Gaon, *Berakhoth* 27b, s.v. *Noki; Kesef Mishneh, Sanhedrin* 2:9. See above, note 17.
50. *Sanhedrin* 36b; *Yevamoth* 102a; *Yad, Sanhedrin* 2:9.
51. *Horioth* 1:4 (4b); *Yad, Shegagoth* 13:1.
52. *Sanhedrin* 4:2 (32a); *Kiddushin* 4:5 (76a); *Niddah* 49b.
53. *Sanhedrin* 36b; *Kiddushin* 76b; *Yad, Sanhedrin* 2:1.
54. *Sanhedrin* 36b; *Yad, Sanhedrin* 2:9
55. *Horioth* 1:4 (4b); *Yad, Shegagoth* 13:1.

10:23   A woman cannot be appointed as a member of the Sanhedrin or any other court.[56]

10:24   It is preferable that the Sanhedrin contain cohen-priests and Levites as members. It is thus written, "You shall come to the cohen-priest and Levites, and to the judge who shall be in those days" (Deuteronomy 17:9). Nonetheless, a Sanhedrin is valid even without cohen-priests and Levites.[57]

10:25   Every member of the Sanhedrin must be ordained,[58] following a tradition from Moses. It is thus written, "Moses did as God commanded him. He took Joshua . . . and laid his hands on him, commanding him, as God spoke through Moses" (Numbers 27:22,23). Moses also laid his hands on the other elders, ordaining them as members of the Sanhedrin.[59] These, in turn, ordained others, generation after generation, in an unbroken line of ordination from Moses.[60]

10:26   Although Moses ordained the first Sanhedrin with the actual laying of hands, this was a special case, and was only done that one time.[61] All subsequent ordinations were performed orally, granting the subject the title of "Rabbi"

---

56. *Yerushalmi, Sanhedrin* 3:9 (18a); *Yerushalmi, Shevuoth* 4:1 (19a); *Tosafoth, Bava Kama* 15a, s.v. *Asher, Shevuoth* 29b, s.v. *Shevuoth, Niddah* 50a, s.v. *Kol; Chinukh* 83; *Choshen Mishpat* 7:4. Also see *Tosafoth, Yevamoth* 45b, s.v. *Mi, Gittin* 88b, s.v. *VeLo;* Rabbi Yehudah Leib Margolioth, *Teshuvoth P'ri Tevuah* 46 (Novydvor, 1796). Nevertheless, a woman can render a decision in questions of Torah law; *Chinukh* 152 (end): *Birkey Yosef, Choshen Mishpat* 7:12; *Pithchey Teshuvah, Choshen Mishpat* 7:5; cf. *Shaarey Teshuvah, Orach Chaim* 461:17. Regarding Deborah, see *Tosafoth, loc cit.*
57. *Sifri, Yalkut* (911), *ad loc.; Yad, Sanhedrin* 2:2.
58. *Yad, Sanhedrin* 1:8. Cf. *Sanhedrin* 4:4 (37a).
59. From *Yad, Sanhedrin* 4:1, it appears that Moses also laid his hands on the members of the Sanhedrin. However, in Numbers 11:16,24 there is no mention of it. See *Margolioth HaYam* 13b 19. See below, note 61.
60. *Sanhedrin* 13b; *Yad, Sanhedrin* 4:1; *Sefer Meirath Eynayim (Sema)* 1:9. Cf. Numbers 8:10, 11:17, 27:18, Deuteronomy 34:9.
61. The laying of hands may have been to confer the gifts of prophecy; *Margolioth HaYam* 13b 13, 19.

(רַבִּי)[62] and declaring that he is "ordained with the right to judge cases involving fines."[63]

10:27 Ordination must be conferred by a court of three,[64] containing at least one ordained member.[65] It can be done either in person, or by messenger or letter.[66] A single court can ordain many individuals at once.[67]

10:28 Therefore, as long as a single ordained person is alive, the tradition of ordination can remain unbroken. The ordained person can form a court with two unordained men, and ordain as many others as needed.[68] The unordained members of the court, however, could then never be ordained themselves,[69] since that would give them an interest in the case.[70]

10:29 Some authorities maintain that ordination must be performed by day.[71] In this respect, it is no different than any other judgment.[72]

62. Cf. *Bava Metzia* 86a (top); Rashi, *Kethuvoth* 43b, s.v. *Amar Rav Zeira, Bava Metzia* 85a, s.v. *Asmechey.* Also see *Tosefta, Edduyoth* 3:4; Rambam, Introduction to *Mishnah; Arukh* s.v. *Abuya; Iggereth Rav Sherira Gaon* 2 (p. 125 ff); Rabbi Shimon ben Tzemach Duran (Rashbatz), *Magen Avoth* on Avoth/2:1; *Sefer HaTishbi,* s.v. *Rav; Margolioth HaYam* 13b 16. Also see *Tikkuney Zohar* 21 (43b); *Tikkuney Zohar Chadash* 98a; *Shaarey Zohar, Kethuvoth* 43b; *Etz Chaim, Shaar Anakh* 3 (Tel Aviv, 1960), p. 272; *Shemonah Shaarim, Shaar Rashbi,* beginning.
63. *Sanhedrin* 13b; *Yerushalmi, Horioth* 3:2 (16b, end); *Yad, Sanhedrin* 4:2. There may have been a special ordination for membership in the Sanhedrin; cf. *Sanhedrin* 4:4 (37a); *Melekheth Sh'lemah ad loc.*
64. *Sanhedrin* 1:3 (2a), 13b; *Yerushalmi* 1:2 (6a, end).
65. *Yad, Sanhedrin* 4:3; *Kesef Mishneh,* Radbaz, ad loc.; Ran, Meiri, *Sanhedrin* 14a; *Sheyarey Karban* on *Yerushalmi* 1:2 (6a), s.v. *Semikhath.* Cf. Rashi, *Sanhedrin* 14a, s.v. *Lo;* Rambam on *Sanhedrin* 1:3.
66. *Yad, Sanhedrin* 4:6; *Kesef Mishneh ad loc.* Cf. Rashi, *Sanhedrin* 14a, s.v. *Somkhin.*
67. *Yad, Sanhedrin* 4:7. Cf. *Sanhedrin* 14a; *Yerushalmi, Sanhedrin* 10:2 (52b).
68. *Yad, Sanhedrin* 4:11. Cf. *Sanhedrin* 14a.
69. Thus, Yehudah ben Bava had two others with him when he ordained his five disciples; *Sanhedrin* 14a. He could not have used two of the five, who in turn could have been ordained by their fellows. This is also indicated by the wording of *Yad, Sanhedrin* 4:11.
70. Cf. *Choshen Mishpat* 7:12, from *Bava Bathra* 43a.
71. *Minchath Chinukh* 491.
72. *Sanhedrin* 4:1 (32a); *Yad, Sanhedrin* 11:1; *Choshen Mishpat* 8:2.

10:30   Ordination can only be conferred in the Land of Israel. The entire area included in the First Commonwealth is valid for such ordination.[73] Both the ordaining court and the persons being ordained must be within its borders.[74] If a Sanhedrin was ordained in the Holy Land, however, it can then function in other lands as well.[75]

10:31   To qualify for ordination, a man must have all the qualifications necessary for membership in the Sanhedrin.[76] However, if he later becomes disqualified from membership in the Sanhedrin because of age or physical disability, his ordination is still valid.[77]

10:32   To qualify for ordination, one must be expert in all areas of Torah law.[78] However, now that the Oral Torah has been committed to writing, it is sufficient that one be familiar enough with all the written authorities to render judgment in all cases.[79]

10:33   The greatest Torah scholars of each generation are automatically qualified for ordination. It is thus written, "You shall go to the . . . judge who shall be *in those days*" (Deuteronomy 17:9). This indicates that each generation has its own standard.[80]

73. *Yad, Sanhedrin* 4:7; *Kesef Mishneh*, Radbaz, *ad loc.* Cf. *Yerushalmi, Bikkurim* 3:3 (11b).
74. *Sanhedrin* 14a; *Yerushalmi, Bikkurim* 3:3 (11b); *Yad, Sanhedrin* 4:7.
75. *Makkoth* 1:10 (7a); *Sanhedrin* 14a; *Yad, Sanhedrin* 4:12.
76. *Yerushalmi, Chagigah* 1:8 (7a); *Yerushalmi, Nedarim* 10:8 (35b); *Yad, Sanhedrin* 4:9; Rambam on *Berkhoroth* 4:3.
77. *Ketzoth HaChoshen* 7:2 (end); *Minchath Chinukh* 491 (end).
78. *Yad, Sanhedrin* 4:8; *Sifethey Cohen, Yoreh Deah* 242:22. Cf. *Yad, Sanhedrin* 1:5. Some sources, however, question this; *Minchath Chinukh* 491, from *Sanhedrin* 5b. Rabban Gamaliel was likewise not familiar with *Uktzin*; *Horioth* 13b.
79. Cf. *Teshuvoth Shevuth Yaakov* 2:64; *Pith'chey Teshuvah, Yoreh Deah* 242:3; Maharsha, *Sotah* 22a, s.v. *Yirah*.
80. *Sifri* (153), *Yalkut Shimoni* (911), Rashi, *ad loc.; Rosh HaShanah* 25b. Cf. *Chinukh* 495 (end); Rashash, *Yoma* 80a.

10:34   It is forbidden to appoint a man to the Sanhedrin or any other court if he does not have the necessary qualifications, even if he has other good qualities. To do so is to violate the commandment, "You shall not respect persons in judgment" (Deuteronomy 1:17).[81]

10:35   The Sanhedrin originally convened in the Temple area,[82] in the Chamber of Cut Stones (*Lishkath HaGazith,* לִשְׁכַּת הַגָּזִית).[83] This was a chamber built into the north wall of the Temple, half inside the sanctuary and half outside, with doors providing access both to the Temple and to the outside.[84]

10:36   The place where the Sanhedrin convened was actually outside the sanctuary area. The Sanhedrin would sit while in judgment, and it is forbidden to sit within the sanctuary area.[85] On the other hand, part of this chamber had to be inside the sanctuary area, since the Sanhedrin judged many things involving priests and the Temple service, and this had to be done within the Temple grounds.[86] Moreover, questions would often arise during the divine service, when it is forbidden for a cohen-priest to leave the sanctuary

81. *Sifri Yalkut* (802), Rashi *ad loc.; Sanhedrin* 7b; *Yad, Sanhedrin* 3:8; *Sefer HaMitzvoth,* Negative Commandment 284; *Sefer Mitzvoth Gadol,* Negative Commandment 194; *Chinukh* 414; *Choshen Mishpat* 8:1. Cf. *Yerushalmi, Bikkurim* 3:3 (11b).
82. *Yerushalmi, Makkoth* 2:6 (7a); *Mekhilta* on Exodus 20:23 (74a), 21:14 (81a); Rashi on Exodus 21:1.
83. *Sanhedrin* 11:2 (86b); *Middoth* 5:4; *Yad, Sanhedrin* 1:3. Cf. *Peah* 2:6; *Tanchuma, VaYakhel* 8.
84. *Yoma,* 25a; *Yad, Beth HaBechirah* 5:17.
85. *Yoma* 25a. If there was no entrance to the outside, the entire room would have the status of inside the sanctuary; *Yoma* 25a; *Pesachim* 86a; *Zevachim* 56a; *Maaser Sheni* 3:8. Moreover, if there were no entrance from the outside, people would have to go through the Temple in order to come to the Sanhedrin, and it is forbidden to make use of the Temple as a thoroughfare to go to a place outside the sanctuary area; *Berakhoth* 9:5 (54a).
86. *Yoma* 25a; commentaries on Psalms 52:16. This was an important task of the Sanhedrin; *Middoth* 5:4; *Yad, Biyath HaMikdash* 6:11.

area.[87] There was also a requirement that there be direct access from the Great Altar (*mizbeach*, מִזְבֵּחַ) to the Sanhedrin.[88]

10:37   It was only in this chamber that the Sanhedrin could perform all its functions,[89] including the trial of capital offenses.[90]

10:38   However, in the year 3788 (28 c.e.),[91] when the Sanhedrin relinquished its power to try capital offenses,[92] it moved to another room on the Temple Mount,[93] and then into the city itself. When Jerusalem was destroyed in 3828 (68 c.e.), the Sanhedrin moved to Yavneh.[94] During the ensuing century, the location of the Sanhedrin alternated between Yavneh and Usha.[95] From there it moved consecutively to Shafar'am,[96] Beth She'arim, Sephoris, and

---

87. *Yad, Biyath HaMikdash* 2:5; *Chinukh* 151; from Leviticus 10:7, 21:2.

88. *Mekhilta* on Exodus 20:23 and 21:14. Both derivations are required, one to teach that they must be in proximity to one another, and the other to require that there be direct access from one to the other. Cf. *Sanhedrin* 7b; *Tosafoth, Avodah Zarah* 8b, s.v. *MeLamed.*

89. Some maintain that the Sanhedrin lost all its prerogatives when they left the Temple; Ramban on *Sefer HaMitzvoth*, Positive Commandment 153. Others, however, state that this is not the accepted view; *Megillath Esther ibid.*

90. *Sanhedrin* 52a; *Yad, Sanhedrin* 14:11; *Tosafoth, Shabbath* 15a, s.v. *Eleh, Sanhedrin* 14b, *Avodah Zarah* 8b, s.v. *MeLamed, Sanhedrin* 37b, s.v. *MiYom; Yad Rama,* Meiri, *Sanhedrin* 51a; *Sefer HaMitzvoth,* Shoresh 14 (end); Maharatz Chajas, *Shabbath* 15a.

91. *Shabbath* 15a; *Sanhedrin* 41a; *Avodah Zarah* 8b; *Yad, Sanhedrin* 14:13. Cf. *Yoma* 39b. This is also when Rabbi Tzadok began fasting that the Temple not be destroyed; *Gittin* 56b.

92. *Avodah Zarah* 8b; Rashi, *Sanhedrin* 41a, s.v. *Eleh, Rosh HaShanah* 31a, s.v. *MiLishkath; Yad Rama,* Sanhedrin 51a.

93. Cf. Rashi, *Avodah Zarah* 8a, s.v. *BaChanuth, Rosh HaShanah* 31a (end), s.v. *MiLishkath.* But see Jeremiah 37:16. Also see *Margolioth HaYam* 41a 22.

94. Cf. *Gittin* 56b; *Koheleth Rabbah* 7:15.

95. Rashi, *Rosh HaShanah* 31b, s.v. *U'MiYavneh.* Cf. *Yerushalmi, Peah* 1:1 (3a). The move apparently took place about 3900 (140 c.e.); cf. *Shir HaShirim Rabbah* 2:16. It was where Rabbi Yehudah the Prince was ordained; *Tosefta, Megillah* 2:8. Cf. *Bava Bathra* 28b; *Yerushalmi, Moed Katan* 3:1; *Yerushalmi, Kethuvoth* 4:8. See *Sanhedrin* 14a.

96. Cf. *Sanhedrin* 14a; *Avodah Zarah* 8b; *Tosefta, Moed Katan* 6:2. The ordination of Rabbi Meir may have taken place during the transition; *Margolioth HaYam, Sanhedrin* 14a 3.

Tiberias.[97] It remained functioning in Tiberias[98] until shortly before the completion of the Talmud.[99] During the persecutions of Constantinius (4097-4121; 337-361 c.e.), the Sanhedrin had to go into hiding,[100] and it was eventually disbanded. There is a tradition that it will be in Tiberias that the Sanhedrin will be restored.[101]

10:39 The traditional ordination (*semikhah*, סְמִיכָה) was thus abolished in the year 4118 (358 c.e.).[102] The Sanhedrin and other duly constituted courts cannot be established until this ordination is reinstituted.[103]

10:40 What is called "ordination" today is not true ordination, but rather, a certification that the individual is expert in certain areas of Torah law.[104] Moreover, it implies that he has the permission of his teachers to render public decisions;[105] without such permission it is forbidden.[106]

---

97. *Rosh HaShanah* 31a,b; *Yad, Sanhedrin* 14:12. These last three places were the seat of the Sanhedrin during the time of Rabbi Yehudah the Prince; *Sanhedrin* 32b; *Kethuboth* 103b; Rashi, *Rosh HaShanah* 31b, s.v. *Beth She'arim*. Cf. *Margolioth HaYam* 3b 6.
98. Cf. *Sanhedrin* 12a; *Yerushalmi, Pesachim* 4:2 (26a); *Yad, Kiddush HaChodesh* 5:3.
99. Cf. *Bava Metzia* 86a; *Yad*, Introduction.
100. *Bereshith Rabbah* 31:12.
101. *Rosh HaShanah* 31b; *Yad, Sanhedrin* 14:12. Cf. Rabbi Yosef Rosen, *Tzofnath Paaneach*, Part 2, 143:2 (Warsaw, 1936); *Margolioth HaYam* 13b 4 (end). Also see *Yalkut Shimoni* 1:161; *Nitzutzey Zohar* 1:119a 4.
102. Ramban, *Sefer HaZakhuth, Gittin* (on Rif 18a); *Tzemach David* 4118; *Seder HaDoroth* 4118; cf. Ramban on *Sefer HaMitzvoth*, Positive Commandment 153; Rabbi Avraham ben Chiya, *Sefer HaIbbur* (London, 1851), p. 97; Rabbi Yitzchak HaYisraeli, *Yesod Olam* 4:9, 4:18 (end); *Teshuvoth Tashbatz* 1:136; *Teshuvoth Ralbach* 147 (end); Tashbatz, *Zohar HaRakia* 54; Note on *Machzor Vitri*, p. 478. Some say that this was when people stopped counting from "shetaroth" and began counting from creation; *Shalsheleth HaKabbalah*, p. 78.
103. *Yad, Sanhedrin* 4:4; Ramban on Deuteronomy 16:16; *Chinukh* 491.
104. *Teshuvoth Rivash* 271 (end); *Yoreh Deah* 242:14 in Hagah; *Sifethey Cohen, Yoreh Deah* 242:22; *Choshen Mishpat* 1:4; *Sefer Meirath Eynayim (Sema)* 1:9; *Pachad Yitzchak*, s.v. *Semikha* (51b).
105. Cf. *Sanhedrin* 5b; Rabbi Shmuel (ben Avraham) Abohab, *Teshuvoth Devar Sh'muel* 206 (Venice, 1702); *Gilyon Maharsha, Yoreh Deah* 242:14.
106. *Eruvin* 63a; *Yad, Talmud Torah* 5:2; *Yoreh Deah* 242:4.

Such ordination, however, in no way implies competence to serve on the Sanhedrin.[107]

10:41   Therefore, no rabbinical court today can judge cases on its own authority.[108] The only authority that such courts have is as agents of the earlier ordained courts.[109] In this capacity, they can only judge commonly occurring cases involving actual loss on the part of the litigants.[110] However, infrequently occurring cases, and those involving punitive damages or fines, require duly ordained judges, and therefore cannot be judged in contemporary rabbinical courts.[111]

10:42   Some say that like all other positions of authority, ordination can be established by common consent as well as by unbroken tradition.[112] However, only those living in the Land of Israel are counted with regard to matters dealing with authority.[113] Therefore, ordination can be re-established by the consent of the religious leaders in the Holy Land, even if they represent a minority of world Jewry.[114]

10:43   Therefore, if all the religious leaders and authorities living in the Land of Israel were to agree to ordain a suitable individual, he would be considered duly ordained. He would then have the authority to set up a court and ordain others. Thus, the Sanhedrin and other courts could be restored.[115]

107. Yad, Sanhedrin 4:4.
108. Cf. Kesef Kedoshim, Choshen Mishpat 1:1.
109. Tosafoth, Gittin 88b, s.v. BeMiltha; Sefer Meirath Eynayim (Sema) 1:1.
110. Gittin 88b; Bava Kama 84b; Yad, Sanhedrin 5:8,9.
111. Rosh, Bava Kama 1:20, 8:3; Choshen Mishpat 1:1.
112. Cf. Urim VeThumim, Thumim 7:1. Thus, the elders of the Israelites in Egypt had the status of a Sanhedrin without being ordained; cf. Exodus 24:1; 3:16, 4:29, 12:21, 17:6, 18:12, 24:9; Rashi on Numbers 11:16.
113. Horioth 3a; Yad, Shegagoth 13:2; Yesod HaMishnah, pp. 36, 37.
114. Rambam on Bekhoroth 4:3.
115. Rambam on Sanhedrin 1:3; Bertenoro, Tosefoth Yom Tov, Ibid.; Yad, Sanhedrin 4:11; Rashba, Bava Kama 36b, s.v. Ho'il; Rosh. Bava Metzia 3:2; Pilpula Charifta

10:44   It is foretold that the restoration of the Sanhedrin will precede the coming of the Messiah. God thus told His prophet, "I will restore your judges as at first, and your councelors as in the beginning; afterward you will be called the city of righteousness, the faithful city. Zion shall be redeemed with justice, and those who return to her, with righteousness" (Isaiah 1:26,27).[116] This restoration, however, can only take place in such a time as willed by God.[117]

10:45   The Messiah will be a king of Israel, and as such, he can only be recognized by a duly ordained Sanhedrin.[118]

10:46   There is a tradition that the Sanhedrin will be restored after a partial ingathering of the Jewish exile, before Jerusalem is rebuilt and restored.[119] There is also a tradition that Elijah will present himself before a duly ordained Sanhedrin when he announces the coming of the Messiah.[120] Like all events in the Messianic drama, the restoration of the Sanhedrin can only occur at the time decreed by God.[121]

ad loc. 3; *Pachad Yitzchak*, s.v. *Semikhah* (51b); *Teshuvoth Rabbi Yaakov Berab, Kuntres HuChukhum* (Jerusalem, 1958), p. 199ff; *Beth Yosef, Choshen Mishpat* 295; *Birkey Yosef, Choshen Mishpat* 1:7; *Sifethey Cohen, Yoreh Deah* 242:22; *Sefer Meirath Eynayim (Sema)* 1:9; *Minchath Chinukh* 491; Rabbi Yaakov Emden (Maharibatz), *Sanhedrin* 14a. In 5298 (1538 c.e.), Rabbi Yaakov Berab temporarily restored this practice, ordaining several scholars in Safed, including Rabbi Yosef Caro and Rabbi Moshe di Trani, but it was later discontinued. Opposing the restoration of ordination were *Teshuvoth Ralbach, Kuntres HaSemikha*; Radbaz on Yad, *Sanhedrin* 4:11; Chazon Ish, *Maasroth* 13. For further discussion, see Rabbi Yaakov Pieterkovski, *Adath Yaakov* (Jerusalem, 1935, 1940); Rabbi Tzvi Makovski, *VeAshiva Shoftaych* (Tel Aviv, 1938); Rabbi Aryeh Leib Frumkin, *Evven Sh'muel*, Part 1 (Vilna, 1874); Rabbi Aaron Mendel HaCohen, *Semikhath Chakhamim* (Kehir, 1911); Rabbi Yehudah Leib Maimon (Fishman), *Chidush HaSanhedrin* (Jerusalem, 1951). See above, note 101.

116. Rambam on *Sanhedrin* 1:3. Cf *Seder Arkim*, quoted in Rabbi Chaim Meir HaLevi Horowitz, *Kevod Chupah*, p. 19 (Frankfurt am Mein, 1888), and in *Otzar Midrashim*, p. 72. Also see *Shemoth Rabbah* 30:23. See below, note 119.

117. *Urim VeThumim, Thumim* 1:2 (3a).

118. See above, 8:54, below, 11:5.

119. *Megillah* 17b, Rashi ad loc. s.v. *VeKevan*. This would also appear to indicate that the Sanhedrin will be restored before the Messiah.

120. *Eruvin* 43b; Maharatz Chajas ad loc.; Ritva (in *Eyn Yaakov*) ad loc.; Rashash, *Sanhedrin* 13b. Cf. *Kerethi U'Phelethi* 110. *Beth HaSafek* (end).

ELEVEN

AUTHORITY

11:1   As long as the Sanhedrin remained in existence, it stood at the head of the judicial system in Israel.[1]

11:2   The lowest courts in this system were those consisting of three ordained judges. These courts had jurisdiction over all monetary cases, including those involving theft, fines, and punitive damages.[2] They also judged cases involving corporal punishment for the violation of negative commandments.[3]

11:3   The Great Sanhedrin in Jerusalem would also appoint minor Sanhedrins, consisting of 23 justices, in each major city.[4] These higher courts were the final authority in all questions of Torah law in their area of jurisdiction.[5] They also had jurisdiction in all regular cases involving capital punishment.[6]

1. See below, 11:14. Also see *Sanhedrin* 31b; *Yad, Sanhedrin* 6:6-8; *Choshen Mishpat* 14:1.
2. *Sanhedrin* 1:1 (2a); *Yad, Sanhedrin* 5:8.
3. *Sanhedrin* 1:2 (2a); *Yad, Sanhedrin* 5:4.
4. *Sanhedrin* 1:5 (2a); *Yad, Sanhedrin* 5:1.
5. *Sanhedrin* 88b. See below, 11:14. It is for this reason that every locality has a degree of autonomy with regard to Torah law, see below, 12:41, 13:6, 13:24.
6. *Sanhedrin* 1:4 (2a); *Yad, Sanhedrin* 5:2.

11:4   However, all major or unusual cases, as well as those involving all Israel, were judged only by the Great Sanhedrin in Jerusalem. The Torah thus says of the first Sanhedrin under Moses, "Every great matter, they shall bring to you" (Exodus 18:22).[7]

11:5   Therefore, only the Sanhedrin had the authority to appoint a king[8] or High Priest[9] over Israel. Only the Sanhedrin could appoint minor Sanhedrins,[10] declare voluntary war, or add to the area of the Temple or Jerusalem.[11] Similarly, only the Sanhedrin had the jurisdiction·to judge an entire tribe, an apostate city,[12] a false prophet,[13] or a rebellious elder.[14] If a High Priest (*Cohen Gadol*, פֹּהֵן גָּדוֹל) was guilty of a capital offense, he could be judged only by the Sanhedrin.[15]

11:6   The Sanhedrin likewise had jurisdiction in such unusual cases as the administration of the bitter waters to a suspected adultress,[16] as well as the calf slaughtered to expiate an unsolved murder.[17]

11:7   As representatives of all Israel, the Sanhedrin also administered the Temple. The Sanhedrin would judge the fitness of cohen-priests for service[18] and prepare the Red

---

7. *Sanhedrin* 16a; *Yad, Sanhedrin* 5:1, *K'ley HaMikdash* 4:15.
8. See above, 8:54.
9. *Mishpat HaMelukhah*, p. 27. *Tosefta, Sanhedrin* 3:2; *Yad, K'ley HaMikdash* 4:15.
10. The Mishnah, *Sanhedrin* 1:5 (2a), only mentions minor Sanhedrin for each tribe. In *Yad, Sanhedrin* 5:1, however, a Sanhedrin for each city is also included. See *Horioth* 4b; Ramban on Deuteronomy 16:18, Genesis 19:8; *Margolioth HaYam* 2a 36.
11. *Sanhedrin* 1:5 (2a); *Yad, Sanhedrin* 5:1.
12. *Ir HaNidachath* (עִיר הַנִּדַּחַת); Deuteronomy 13:13-19.
13. See above, 8:27. Also see 8:21.
14. See below, 11:56.
15. *Sanhedrin* 1:5 (2a); Yad, Sanhedrin 5:1.
16. *Sotah* (סוֹטָה); Numbers 5:11-31; *Sotah* 1:4 (7a); *Yad, Sanhedrin* 5:1, *Sotah* 3:1.
17. *Egla Arufa* (עֶגְלָה עֲרוּפָה); Deuteronomy 21:1-9; *Sotah* 9:1 (44b), *Yad, Sanhedrin* 5:1, *Rotzeach* 9:1.
18. *Middoth* 5:4; *Tosefta, Chagigah* 2:4; *Yad, Biyath HaMikdash* 6:11. See above, 10:36.

Heifer.[19] They would also provide corrected copies of the Torah.[20]

11:8   But most important, as long as the Sanhedrin was in existence, it was the final authority in all questions of Torah law. Whoever believes in the authority of the Torah must accept the decisions of the Sanhedrin as binding.[21]

11:9   It is a positive commandment to obey the Sanhedrin in all questions of Torah law. It is thus written, "You must follow . . . all that they declare to you, from the place that God shall choose, and you must observe all that they teach you" (Deuteronomy 17:10).[22] This includes all questions of tradition and Torah interpretation, as well as legislation passed by the Sanhedrin.[23]

11:10   It is, moreover, forbidden to dispute the authority of the Sanhedrin. It is thus written, "You must follow the law that they teach you and the judgment that they declare to you; you must not turn aside . . . to the right or to the left" (Deuteronomy 17:11).[24]

11:11   Therefore, the decisions of the Sanhedrin must be accepted even when they appear to be mistaken or illogical.[25] By definition, their decisions represent the will of God.[26]

---

19. *Parah Adumah* (פָרָה אֲדֻמָה); Numbers 19; *Tosefta, Sanhedrin* 3:2; *Yad, Parah Adumah* 3:2.
20. See above, 7:41.
21. *Yad, Mamrim* 1:1.
22. Ibid.; *Sefer HaMitzvoth,* Positive Commandment 174; *Sefer Mitzvoth Gadol,* Positive Commandment 111; *Chinukh* 495.
23. *Sifri ad loc.;* quoted in *Yad, Mamrim* 1:2; *Chinukh* 495.
24. *Yad, Mamrim* 1:2; *Sefer HaMitzvoth,* Negative Commandment 312; *Sefer Mitzvoth Gadol, Negative Commandment* 217; *Chinukh* 496. Cf. *Torath HaNevi'im, Maamar Lo Thasur* 3 (p. 97).
25. *Sifri, Yalkut* (911), Rashi, on Deuteronomy 17:11.
26. Ramban on Deuteronomy 17:11; Ramban on *Sefer HaMitzvoth, Shoresh* 1 (p. 7b); *Derashoth HaRan* 7 (p. 114).

11:12   Nevertheless, if the Sanhedrin permits something, and a Torah authority has a clear tradition or argument that it is forbidden, he must take the stricter course until he is able to confront the Sanhedrin with his opinion.[27] However, if the Sanhedrin hears his argument and rejects it, he is bound to follow the opinion of the Sanhedrin.[28]

11:13   The judiciary system in Israel included minor Sanhedrins, consisting of 23 sages, in each major city.[29] There were also two superior courts, also consisting of 23 members, one on the Temple Mount, and another near the door of the Temple.[30] Members of these superior courts would be chosen by the Sanhedrin from among the greatest sages of the regional minor Sanhedrins.[31] These courts kept records of all decisions handed down by the Sanhedrin, and decided accordingly in all cases of Torah law.

11:14   Whenever any question of Torah law would arise, it would be brought to the local minor Sanhedrin for decision. If they did not have a clear precedent or tradition, they would send their agents,[32] along with the questioner, to the superior court on the Temple Mount for a decision. If this court could not give a decision, the case would be brought to the Superior Court near the Temple door, which was second only to the Sanhedrin itself in authority. If this court could not decide the case, it would be brought to the Sanhedrin.[33]

27. Horioth 2b; Yad, Shegagoth 13:5; Ramban on Sefer HaMitzvoth, Shoresh 1 (7b).
28. Sanhedrin 11:2 (86b); Yad, Mamrim 3:8, 4:1. Cf. Rosh HaShanah 2:9 (25a).
29. There were also superior courts of 23 members for each tribe, above, note 10; Radbaz on Yad, Sanhedrin 1:2; Yad, Shegagoth 13:1. Cf. Sifri, Rashi, on Deuteronomy 16:18; Sanhedrin 16b; Makkoth 7a.
30. Sanhedrin 11:2 (86b); Yad, Sanhedrin 1:3, Mamrim 3:8.
31. Sanhedrin 88b; Tosefta, Shekalim 3:17; Tosefta, Chagigah 2:4; Yad, Sanhedrin 2:8. Members of the Sanhedrin were chosen from these courts.
32. Some question this; Lechem Mishneh on Yad, Mamrim 1:4. However, this is specifically mentioned in Tosefta, Sanhedrin 7:1; Yerushalmi, Sanhedrin 1:4 (8b). Apparently, the agents were needed to report the decision back to the local court.
33. Sanhedrin 88b; Tosefta, Sanhedrin 7:1; Tosefta, Chagigah 2:4; Yerushalmi,

11:15   When a question was brought before the Sanhedrin, it would first seek a precedent from previous assemblies.[34] If any member of the Sanhedrin had a clear tradition that such a precedent existed, it would be accepted immediately,[35] unless the membership saw fit to oppose it.[36]

11:16   Where there was no clear tradition or precedent, the Sanhedrin would place the question on its agenda, to be discussed and decided by common consent or majority vote. In either case, the decision of the Sanhedrin would be binding on all Israel.[37]

11:17   In the case of any controversy within the Sanhedrin, the question would be put to a vote, and the majority opinion would be accepted by the entire assembly. This is in accordance with the commandment, "Incline after the majority" (Exodus 23:2).[38]

11:18   Once a vote is taken, the minority opinion must be neglected completely.[39] Nevertheless, the minority opinion was also recorded, so that there not arise a need to debate the question a second time.[40]

11:19   A Sanhedrin is not bound to follow precedent in questions of Torah law. It is thus written, "You shall go to

Sanhedrin 1:4 (8b); Yad, Mamrim 1:4. This was also true in monetary cases, see *Bava Kama* 112b; Yad, *Sanhedrin* 6:6-8; *Choshen Mishpat* 14:1. The Sanhedrin could only give an opinion, but it could not render a decision in the absence of the litigants; *Nimukey Yosef*, *Sanhedrin* (Rif 10a, top), s.v. *Koth'vin*; *Choshen Mishpat* 13:6.

34. See note 33.
35. Cf. *Yevamoth* 8:3 (76b); *Tosafoth*, *Yevamoth* 77b, s.v. *Halakha*; *Yadayim* 4:3; *Bertenoro ad loc.*; *Yad Malachi* 663.
36. See below, 11:19.
37. See note 33. If the question is not brought to the Sanhedrin, each local court's decision is binding in its area of jurisdiction.
38. *Bava Metzia* 59b; *Tosefta, Berakhoth* 4:1; *Yad, Mamrim* 1:4; *Sefer HaMitzvoth*, Positive Commandment 175; *Sefer Mitzvoth Gadol*, Positive Commandment 98; *Chinukh* 78.
39. *Horayoth* 3b; *Tosafoth, Bava Kama* 27b, s.v. *Ka Mashma Lan*; *Get Pashut*, Rules (end); *Ketzoth HaChoshen, Kuntres HaS'fekoth* 6:2.
40. *Edduyoth* 1:6.

the . . . judge who shall exist in *those days*" (Deuteronomy 17:9). This indicates that it is always the opinion of the contemporary Sanhedrin that is binding on each generation. Therefore, any Sanhedrin can overrule its predecessors in questions involving decision or interpretation of Torah law.[41]

11:20   However, an opinion accepted by all Israel is binding forever, and it cannot be overruled by a later Sanhedrin.[42] Therefore, any opinion recorded in the Bible is permanently binding.[43] Similarly, when the Mishnah, and later the Talmud, were published, they were universally accepted; therefore their opinions cannot be reversed by any later Sanhedrin.[44]

11:21   It was for this reason that minority opinions were preserved when the Mishnah and the Talmud were written. Where a majority opinion was not universally accepted, it could be overruled by a later Sanhedrin.[45]

11:22   Originally, all majority opinions were accepted without reservation by the minority, and therefore, no permanent disputes existed.[46] However, in the generation following Hillel and Shamai (3768; 7 c.e.), many issues became so confused that a clear majority could not be obtained to

---

41. *Yad, Mamrim* 2:1. Cf. *Sotah* 5:2 (27b), Rashi *ad loc.* s.v. *Athid*; Maharatz Chajas *ad loc.*; *Yoma* 80a; *Arukh HaShulchan HeAthid, Mamrim* 65:3. See *Yad Ramah, Sanhedrin* 33a, s.v. *Velbeya* (end), from *Bava Bathra* 130b.
42. See below, 12:9. Cf. *Zevachim* 12b; *Margolioth HaYam* 86b 14.
43. Cf. *Tosafoth, Bava Kama* 82b, s.v. *Atha.*
44. *Kesef Mishneh, Mamrim* 2:1. Cf. *Chazon Ish, Kobetz Iggeroth* 2:24. See above, 9:52; below, 12:10.
45. Raavad, *Tosafoth Shantz, Edduyoth* 1:5. See *Tosefta, Edduyoth* 1:2; *Margolioth HaYam* 86b 14. See above, 9:41.
46. See note 33. Also see *Temurah* 16b; *Yerushalmi, Chagigah* 2:2 (10b); *Tosafoth, Chagigah* 16a, s.v. *Yosi; Tosafoth Yeshanim, Yoma* 59a, s.v. *Sh'nei; Teshuvoth Chavath Yair* 192 (additions); Maharatz Chajas, *Chagigah* 16a, *Sanhedrin* 88b; *Margolioth HaYam* 88b 4.

decide them,[47] and the disputes remained unresolved.[48] Likewise, due to later persecutions, many questions could not be discussed and voted upon by the Sanhedrin.[49]

11:23   There are many Torah laws whose observance depends strongly upon the circumstances of the time, and therefore, they were not rigidly fixed for all times. In such cases, the details of the law were neither written in the Torah nor included in the Oral Torah, but left to the discretion of the Sanhedrin. Although the details of such laws are decided by the Sanhedrin, they are considered part of the observance required by the Torah.[50]

11:24   The Sanhedrin likewise had the authority to enact legislation according to the needs of the time. It is thus written, "you must follow . . . the Torah that they teach you" (Deuteronomy 17:11).[51] Any legislation enacted by the Sanhedrin is called a Rabbinical Commandment (*Mitzvah de-Rabanan*, מִצְוָה דְרַבָּנָן), as distinguished from a commandment from the Torah (*Mitzvah de-Oreitha*,

47. *Karban HaEdah* on *Yerushalmi, Chagigah* 2:2 (10b), s.v. *Eleh; Maharatz Chajas, Shabbath* 15a, *Yoma* 59a. Also see *Yevamoth* 14a; *Sanhedrin* 42a.

48. Cf. *Eruvin* 46a; *Niddah* 6b, 9b. Also see *Iggereth Rav Sherira Gaon*, pp. 10, 41; *Beth Elohim, Shaar HaYesodoth* 36; Maharatz Chajas, *Mavo HaTalmud* 14 (p. 311); *Yesod HaMishneh*, pp. 12, 43.

49. *Mavo HaTulmud, loc. cit.; Atereth Tzvi, Mishpat HaTorah* 7 (p. 387). Although the Sanhedrin existed until much later, after the destruction of the Temple it was only able to convene sporadically. There were also earlier times when the Sanhedrin was not legally constituted; cf. *Megillath Taanith* 10.

50. *Chagigah* 18a; *Bekhoroth* 26b; Rashi, *Chagigah* 18a, s.v. *Hah, Kiddushin* 11b, s.v. *VeTenan, Bekhoroth* 26c, s.v. *Lo, Temurah* 27a, s.v. *Velm;* Tosafoth, *Yoma* 45b, s.v. *Tamid*, 54b, s.v. *Keruvim* (end); Ramban on Leviticus 23:24; Ran, *Yoma* (Rif 1a), s.v. *Yom;* Rosh, *Sukkah* 3:14 (end); *Kesef Mishneh* on *Yad, Avodath Kokhavim* 11:2, *Keriath Sh'ma* 1:10, *Chametz U'Matzah* 2:2; *Beth Yosef, Yoreh Deah* 178; *Orach Chaim* 530:1 in *Hagah; Magen Avraham ad loc.* 530:1; HaGra, *Biur Halakha, Ibid.; Turey Zahav, Yoreh Deah* 117:1, 178:5; *Sh'nei Luchoth HaB'rith, Torah SheB'al Peh*, s.v. *K'lal Rabanan* (3:240b); *Teshuvoth Chakham Tzvi* 9; *Yad Malachi* 216. Also see *Yerushalmi, Peah* 1:1 (2a); *Yerushalmi, Chagigah* 1:2 (4b); Maharatz Chajas, *Yoma* 80a.

51. *Sifri ad loc.; Yad, Mamrim* 1:2, *Berakhoth* 6:2, 11:3; *Chinukh* 496; Maharatz Chajas, *Sukkah* 46a.

מִצְוָה דְּאוֹרַיְיתָא). Even legislation enacted by the Sanhedrin of Moses is considered a Rabbinical Commandment.[52]

11:25   Although God gave many laws in the Torah, He also wanted other laws to be created by human minds through the Sanhedrin.[53] These laws would be tailored to meet specific situations that would arise in the course of time.[54] In many cases, laws would be enacted to strengthen religious practice and unify the people.[55] God assured that the reward for obeying such legislation would be equal to that for keeping the Torah itself.[56]

11:26   Some authorities maintain that to disregard a Rabbinical Commandment is to violate the commandment, "You shall not turn aside from the law that they declare to you" (Deuteronomy 17:11).[57] Other authorities, however, state that this commandment only applies to the decisions of the Sanhedrin, but not to their legislation.[58]

11:27   It is forbidden to add any commandment to the Torah, as it is written, "You shall not add onto the word which I command you" (Deuteronomy 4:2).[59] Therefore, the Sanhedrin[60] was careful to distinguish between their

52. Ramban on *Sefer HaMitzvoth, Shoresh* 2 (27b).
53. Rabbi Moshe Chaim Luzzatto, *Maamar Halkkarim*, end.
54. *Beth Elohim, Shaar HaYesodoth* 38. See below, notes 82, 134.
55. Rabbenu Yonah, *Shaar Teshuvah* 3:7,8.
56. *Derashoth HaRan* 7 (p. 116).
57. *Yad*, Introduction, *Mamrim* 1:2; *Kuzari* 3:39 (46a); Rabbenu Yonah, *Shaarey Teshuvah* 3:4; *Derashoth HaRan* 7 (p. 115); *Nimukey Yosef, Yevamoth* (Rif 4a), s.v. *Mitzvah*. Cf. *Berakhoth* 19b; *Shabbath* 23a; *Sukkah* 46a; *Avney Milu'im, Teshuvoth* 2:14; *Machaneh Ephraim, Nedarim* 10; Maharatz Chajas, *Nedarim* 12a.
58. Ramban on *Sefer HaMitzvoth, Shoresh* 1 (4a ff); *Chinukh* 496; *Teshuvoth Tashbatz* 1:141.
59. *Yad, Mamrim* 2:9; *Sefer HaMitzvoth*, Negative Commandment 313; *Sefer Mitzvoth Gadol*, Negative Commandment 364; *Chinukh* 454; cf. *Torath HaNevi'im, Maamar Bal Tosif* 2 (p. 90).
60. Some authorities, however, maintain that the commandment does not apply to the Sanhedrin at all; Raavad, *Mamrim* 2:9; *Kuzari* 3:41 (50a); Rashba, *Rosh HaShanah* 16b; *Yad Malachi* 107; *Pri Megadim*, Introduction 1:35; Maharsha, *Megillah* 7a,

legislation and commandments of the Torah.[61] Hence, they made the observance of Rabbinical Commandments more lenient in many special instances, such as in the case of a questionable prohibition[62] where personal honor is at stake,[63] and in the case of severe illness.[64]

1:28   However, this does not mean that one may be lax in observing Rabbinical Commandments. It is taught that one must be more careful in obeying Rabbinical Commandments than those written in the Torah.[65]

1:29   Obedience to the Sanhedrin is the basis for Jewish unity.[66] Therefore, one who disregards a Rabbinical Commandment is considered a sinner.[67] It is taught that he is

14a; *Amudey Yerushalayim*, on *Yerushalmi, Megillah* 1:5 (7a). Cf. Ritva, *Makkoth* 23b; *Chidushey HaRan, Sanhedrin* 81b.

61. *Yad, Mamrim* 2:9; *Ramban* on Deuteronomy 4:2 (end); *Derashoth HaRan* 7 (p. 114); *Beth Elohim, Shaar HaYesodoth* 35. It was for this reason that the sages did not forbid work on Chanukah and Purim as it is forbidden on festivals prescribed by the Torah; *Maharatz Chajas, Megillah* 14a; cf. *Megillah* 5b, 7a; *Yerushalmi, Megillah* 1:5 (7a).

62. *Lechem Mishneh* on *Yad, Mamrim* 1:2; *Mabit, Kiryath Sefer*, Introduction 5; *Derashoth HaRan* 7 (p. 114), *Megilluth Esther* on *Sefer HaMitzvoth, Shoresh* 1 (5b); *Chayay Adam* 127:1; *Teshuvoth Binyamin Zeev* 407. See *Shabbath* 34a; *Eruvin* 5a, 45b; *Betzah* 3b; *Kethuvoth* 56b, *Yerushalmi, Eruvin* 3:4; *Yerushalmi, Yevamoth* 7:3 (end). Cf. *Yerushalmi Orlah* 3:7 (20a). Some authorities, however, maintain that even in the case of something forbidden by the Torah, a question is only forbidden by Rabbinical law; *Yad, Issurey Biyah* 18:17, *Kelayim* 10:27, *Tumath Meth* 9:12; Raavad, *Kelayim* 10:27. Others, however, maintain that this is a law from the Torah, Rashba on *Kiddushin* 73a; *Idem., Torath HaBayith* 4:1 (Josefov, 1883), Part 2 p. 11b. For discussion, see *Shev Shematha* 1:1; Rabbi Shimon Schkop, *Shaarey Yosher* 1:1; *Maley HaRo'im*, s.v. *Sefeka* (77b).

63. *Berakhoth* 19b; *Shaar Ephraim* 93; Rabbi Avraham Yitzchakl, *Teshuvoth Zera Avraham, Yoreh Deah* 1:17 (Constantinople, 1732); *Yad Malachi* 122; *Derashoth HaRan* 7 (p. 114).

64. Ramban, *Torath HaAdam* (in Kithvey Ramban), pp. 21,22; Ran, *Shabbath* (Rif 39b), s.v. *U'MeHa*; Rosh, *Avodah Zarah* 2:10, from *Avodah Zarah* 28b; *Orach Chaim* 328:8; *Turey Zahav ad loc.* 328:11; *Magen Avraham* 328:13; *Chayay Adam* 69:13; *Mishnah Berurah* 328:57; "*Rav*" *Shulchan Arukh* 328:19. However, see *Yad, Shabbath* 2:10; *Maggid Mishneh, Kesef Mishneh, ad loc.* For other cases where rabbinical laws are more lenient, see *Pesachim* 4a; *Shabbath* 154b; *Betza* 9b; 10a; *Derashoth HaRan* 7 (p. 114). See note 84.

65. *Eruvin* 21b, from Ecclesiastes 12:12.

66. Rabbeinu Yonah, *Shaarey Teshuvah* 3:8. See below, note 134.

67. *Shabbath* 40a; *Eruvin* 101b; *Yevamoth* 20b; *Niddah* 12a; *Choshen Mishpat* 34:3;

worthy of death,[68] as it is written, "he who breaks a fence
shall be bitten by a snake" (Ecclesiastes 10:8).[69]

11:30   Legislation would be enacted by a majority vote of the
Sanhedrin,[70] and it would thereby become binding on all
Israel.[71] However, even if they are not sitting in formal
session as a Sanhedrin, the majority of ordained sages can
enact legislation binding on all Israel.[72]

11:31   Just as they had rules for interpreting the Torah, the
Sanhedrin also had rules concerning when and under what
conditions legislation should be enacted, as well as how it
should be applied.[73] These rules would occasionally be used
to institute customs before they were formally enacted as
law.[74]

11:32   In many cases, rabbinical laws are based on verses in the
Torah. This indicates that the logic for the particular
legislation is derived from the particular verse.[75] Since such
laws are suggested by the Torah, they are not considered

Teshuvoth Chut HaShani 18 (21a); Yad Malachi 310; Likutey Amarim (Tanya),
Sefer Shel Benonim 1 (5a). Cf. Sotah 44a.
68. Berakhoth 4b; Eruvin 21b; Sotah 4b; Tosafoth ad loc. s.v. Ne'ekar; Rabbenu Yonah,
Shaarey Teshuvah 3:5; Derashoth HaRan 7 (p. 117); Eliah Rabbah (on Orach
Chaim) 158:9.
69. Yerushalmi, Berakhoth 1:4 (8b); Yerushalmi, Sanhedrin 11:4 (55b); Yerushalmi,
Avodah Zarah 2:7 (15a); Rashi, Eruvin 21b, s.v. Avel, Sotah 4b, s.v. Ne'ekar;
Rambam, Introduction to Mishnah.
70. Yad, Mamrim 1:4. See above, 11:17
71. Rambam, Introduction to Mishnah.
72. Rambam on Shabbath 1:4 (13b). Cf. Chayay Adam 127:1. See below Chapter 12,
note 35. Also see 13:28.
73. See above, 9:29.
74. Rambam, Introduction to Mishnah, from Shabbath 130a.
75. Maharal, Be'er HaGolah 1 (4a). Cf. Chulin 106a; Tanna DeBei Eliahu Rabbah 15
(74a); Teshuvoth Zera Avraham 1:8 (10c); Yad Malachi 32. Such a derivation is
known as an asmachta (אסמכתא); see Berakhoth 41b; Eruvin 74a; Yoma 74a;
Yevamoth 72a; Bava Metzia 88b; Chulin 64b, 77a; Tosafoth, Sotah 32b, s.v.
U'Rabbi (end); Yad Malachi 19. The asmachta may also contain a prediction of the
legislation; Kethuvoth 10b; Rabbi Moshe Chaim Luzzatto, Maamar Halkkarim, end.

additions.[76] Therefore,[77] they were occasionally[78] made as binding as the commandments of the Torah.[79]

11:33   The Sanhedrin is commanded to enact safeguards to prevent people from violating actual commandments of the Torah. It is thus written, "You shall safeguard My charge" (Leviticus 18:30).[80] It is likewise taught, "Make a fence for the Torah."[81]

11:34   Such safeguards were enacted at various periods according to the needs of the time.[82] Once they were passed by the Sanhedrin and accepted by the majority of Israel, they could never be repealed by a later Sanhedrin.[83]

11:35   The Sanhedrin was only enjoined to safeguard commandments of the Torah, and not Rabbinical Commandments.[84] This, however, was only true of existing

---

76. Hence, they are not bound by the strictures above, 11:27.
77. *Tosafoth, Bava Bathra* 49b, s.v. *U'KeDeRav; Pri Megadim*, Introduction 1:20; Rabbi Moshe HaCohen, *Kehunath Olam* (Constantinople, 1740), p. 87; *Yad Malachi* 286.
78. But only when this fact is mentioned in the Talmud; *Teshuvoth Chavath Yair* 9; *Yad Malachi* 287.
79. *Eruvin* 77a, 85b; *Yevamoth* 36b; *Kethuvoth* 56a, 83b, 84a; *Bava Metzia* 55b; *Zevachim* 55b.
80. *Sifra* (86d), Rashi, *ad loc.; Yevamoth* 21a; *Moed Katan* 5a; Rambam, Introduction to Mishnah; *Yad*, Introduction; *Moreh Nevukhim* 3:41; Raavad, *Mamrim* 2:9; Rambam, Rabbenu Yonah, Bertenoro, on *Avoth* 1:1, s.v. *Assey; Minchath Chinukh* 454. Cf. *Berakhoth* 1:1 (2a), 4b; *Zevachim* 57b.
81. *Avoth* 1:1; *Avoth deRabbi Nathan* 1:5; *Mekhilta* (6a) on Exodus 12:8; *BaMidbar Rabbah* 10:22.
82. *Sh'nei Luchoth HaB'rith, Beth Chakhmah* (1:39b). See notes 54, 134.
83. *Yad, Mamrim* 2:4; *Moreh Nevukhim* 3:41; Rambam, Introduction to Mishnah, from *Avodah Zarah* 36a. Others, however, maintain that the only laws which can never be repealed are specifically the 18 passed by Beth Shammai (*Shabbath* 1:4), since they risked their lives for them; *Tosafoth, Gittin* 36b, s.v. *Eleh, Avodah Zarah* 36a s.v. *VeHaT'nan;* from *Yerushalmi, Shabbath* 1:4 (11a). On the opposite extreme, there is an opinion that any legislation accepted by the majority of Israel can never be repealed; Raavad, *Mamrim* 2:2; Ran, *Avodah Zarah* (Rif 14b), s.v. *Rabbi.* See below, 11:46.
84. *Shabbath* 11a, 21a; *Eruvin* 4b, 99a; *Betza* 3a; *Yoma* 11a, 44b; *Sukkah* 6b; *Yevamoth* 21b, 109a; *Avodah Zarah* 21a; *Chulin* 85b, 104a; *Niddah* 67b; Rashi, *Betza* 2b, s.v. *VeHaTana; Tosafoth, Chulin* 104a, s.v. *U'Mana; Yad Malachi* 656. This may also be another way in which rabbinical laws are distinguished from laws of the Torah; see above, 11:27.

rabbinical laws, and the rule did not prevent the Sanhedrin from including safeguards in their legislation to assure that they would be obeyed.[85]

11:36   The Sanhedrin only had an obligation to enact legislation to enact safeguards to prevent likely violations. Safeguards were not enacted to protect against the unlikely.[86]

11:37   The Sanhedrin also enacted many laws to prevent even the suspicion of sin. This is in keeping with the injunction, "You shall be innocent before God and before Israel" (Numbers 32:22).[87] Where such legislation exists, however, no distinction is made, and the prohibition exists even in private.[88]

11:38   There were many other ordinances which were enacted by the Sanhedrin to fulfill a particular need, even though they had no relation to commandments of the Torah.[89]

11:39   An ordinance that is not a safeguard for a commandment of the Torah can be repealed by a later Sanhedrin. The only condition is that the later Sanhedrin be superior in wisdom[90]

85. This is why safeguards are sometimes found for rabbinical laws; Rashi, *Betza* 3a, s.v. *Chad*; *Tosafoth, Berakhoth* 53a, s.v. *Gezarah*; Rambam on *Shabbath* 4:1; *Sh'nei Luchoth HaB'rith, Torah SheB'al Peh, Gimel* (3:230b).
86. *Eruvin* 63b; *Betza* 2b, 18a; *Yevamoth* 31a; *Kethuvoth* 56b; *Kiddushin* 28b; *Gittin* 5a, 44a; *Nazir* 55a; *Bava Metzia* 46b, 47a; *Bekhoroth* 3a; *Niddah* 34a; *Kenesseth HaGedolah, K'laley HaGemara* 186; *Teshuvoth Shaar Ephraim* 68; *Teshuvoth Chakham Tzvi* 68; *She'erith Yehudah* 25; *Kenesseth HaGedolah, Choshen Mishpat* 225; *Teshuvoth Divrey Yosef* 43 (end); *Yad Malachi* 435.
87. *Shekalim* 3:2; *Pesachim* 13a, *Yoma* 38a; *Sotah* 3a; *Tosefta, Peah* 4:15; *Tosefta, Yoma* 2:5,6; *Tosefta, Shekalim* 2:3; *Kitzur Shulchan Arukh* 29:20.
88. *Shabbath* 64b, 146b; *Betza* 9a; *Avodah Zarah* 12b; *Yerushalmi, Kelayim* 9:1 (40b); *Tosafoth, Chulin* 41a, s.v. *U'VeShuk*; *Yad, Shabbath* 22:20, *Yom Tov* 5:4; *Orach Chaim* 301:45.
89. Rambam, Introduction to Mishnah.
90. Some authorities, however, only require that the *Nasi* (president) be superior in wisdom; Rambam, Bertenoro, on *Edduyoth* 1:5.

and prestige[91] to the one which enacted the ordinance.[92] It can then repeal the ordinance, even if it has been accepted by the majority of Israel.[93]

11:40   The Sanhedrin likewise had the responsibility to judge customs.[94] It would also pattern its legislation after ancient common practices, following the injunction, "Do not remove the ancient landmark that your fathers have set up" (Proverbs 22:28).[95] Thus, for example, the three daily prayers were first instituted by the Patriarchs, but they were later enacted as law by the Sanhedrin.[96] Nonetheless, the Sanhedrin also instituted numerous customs without making them binding by legislation.[97]

11:41   The Sanhedrin had the authority to suspend temporarily any Biblical commandment if the situation warranted it. Likewise, it could temporarily suspend any decree enacted by a previous Sanhedrin.[98] It is thus written, "It is a time to

91. That is, the number of sages supporting the Sanhedrin's decision; *Yad, Mamrim* 2:2. Others, however, write that this refers to the prestige of the *Nasi* (president) and the number of his students; Bertenoro, *Edduyoth* 1:5. Others state that it refers to the age of the Sanhedrin; Raavad on *Edduyoth* 1:5, quoting *Yerushalmi.* Cf. *Avoth* 5:7; Rashi, *Tosefoth Yom Tov, ad loc.* s.v. *U'VeMinyan;* *Berakhoth* 17a; Maharatz Chajas *ad loc;* *Avodah Zarah* 7a; Ritva, Meiri, *ad loc.* *Yesod Hamishnah,* p. 44; *Margolioth HaYam* 86b 12. Cf. *Teshuvoth Radbaz* 1490 (5:117).
92. *Edduyoth* 1:4; *Avodah Zarah* 36a; *Moed Katan* 3b; *Megillah* 2a; *Gittin* 36b; *Yerushalmi, Shabbath* 1:4 (10h); *Yerushalmi, Shevi'ith* 1:1 (1a); *Yerushalmi, Avodah Zarah* 2:8 (16a); *Yad, Mamrim* 2:2.
93. However, some authorities hold that an ordinance accepted by the majority of Israel can never be abolished; see note 83. There are some cases, however, where the legislation specifically included a condition that any Sanhedrin could repeal it; cf. *Masser Sheni* 5:2; *Moed Katan* 3b; *Tosafoth, Bava Kama* 82b, s.v. *Atha.*
94. Cf. *Yad, Mamrim* 1:2, 1:3, 2:2; *Chinukh* 495.
95. *Yalkut Shimoni* (960), Rashi, *ad loc.* Cf. *Peah* 5:6, 7:3; *Tanchuma, VaYishlach* 10. See *Derashoth HaRan* 7 (p. 115).
96. *Berakhoth* 26b; Maharatz Chajas *ad loc.;* *Yad, Tefillah* 5:8, *Melakhim* 9:1.
97. *Sukkah* 44a; Rashi *ad loc.* s.v. *Minhag;* *Pri Megadim,* Introduction 1:41. Cf. *Yad, Berakhoth* 11:16; Raavad *ad loc.*
98. *Yad, Mamrim* 2:4; from *Yevamoth* 90b; cf. *Tosafoth ad loc.* s.v. *VeLiG'mor;* *Tosafoth Yeshenim ibid.* s.v. *Kemo;* *Tosafoth, Sanhedrin* 89b, s.v. *Eliahu.* Also see Rabbi Yitzchak Plurintin, Commentary on *Yad, Mamrim* 2:4, in Rabbi Chaim Shmuel Plurintin, *Meil Sh'muel* (Salonika, 1725); *Tumath Yesharim* 168 (Venice, 1620); *Yad Malachi* 67; *Torath HaNevi'im, Hora'h Sha'ah* 5 (p. 31).

work for God, suspend your Torah" (Psalms 119:126).[99]
Therefore, when the situation warrants it, the Sanhedrin, or
any other duly appointed court,[100] could issue sentences
involving punishments not prescribed by law.[101]

11:42   The Sanhedrin had the authority to enact a decree, even
where it would result in a passive[102] violation of a commandment of the Torah.[103] Thus, for example, legislation
was enacted which forbade the use of the Shofar[104] and
Lulav and Ethrog[105] on the Sabbath, even though they are
commandments of the Torah; using them might result in an
accidental violation of the Sabbath.

11:43   Nonetheless, the Sanhedrin cannot enact a decree that
will completely abolish a commandment of the Torah.[106]
Similarly, the Sanhedrin cannot prohibit something which
the Torah expressedly permits.[107]

99. *Yad, Mamrim* 2:9. *Cf. Rashi ad loc.; Berakhoth* 63a. Also see above, 9:43. *Cf.
    Menachoth* 99a,b.
100. *Choshen Mishpat* 2:1; from *Rif, Bava Kama* 34a; *Teshuvoth Ramban* 279;
    Teshuvoth Maharam Lublin 138. However, some maintain that only the Sanhedrin
    itself has this authority; *Nimukey Yosef, Sanhedrin* (Rif 16a), s.v. *Garsinin.* See
    Birkey Yosef, Choshen Mishpat 3:2.
101. *Yevamoth* 90b; *Sanhedrin* 46a; *Yerushalmi, Chagigah* 2:2 (11b); *Yad, Sanhedrin*
    24:4; *Choshen Mishpat* 2:1; *Yad Malachi* 118.
102. Some authorities maintain tht they can even legislate an active violation if there is
    sufficient reason; *Tosafoth, Yevamoth* 88a, s.v. *MiTokh, Nazir* 43b, s.v. *VeHa,
    Avodah Zarah* 13a, s.v. *Amar; Teshuvoth Rashba* 127; *Kesef Mishneh* on *Yad,
    Nedarim* 3:9 (end); *Beth Yosef, Orach Chaim* 411 (end); *Teshuvoth Radbaz*
    (Leshanoth HaRambam) 1461 (5:88); *Teshuvoth Tamim Deyim* 203; *Teshuvoth
    Beth Yaakov* 159; *Yad Malachi* 103.
103. *Yevamoth* 89b, 90a; *Rashba, Rosh HaShanah* 16b. *Cf. Rosh HaShanah* 26b; *Pri
    Chadash* 455:1, 588:5; *Yavin Shemuah* 453; *Yedey Eliahu* 25; *Yad Malachi* 101,
    102; *Torath HaNevi'im, Hora'ah Sha'ah* 6 (p. 32).
104. *Rosh HaShanah* 29b; *Yad, Shofar* 2:6.
105. *Sukkah* 42b; *Yad, Lulav* 7:13.
106. *Magen Avraham* 588:4; *Turey Zahav, Orach Chaim* 588:5; Maharatz Chajas,
    Yoma 14b.
107. *Tosafoth, Bava Metzia* 64b, s.v. *VeLo,* 70b, s.v. *Tashikh; Turey Zahav, Orach
    Chaim* 588:5, *Yoreh Deah* 117:1; *Kesef Mishneh, Melakhim* 3:7; *Beth Chadash,
    Yoreh Deah* 159; *Teshuvoth Chavath Yair* 142; *Teshuvoth Divrey Yosef* 48;
    Teshuvoth Chakham Tzvi 46; *Teshuvoth Nodeh BeYehudah, Yoreh Deah* 41;
    Peney Yehoshua, Kiddushin 73a, s.v. *Rashi; Shaar HaMelekh* on *Yad, Yesodey
    HaTorah* 5:8; *Yad Malachi* 295; Rabbi Akiba Eiger, *Gilyon Maharsha, Yoreh Deah*
    117:1.

11:44　The Sanhedrin can likewise enact legislation that involves the seizure or transfer of property.[108] Where the situation requires it, lower courts also have this power.[109] It is thus written, "Whoever did not come . . . according to the council of the leaders and elders, all his property would be forfeit" (Ezra 10:8).[110]

11:45　Such is the power of the Sanhedrin, that a transfer of property according to their legislation is valid even if serious laws of the Torah are concerned.[111] Similarly, under certain conditions, the Sanhedrin can enact laws that annul a marriage[112] or invalidate any other religious observance.[113]

11:46　Legislation is not binding unless the majority of Israel is able to abide by it.[114] It is thus written, "You have accepted it with an oath . . . the entire nation" (Malachi 3:9).[115]

11:47　Therefore, before a Sanhedrin enacts any law or safeguard, it must carefully determine whether the majority of Israel will be able to abide by it.[116]

---

108. Even placing that property in another person's possession; Rashi, *Gittin* 20a, s.v. *Aknuy*, 55a, s.v. *Ukmua*; *Yam Shel Shlomo*, *Yevamoth* 10:19; *Beth Yosef, Evven HaEzer* 28; *Choshen Mishpat* 66; *Teshuvoth Rivash* 99; Rashba, *Gittin* 36b, s.v. *Rava*; Rabbi Yitzchak ben David, *Divrey Emeth, Kuntresim* (Constantinople, 1760), p. 93; *Pith'chey Teshuvah, Choshen Mishpat* 2:2; *Tzion Yerushalayim* on *Yerushalmi, Shekalim* 1:2 (3a). Other authorities, however, dispute this; *Tosafoth, Sukkah* 30b, s.v. *Shinuy*; Rabbi Ephraim Navon, *Machaneh Ephraim* on *Yad, Zekhiah* 4 (Constantinople, 1738); *Teshuvoth Beth Ephraim, Choshen Mishpat* 61; Maharatz Chajas, *Sukkah* 30b, *Moed Katan* 16a, *Gittin* 14a, 20a, 55a. Cf. *Birkey Yosef, Choshen Mishpat, Kuntres Acharon* 3.
109. *Yad, Sanhedrin* 24:6; *Choshen Mishpat* 2:1 in *Hagah.*
110. *Yevamoth* 89b; *Gittin* 36b; *Yerushalmi, Peah* 5:1 (25a); *Yerushalmi, Shekalim* 1:2 (3a); Rashi, *Moed Katan*, s.v. *Hu; Yad, Sanhedrin* 24:6.
111. *Gittin* 55b.
112. *Yevamoth* 90b, 110a; *Kethuvoth* 3a; *Gittin* 33a, 73a; *Bava Bathra* 48b.
113. Cf. Maharatz Chajas, *Sukkah* 23a, *Sotah* 24a.
114. *Bava Kama* 79b; *Yerushalmi, Shabbath* 1:4 (10b); *Yerushalmi, Avodah Zarah* 2:8 (16a). Cf. *Sefer Chasidim* 298.
115. *Bava Bathra* 60b; *Avodah Zarah* 36b; *Ritva Ad loc.; Horioth* 3b; *Midrash Tehillim* 137:6. See above, Chapter 5, note 33.
116. *Yad, Mamrim* 2:5. Cf. *Tosefta, Shevi'ith* 3:7.

11:48   If a Sanhedrin enacts a law under the erroneous assumption that the majority of Israel will be able to keep it, and later discovers that it was wrong and the law is not accepted, then it is considered erroneous legislation and is automatically null and void.[117] Some authorities, however, dispute this, and maintain tht even such legislation must be formally repealed. It can even be done, however, by a Sanhedrin inferior to the first.[118]

11:49   Legislation is considered erroneous only if it was never accepted, and it is immediately apparent that it is not acceptable to the community at large. However, if it is not immediately apparent, but discovered at a later date, the legislation is considered binding until formally repealed by a later Sanhedrin. In such a case also, the later Sanhedrin can repeal the legislation even if it is inferior to the first.[119]

11:50   Some say that if the community is able to keep the legislation, but purposely refuses to do so, then the legislation is not considered improper. Then, like any other legislation, it can only be repealed by a Sanhedrin greater in wisdom and prestige than the first.[120]

11:51   Where it is known that a legislated ordinance or safeguard cannot be observed by the majority of Israel, it can be repealed by any later Sanhedrin, even one that is inferior to the Sanhedrin that enacted the law.[121] Such legislation could even be repealed by a contemporary Sanhedrin.[122]

117. *Yad, Mamrim* 2:6. Cf. *Yad, Keriath Sh'ma* 4:8.
118. *Tosafoth, Avodah Zarah* 36b, s.v. *Iy, Bava Kama* 82a, s.v. *Atha*; Rabbenu Yonah, *Berakhoth* (Rif 13b), s.v. *Ki Atha*. Cf. *Magen Avraham* 88:1; also see *Betza* 5a; *Sanhedrin* 59b. See above, 11:39.
119. *Yad, Mamrim* 2:7; *Lechem Mishneh ad loc.* See above, 11:39.
120. Ran, *Avodah Zarah* (Rif 14b), s.v. *Rabbi*. See above, 11:39.
121. This is a universal opinion; Ran, *loc. cit.*
122. Ran, *loc. cit.* quoting Ramban.

11:52   If a law is enacted only for a specific place, it becomes binding as soon as it is accepted by the majority of people in that place, even though they are a minority of all Israel.[123]

11:53   If a law is enacted for a specific time, then it does not have to be formally repealed after that time has passed.[124]

11:54   Even where the reason for legislation no longer exists, the law is binding until it is formally repealed by another Sanhedrin.[125] Some authorities maintain that this later Sanhedrin must be greater than the first in wisdom and prestige,[126] but in this case, others do not require it.[127]

11:55   However, legislation may be enacted specifically[128] for a well known [129] reason. In such a case, it is assumed that the legislation included exceptions in instances[130] and places[131] where the reason does not exist. In such cases, where the reason does not exist, the law is not binding.[132]

11:56   It is an extremely serious sin to dispute the authority of the Sanhedrin. In certain cases, one who does so can be worthy of death, as it is written, "If a man acts presumptuously and does not listen to . . . the judge, that man shall die; you shall eliminate the evil from Israel"

---

123. *Tosafoth, Gittin* 36b, s.v. *Eleh* (end).
124. *Tosafoth, Betza* 5a, *Sanhedrin* 59b, s.v. *LeKhol.* Some authorities, however, dispute this and maintain that it must be repealed formally; Rashi, *Sanhedrin* 59b, s.v. *LeKhol.*
125. Rashi, *Betza* 5a, s.v. *Mana; Tosafoth, Sanhedrin* 59b, s.v. *LeKhol; Tosefoth Yom Tov, Maaser Sheni* 5:2. Cf. *Yevamoth* 41b; *Tosafoth, Pesachim* 50a, s.v. *Makom, Avodah Zarah* 5b, s.v. *VeHaTenan.*
126. *Yad, Mamrim* 2:2; *Magen Avraham* 9:7, 690:22.
127. Raavad, *Mamrim* 2:2.
128. *Tosafoth, Betza* 6a, s.v. *VeHaldna; Yoreh Deah* 116:1; *Magen Avraham* 690:22; *Beer Hetiv, Orach Chaim* 690:15.
129. *Magen Avraham* 9:7.
130. *Mateh Yehonathan, Yoreh Deah* 116:1.
131. *Magen Avraham* 468:1; *Pri Chadash, Yoreh Deah* 116:1; *HaGra ibid.*
132. *Shita Mekubetzeth, Kethuvoth* 15b; *Yad Malachi* 65. See below 13:57.

(Deuteronomy 17:12).[133] The authority of the Sanhedrin is all important, since it is this authority that makes Judaism unique and unified.[134]

133. This is the case of the Rebellious Elder (*zaken mamra*, זָקֵן מַמְרֵא), see *Sanhedrin* 11:1 (84b); *Yad, Mamrim* 3:4.
134. Cf. *Kuzari* 3:38 (42b). See above, notes 54, 66, 82.

TWELVE

HALAKHAH

12:1 It is God's will that there exist a certain degree of uniformity in Jewish practices, as well as in the interpretation of the Law. It is thus written, "There shall be one Torah and one law for you" (Numbers 15:16).[1]

12:2 Therefore, even when no formal central authority, such as the Sanhedrin, exists, God has provided guidelines to insure the continuance of Judaism as a unified way of life. These guidelines provide the basis for the system of Torah law known as *halakhah* (הֲלָכָה).[2]

12:3 Moreover, it was impossible to include every possible case in the Oral Torah. It would also be impossible for the

---

1. *Kuzari* 3:38 (42b); Ramban on *Megillah* 2a; Ran, *Megillah* (Rif 1a) s.v. *VeYesh.* Cf. *Sanhedrin* 88b; *Sotah* 47b; *Tosefta, Chagigah* 2:7; Rashi, *Yevamoth* 13b, s.v. *Lo Thaasu,* s.v. *Amar Lo, Sukkah* 44a (top), s.v. *LeDidehu;* Rashba, *Yevamoth* 14a, s.v. *Amar* (end); *Beth Yosef,* Introduction (beginning); *Turey Zahav,* Introduction to *Yoreh Deah.*

2. Literally "going." It is thus the way in which the Jewish people go; *Arukh,* s.v. *Halakh.* Also see *Sefer HaTishbi,* s.v. *Halakhah; Ragley Mebhasser ad loc.;* quoting Rabbi Menachem Mendel (ben Chaim) Hager of Viznetz, *Tzemach Tzadik* (Chernowitz, Lvov, 1885-1892). Cf. *Targum Yonathan* on Leviticus 5:10, 9:16; *Targum* on Joshua 6:15, 2 Kings 11:14. The word *halakhah* is certainly also related to the concept expressed in the verse, "You shall teach them the way in which they shall *go*" (Exodus 18:20). Also see Deuteronomy 8:6, 10:12, 11:22, 19:9, 26:17, 28:9, 30:16, 1 Kings 2:3, 8:58; *Targum ad loc.* Cf. Rabbi Shneur Zalman of Liadi, *Torah Or, Mishpatim* (75c).

Sanhedrin to decide in every possible case. Therefore, God gave each qualified Torah scholar the right to decide questions of Torah law.[3] Then, even if laws were forgotten, they could be restored through the halakhic process.[4]

12:4   It is a positive commandment for a duly qualified Torah scholar to render decisions in questions of Torah law when asked. It is thus written, "You shall teach the children of Israel all the decrees which God told them through Moses" (Leviticus 10:11).[5]

12:5   It is forbidden to render any decisions in the Torah law while intoxicated. The commandment to render decisions is therefore immediately preceded by the warning, "Do not drink any wine or strong drink" (Leviticus 10:9).[6] However, if a law is perfectly obvious in the Torah itself,[7] it may be related even when one is intoxicated.[8]

3. *Yerushalmi, Sanhedrin* 4:2 (29a,b); *Karban HaEdah, Yeffeh Mareh, ad loc.; Sofrim* 16:5; *Imrey Binah* 8 (in *Kithvey Maharatz Chajas*), pp. 946,47.
4. *Imrey Binah loc. cit.* Cf. *Temurah* 16a; *Tosafoth, Eruvin* 21b, s.v. *Mipney Mah; Teshuvoth Chavath Yair* 192. See Chapter 9, note 36.
5. *Sefer Mitzvoth Katan* 111; *Cheredim,* Positive Commandments 4:20. See *Pri Megadim,* Introduction to *Orach Chaim, Seder Hanhagath HaShoel im HaNish'al* 4; *Hagahoth Maharshak ad loc.*
6. *Kerithoth* 13b; *Eruvin* 64a; *Kethuvoth* 10b; *Yad, Biyath HaMikdash* 1:3; *Sefer HaMitzvoth,* Negative Commandment 73; *Sefer Mitzvoth Gadol,* Negative Commandment 300; *Chinukh* 152; *Yoreh Deah* 242:13 in *Hagah.* Also see Ramban on *Sefer HaMitzvoth loc. cit.* This also includes women, see above, Chapter 10, note 56. It is this commandment that essentially defines the essence of decision making.
7. See *Turey Zahav, Yoreh Deah* 242:3; *Sifethey Cohen* 242:30. Cf. *Teshuvoth Maharik* 170; *Terumath HaDeshen* 42; *Teshuvoth Chavath Yair* 177.
8. *Kerithoth* 13b; *Yad, Biyath HaMikdash* 1:3. Some authorities write that it is permitted to participate as a member of a rabbinical court (*beth din*) while intoxicated; *Tosafoth, Sanhedrin* 42a, s.v. *HaOskim; Choshen Mishpat* 7:5; *Teshuvoth Shevuth Yaakov* 140. Many authorities, however forbid it; *BaMidbar Rabbah* 10:8; *Teshuvoth Beth Chadash* 41; *Kenesseth HaGedolah, Hagahoth Beth Yosef, Choshen Mishpat* 7; *Teshuvoth Mishkenoth Yaakov* 6; cf. *Urim VeThumim, Thumim* 7:6. There is some indication that merely to forbid something does not constitute a decision; *Kethuvoth* 7a; Rashi *ad loc. s.v. U'Mi Ikka; Halikhoth Olam* 3:1; *Teshuvoth Binyamin Zeev* 107; *Sh'nei Luchoth HaB'rith, Torah SheB'al Peh, Heh* (3:232a); *Pachad Yitzchak, s.v. Horah* (11c); cf. *Eruvin* 63a; *Yoreh Deah* 242:11. But see below, 12:43.

12:6   The unique relationship between God and Israel guarantees that we will always be able to ascertain His will. It is thus written, "You will seek God your Lord, and you will find Him, as long as you search after Him with all your heart and with all your soul" (Deuteronomy 4:29).[9]

12:7   This relationship also guarantees that collectively Israel will always obey God's will in the long run. It is thus written, "God will not abandon His people, nor will He forsake His inheritance. For [Torah] law will return to righteousness, and all upright men will follow it" (Psalms 94:14,15).[10]

12:8   God therefore granted the Jewish people as a whole a sort of collective Divine Inspiration so that they would be able to recognize the correct opinion in questions of Torah law.[11] Therefore, when there is any question, it is ultimately decided on the basis of what becomes common practice.[12] Hence, when a decision is accepted as a general custom, it becomes universally binding.[13]

9. This clearly only applies to those who actively seek to do God's will, and not to those who wish to cast off the yoke of His commandments; see below, note 197. Also see Deuteronomy 26:18.
10. Cf. *Shabbath* 138b; *Tana DeBei Eliahu Zuta* 16 (31b). There will be disputes, but there will be a way of resolving them; Rashi, *Shabbath* 139a, s.v. Halakhah.
11. In such cases, "If they are not prophets, they are sons of prophets;" *Pesachim* 66a; *Yerushalmi, Pesachim* 6:1 (39b); *Yerushalmi, Shabbath* 19:1 (86b). (Regarding "sons of prophets," see above, 6:55.) This may have been the significance of the *Bath Kol* in the case of Beth Hillel and Beth Shamai; see *Eruvin* 13b; *Tosefta, Terumoth* 3:11; *Imrey Binah* 6:5,8 (in *Kithvey Maharatz Chajas*), pp. 941, 944. See above, chapter 6, note 38.
12. *Yerushalmi, Peah* 7:5 (34b); *Yerushalmi, Maaser Sheni* 5:2 (30a); *Yerushalmi Yevamoth* 7:3 (40a); *Berakhoth* 45a; *Pesachim* 54a, *Menachoth* 35b; Rashi, *Berakhoth* 45a, s.v. *Mai*; *Teshuvoth Ramban* 260; *Teshuvoth Harosh* 55:10; *Halikhoth Olam* 5:3 (end), s.v. Halakhah; *Sh'nei Luchoth HaB'rith, Torah SheB'al Peh, s.v. Kol Halakhah* (3:249a). Also see *Berakhoth* 52b; *Pesachim* 103a; *Taanith* 26b; *Rosh HaShanah* 15b; *Yerushalmi, Shevi'ith* 5:1 (13a); *Teshuvoth Rabbi Meir of Rothenberg* (Shaarey Teshuvah) 386 (Berlin, 1891); *Teshuvoth Maharik* 171. See below, Chapter 13, note 69.
13. *Sofrim* 14:18; *Sefer Kerithoth, Yemoth Olam* 3:19 (21b). See above, 11:46.

12:9   Therefore, any practice, decision or code that is universally accepted by the Jewish people is assumed to represent God's will and is binding as such.[14] Even when a decision is initially disputed, the commonly accepted opinion becomes binding as law.[15]

12:10   Since the Talmud was accepted by all Israel, it is the final authority in all questions of Torah law.[16] Since such universal acceptance is a manifestation of God's will, one who opposes the teachings of the Talmud is like one who opposes God and His Torah.[17] All later codes and decisions are binding only insofar as they are derived from the Talmud.[18]

12:11   Other works, written prior or contemporary to the Babylonian Talmud are likewise very important for the understanding of laws, beliefs and history.[19] However, since they were all known to the compilers of the Talmud, it is assumed that when the Talmud disputes these works, it does

14. A rabbi who opposes such a decision is considered to be "mistaken in a matter of Mishnah;" Rosh, *Sanhedrin* 4:6; Tur, *Choshen Mishpat* 25; *Choshen Mishpat* 25:1; *Pith'chey Teshuvah ad loc.* 25:2. See *Sanhedrin* 6a, 33a; *Bava Kama* 100a, 117b; *Berakhoth* 28a; *Yad Ramah, Sanhedrin* 6a; *Yerushalmi, Sanhedrin* 1:1 (1b); *Sifethey Cohen, Choshen Mishpat* 25:30. Cf. *Yerushalmi, Gittin* 5:5 (30a). Also see *Yoreh Deah* 242:8; *Tosafoth, Eruvin* 62b, s.v. *Afilu;* Rosh, *Eruvin* 6:2.
15. A rabbi who disputes this is considered "mistaken in estimation " (*to'eh be-shikul ha-daath,* טוֹעֶה בְּשִׁיקוּל הַדַעַת); *Sanhedrin* 6a, 33a, *Bava Kama* 100a, 117b; *Bekhoroth* 28a; *Yad, Sanhedrin* 6:2; *Choshen Mishpat* 25:2; *Sifethey Cohen ad loc.* 25:88. This may be related to the concept of following the majority (below, 12:33); cf. Rashi, *Sanhedrin* 33a, s.v. *Sugya;* Tur, *Choshen Mishpat* 25; see *Sofrim* 16:7. Also see *Maor HaGadol, Sanhedrin* (Rif 12a); *Sefer VeHaz'hir, Mishpatim* (Leipzig, 1873), p. 51a; Rabbi Moshe Teitelbaum, *Yismach Moshe, Yeyn Rokeach* (Sighet, 1908). p. 29c).
16. *Maor HaGadol, Sanhedrin* (Rif 12a); Rosh, *Sanhedrin* 4:6; *Yad, Sanhedrin* 5:1; Tur, *Choshen Mishpat* 25. The Talmud was accepted by all sages together; *Sefer Mitzvoth Gadol,* Negative Commandments, Introduction (3a). Also see above, 9:15, 11:20.
17. See Chapter 9, note 106.
18. Cf. Rashbam, *Bava Bathra* 103b, s.v. *Ad; Tosefoth Yom Tov, Shevi'ith* 4:10. See below, note 126.
19. Cf. Maharatz Chajas, *Gittin* 7a, 17a.

so for a reason.[20] Therefore, whenever they disagree with the Talmud,[21] decisions found in the Jerusalem Talmud,[22] Midrash and Tosefta are ignored.[23] There are, however, certain special cases, where, because of long established custom, the opinions of other early works are accepted, even when they disagree with the Talmud.[24]

12:12 All the opinions found in the Talmud are equally sacred.[25] Still, there is always one binding opinion whenever questions of actual practice are concerned.[26] This is known either from the Talmudic discussions itself,[27] or from later tradition.[28]

20. Cf. Rashi, *Taanith* 16a, s.v. *VeLama*, *Nazir* 20b, s.v. *Hashta*, *Niddah* 8a (end), s.v. *VeOmar*; Maharatz Chajas, *Taanith* 16a, *Nazir* 20b, *Bava Kama* 60a.

21. *Tosafoth, Berakhoth* 48a, s.v. *VeLeth*. However, where they do not disagree with the Talmud, they can be accepted, *Magid Mishneh* on *Yad, Shabbath* 18:2; *Beth Chadash, Orach Chaim* 124; *Mayim Chaim* 1b; *Lechem Yehudah* 14b (end); *Yad Malachi, Kelaley Sh'nei HaTalmudim* 4; *Darkey HaHorah* 2 (in *Kithvey Maharatz Chajas*), p. 243.

22. *Bereshith Rabbah* 33:3; *Rif, Eruvin* 35b; *Migdal Oz* on *Yad, Shofar* 1:5; *Teshuvoth Rashbash* 151; *Kesef Mishneh* on *Yad, Nedarim* 6:17 (end); *Beth Yosef, Orach Chaim* 59 (end); *Yad Malachi, Kelaley Sh'nei HaTalmudim* 2; *Beer Sheva, Horioth* p. 6a.

23. *Yerushalmi, Peah* 2:4 (13a); *Yerushalmi, Chagigah* 1:8 (7b); *Rashbam, Bava Bathra* 130b, s.v. *Ad*; *Ran, Nedarim* 40b, s.v. *U'LeInyan; Teshuvoth Rashbu* 335; *Tosefoth Yom Tov, Berakhoth* 5:4; *Teshuvoth Radbaz* 3:647; *Teshuvoth Nodeh BeYehudah, Tinyana, Yoreh Deah* 161; *Beer Yaakov, Evven HaEzer* 119; *Yad Malachi* 72; Maharatz Chajas, *Nedarim* 40b.

24. *Tosafoth, Berakhoth* 18a, s.v. *LeMachar, Pesachim* 40b, s.v. *Aval, Megillah* 32b, s.v. *Rosh, Bava Bathra* 74a s.v. *Piskey, Avodah Zarah* 65b, s.v. *Aval; Teshuvoth Maharik* 9, 54; *Magen Avraham* 690:22, quoting Rabbi Yitzchak Stein on *Sefer Mitzvoth Gadol*, Positive Commandments (56c). See below, 13:43.

25. "Both are the words of the Living God;" *Gittin* 6b; *Eruvin* 13b; *Ritva ad loc.*; *Yerushalmi, Berakhoth* 1:4 (9a); *Yerushalmi, Yevamoth* 1:6 (9a); *Yerushalmi, Sotah* 3:4 (16a); *Yerushalmi, Kiddushin* 1:1 (4a); Rashi, *Kethuvoth* 57a, s.v. *Mah; Tosefoth Shuntz, Edduyoth* 1:5; *Tikuney Zohar Chadash* 107a; *Tosefoth Yom Tov*, Introduction; *Avodath HaKodesh, Shaar HaTachlith* 23; *Sh'nei Luchoth HaB'rith, Beth David* (1:39b); *Derashoth HaRan* 7 (p. 111); *Peney Moshe* on *Yerushalmi, Sanhedrin* 4:2 (21a end), s.v. *Lo*. Also see *Chagigah* 3b; *Sofrim* 16:6,7; *BaMidbar Rabbah* 14:11; *Pirkey Rabbi Eliezer* 18 (42a).

26. Cf. *Yerushalmi, Sanhedrin* 4:2 (21b); *Sofrim* 16:5; *Midrash Tehillim* 12:14. Also see *Avodah Zarah* 7a; *Choshen Mishpat* 25:2 in *Hagah*.

27. *Rif, Sanhedrin* 12b; *HaMaor HaGadol, Sanhedrin* (Rif 12a) (end); *Rosh, Sanhedrin* 4:6; *Tur, Choshen Mishpat* 25; *Sifethey Cohen, Choshen Mishpat*, 25:9; *Teshuvoth Rashba* 1230.

28. Rabbi Shumel HaNaggid, *Mavo HaTalmud; Machzor Vitri*, p. 490; *Sefer Kerithoth, Yemoth Olam* 3.

12:13   However, when a dispute involves questions of opinion or history,[29] and has no special consequences,[30] any opinion found in the Talmud is equally acceptable.[31] Similarly, no final decision is normally rendered between conflicting Talmudical opinions in the case of laws that are no longer applicable.[32]

12:14   The main work of the Talmud came to an end with the death of Ravina in 4259 (499 c.e.).[33] This initiated the period of the Savoraim (סָבוֹרָאִים),[34] who made some additions to the Talmud and placed it in its final form.[35] The period of the

29. Cf. Yerushalmi, Shevi'ith 1:1 (1a); Ramban on Sefer HaMitzvoth, Shoresh 3 (39b); Maharatz Chajas, Chagigah 6b.

30. Cf. Yoma 5b, Maharatz Chajas ad loc.; Rosh, Chulin 1:23; Rashi, Chulin 17a, s.v. SheHikhniso. Also see Maharatz Chajas, Sotah 2a, Bava Kama 2b.

31. Rambam on Mishnah, Sotah 3:5, Sanhedrin 10:3, Shevuoth 1:4; Iggereth Techiyath HaMethim (in Iggereth HaRambam), pp. 11, 15; Tosafoth, Yoma 5b, Chagigah 6b, s.v. Mai Sanhedrin 15b, s.v. Shor; Rashash, Shabbath 63a; Maharatz Chajas, Yevamoth 86b. Cf. Makkoth 23b; Tosafoth Yom Tov, Makkoth 3:16, Sotah 3:5. Carefully compare Gittin 6b and Eruvin 13b.

32. Zevachim 45a; Rashi ad loc. s.v. Amar; Tosafoth, Zevachim 45a, 87a, 51b, s.v. Hilkhatha, Menachoth 45b, 52b, s.v. Halakhah, Shabbath 133a, s.v. U'Tenan, Yoma 13a, s.v. Halakhah; Tosefoth Yeshenim, Yoma 13a; Nimukey Yosef, Bava Bathra (Rif 12b end), s.v. Mathnithin; Tosefoth Tom Tov, Bava Bathra 7:7; Maharik 165; Kenesseth HaGedolah, Kellaley HaGemara 99; Magen Avraham 218:3; Teshuvoth Chavath Yair 94; Teshuvoth Panim Meiroth 2:51; Teshuvoth Yavin Shamua 301; Yad Malachi 234; Pachad Yitzchak, s.v. Halakhah LeMeshikha (27a).

33. Rav Ashi and Ravina were thus the end of decision making (horaah, הוֹרָאָה); Bava Metzia 86a; horaah denotes the Talmud; Berakhoth 5a. See Iggereth Rav Sherira Gaon, p. 97; Sefer HaKabbalah p. 19; Machzor Vitri, p. 483. See above, Chapter 9, note 101. Some sources state that this was in 4239 (379 c.e.); Meiri on Avoth, Introduction, p. 50. Also see Seder Olam Zuta, end (p. 114).

34. This is the term used by many modern writers, but it is also found in such ancient sources as Machzor Italki, Tefillah al Parnassah (Livorno, 1856) 2:15b. The usual term, however, is Rabanan Savorai (רַבָּנָן סָבוֹרָאֵי). Other sources, however, give the vocalization as Sevorai (סְבוֹרָאֵי); Arukh HaShalem, s.v. Savar (p. 14). The word Savora (סָבוֹרָא) denotes a student; Yerushalmi, Shabbath 3:3 (24a top); Karban HaEdah ad loc. s.v. Mah Yaavid; Yerushalmi, Kiddushin 3:2 (34a). Cf. Targum on Leviticus 19:32; Shabbath 6a. Some say that these rabbis could explain (savar, סבר) but not render universally binding decisions, Shalsheleth HaKabbalah, p. 79. Also see Sefer HaKabbalah p. 24; Sefer Kerithoth, Yemoth Olam 2:2 (20b); Sefer HaYuchsin 3 (69b); Tzemach David 4235; Seder HaDoroth 4235; Rabbi Binyamin Menashe Levin, Rabanan Savorai VeTalmudam (Jerusalsm, 1937). Cf. Rif, Megillah 13a.

35. Iggereth Rav Sherira Gaon, pp. 69-71; Sefer Kerithoth, Yemoth Olam, Introduction; Halikhoth Olam, quoted in Sh'nei Luchoth HaB'rith, Torah SheB'al Peh, s.v. Kelal Bathrai (3:21a); Ritva, Kiddushin 3a, s.v. Elah. Cf. Tosafoth, Zevachim 102, s.v.

Savoraim lasted for 90 years until 4349 (589 c.e.).[36] They reached final decisions in all questions that had not been decided in the Talmud.[37] Since the Savoraim headed academies including all the sages of the time, their decisions are as binding as those of the Talmud.[38]

12:15 Following the Savoraim came the period of the Geonim (גְּאוֹנִים),[39] which lasted until the death of Rav Hai Gaon in 4798 (1038 c.e.).[40] They headed the great academies of Sura and Pumbetitha in Babylonia, which had been founded in Talmudic times, and were accepted as centers of authority in all matters of Torah law.[41] The decisions of the Geonim were

Parikh, Kethuvoth 2b, s.v. *Pashit; Shem HaGedolim, Alef* 145; *Doroth HaRishonim* 3:23 (p. 28f). It is taught that the Savoraim studied the Talmud by heart; Meiri, Introduction to *Avoth* p. 50; see Rabbi Raphael Yosef (ben Chaim) Chazan, *Chikrey Lev, Orach Chaim* 12, *Yoreh Deah* 1, *Kuntres Konen LeChaker* 310. The Savoraim also made decrees; *Sefer Mitzvoth Gadol*, Positive Commandment 93 (175b). Also see *Yad, Malveh U'Loveh* 2:2; *Hagahoth Maimoni* ad loc. 2, which also indicates that the Rambam referred to the *Savoraim* as "the first Geonim." The *Savoraim* also wrote the *Mesekhtoth Ketanoth; Doroth HaRishonim* 3:17 (19b), from *Piskey HaRosh* on Rif, *Halakhoth Ketanoth, Sefer Torah* 4a (top). They may also have compiled a number of *Midrashim*.

36. *Seder HaDoroth* 4349; *Iggereth Rav Sherira Gaon*, pp. 99, 100. In *Machzor Vitri*, p. 484, we find that they existed until 928 of *Shetaroth*, that is, until 4376 (616 c.e.). Other sources state that they existed from 4265 (505 c.e.) (the time of the redaction of the Talmud) until 4451 (691 c.e.); Meiri, Introduction to *Avoth*, p. 50; cf. *Sefer HaKabbalah*, p. 26. For further discussion, see Rabbi Yaakov Eliahu Ephrathi, *Tekufoth HaSavoraim VeSafruthah* 3 (Jerusalem, 1973), p. 33ff. Note that the Islamic calendar begins in 622 c.e.; cf. *Teshuvoth Radbaz* 3:509 (944). It is also known that the Geonate in Pumbetitha began in 589 c.e., while that in Sura began in 609 c.e. See *Sefer HaPeliah* (Koretz, 1884), p. 81c.
37. *Iggereth Rav Sherira Gaon*, p. 69.
38. *Doroth HaRishonim* 3:17 (20b); cf. *Sefer HaYuchsin* 2 s.v. *Eleh HaMaaloth* (Jerusalem, 1962), p. 66d. Cf. *Chulin* 59b, regarding Rabbenu Achai; see *Tosafoth, Zevachim* 102b, s.v. *Parikh*. Also see Rif, *Megillah* 13a; Ritva, *Rosh HaShanah* 35a, s.v. *Amar* (end).
39. Gaon (גָּאוֹן) in the singular; cf. Leviticus 26:19, Sifra, Yalkut (673) ad loc.; Isaiah 4:5; Psalms 47:5. See *Yad*, Introduction; *Arukh* s.v. *Abaya*. The Rambam also refers to the *Savoraim* as Geonim, see above, note 35. Some say that the word *Gaon* has a numerical value of sixty, indicating that a Gaon must be expert in the sixty volumes of the Talmud; Meiri, Introduction to Avoth; *Sefer HaTishbi*, s.v. *Gaon; Shem HaGedolim, Kuntres Acharon, Gimel* 5; Rabbi Yeshiah Berlin, *Sheilath Shalom* on Sheiltoth, Introduction; *Sedey Chemed, P'ath HaSadeh, Gimel* 25 (2:50).
40. *Sefer HaYuchsin* 4 (beginning) (74a); *Tzemach David* 4797; *Seder HaDoroth* 4797; cf. Meiri, Introduction to *Avoth*, p. 51; *Sefer HaKabbalah*, pp. 33, 39; *Teshuvoth Tashbatz* 1:72.
41. *Iggereth Rav Sherira Gaon*, p. 100 ff; *Yad*, Introduction; *Sefer Mitzvoth Gadol*,

based on traditions from the masters of the Talmud, and were almost universally accepted.[42] Therefore, they cannot be disputed by any later authority without uncontestable proof.[43]

12:16   With the closing of the great Babylonian academies, there ceased to be any formally acknowledged center of Torah authority. However, numerous codes, based on the Talmud and the decisions of the Geonim were compiled by leading rabbis, and they achieved almost universal recognition.[44]

12:17   Most noteworthy among these[45] were the codes of Rabbi Yitzchak AlFasi (Rif; 1013-1103 c.e.)[46] and Rabbi Asher ben Yechiel (Rosh; 1250-1328 c.e.),[47] as well as the *Yad HaChazakah* (יָד הַחֲזָקָה)[48] of Rabbi Moshe Maimonides

Negative Commandments, Introduction (3a); Meiri, Introduction to *Avoth*, pp. 50,51; *MeAm Lo'ez*, Introduction. Also see *Sefer HaYuchsin* 2, s.v. *Eleh HaMaaloth* (66c ff). Unlike the *Savoraim* who were elected by all the sages together, the *Geonim* were appointed by the exilarch (*resh galutha*, רֵישׁ גָּלוּתָא), and hence, their authority was less. Moreover, the group that elected the *Savoraim* was the same that had formally closed the canon of the Talmud.

42. *Nimukey Yosef, Bava Metzia* (Rif 66b), s.v. *Garsinin* (end); Ritva, *loc. cit.*

43. *HaMaor HaGadol, Sanhedrin* (Rif 12a); *Rosh, Sanhedrin* 4:6; *Tur, Choshen Mishpat* 25; cf. *Teshuvoth Maharik* 84, 96; *Choshen Mishpat* 25:2 in *Hagah*. Also see *Hagahoth Maimonioth* on *Yad, Talmud Torah* 5:2 3; *Yoreh Deah* 242:9; Bertenoro, *Sanhedrin* 3:1. With adequate proof, however, they could be disputed, since their teachings were not universally accepted; *Doroth HaRishonim* 3:17 (20b); cf. *Teshuvoth Rabbi Eliahu Mizrachi* 1:75; *Kenesseth HaGedolah, Kelalim BeDarkey HaPoskim* 76; *Pachad Yitzchak*, s.v. *Geonim* (lc).

44. *Sefer Mitzvoth Gadol*, Negative Commandments, Introduction (3a); *Beth Yosef*, Introduction.

45. *Beth Yosef*, Introduction; *Teshuvoth Radbaz* 626; *Sh'nei Luchoth HaB'rith, Torah SheB'al Peh*, s.v. *BeMesekhta Eruvin* (3:249b); *Maadney Yom Tov*, Introduction s.v. *U'MeAz Birkey Yosef,* *Choshen Mishpat* 25:29. Cf. *Teshuvoth Rashba* 253.

46. Mordecai, *Kethvoth* 170; *Sefer Meirath Eynayim (Sema), Choshen Mishpat* 25:19; Rabbi Menachem ben Zerach, *Tzedah LaDerekh*, Introduction. Cf. *Sefer HaKabbalah*, p. 46.

47. *Maadney Yom Tov*, Introduction, s.v. *U'MeAz; Teshuvoth Rabbi Betzalel Ashkenazi* 52 (Venice, 1590); *Birkey Yosef Choshen Mishpat* 25:29.

48. "The Strong Hand." The numerical value of *Yad* (יָד) is fourteen, alluding to the number of sections in this work. It is also known as *Mishneh Torah* (מִשְׁנֶה תּוֹרָה), from Deuteronomy 17:18.

(Rambam; 1135-1204 c.e.).[49] The rabbis of this period are known as *Rishonim* (רִאשׁוֹנִים) or "first [codifiers]."[50]

12:18 The work that was most widely accepted, however, was the *Shulchan Arukh* (שֻׁלְחָן עָרוּךְ)[51] written by Rabbi Yosef Caro (1488-1575 c.e.), which took into account almost all of the earlier codes.[52] Since the *Shulchan Arukh* followed the practices of the Sephardic[53] practices, a gloss was added to it by Rabbi Moshe Isserles (1520-1527 c.e.), including all the Ashkenazic customs.[54]

12:19 With the publication of the *Shulchan Arukh*, the period of the *Rishonim* came to an end, and the period of the *Acharonim* (אַחֲרוֹנִים) or "later [codifiers]" began. The opinions of the Rishonim gained almost universal acceptance through the *Shulchan Arukh*, and therefore, the

---

49. *Teshuvoth Tashbatz* 251; *Teshuvoth Radbaz* 825; *Bedek HaBayith, Choshen Mishpat* 25 (37b); *Birkey Yosef, Choshen Mishpat* 25:26,32.
50. Cf. Meiri, Introduction to *Avoth*, p. 51ff. They are distinguished from the *Acharonim*; see below, 12:18.
51. Literally, the "Set Table." It was based on the *Arbah Turim* (or *"Tur"*) of Rabbi Yaakov ben Asher (1270-1343), son of the Rosh. Following the divisions of the *Tur*, the *Shulchan Arukh* consists of four parts: *Orach Chaim* (אוֹרַח חַיִּים, "way of life," from Psalms 16:11) dealing with daily observances, the Sabbath and the festivals; *Yoreh Deah* (יוֹרֶה דֵּעָה, "teacher of knowledge," from Isaiah 28:9), dealing with areas requiring rabbinical decision-making, such as the dietary laws; *Evven HaEzer* (אֶבֶן הָעֵזֶר, "rock of help," from 1 Samuel 7:12), dealing with marriage, divorce and related topics; and *Choshen Mishpat* (חֹשֶׁן מִשְׁפָּט, "breastplate of judgment," from Exodus 28:30), dealing with civil law and torts; see Introduction to *Tur*.
52. *Shulchan Arukh*, Introduction; *Beth Yosef*, Introduction. The *Shulchan Arukh* was first published in Venice, 1525.
53. Literally "Spanish." With the expulsion from Spain in 1492, however, Sephardic Jews spread all over the Mediterranean region. See Obadiah 1:20; *Targum Yonathan*, Rashi, Ibn Ezra, Radak, *ad loc.; Seder Olam Zuta*, p. 111 (top); *Siddur Rav Amram Gaon, Seder Birkoth HaShachar* (Jerusalem, 1971), p. 2.
54. This was known as the *Mappah* (מַפָּה), literally the "Tablecloth," and it was first published together with the *Shulchan Arukh* in Cracow, 1578. The term Ashkenaz normally denotes Germany; cf. Genesis 10:3; *Targum* on 1 Chronicles 1:5; *Yoma* 10a; Rashi, *Chulin* 93a (top), s.v. *Chelev* (end); *Rosh. Shabbath* 2:1; *Teshuvoth HaRosh* 20:20; *Teshuvoth Maharik* 91; *Pele Yoetz*, s.v. *Ger; Teshuvoth Chatham Sofer, Orach Chaim* 16. With the spread of German Jews to Eastern Europe in the fifteenth and sixteenth centuries, the term came to designate all northern European Jews.

Acharonim usually do not oppose them. While the *Acharonim* may decide among opinions found in the *Rishonim* they do not dispute them without conclusive evidence.[55]

12:20   The *Shulchan Arukh* was not the individual opinion of its authors, but a compilation of opinions found in the works of the *Rishonim* which had gained the widest acceptance. Because of the near universal acceptance of the *Shulchan Arukh*, its decisions are considered binding, unless otherwise indicated by the leading authorities of succeeding generations.[56]

12:21   Since the *Shulchan Arukh* was the standard of Torah law, it became the subject of many commentaries which expounded, and occasionally disputes its opinions.[57] Many of those which were printed alongside the *Shulchan Arukh*[58] were almost universally accepted.[59]

---

55. *Sifethey Cohen, Yoreh Deah* 242, *Kitzur BeHanhagoth Horah* 8; *Urim VeThumim, Urim* 25:22. Cf. *Teshuvoth Alshekh* 39; *Teshuvoth Maharam Alshakar* 24; *Sifethey Cohen, Choshen Mishpat* 25:21; *Chikrey Lev, Yoreh Deah* 3:82 (72c); *Sedey Chemed, Keleley HaPoskim* 16:66 (9:206). See above, note 43.

56. *Teshuvoth Menachem Azariah of Fano* 97; *Teshuvoth Chavath Yair*, additions (p. 262); quoted in *Pith'chey Teshuvah, Choshen Mishpat* 25:2; *Urim VeThumim, Urim* 25:22; *Nethivoth HaMishpat* 25:20; *Teshuvoth Tzemach Tzedek* 9 (end); *Avodath HaGershoni* 48; *Shaar Ephraim* 113 (Sulzbach, 1688), p. 81 (end); *Birkey Yosef, Choshen Mishpat* 25:26,27,29.

57. Most important of these were the *Magen Avraham* by Rabbi Avraham Abele Gombiner (1665 c.e.) and the *Magen David* or *Turey Zahav* of Rabbi David ben Sh'muel HaLevi (1646 c.e.). Both of these were published together with the *Shulchan Arukh* under the name of *Meginey Eretz* (מְגִינֵי אֶרֶץ, "protectors of the land," from Psalms 47:10) in Dyhernfurth, 1692. Other major commentaries were the *Turey Zahav, (Taz)* on all four sections of the *Shulchan Arukh;* the *Sifethey Cohen* (Shakh) of Rabbi Shabbethai ben Meir HaCohen (1647 c.e.) on *Yoreh Deah* and *Choshen Mishpat; Chelkath Mechokek* by Rabbi Moshe (ben Yitzchak) Lima (1670 c.e.) on *Evven HaEzer;* the *Beth Sh'muel (Bash)* of Rabbi Sh'muel (ben Uri Shraga) Pheobus (1689 c.e.) on *Evven HaEzer;* and the *Sefer Meirath Eynayim (Sema)* of Rabbi Yehoshua (ben Alexander HaCohen) Falk (1606 c.e.) on *Choshen Mishpat.*

58. Most notable was the *Meginey Eretz*, see above note.

59. *Teshuvoth Chavath Yair*, additions (p. 262), quoted in *Pith'chey Teshuvah, Choshen Mishpat* 25:2; *Urim VeThumim, Urim* 25:22; *Nethivoth HaMishpat* 25:20.

12:22   There were a great many accepted authorities, both among the commentators to the *Shulchan Arukh*, and among the writers of responsa (*teshuvoth*, תְּשׁוּבוֹת). These applied Torah law to individual cases, and often set binding precedents. Over the years, various compilations of these later opinions were published.[60]

12:23   The opinions found in any generally accepted code or responsum is considered a binding precedent.[61]

12:24   Nevertheless, a recognized Torah scholar may dispute such a decision if he has ample Talmudic proof[62] or an unequivocal tradition that a particular decision was not generally accepted.[63] In such cases, it is preferable to follow the rulings of a living authority, as it is written, "You shall come ... to the judge who shall be in those days" (Deuteronomy 17:9).[64]

12:25   In every generation, there are certain rabbis who, because of their great scholarship and piety, are generally accepted as religious leaders and authorities, as it is written, "You must observe all that they decide for you" (Deuteronomy 17:10).[65] Although this commandment relates specifically to

60. Most notable were the "*Rav*" *Shulchan Arukh* by Rabbi Sh'neur Zalman of Liadi (1747-1812); the *Chayay Adam and Chokhmath Adam* by Rabbi Avraham Danzig (1748-1820); the *Kitzur Shulchan Arukh* by Rabbi Shlomo Ganzfried (1804-1886); the *Mishnah Berurah* by Rabbi Yisrael Meir Kagen, the "*Chafetz Chaim*" (1839-1933); and the *Arukh HaShulchan* by Rabbi Yechiel Michel Epstein (1839-1908).
61. *Rosh, Sanhedrin* 4:6; *Choshen Mishpat* 25:1; *Terumath HaDeshen, Pesakim U'Kethavim* 241, 271; *Kenesseth HaGedolah, Orach Chaim, Kellaley Poskim* 64; *Pri Megadim*, Introduction to *Yoreh Deah, Kellaley Horah* 6. Cf. *Eruvin* 41a.
62. *Rosh, Sanhedrin* 4:6; *Tur, Choshen Mishpat* 25; *Choshen Mishpat* 25:1 in *Hagah*. Without ample proof, however, such a decision cannot be disputed on the basis of mere logic; *Terumath HaDeshen, Pesakim U'Kethavim* 241; *Teshuvoth Rashba* 2:322; *Birkey Yosef, Choshen Mishpat* 25:2,3; *Pith'chey Teshuvah* 25:3. See below, note 109.
63. *Terumath HaDeshen, Pesakim U'Kethavim* 241; *Choshen Mishpat* 25:1 in *Hagah; Sefer Meirath Eynayim (Sema)* 25:2; *HaGra* 25:7.
64. *Rosh, Sanhedrin* 4:6, from *Rosh HaShanah* 25b; cf. *Tosafoth ad loc. SheHaYamim.* See above, 10:33.
65. See above, 11:9. Also see 12:4.

the Sanhedrin, it also applies to the religious leaders of each generation.[66]

12:26   Just as a religious leader must be outstanding in wisdom and scholarship, so must he be distinguished in piety and observance.[67] It is thus written, "They shall seek the Torah from his lips, for he is an angel of the Lord of Hosts" (Malachi 2:7). This is interpreted to mean that we should only seek to learn the Torah from a rabbi who resembles an angel in holiness and piety.[68] If a person is not outstanding in piety and observance, he is not worthy of the prestige and authority of a religious leader, no matter how great his scholarship.[69]

12:27   An unopposed decision, whether given by a contemporary religious leader or found in an accepted code, should be accepted, even if it is not mentioned by other authorities.[70]

12:28   Whenever there is a dispute between two equally great authorities, whether they are contemporary to each other or not,[71] we decide the same as in the case of any other questionable circumstance.[72] If the case involves a law from the Torah, the stricter opinion must be followed,[73] while if it

---

66. *Chinukh* 495; *Minchath Chinukh* 496; *Pri Megadim,* Introduction to *Yoreh Deah; Chayay Adam* 127:1. *Cf.* Rambam on Mishnah, *Shabbath* 1:4; Maharatz Chajas, *Shabbath* 3b.
67. *Avoth* 1:17, 3:9, 3:17.
68. *Moed Katan* 17a; *Chagigah* 15b; *Yad, Talmud Torah* 4:1; *Yoreh Deah* 246:8, *Sifethey Cohen* 246:8.
69. *Yoma* 72b; *Yoreh Deah* 243:3.
70. *Chulin* 7a; *Kenesseth HaGedolah, Orach Chaim, Kelaley Poskim* 60. See above, 12:8.
71. *Yad, Mamrim* 1:5.
72. *Rif, Pesachim* 12a; *Teshuvoth Rashba* 253.
73. *Cf. Bava Bathra* 57b, Rashbam *ad loc.* s.v. *LeChumra; Kethuboth* 73b; *Gittin* 63b; *Nedarim* 53a; *Chulin* 134a; *Niddah* 25a. See above, Chapter 11, note 62.

involves rabbinical law, the more lenient opinion is followed.[74] This is a general rule.[75]

12:29 The same rule also applies where there is equal reason to forbid as to permit, and therefore, no final decision is possible.[76] However, if there is absolutely no basis whatever for a decision, then the stricter course must be taken, even in cases of rabbinical law.[77]

12:30 In the case of a Biblical law, the stricter opinion is always followed, even if it is that of the leser of two authorities.[78] However, in a question of rabbinical law, the opinion of the greater authority is followed, whether it is stricter or more lenient.[79]

12:31 The religious leader with the largest following is always considered the greater authority.[80] However, if two authorities have an equal following, the one generally recognized as a superior scholar is considered the greater.[81]

74. *Shabbath* 34; *Eruvin* 5b, 45b; *Betza* 3b. See Chapter 11 note 62.
75. *Avodah Zarah* 7a; *Tosafoth ad loc.* s.v. *BeShel*; *Yad, Mamrim* 1:5; *Choshen Mishpat* 25:2 in *Hagah*; *Teshuvoth Rashba* 253; *Sifethey Cohen, Yoreh Deah* 252, *Kitzur Hanhagoth Horaoth Issur VeHeter* 2; *Yad Malachi* 82, 83.
76. As in the case where the Talmud does not reach a decision and states that the question is left hanging (*teku*, תיקו; see Chapter 8, note 68); Rif, *Shabbath* 30a; Rosh, *Shabbath* 6:16; *Hagahoth Maimonioth, Chametz U'Matzah* 2:16 1; *Sefer Yereyim* (HaShalem) 12; *Kesef Mishneh* on *Yad, Sefer Torah* 9:14, *Tzitzith* 1:18 (end) *Shabbath* 28:3, *Yom Tov* 19:8, 6:10, 8:3; *Tamim Deyim* 242 (71a); *Pri Chadash, Orach Chaim* 672.2, *Yoreh Deah* 110, *Kelaley Sefek Sefekah* 17; *Yavin Shemua* 288; *Teshuvoth Chavath Yair* 94; *Yam Shel Shlomo, Bava Kama* 1:43 (end); *Sh'nei Luchoth HaB'rith, Torah SheB'al Peh*, s.v. *VeHoil* (3:246b); *Yad Malachi* 634; *Pachad Yitzchak*, s.v. *Teku* (33a,b).
77. *Teshuvoth Radbaz* 205; *Teshuvoth Rashdam, Orach Chaim* 165; *Teshuvoth Chavath Yair* 94; Rabbi Meyuchas ben Shmuel, *Pri HaAdamah* (Salonika, 1752), p. 40c; Rabbi Yehudah (ben Moshe) Saltro, *Mikvey Yisrael* (Venice, 1607), p. 16b; *Teshuvoth Zaken Aaron* 24 (end), 183; *Yad Malachi* 82, 83. Cf. *Berakhoth* 51a (end).
78. *Sifethey Cohen, Yoreh Deah* 242, *Kitzur Hanhagoth Horaoth Issur VeHeter* 2; from *Yad, Mamrim* 1:2, where no distinction is made between a greater and a lesser scholar.
79. *Sifethey Cohen loc. cit.* from *Avodah Zarah* 7a; *Choshen Mishpat* 25:2 in *Hagah*.
80. See Chapter 11, note 91.
81. *Hagahoth Asheri, Avodah Zarah* 1:3; *Sefer Meirath Eynayim (Sema)* 25:18; *Sifethey Cohen, loc. cit.* Cf. *Teshuvoth Chatham Sofer* 7:27 (Munkatch, 1912); *Yesod HaMishnah* p. 45.

Although experience is also taken into consideration,[82] age alone is not enough to distinguish an authority.[83]

12:32   It is forbidden for a student to oppose his teacher.[84] Therefore, the opinion of a student who opposes his teacher is never followed.[85] This is even true when the student has a stricter opinion in the case of Biblical law.[86]

12:33   This, however, is only true during the lifetime of the teacher. After his death, his students are no different from any other independent scholars.[87] Similarly, if a student surpasses his master in scholarship, he is no longer subservient to his master's opinions.[88]

12:34   It is written, "You shall incline after a majority" (Exodus 23:2).[89] Although this commandment relates specifically to the Sanhedrin, it also applies to any controversy between religious leaders.[90] In particular, if an individual opinion is opposed by that of the majority, the former is ignored.[91]

82. Ritva, *Avodah Zarah* 7a, s.v. *Hayu*; Rashi, *Tosefoth Yom Tov, Avoth* 5:7; Maharatz Chajas, *Berakhoth* 17a. Also see Chapter 11, note 91. Cf. *Pri Megadim*, Introduction to *Yoreh Deah, Kelalim BeHorah* 5.
83. *Sifethey Cohen, Yoreh Deah* 242, *Kitzur Hanhagoth Horaoth* 2. Cf. *Bava Bathra* 142b.
84. *Eruvin* 63a; *Berakhoth* 31b; *Yoma* 53a; *Yerushalmi, Shevi'ith* 6:1 (16a); *Yerushalmi, Gittin* 1:2 (5b); *Sifra* on Leviticus 10:1 (45c); *Pesikta* 2b (172a); *Yad, Talmud Torah* 5:2; *Yoreh Deah* 242:4.
85. Rabbi Sh'muel HaNaggid, *Mavo HaTalmud*, s.v. *VeHaTanaim*; *Machzor Vitri*, p. 491; *Tosafoth, Kiddushin* 45b, s.v. *Hava*; *Yad Malachi* 38,39; *Teshuvoth Zaken Aaron* 3 (8b). Cf. *Niddah* 14b; *Kiddushin* 42b; *Sanhedrin* 29a.
86. *Sifethey Cohen, Yoreh Deah* 242, *Kitzur Hanhagoth Horaoth* 2. See *Tosafoth, Berakhoth* 24b, s.v. *Pesak*; *Sedey Chemed, Alef* 339 (1:89).
87. *Ran, Sukkah* (Rif. 1a), s.v. *U'LeRabbi; Sh'nei Luchoth HaB'rith, Torah SheB'al Peh*, s.v. *Ain* (3:249b). Also see *Rosh, Bava Metzia* 1:49, *Eruvin* 2:4; *Halikhoth Olam* 5:3; *Sefer HaKerithoth, Yemoth Olam* 3:6; *Yam Shel Shlomo, Bava Kama* 2:15; *Yad Malachi* 17; *Sedey Chemed, P'ath HaSadeh, Alef* 42 (1:168). Cf. *Yoreh Deah* 242:12 in Hagah.
88. *Sifethey Cohen, Yoreh Deah, Kitzur Hanhagoth Horaoth* 2. Cf. *Teshuvoth Rivash* 271; *HaGra, Yoreh Deah* 242:12
89. See above, 11:17.
90. *Chinukh* 78; *Pri Megadim*, Introduction to *Yoreh Deah, Kelalim BeHorah* 5. Cf. *Yerushalmi, Sanhedrin* 4:2 (12b); *Midrash Tehillim* 12:4. Also see *Chulin* 11a; *Sefer HaMitzvoth*, Positive Commandment 175; *Yad Malachi* 296.
91. *Berakhoth* 9a, 37a; *Shabbath* 60b, 130b; *Betza* 11a; *Yoma* 36b; *Yevamoth* 40a, 46b;

12:35   Therefore, if two factions oppose each other in a question of law, the opinion of the faction including the greatest number of sages is that which must be followed.[92] However, if it is well established that the smaller group is superior in wisdom and scholarship, then its opinion must be followed. Wisdom take precedence over number.[93]

12:36   Some authorities maintain that in order to constitute a clear majority, the larger group must agree regarding their reasons as well as regarding their decision.[94] Therefore, in a case involving Biblical law, a lenient decision of the majority can only be followed if they all agree as to its reason.[95] In any case, if they are able to discuss the case, they are

Bava Kama 102a; *Avodah Zarah* 7a; *Berakhoth* 37a; *Niddah* 30b, 49a; *Kenesseth HaGedolah, Orach Chaim, Kelaley Poskim* 47. In the case of monetary cases, however, we do not follow a majority; *Bava Kama* 27b (top), 46b; *Bava Bathra* 92b. Therefore, the party having possession can argue that he holds (*kim li*, קים לי) like the minority or individual opinion; Rabbi Aaron Sassoon, *Torah Emeth* 207 (Venice, 1627); Rabbi Sh'muel (ben Moshe) LeBeth Kaley, *Mishpetey Sh'muel* 60 (end) (Venice, 1599); *Kenesseth HaGedolah, Choshen Mishpat* 25; *Shaar Ephraim* 127; *Sifethey Cohen, Choshen Mishpat* 25:17; *Sefer Meirath Eynuyim (Sema)* 25:16; *Beney Chayay, Choshen Mishpat* 25; *Birkey Yosef, Choshen Mishput* 25:8; *Pachad Yitzchak*, s.v. *Kim* (193a). Cf. *Bava Bathra* 55a (top), Rabbi Yaakov Emden (Maharibatz) *ad loc.*; Rashi, *Sanhedrin* 6a, s.v. *VeSugia*; *Teshuvoth Maharik* 94:4; *Teshuvoth Rashdam* 4:61; *Teshuvoth Rabbi David Cohen of Cortu, Beth* 3 (Constantinople, 1538). Some say that this is a Biblical law; *Chikrey Lev, Yoreh Deah* 2:46 (end), *Evven HaEzer* 45; *Mishpetey Sh'muel* 26 (end); Rabbi Chaim (ben David) Abulafia, *Nishmath Chaim* 1 (Salonika, 1800); Rabbi Nissim Palombo, *Yeffeh Anaf* (Izmir, 1877), p. 61a 5. Others, however, maintain that it is rabbinical; Rabbi Sh'muel Yitzchak, *Ne'eman Sh'muel* 51 (Salonika, 1723). Cf. *Sedey Chemed, Kof* 19 (4:481).

92. *Choshen Mishpat* 25:2 in *Hagah*. This is even true if 1000 are opposing 1001; Rambam, Introduction to Mishnah. See *Teshuvoth Rashba* 253; *Kenesseth HaGedolah, Orach Chaim, Kelaley Poskim* 92. Cf. *Niddah* 10b.

93. *Chinukh* 78; from *Yevamoth* 14a; cf. Meiri, Maharsha *ad loc.*; Ritva, *Rosh HaShanah* 14b, s.v. *U'Mi*; *Minchath Chinukh* 78:1; *Kenesseth HaGedolah, Orach Chaim, Kelaley Poskim* 39. Cf. *Ikkarim* 3:23; *Sheiltoth, Shemoth* 38.

94. *Sifethey Cohen, Yoreh Deah* 242, *Pilpul BeHanhagath Horaoth*, s.v. *U'Kethav; Idem. Choshen Mishpat* 25:19; Rabbi Akiva Eiger *ad loc.*; cf. *Yad, Sanhedrin* 10:5. Others, however, dispute this; *Choshen Mishpat* 25:2 in *Hagah*; HaGra *ad loc.* 25:21; cf. *Sanhedrin* 18b. Cf. *Teshuvoth Shaar Ephraim* 10:8; *Get Pashut* 122:8; *Beth Ephraim, Kuntres HaSefekoth* 39:13; *Teshuvoth Maharit* 2:19; *Teshuvoth Nodeh BeYehudah, Tinyana, Choshen Mishpat* 3; *Birkey Yosef, Choshen Mishpat* 25:25.

95. *Sifethey Cohen, Yoreh Deah* 242, *Kitzur Kelaley Horaoth* 7.

considered a clear majority even when they disagree as to their reasons for the decision.[96]

12:37   When two factions actually have the opportunity to debate a question, the majority opinion must be followed even if it is the more lenient.[97] In such a case, one who follows even a stricter opinion of the minority is guilty of violating the commandment to follow the majority[98] and is liable to death.[99] However, where there is no actual debate between the factions, as in the case of published opinions, one may follow the stricter opinion of the minority; if an actual debate were to have occurred, they might have been able to convince the majority.[100]

12:38   When rabbinical laws were legislated by the Sanhedrin, a condition was made that any valid opinion could be relied upon where there is a question of great monetary loss.[101] Therefore, where a question of r، bbinical law involves the possibility of great monetary loss, one may even follow the lenient opinion of a minority, a lesser scholar opposing a greater one, or a student opposing his teacher.[102]

96. Baer Hetiv, Choshen Mishpat 25:12.
97. Sifethey Cohen, Pilpul BeHannagath Horaoth, s.v. U'Mashma; cf. Sedey Chemed, Yod 35 (3:63).
98. Minchath Chinukh 78:6.
99. Berakhoth 1:3 (10b); Yerushalmi, Sotah 3:4 (16a); Yerushalmi, Kiddushin 1:1 (4a); Mesilath Yesharim 20 (30b). Cf. Yerushalmi, Shevi'ith 4:2 (11a); Rashba, Berakhoth 11a, s.v. Amar; Teshuvoth Rama 91; Teshuvoth Rashdam, Yoreh Deah 192; Tifereth Yisrael, Berakhoth 1:25, Boaz 3. See below, note 131. Cf. Avoth 1:11.
100. Get Pashut, Kuntres HaKelalim (end); Minchath Chinukh 78:1 (end); Sedey Chemed, Yod 35 (3:63)
101. Hefsed Merubah (הֶפְסֵד מְרוּבָּה); Sifethey Cohen, Pilpul BeHanhagath Horaoth, s.v. U'Mashma. Atereth Tzvi, Mishpat HaHorah 5 (p. 379). Cf. Shabbath 154b; Pesachim 15b, 20b, 55b; Betza 36a; Bava Kama 117a; Bava Metzia 38b. See above, note 11:27. Also see Rosh HaShanah 27a.
102. Eruvin 46a; Niddah 6b, 9a; Choshen Mishpat 25:2 in Hagah; Teshuvoth Rashba 253; Teshuvoth Rashbash 513; Sifethey Cohen, Yoreh Deah 242, Kitzur Kelaley Horah 2,3; Kenesseth HaGedolah, Orach Chaim, Keleley Poskim 92. See Beth Chadash, Yoreh Deah, Kuntres Acharon, Pesak BeHanhagoth Horaah DeIssur VeHeter; Birkey Yosef, Choshen Mishpat 25:34; Sedey Chemed, Heh 90,91 (2:187).

Nonetheless, even in such a case, one may not rely upon an opinion opposing one that has been universally accepted.[103]

12:39   Torah law depends on legal precedent rather than on historical scholarship.[104] Therefore, it is usually the most recent valid decision that is followed.[105] This is even true when it disputes an earlier majority.[106]

12:40   However, a later authority is only followed when he is known to be fully aware of the earlier decision[107] and worthy of disputing it.[108] Moreover, he must refute the earlier decision with clear and unambiguous proof rather than with mere logic.[109] When the earlier opinion is not generally known, however, it can be assumed that the later authority would have accepted it if he would have been aware of it; therefore, the earlier opinion can be followed.[110]

103. *Eruvin* 46a; *Niddah* 6b, 9b. Cf. Rashi, *Sanhedrin* 6a, s.v. *VeSugia*; above, note 91.
104. Cf. *Bava Bathra* 142b.
105. *Teshuvoth Maharik* 84, 102; *Choshen Mishpat* 25:2 in *Hagah.* Cf. Rabbi Sh'muel HaNaggid, *Mavo HaTalmud,* s.v. *VeHaTanaim; Machzor Vitrl,* p. 491; *Sefer HaKerithoth, Yemoth Olam* 3:6; Rosh, *Sanhedrin* 4:6; *Tosafoth, Kiddushin* 45b, s.v. *Hava; Sh'nei Luchoth HaB'rith, Torah SheB'al Peh,* s.v. *Ain* (3:249b); *Tosefoth Yom Tov,* Introduction to *Bava Kama; Yad Malachi* 168, 194; *Atzmoth Yosef, Kiddushin* 62b; *Lev Shomea,* Alef 3; *Sedey Chemed, P'ath HaSadeh, Heh* 27 (2:258). Also see Rif, *Berakhoth* 31b, *Bava Metzia* 14b; *Tosafoth, Yoma* 37b, s.v. *Amar;* Rosh, *Shabbath* 23:1, *Bava Metzia* 3:10, 4:21; *Pachad Yitzchak,* s.v. *Halakhah* (21d).
106. *Teshuvoth Binyanim Zeev* 126; *Teshuvoth Rabbi Moshe Alshaker* 93; *Kennesseth HaGedolah, Orach Chaim, Kelaley Poskim* 39; *Yad Malachi* 169; *Pri Megadim,* Introduction to *Yoreh Deah, Kitzur Kelaley Horaah* 8; *Pith'chey Teshuvah, Choshen Mishpat* 25:8. Also see *Tosafoth Shantz,* Raavad, *Edduyoth* 1:5; *Sifethey Cohen, Yoreh Deah* 242, *Pilpul BeHanhagoth Horaoth,* s.v. *VeKi Tomar.* Also see Chida, *Eyn Zokher, Heh* 48, 51.
107. *Choshen Mishpat* 25:2 in *Hagah; Sifethey Cohen* ad loc. 25:21; *Teshuvoth Rabbi Moshe Alshekh* 39 (61b).
108. *Sifethey Cohen, Kitzur BeHanhagath Horaoth* 8; *Idem., Choshen Mishpat* 25:21; *Nesivoth HaMishpat* 25:20.
109. *Pith'chey Teshuvah, Choshen Mishpat* 25:3, 25:8; *Teshuvoth Rabbi Moshe MeRothenberg, Yoreh Deah* 60 (Lvov, 1857). See above, note 62.
110. *Teshuvoth Maharik* 96; *Choshen Mishpat* 25:2 in *Hagah; Sedey Chemed, Kelaley Poskim* 16:46 (9:201). Cf. *Shabbath* 61a; Rosh, *Berakhoth* 3:35; *Teshuvoth Chatham Sofer, Yoreh Deah* 233, s.v. *BeHah.* Also see *Tumath Yesharim* 16; *Kennesseth HaGedolah, Orach Chaim, Kelaley Poskim* 44.

12:41   When a community accepts a rabbi as their religious leader, his decisions are binding in all cases.[111]

12:42   The rabbi of a community may even reverse the decisions of his predecessors.[112] This is true even if the current rabbi's decisions are more lenient.[113]

12:43   If the community rabbi is a recognized Torah authority, he must be followed, even when he disagrees with the majority of contemporary rabbis.[114]

12:44   In all such cases, the rabbi must depend on his own judgment.[115] He can be secure in the promise of divine guidance, as it is written, "Consider what you do, for you judge not for man, but for God, and He is with you in your decision" (2 Chronicles 19:6).[116]

---

111. *Teshuvoth Rashba* 253; *Teshuvoth HaRan* 48; *Choshen Mishpat* 25:2 in *Hagah*; *HaGra ad loc.* 25:22. See *Shabbath* 130a; *Yevamoth* 14a; *Chulin* 116a; *Kenesseth HaGedolah, Orach Chaim, Kelaley Poskim* 93; *Pri Chadash, Orach Chaim* 496, *Diney Minhagey Issur* 11. Also see *Choshen Mishpat* 14:1. The rabbi of a city is known as *Chakham Halr* (חֲכַם הָעִיר) or *Mara DeAthra* (מָרָא דְּאַתְרָא). We see that with regard to courts the Torah gives each city autonomy; see Chapter 11, note 5. Regarding appointing a rabbi, see *Teshuvoth HaRosh* 6:1; *Orach Chaim* 53:24; *Beur Halakhah ad loc.* s.v. *Sh'liach Tzibbur; Choshen Mishpat* 163:1 in *Hagah*. Also see *Tanna DeBei Eliahu Rabbah* 11 (Ed. Meir Freidman; Vienna, 1902), p. 54; *Teshuvoth Rabbi Yosef (ben David) ibn Lev* 3:97 (Constantinople, 1573); *Teshuvoth Rabbi Shlomo (ben Avraham) Cohen (Maharshakh)* 2:143 (Venice, 1592). Cf. *Teshuvoth Rashdam, Orach Chaim* 36; *Kenesseth HaGedolah, Orach Chaim* 53; *Beer Hetiv, Orach Chaim* 53:29. Regarding dismissing a rabbi without adequate cause, see *Teshuvoth Chatham Sofer, Orach Chaim* 206; *Mishnah Berurah* 53:86. Cf. *Pachad Yitzchak,* s.v. *Chakham* (4a).
112. *Teshuvoth Rashba* 253; *Choshen Mishpat* 25:2 in *Hagah*. Cf. *Eruvin* 41a.
113. *Beth Chadash, Choshen Mishpat* 25 (37b); *Sifethey Cohen, Choshen Mishpat* 25:20; *Urim VeThumim, Thumim* 25:7; *Birkey Yosef, Choshen Mishpat* 25:36; Rabbi Yosef HaLevi Nazir, *Matteh Yosef, Yoreh Deah* 2 (Constantinople, 1717), p. 22. Cf. *Shiltey Gibborim, Avodah Zarah* (Rif 1b) 3.
114. *Pri Chadash, Orach Chaim* 496, *Diney Minhagey Issur* 11 (end). Cf. *Yevamoth* 14a. See below, Chapter 13, note 70.
115. *Bava Bathra* 131a; *Sanhedrin* 6b; *Niddah* 20b.
116. *Sanhedrin* 6b; *Rashbam, Bava Bathra* 131a, s.v. *VeAl*. Cf. *Yerushalmi, Sanhedrin* 1:1 (2b end); *Tosefta, Sanhedrin* 1:4; *Shemoth Rabbah* 30:13; *Tanchuma, Mishpatim* 6; *Shoftim* 7. Also see *Yad, Sanhedrin* 23:9; *Choshen Mishpat* 8:9 in *Hagah*. See above, Chapter 6, note 38.

12:45   The authority of a community rabbi depends on his general acceptance.[117] Therefore, other religious scholars living in the community may follow stricter opinions according to their own judgment.[118] However, they may not openly oppose the community rabbi[119] or publicly display their dissent.[120]

12:46   If there are many Torah scholars in the community who disagree with the rabbi, he should yield to the opinion of the majority.[121] This is only true, however, where the majority are the rabbi's equals in wisdom and Torah knowledge. Under no condition should the rabbi yield to the ignorant laity in any question of Torah law, no matter how great their number.[122]

12:47   In rendering a decision, a rabbi must carefully consider all its aspects.[123] Wherever possible, he should strive to find a precedent for his decisions from the opinions of earlier authorities.[124]

12:48   An opinion should not be based on abridged codes[125] unless the rabbi knows their sources in the Talmud.[126]

117. Cf. Netziv, *Meshiv Davar, Yoreh Deah* 9; *Sedey Chemed, Cheth* 76 (3:412), s.v. *VeAl.*
118. *Pri Chadash, Orach Chaim* 496, *Diney Minhagey Issur* 11 from *Teshuvoth Rashba* 253 (end). Cf. *Chulin* 37b, 44b; *Yoreh Deah* 116:7 in *Hagah.* See Meiri, *Yevamoth* 14a, s.v *Kol.*
119. See below, 12:49.
120. See below, 13:81.
121. *Pri Chadash, Orach Chaim* 496, *Diney Minhagey Issur* 11; from *Berakhoth* 37a; *Tosefta, Berakhoth* 4:12. Also see *Berakhoth* 9a.
122. *Ikkarim* 3:23. See above, note 93.
123. *Avoth* 1:1; *Avoth deRabbi Nathan* 1:4; *Sanhedrin* 7b; *Sifri* (16) on Deuteronomy 1:16; *Yad, Sanhedrin* 20:7; *Choshen Mishpat* 10:1.
124. *Kenesseth HaGedolah, Orach Chaim, Kelaley Poskim* 59. Cf.*Teshuvoth Rabbi Yaakov Weil* 164 (Venice, 1523).
125. *Sotah* 22a; *Maharsha, Chikushey Agaddoth* ad loc. s.v. *Yireh Eth; Pith'chey Teshuvah, Yoreh Deah* 242:8; *Teshuvoth Rashba* 335; *Teshuvoth Chavath Yair* 94; *Pachad Yitzchak,* s.v. *Halakhah* (21a). See Rav Paltoi ben Abaye Gaon, *Chemdah Genuzah* 110; *Teshuvoth HaGeonim MiTokh HaGenizah* (Jerusalem, 1929), p. 81; cf. *Iggereth Rav Sherira Gaon,* p. 47.
126. *Teshuvoth HaRosh* 31:19; *Yam Shel Shlomo, Bava Kama,* Introduction; *Levush,*

12:49   A rabbi should not base his decision upon the mere action of an earlier authority[127] unless he thoroughly understands the issue, and knows that the reason for the action is completely unambiguous.[128] However, if the act was accompanied by a formal decision, it is the most valid of precedents.[129]

12:50   Just as a rabbi may not permit that which is forbidden, so must he be careful not to forbid that which is permitted.[130] Therefore, if a rabbi must forbid something merely because of a question of law, because of a custom, or because of special circumstances, he must state his reason so as not to establish an erroneous precedent.[131] Similarly, if he must permit something in an emergency, he must clarify his reason for that particular case.[132]

12:51   A rabbi should be careful not to render an unusual or anomalous decision,[133] unless he carefully explains the reasons for it.[134] Therefore, any uncommon decision that depends on subtle or esoteric reasoning should not be publicized, lest it lead to erroneous conclusions.[135] It is for

Introduction; *Maadney Yom Tov*, Introduction, s.v. *U'MeAz*; Maharal, *Nethivoth Olam, Nethiv HaTorah* 15; *Derekh Chaim* on *Avoth* 66. Cf. Raavad on *Yad*, Introduction, s.v. *VeYodea*. See above, note 18.

127. *Bava Bathra* 130b; *Pachad Yitzchak*, s.v. *Halakhah* (21b); *Darkey HaHorah* 1 (in *Kithvey Maharatz Chajas*), p. 217. Cf. *Niddah* 7b; *Yerushalmi, Peah* 2:4 (13a).

128. *Kenesseth HaGedolah, Orach Chaim, Kelaley Poskim* 63; *Teshuvoth Binyamin Zeev* 131; *Teshuvoth Rivash* 301.

129. Cf. *Shabbath* 21a, 136b; *Bava Bathra* 83a, 130b; *Niddah* 65b.

130. *Yerushalmi, Terumoth* 5:3 (30b); *Yerushalmi, Chagigah* 1:8 (8a); *Yerushalmi, Sotah* 8:2 (34b); *Teshuvoth Binyamin Zeev* 326; *Teshuvoth Zaken Aaron* 144; *Pachad Yitzchak*, s.v. *Horah* (11c). Cf. *Yerushalmi, Avodah Zarah* 2:9 (17b); *Tosafoth, Avodah Zarah* 40a, s.v. *Amar*.

131. Cf. *Tosefta, Damai* 5:26. Also see *Berakhoth* 11a; *Pesachim* 100a; *Kethuvoth* 50b.

132. *Sifethey Cohen, Yoreh Deah* 242, *Kitzur BeHanhagoth Horaoth* 9.

133. *Yoreh Deah* 242:10; *Hagahoth Maimonioth* on *Yad, Talmud Torah* 5:3 6. Cf. *Sanhedrin* 5b; *Niddah* 20b (top); *Bekhoroth* 3b (end); *Eruvin* 13b. Also see *Avoth* 1:11, 2:4; Maharatz Chajas, *Yoma* 40b.

134. *Sifethey Cohen, Yoreh Deah* 242:17; *Sheyarey Berakhah ad loc.; Pri Megadim*, Introduction to *Orach Chaim, Seder Hanhagath HaShoel im HaNish'al* 1:10.

135. *Shabbath* 12b; *Menachoth* 36b; *Bava Kama* 30b, Maharatz Chajas *ad loc.; Yad, Tefillin* 4:14, *Yom Tov* 4:9. Also see *Taanith* 26b; *Nedarim* 23b; *Pesachim* 30b;

this reason that there are cases which are permitted only in the case of a scholar,[136] and which may not be taught to the ignorant.[137]

12:52 When a rabbi renders a decision in a case in which there are no clear precedents, he must strive to bring as many proofs as possible.[138]

12:53 When a rabbi is positive of his conclusions, he may even make use of dubious proofs to strengthen his decision.[139] He may even, if the situation warrants, ascribe the decision to a great sage so that it will be generally accepted.[140] Where it is not absolutely necessary, however, this is forbidden.[141]

12:54 When a rabbi renders a decision in a question of law, the Torah recognizes it as binding.[142] Therefore, when a rabbi decides on a case and forbids something, it becomes intrinsically forbidden.[143]

Sukkah 34b; Maharatz Chajas, *Chulin* 12a, 15a; *Darkey Horaah* 1 (p. 217); *Yad Malachi* 191 (28b).

136. *Nedarim* 14a; *Bava Metzia* 71a; *Tosafoth, Bava Kama* 99b, s.v. *Menacha;* Maharatz Chajas *ad loc.*

137. *Menachoth* 99b; *Nedarim* 49a; Rashi, *Taanith* 13a, s.v. *KeSheAmru; Pachad Yitzchak, s.v. Halakhah* (21c); *Darkey Horaah* 1 (p. 218).

138. *Yerushalmi, Berakhoth* 2:3 (14b); *Nimukey Yosef, Bava Kama* (Rif 30a), s.v. *Gemara;* Maharatz Chajas, *Yoma* 32a.

139. *Nimukey Yosef, loc. cit.*

140. *Magen Avraham* 156:2; from *Eruvin* 51a; *Pesachim* 112a; Rashi, Rashbam, *ad loc.* s.v. *Hithla.* Cf. *Birkey Yosef, Yoreh Deah* 242:24, quoting *Teshuvoth HaGeonim* 324; *Tanna DeBei Eliahu Rabbah* 4 (31b); *Ramathaim HaTzofim ad loc.* 4:2; *Makor Chesed* on Sefer Chasidim 977:2. Also see *Shabbath* 115a; Rashi *ad loc.* s.v. *Atha; Pesachim* 27b; *Gittin* 20a. If a rabbi wants his decisions to be followed, he should carefully abide by them; *Shemoth Rabbah* 43:5.

141. *Yerushalmi, Nazir* 7:1 (34b top); *Berakhoth* 27b; *Mesekhta Kallah* (end); HaGra *ad loc.* 3; *Yoreh Deah* 242:24. Cf. *Shevuoth* 31a; *Kethuboth* 17a; *Yevamoth* 65b; *Sefer Mitzvoth Gadol,* Positive Commandment 107; from Exodus 23:7.

142. See above 12:4, 5. Also see Netziv, *Meshiv Davar, Yoreh Deah* 9; *Sedey Chemed, Cheth* 76 (2:412). Cf. *Teshuvoth Shoel U'Meshiv* 1:5.

143. Rashba, *Chulin* 44b; Ran, *Avodah Zarah* (Rif 1b), s.v. *HaNish'al,* quoting Raavad; Meiri, Ritva, *Avodah Zarah* 7a; cf. *Yevamoth* 92a. Others, however, state that it does not become intrinsically forbidden, but the decision cannot be overruled out of respect for the first rabbi; Ran, Meiri, *loc. cit.;* Meiri, *Horioth* 3a, s.v. *Gedoley; Shiltey Gibborim, Avodah Zarah* (Rif 1b) 3; cf. Rashi, *Niddah* 20b, s.v. *A'Garmai.* Also see *Teshuvoth Tashbatz* 66, s.v. *Od; Teshuvoth Radbaz* 362; Rabbi

12:55   Hence, when one rabbi forbids something in a specific case, another rabbi may not permit it in the same case.[144] One rabbi can overturn the decision of another only if he can prove the initial decision to be erroneous.[145]

12:56   Since the initial decision renders the subject of a case intrinsically forbidden, it cannot be permitted even by a greater sage[146] or by a majority rule.[147]

12:57   An erroneous decision cannot render a case intrinsically forbidden. Therefore, if a second rabbi is able to show that the original decision is refuted by generally accepted authorities or codes,[148] he may reverse the original decision.[149]

12:58   Similarly, a decision that is retracted with good reason does not render a case intrinsically forbidden. Therefore, if a second rabbi is able to determine that common practice

Menachem Mendel of Lubavitch, *Teshuvoth Tzemach Tzedek*, Yoreh Deah 197. cf. *Kethuboth* 22a, 23b.

144. *Chulin* 44b; *Niddah* 20b; *Berakhoth* 63b; *Yoreh Deah* 242:31 in *Hagah*; *Hagahoth Maimonioth* on *Yad*, Mamrim 1:5 1; *Pachad Yitzchak*, s.v. *Chakham* (7d). Also see *Avodah Zarah* 7a; *Tosefta, Edduyoth* 1:3; *Yerushalmi, Shabbath* 19:1 (86b).
145. See above, notes 14,15. See below, 12:26.
146. Ran, *Avodah Zarah* (Rif 1b), s.v. *HaNish'al*; Meiri, *Avodah Zarah* 7a; *Teshuvoth Rivash* 379; *Divrey Chamudoth* on Rosh, *Chulin* 3:7 24. However, those who hold by the second reason in note 143 maintain that a greater sage or a majority can reverse such a decision; Ran, *loc. cit.*; *Teshuvoth Maharik* 171; *Sifethey Cohen, Yoreh Deah* 242:53; *Beer Hetiv* 242:34; *Divrey Chamudoth loc. cit.*; *Teshuvoth Radbaz* 56; *Yad Malachi* 2:232 (147a). Cf. *Yevamoth* 97b; Rashi, *Chulin* 59b, s.v. *VeHiz'hiru.*
147. For the reason given in note 143. See *Berakhoth* 63b; Rabbi Avraham Serano, *Mikneh Avraham* 124 (Salonika, 1858); Rabbi Menachem (ben Shimon Mordecai) of Adrianople, *Minchath Zikaron* (Salonika, 1833), pp. 79a, 80b. Cf. *Sedey Chemed, Cheth* 78 (2:412). ·
148. That is, if he is "mistaken in a matter of Mishnah;" see above, note 14. See *Sedey Chemed, Cheth* 76 (end) (2:412).
149. *Yoreh Deah* 242:31 in *Hagah*; *Tosafoth, Avodah Zarah* 7a, s.v. *HaNish'al*; Rosh, *Avodah Zarah* 1:3, Ran, *Avodah Zarah* (Rif 1b), s.v. *HaNishal*, *Chulin* (Rif 9b), s.v. *Chakham*; cf. *Bekhoroth* 28b, *Sanhedrin* 33a. Also see *Teshuvoth Rivash* 379, 498; *Teshuvoth Maharik* 1:37; *Teshuvoth Zaken Aaron* 2, 138; *Yad Malachi* 2:225 (147b).

traditionally[150] opposes the initial decision, even where it is disputed among authorities,[151] he may convince the first rabbi to retract his decision and permit the case in question.[152] Individual logic and judgment, however, are not considered sufficient reason for a rabbi to reverse even his own decision.[153]

12:59   A case is rendered intrinsically *forbidden* on the basis of a mere decision. On the other hand, however, a case is not considered intrinsically *permitted* until the decision is acted upon.[154] Therefore, if one rabbi permits something in a certain case, a second rabbi may pursue a stricter course and forbid it.[155] However, once the decision has been acted

---

150. Cf. *Niddah* 20b; *Tosafoth ad loc.* s.v. *A'Garmai*; *Tosafoth, Chulin* 44b, s.v. *Heikhi*; Rosh, *Chulin* 3:7. Others, however, maintain that tradition alone is not enough; Ran, *Chulin* (Rif 9b), s.v. *Rabbah*; *Sifethey Cohen, Yoreh Deah* 242:55; *Beer Hetiv* 242:34. Also see *Shiltey Giborim Avodah Zarah* (Rif 1b) 3; *Teshuvoth Mishkenoth Yaakov* 59; *Pith'chey Teshuvah, Yoreh Deah* 242:18; *Teshuvoth Ran Ashkenazi* 53; *Mikveh Yisrael* 62a, 69b; *Yad Malachi* 2:231 (147a); HaGra, *Yoreh Deah* 242:72.

151. That is, an error in estimation; see above, note 15. See *Tosafoth, Avodah Zarah* 7a, s.v. *HaNishal*; Ran, *Avodah Zarah* (Rif 1b), s.v. *HaNishal*; *Anshey Shem ad loc.* *Ritva, Avodah Zarah* 7a, s.v. *Tanu*; Meiri *ibid.*

152. Ran, *Avodah Zarah* (Rif 1b), s.v. *HaNishal*; *Sifethey Cohen, Yoreh Deah* 242:58. Others, however, maintain that in such a case the decision cannot be reversed at all; Ran, *Chulin* (Rif 9b), s.v. *Rabbah*; *Sifethey Cohen, Choshen Mishpat* 25:14 17,18. A third opinion is that a decision need not even be retracted by its originator in such a case; *Tosafoth, Avodah Zarah* 7a, s.v. *HaNishal*, HaGra, *Yoreh Deah* 242:72. Also see *Teshuvoth Panim Meiroth* 1:2; *Pith'chey Teshuvah, Yoreh Deah* 242:19.

153. Rosh, *Avodah Zarah* 1:3; *Sifethey Cohen, Yoreh Deah* 242:58; *Beer Hetiv* 242:36; *Divrey Chamudoth* on Rosh, *Chulin* 3:7 24. However, according to the authorities cited in note 143 who maintain that the reason is respect, the originator can retract his decision in any case; Meiri, *Avodah Zarah* 7a. See Rabbi Ya'udah Covo, *Ye'udah Yaaleh, Yoreh Deah* 1 (Salonika, 1888), *Ibid.* p. 129b, s.v. *Chakham*, Ibid. *Kuntres Haoroth* 53:7.

154. Cf. *Shemoth Rabbah* 43:5; *Or Zarua, Piskey Avodah Zarah* 104; *Hagahoth Aseri, Avodah Zarah* 1:3, s.v. *VeShari*; *Yoreh Deah* 246:21 in *Hagah*; HaGra *ad loc.* 246:68. See *Yerushalmi, Betza* 1:9 (8a); *Or Zarua* 1:406.

155. *Berakhoth* 63b; *Tosafoth, Avodah Zarah* 7a, s.v. *HaNishal*; HaGra, *Yoreh Deah* 242:77. According to the authorities cited in note 143 that the reason is respect, there is no difference between a decision to permit or forbid; *Shiltey Gibborim, Avodah Zarah* (Rif 1b) 3. Also see *Teshuvoth Radbaz* 362; *Mikneh Avraham* 124; Rabbi Shlomo (ben Avraham) Algazi, *Lechem Setharim* (Venice, 1684), p. 114d; *Minchath Zikaron* 121c; *Sedey Chemed, Cheth* 77 (2:412).

upon,[156] a second rabbi should refrain from reversing the decision[157] unless he has a clear proof that it is wrong.[158]

12:60   A case becomes intrinsically forbidden only when there is a valid reason for the ruling. However, when it is forbidden only as a stringent measure due to lack of permissive evidence, it is not intrinsically forbidden.[159] In such a case, the decision can be reversed on the basis of individual judgment alone.[160]

12:61   A decision can only render a case intrinsically forbidden when it is initially unopposed. However, if two or more rabbis are present when the case is presented, any initial decision can be disputed and reversed as long as it is not accepted.[161]

12:62   It is only the particular case under consideration that is rendered intrinsically forbidden. Therefore, although the decision may establish a precedent, the precedent is not absolutely binding, and it can be ignored according to the judgment of rabbis deciding similar cases.[162] However, if it is known that a case was forbidden specifically to safeguard a

---

156. *Turey Zahav, Yoreh Deah* 242:18. This essentially resolves the objection of the *Nekudoth HaKesef ad loc.* and of *Beer Hetiv, Yoreh Deah* 242:37.
157 *Yoreh Deah* 242:31 in *Hagah; Rosh, Avodah Zarah* 1:3, from *Yerushalmi, Shabbath* 19:1 (96b). Other authorities, however, maintain that even such a case may be reversed; *Hagahoth Maimonioth, Mamrim* 1:5 1; *Sefer Mitzvoth Gadol,* Positive Commandment 111; *Yam Shel Sh'lomo, Chulin* 3:18; *Teshuvoth Rivash* 379. Also see *Teshuvoth Radbaz* 362.
158. *Teshuvoth Radbaz* 362, 393; *Pith'chey Teshuvah, Yoreh Deah* 242:20.
159. Cf. *Rashi, Kethuboth* 7a, s.v. *U'Mi Ikka.*
160. Cf. *Beth Lechem Yehudah, Yoreh Deah* 242:31; *Atzey Levonah ibid.*
161. *Tosafoth, Avodah Zarah* 7a, s.v. *HaNishal; Sifethey Cohen, Yoreh Deah* 242:52. Cf. *Ritva, Avodah Zarah* 7a.
162. *Yoreh Deah* 242:31 in *Hagah; Teshuvoth Maharik* 171:3. Cf. *Eruvin* 41a, HaGra, *Yoreh Deah* 242:78. Also see *Ritva, Avodah Zarah* 7a, s.v. *Hayu; Meiri ibid.; Teshuvoth Mabit* 1:156; *Teshuvoth Rashdam, Orach Chaim* 17; *Yad Malachi* 2:224 (147a); *Teshuvoth Shivath Tzion* 25; *Pith'chey Teshuvah, Yoreh Deah* 242:21.

religious law, its precedent should be respected in similar cases.[163]

12:63   In order to prevent controversy, one should not present a case before a rabbi without informing him[164] of any previous decisions associated with that particular case.[165]

12:64   Although the Torah demands a certain degree of uniformity in practice, it does recognize geographical differences.[166] Therefore, different communities may follow varying opinions in minor[167] questions of Torah law.[168]

12:65   However, where there is no geographical or similar justification for varied practices, such differences are liable to be associated with ideological divergences and are forbidden. Within a single community, the Torah requires a high degree of uniformity in religious practice.[169] In no case should it be made to appear that there is more than one Torah.[170]

12:66   It is written, "You are children of God your Lord; you must not mutilate yourselves (*lo tith-godedu*, לֹא תִתְגֹּדְדוּ)" (Deuteronomy 14:1). Just as it is forbidden to mutilate one's

---

163. *Yam Shel Shlomo, Chulin* 3:18; *Sifethey Cohen, Yoreh Deah* 242:60; Beer Hetiv 242:38. Cf. Mordechai, *Chulin* 611. See above, 11:34.

164. *Tosafoth, Avodah Zarah* 7a, s.v. HaNishul; Rosh, *Avodah Zarah* 1:3; *Yoreh Deah* 243:31 in *Hagah*.

165. *Avodah Zarah* 7a; *Tosefta, Edduyoth* 1:3; *Yerushalmi, Shabbath* 19:1 (86b).

166. Cf. *Chulin* 18b, Rashi *ad loc.* s.v. *Nahara*, 57a, Rashi *ad loc.* s.v. *Nahara; Sifethey Cohen, Yoreh Deah* 242, *Pilpul BeHanhagath Horaoth, s.v. VeKhi Tomar.* Cf. *Shabbath* 153a; *Pesachim* 3a; *Betza* 15a; *Yoma* 55a; *Nedarim* 49a, 52b; *Bava Metzia* 40a, 117a; *Bava Bathra* 12b; *Bekhoroth* 32b; *Chulin* 66a.

167. But not in major areas; Rashi, *Sukkah* 44a (top), s.v. *LeDidehu*; Ran, *Rosh HaShanah* (Rif 10b), s.v. *Iskin* (end) [s.v. is on 10a]; *Teshuvoth Rashdam, Yoreh Deah* 153; *Sedey Chemed, Lamed* 79, s.v. *VeDa* (3:294).

168. *Shabbath* 130a; *Yevamoth* 14a; *Chulin* 116a. See above, note 111. Also see Chapter 11, note 5. The Torah grants autonomy to courts (*batey dinim*, בָּתֵּי דִינִים), and hence the Talmud expresses this rule in terms of courts; *Yevamoth* 14a.

169. *Yevamoth* 14a.

170. Rashi, *Yevamoth* 13b, s.v. *Lo Thaasu*, s.v. *Amar Lo, Sukkah* 44a (top), s.v. *LeDidehu*; Rashba, *Yevamoth* 14a, s.v. *Amar* (end). See above, note 1.

body, so is it prohibited[171] to mutilate the body of Judaism by dividing it into factions.[172] To do so is to disaffirm the universal fatherhood of God[173] and the unity of His Torah.[174]

12:67   It is therefore forbidden for members of a single congregation to form factions, each following a different practice or opinion.[175] It is likewise forbidden for a single rabbinical court to issue a split decision.[176]

12:68   However, where a city has more than one congregation,[177] or more than one rabbinical court,[178] the following

171. Some authorities maintain that this is a Biblical commandment; *Kesef Mishneh* on *Yad, Avodath Kokhavim* 12:14; *Mayim Chaim* ibid.; Maharal, *Gur Aryeh* on Deuteronomy 14:1; Rabbi Raphael Yosef (ben Chaim) Chazan, *Chikrey Lev, Yoreh Deah* 1:84 (Livorno, 1794); Rabbi Chaim David (ben Raphael Yosef) Chazan, *Nadiv Lev* (Jerusalem, 1866), Volume 2, p. 93d; Rabbi Yaakov (ben Yom Tov) Algazi, *Ara'a DeRabanan*, s.v. *Lo Tithgodedu* (Constantinople, 1745); Rabbi Yehudah Yaish, *Afra DeAra'a ad loc.* (Livorno, 1783); *Teshuvoth Meil Tzadakah* 49 (Prague, 1756), p. 62b; *Teshuvoth Chaim Sha'al* 2:18. Others, however, maintain that it is a rabbinical commandment, and an *asmakhta*; Mizrachi on Deuteronomy 14:1; *Minchath Chinukh* 467, quoting *Yesh Seder LaMishneh.* This also seems to be the opinion of *Sefer HaMitzvoth*, Negative Commandment 45; see Chida, *Eyin Zokher, Beth* 8, *Lamed* 18; Rabbi Chaim HaCohen of Trieves, *Mitzvoth HaMelekh, Hiddur Mitzvah* 169, 170 (Livorno, 1879), p. 114a (end). See *Sedey Chemed, Cheth* 78 (3:288).
172. Sifri (96), *Yalkut Shimoni* (891), Hirsch, *ad loc.; Yevamoth* 13b; Rashba *ad loc.* s.v. *VeEima;* Ritva ibid. s.v. *Mai; Yerushalmi, Pesachim* 4:1 (26a); *Yad, Avodath Kokhavim* 12:14; *Sefer HaMitzvoth*, Negative Commandment 45; *Sefer Mitzvoth Gadol*, Negative Commandment 62; *Chinukh* 467; *Orach Chaim* 493:3 in *Hagah.* Cf. *Tosefoth Yom Tov, Yevamoth* 1:4; *Teshuvoth Rabbi Moshe Alshekh* 59; Rashi *Pardes* 204; *Pachad Yitzchak*, s.v. *Lo Tithgodedu* (7d, 8a); *Gilyoney HaShas, Yevamoth* 13b.
173. Ritva, *Yevamoth* 13b, s.v. *Mai* (end). Cf. *Yad, Matnoth Ani'im* 10:2; *Teshuvoth HaRambam* (*P'er HaDor*) 151.
174. See above, note 170. Also see Rabbi David Lida, *Ir Miklat* 467 (Dyherenfurth, 1690); Rabbi Yitzchak Zaler, *Yalkut Yitzchak* 467:2 (Warsaw, 1898).
175. *Chinukh* 467; *Kesef Mishneh* on *Yad, Avodath Kokhavim* 12:14; *Pri Chadash, Orach Chaim* 493:3 (end). See *Mishnah Berurah* 31:8; *Sedey Chemed, Lamed* 79 (3:290,291); Ibid., *Chol HaMoed* 14 (8:23).
176. *Yevamoth* 14a; *Meiri ad loc.* s.v. *Zu; Yad, Avodath Kokhavim* 12:14; *Kesef Mishneh, Lechem Mishneh, ad loc.; Arukh HaShulchan* 493:8; *Sedey Chemed, Lamed* 105 (3:307).
177. *Teshuvoth Rabbi Eliahu Mizrachi* 1:37; *Teshuvoth Rashdam Orach Chaim* 36, *Magen Avraham* 493:6; *Pri Chadash, Orach Chaim* 496, *Diney Minhagey Issur* 20. Cf. Ran, *Megillah* (Rif 1b), s.v. *VeYesh.*

of each one is counted as a separate community, and each one may follow different practices.[179] Nevertheless, it is forbidden for a city to split into two congregations primarily because of a dispute over law or practice.[180]

12:69   It is forbidden for members of a community to follow different opinions even when it does not result in any strife.[181] Where the differences in practice also result in strife and conflict, there is also the violation of the commandment, "You shall not be like Korach and his company" (Numbers 17:5), who caused strife and dissension in Israel.[182]

12:70   Therefore, if a community does not have a regular rabbi whose opinions are universally binding, all questions regarding practice must be discussed and debated until an agreement regarding a uniform practice is reached.[183] Whenever a clear majority exists, it can compel the minority to abide by their decisions and practices.[184] In the absence of a clear majority, the dispute must be treated like any other question of practice; in questions of Biblical law the stricter opinion is followed, while in questions of rabbinical law, the lighter opinion is accepted.[185]

178. *Yevamoth* 14a. See above, 168.
179. *Ibid.*; *Rosh, Yevamoth* 1:9; *Kesef Mishneh* on *Yad, Avodath Kokhavim* 12:14.
180. *Sifethey Cohen, Yoreh Deah* 242, *Kitzur Hanhagoth Horaoth* 10. See below, 13:78.
181. *"Rav" Shulchan Arukh* 493:7 (end). Cf. *Hagahoth Ben HaMechaber, Minchath Chinukh* 467.
182. *Sanhedrin* 110a; *Rif, Sanhedrin* 20a; *Rosh, Sanhedrin* 11:8; *Rabbenu Yonah, Shaarey Teshuvah* 3:48; *Sefer Mitzvoth Gadol,* Negative Commandment 157; *Sefer Mitzvoth Katan* 132; *Cheredim, Negative Commandment* 4:42. Cf. *Sefer HaMitzvoth,* Negative Commandment 42; Ramban on *Sefer HaMitzvoth, Shoresh* 8 (57a).
183. *Chinukh* 467; *Sifethey Cohen, Yoreh Deah* 242, *Kitzur Hanhagoth Horaoth* 10.
184. *Magen Avraham* 493:6; *Pri Chadash, Orach Chaim* 496, *Diney Minhagey Issur* 21. Cf. *Hagahoth Maimonioth* on *Yad, Tefillah* 11:1 2; *Shiltey Gibborim, Yevamoth* (Rif 3b) 1; *Teshuvoth Rashdam* 1:20; *Teshuvoth Rabbi David Cohen of Corfu* 2:13; *Teshuvoth Rabbi Moshe Alshekh* 59; *Yad Malachi* 2:356 (151a). But see below, 12:71.
185. See above, note 183. Also see above, 12:30.

12:71   The prohibition against dividing into factions only applies involving obvious questions of law. It does not apply to cases that merely involve a question of custom[186] or commitment.[187] Similarly, one may unobtrusively follow a stricter opinion in a case where it is not obvious that he is dissenting from the accepted practice of his community.[188]

12:72   A person is not guilty of forming separate factions when he has a valid reason for following a different practice than the community at large.[189] Therefore, one may follow a stricter opinion because of his station[190] or origin.[191] However, when people from different communities form a gathering, they must all agree to abide by a common practice[192] regarding all questions of law.[193]

12:73   *Halakhah* does not represent mere legal decisions, but the will of God. Therefore, through the study of *halakhah*, one

---

186. *Yevamoth* 13b; *Rashba, Ritva, ad loc.; Eshel Avraham, Orach Chaim* 493:6; *Hagahoth ben HaMechaber, Minchath Chinukh* 467; Rabbi Mordecai Galante, *Divrey Mordecai, Gedulath Mordecai* 6 (Livorno, 1860); *Tamim Deyim* 170; *Kitzur Piskey HaRosh, Yevamoth* 1:9; *Teshuvoth Rashdam, Yoreh Deah* 153; *Mishpat Tzedek* 2:47. Others, however, maintain that this is only the initial supposition of the Gemara which is rejected at the conclusion of the discussion, and this is indicated by the wording of the *Yad, loc cit.; Magen Avraham* 493:6; *Teshuvoth Chatham Sofer* 6:86 s.v. *U'MiKol.* See *Sedey Chemed, Lamed* 79 (3:289,290). Cf. *Tosafoth, Pesachim* 14a, s.v. *Shtei; Yerushalmi, Pesachim* 1:5 (5b).
187. *Magen Avraham* 493:6; *Tumath Yesharim* 168,170; *Yad Malachi* 2:354 (151a); *Teshuvoth Rabbi Moshe Alshekh* 59; *Sedey Chemed, Lamed* 105 (3:307)
188. *Yam Shel Sh'lomo, Yevamoth* 1:10; *Karban Nathanel* on *Rosh, Yevamoth* 1:9 4; *Eshel Avraham* 493:6; *Hagahoth Ben HaMechaber, Minchath Chinukh* 467. This opinion also seems to be shared by *Tosafoth, Yevamoth* 14a, s.v. BiMekomo, s.v. Lo. However, some authorities also dispute this, *Magen Avraham* 493:6. See below, 13:81.
189. *Rosh, Yevamoth* 1:9; *Rashba ibid.* s.v. *VeHikshu.*
190. Cf. *Shabbath* 142b; *Moed Katan* 11b, 12b; *Bava Metzia* 73b; *Avodah Zarah* 8b; *Teshuvoth Divrey Yosef* 45; *Yad Malachi* 6 (2b).
191. *Magen Avraham* 493:6; *Yad Malachi* 2:355 (151a). Cf. *Ran, Megillah* (Rif 1b), s.v. *VeYesh.*
192. *Magen Avraham* 493:6; Cf. *Rashi, Sukkah* 44a, s.v. *LeDedehu; Kapoth Temarim ad loc.; Maharatz Chajas, Yevamoth* 14a.
193. But not in questions of custom; *Magen Avraham* 493:6.

can gain a unique closeness to God.[194] It is through *halakhah*
that all things in the world become part of God's ultimate
purpose.[195] It is thus taught that one who studies *halakhah*
everyday is guaranteed a portion in the World to Come.[196]

12:74   The essence of the halakhic process is that as long as it is
not clouded by ulterior motives or the desire for assimilation
or profit, the collective Jewish will parallels the will of
God.[197] Any decision or practice that is instituted exclusively
to serve God therefore joins the mainstream of Jewish
tradition that partakes of the authority of the Torah itself. It
is thus taught that whatever an earnest scholar may innovate
in the future has already been spoken at Sinai.[198]

194. *Likutey Amarim (Tanya), Sefer Shel Benonim* 1:5 (9b), 1:23 (28), *Kuntres Acharon*
    (156b). Also see *Raya Mehemma, Zohar* 3:124b; *Likutey Amarim (Tanya), Iggeroth
    HaKodesh* 26 (142b).
195. *Berakhoth* 8a; *Darkey Hora'ah*, Introduction (in *Kithvey Maharatz Chajas*),
    p. 211ff.
196. *Megillah* 28b; *Niddah* 73a.
197. Cf. *Bava Metzia* 59b; *Avoth* 2:4.
198. *Yerushalmi, Peah* 2:4 (13a).

THIRTEEN

CUSTOM

13:1   It is assumed that the Jewish people are given a degree of Divine Inspiration in ascertaining God's will, and therefore, custom strongly influences Jewish law.[1] Similarly, they are granted a degree of Divine Inspiration in creating customs.[2]

13:2   An accepted Jewish custom is known as a *minhag* (מִנְהָג).[3]

13:3   The authority given to the Jewish people is such that even when the Sanhedrin passed legislation, it would not be binding until accepted by the populace.[4]

13:4   Customs were even instituted by the ancient prophets.[5] Likewise, in many cases, the Sanhedrin would formally ratify customs, making them as binding as any other rabbinical law.[6]

---

1. See above, Chapter 12, note 11.
2. *Teshuvoth Maharik* 9:1, 54:1; Rabbi Yosef HaLevi Nazir, *Teshuvoth Matteh Yosef, Orach Chaim* 2 (Constantinople, 1717); *Pachad Yitzchak*, s.v. *Minhag* (137b).
3. Cf. 2 Kings 9:20; Targum on Ruth 4:7. Also see Rashi, *Taanith* 26b, s.v. *Ora'oy*.
4. See above, 11:46.
5. *Sukkah* 44a; Rashi *ad loc.* s.v. *Minhag; Teshuvoth HaGeonim, Shaarey Teshuvah* 307; *Halakhoth Pesukoth min HaGeonim* 180; Rabbi Yitzchak ibn Ghayyath, *Shaarey Simchah* (Furth, 1861), Volume 1, pp. 112,113; *HaManhig* 40 (Constantinople, 1519), p. 70a; *Shibboley HaLeket* 369 *Sefer Yereyim* (HaShalem) 422. Cf. Ramban on Genesis 29:27. Also see below, note 94. The prophets had to institute the practice as a custom, since they could not institute laws; above, 8:31.
6. *Yad, Mamrim* 1:2,3 2:2,5. Cf. *Pri Megadim*, Introduction 1:41. See above, 11:40.

13:5   To a large degree, Jewish practice depends on custom as much as on law. Therefore, if one wishes to understand Judaism, one must understand the concept of Jewish customs.[7]

13:6   Throughout the world, different Jewish communities observe different customs.[8] Although this may make their observances appear very different in outward form, in essence, the differences are actually very minor. With regard to the basic observances of the laws of the Torah, all traditional Jewish communities are essentially the same.[9]

13:7   Every community differs in history and culture.[10] Individuals have different natures,[11] and so do cities and localities.[12] Just as each river flows along its natural path, so does each community.[13] The customs of each place thus

Also see *Teshuvoth Rashba* 3:411, 1:729, 5:126; Rabbi Yaakov Reischer (author of *Shevuth Yaakov*), *Teshuvoth Minchath Yaakov* 1, at end of commentary on *Torath Chatath* (Prague, 1689). See *Lechem Mishneh, Talmud Torah* 6:14 11.

7. Rabbi Yosef Yozefa (ben Moshe) Kasman, *Nohag KeTz'on Yosef* (Hanau, 1718), Introduction.

8. Cf. *Sukkah* 3:11 (38a); *Pesachim* 119b; *Sofrim* 10:7. The most prominent division in custom was between the Ashkenazim and the Sepharadim; see above, Chapter 12, notes 53,54. Also see Obadiah 1:20; Rashi *ad loc.*; Meiri, *Magen Avoth* (London, 1909). For reasons for these divisions, see *Darkey HaHorah* 2 (in *Kithvey Maharatz Chajas*), pp. 244,245. Also see *Abudarham*, Introduction; Rabbi Yosef (ben Yitzchak) Ibn Ezra (author of *Atzmoth Yosef* on *Kiddushin*), *Maaseh Melekh* 7:15 (Salonika, 1601); *Kenesseth HaGedolah, Hagahoth al HaTur, Yoreh Deah* 214:31; *Pachad Yitzchak,* s.v. *Devarim* (80c). Regarding the different customs in prayer, see *Pri Etz Chaim, Inyan Tefillah* (Koretz, 1782), p. 3d; *Shulchan Arukh HaAri, Kavannoth HaTefillah* 4; *Magen Avraham* 68:0; *Maggid Devarav LeYaakov* 141; *Teshuvoth Chatham Sofer, Orach Chaim* 15; *Teshuvoth Divrey Chaim, Orach Chaim* 2:8; *Teshuvoth Maharam Shik, Orach Chaim* 43; *Sedey Chemed, Mem* 38 (4:100).

9. *Beth Elohim, Shaar HaYesodoth* 38.

10. See *Darkey HaHorah* 2 (in *Kithvey Maharatz Chajas*), p. 225. Jewish communities are also influenced by their gentile surroundings; *Sefer Chasidim* 1101; *Sefer Chasidim* (from manuscript) 1301 (Berlin, 1891), p. 321. Cf. *Yad, Deyoth* 6:1; *Moreh Nevukhim* 3:46.

11. *Berakhoth* 58a; *Sanhedrin* 38a; *Yerushalmi, Berakhoth* 9:1; *BaMidbar Rabbah* 21:2; *Tanchuma, Pinchas* 10; *Yad, Deyoth* 1:1.

12. Cf. *Shabbath* 31a.

13. *Chulin* 18b, 57a; Rashi *ad loc.* s.v. *Nahara; Arukh,* s.v. *Nahar.* Cf. *Gittin* 60b; Rashi *ad loc. s.v. BeMezil.* See *Teshuvoth Binyamin Zeev* 303.

tend to strengthen the Torah according to the character of that place.[14]

13:8 Customs usually involve practices that occur frequently or periodically.[15] Since habit becomes second nature,[16] these customs tend to reinforce Torah values in those areas.

13:9 Customs tend to create a strong bond between people, and therefore are a powerful force against assimilation.[17] Customs also tend to strengthen the bond between succeeding generations.[18]

13:10 In business matters, Torah law recognizes that people usually follow custom.[19] Therefore, where Torah law does not specifically cover a case, it is often decided on the basis of custom.[20]

13:11 There are two ways through which a person can obligate himself by his word: through an oath (*shevuah*, שְׁבֻעָה)[21] and

14. *Darkey HaHorah* 7 (p. 239). Cf. Rashi, *Betza* 25b, s.v. *Dathehem.*
15. See below, 13:50.
16. *Hergel naaseh teva* (הֶרְגֵּל נַעֲשֶׂה טֶבַע); Rabbi Shem Tov (ben Yosef) Falaquera, *HaMaaloth* 2 (Berlin, 1894); *Sheveiley Emunah* 4:5; Rabbi Shaul HaLevi Mortira, *Giva'ath Shuul, Tazria* (Amsterdam, 1645); Rabbi Moshe (ben Menasheh) Chefetz (Gentile), *Melekheth Mach'sheveth Tazria* 2 (Venice, 1710); *Kitzur Shulchan Arukh* 32:8. Cf. *Yad, Deyoth* 2:2; *Yoma* 86b; *Moed Katan* 27b; *Sotah* 22a; *Arkhin* 30b; *Kiddushin* 20a, 40a.
17. *Darkey HaHorah* 7 (p. 339). See above, Chapter 4, note 95.
18. *Teshuvoth Rashba* 3:41; *Kedushath Levi* on *Genesis* 15:8 (Jerusalem, 1958), p. 22. Cf. *Shabbath* 23a, *Sukkah* 46a, from *Deuteronomy* 32:7; *Midrash Lekach Tov, Emor,* p. 66a.
19. *Teshuvoth HaRosh* 55:10, 64:4; *Teshuvoth Rashbash* 562; *Teshuvoth Rashdam, Choshen Mishpat* 380; *Teshuvoth Chavath Yair* 91; Rabb Yitzchak Stein on *Sefer Mitzvoth HaGadol,* Positive Commandments (Venice, 1547), p. 56c. Cf. *Yerushalmi, Kethuboth* 6:4 (40b). Also see *Teshuvoth Rashba* 4:142, 3:411; *Teshuvoth Rivash* 305; *Teshuvoth Tashbatz* 2:132, 2:239.
20. *Bava Metzia* 7:1 (83a); *Kethuboth* 6:4 (66b); *Tosefta, Bava Kama* 11:5 (end); *Tosefta, Kethuboth* 6:4; *Tosefta, Maasroth* 1:11; *Choshen Mishpat* 201:2; *Kenesseth HaGedolah ibid.; Pachad Yitzchak,* s.v. *Minhagey Mamon* (141d). In business law, a custom can even take precedence over the law; *Yerushalmi, Bava Metzia* 7:1 (27b); *Peney Moshe ad loc.* s.v. *Zoth; Rif, Bava Metzia* 52a. See below, note 75.
21. *Leviticus* 19:12; *Yad, Shevuoth* 1:3; *Sefer HaMitzvoth,* Negative Commandment 61; *Sefer Mitzvoth HaGadol,* Negative Commandment 239; *Chinukh* 227.

through a vow (*neder*, נֶדֶר).[22] An oath obligates the person to keep his word, since if he does not, he will have been lying. A vow, on the other hand, gives a person a new obligation that he did not have before.[23]

13:12   It is forbidden to violate an oath or vow, as it is written, "When a man makes a vow to God, or makes an oath to make something forbidden to himself, he must not break his word; he must do all that he expresses" (Numbers 30:3).[24]

13:13   The concept of an oath parallels the oath through which Israel accepted the Torah.[25] Through vows, on the other hand, both individuals and communities can take upon themselves obligations which are not included in the Torah.[26]

13:14   Although Biblical law requires the verbal acceptance of a vow, rabbinical law renders any religious habit or custom binding as a vow, even without verbal acceptance.[27]

22. Deuteronomy 23:24; *Yad, Nedarim* 1:4; *Sefer HaMitzvoth*, Positive Commandment 94; *Sefer Mitzvoth Gadol*, Positive Commandment 124; *Chinukh* 575.
23. Cf. *Rosh HaShanah* 6a; *Nedarim* 7a; *Yad, Nedarim* 1:1,2, *Shevuoth* 4:21. Whereas in the case of oaths there is only a negative commandment not to violate (note 21), in the case of vows, there is also a positive commandment to keep them (note 22). Furthermore, oaths primarily obligate the person (*gavra*, גַּבְרָא), while vows affect their object (*cheftza*, חֶפְצָא); *Nedarim* 2b; *Yad, Nedarim* 3:7; Rashi, *Nedarim* 16b, s.v. *Eleh Amar*; *Tosafoth ibid.* s.v. *Hah, Shevuoth* 25a, s.v. *Hah*; Bertenoro, *Nedarim* 2:2; *Chinukh* 30.
24. *Yad, Nedarim* 1:5; *Sefer HaMitzvoth*, Negative Commandment 157; *Sefer Mitzvoth Gadol*, Negative Commandment 242; *Chinukh* 407.
25. See above, 5:13. Also see Bachya, Introduction to *Mattoth*; Alshekh on Numbers 30:3.
26. Hirsch on Numbers 30:2. Also see *Sifethey Cohen* on Numbers 30:3; Rabbi Eliezer Pappo, *Elef HaMagen ibid.* (Salonika, 1828). Cf. Rabbi Mordecai Yosef of Izbetza, *Mey HaShilo'ach, ibid.* (Vienna, 1860).
27. *Nedarim* 15a; *Ran ad loc.* s.v. *MiShum; Pesachim* 50b; *Megillah* 5b. The reason is that if something forbidden by custom is permitted, people might also permit that which is forbidden by law; *Pesachim* 50b, 51a; *Nimukey Yosef, Nedarim* (Rif 4b, end). s.v. *Iy Atah*. This is a rabbinical law; cf. Rabbi Chaim Palaggi, *Nishmath Kol Chai* 1:46 (Salonika, 1832); *Birkey Yosef, Yoreh Deah* 214:1; *Sedey Chemed, Dalet* 43 (2:66), *P'ath HaSadeh, Dalet* 23 (2:134). However, see *Teshuvoth Chatham Sofer, Yoreh Deah* 107, s.v. *Shavti*. Also see *Sifri*, Rashi, on Deuteronomy 14:21. Some interpret the entire concept differently; *Yad, Nedarim* 3:12; *Yerushalmi, Nedarim* 2:1 (5b).

13:15 Therefore, if a person accustoms himself to observe any religious practice not required by law, he is obligated to adhere to his custom, just as if he actually made a vow to do so.[28]

13:16 A religious practice is established as a binding personal custom as soon as it is performed once with the intent of doing so permanently.[29]

13:17 If a person wishes to stop observing a personal custom he can formally annul it before a rabbinical court, just like any other vow.[30] Regret that one has adopted a custom binding as a vow is sufficient grounds for its formal annulment.[31]

13:18 If a person wishes to adopt a personal custom without having it binding as a vow, he should expressly state this intent when he first begins to practice the custom.[32] Likewise, he should declare that he is only adopting the

---

28. *Rosh, Pesachim* 4:3, *Nedarim* 2:4; *Ran, Nedarim* 81b, s.v. *MiShum; Yoreh Deah* 214:1; *Chayay Adam* 127:7; *Chokhmath Adam* 92:14; *Kitzur Shulchan Arukh* 67:7. Cf. *Sheiltoth* 67. This rule is derived from the verse, "He shall not break his word (*davar*)" (Numbers 30:3). The word *davar* (דָּבָר) also denotes a custom; *Rashash, Nedarim* 15a; *Targum* on 2 Kings 9:20; *Rashi, Pesachim* 54a, s.v. *Ama.*

29. *Mordecai, Pesachim* 602; *Hagahoth Maimonioth, Shevuoth* 12:12 3; *Hagahoth Asheri, Pesachim* 4:3; *Yoreh Deah* 214:1; *Beer Hetiv, Orach Chaim* 581:10; *Mishnah Berurah* 597:6. If he does not have specific intent, it becomes binding after three times; *Perishah, Yoreh Deah* 214:2; *Kitzur Shulchan Arukh* 67:7; *Pri Megadim, Eshel Avraham* 597:2; *Mishnah Berurah* 597:4. Cf. *Choshen Mishpat* 163:3 in *Hagah; HaGra ad loc.* 163:57, from *Yevamoth* 64b; "*Rav*" *Shulchan Arukh* 468:17. Also see *Terumath HaDeshen* 342; Rabbi Yakov Castro (Maharikash), *Teshuvoth Ohaley Yaakov* 61 (end) (Livorno, 1783); *Nachalath Shivah* 27:6 (Warsaw, 1884), p. 70b; *Sedey Chemed, Mem* 37, s.v. *U'Lelnyan* (4:75).

30. *Mordecai, Pesachim* 602; *Rosh, Pesachim* 4:3; *Hagahoth Maimonioth, Shevuoth* 12:12 3; *Yoreh Deah* 214:1; *Chayay Adam* 127:8,9; *Pri Chadash, Orach Chaim* 496, *Diney Minhagey Issur* 1; *Teshuvoth Tashbatz* 2:46; *Teshuvoth Radbaz* 3:527 (962). Other authorities, however, maintain that it cannot be annulled; *Yoreh Deah* 214:1, second opinion; *Teshuvoth Rashba* 3:236; *Ran, Pesachim* (Rif 17b, top); *Ritva, Pesachim* 51a; *Teshuvoth Rivash* 44; *Machzor Vitri,* p. 243 (end); *Otzar HaGaonim, Nedarim* 81b; cf. *Yerushalmi, Pesachim* 4:1 (25b); *Rif, Pesachim* 17a. See below, 13:51, 13:61.

31. *Yoreh Deah* 214:1; *Kitzur Shulchan Arukh* 67:7.

32. That is, he should say that he is doing it "without a vow" (*beli neder,* בְּלִי נֶדֶר); *Yoreh Deah* 214:1.

custom temporarily, and has no intention of making it a permanent practice.[33]

13:19   When a person adopts a personal custom, it is assumed that he does so anticipating certain contingencies that *temporarily* prevent him from observing his custom. Therefore, one may temporarily discontinue a custom because of illness[34] or a religious celebration[35] that prevents its observance. However, it is not assumed that one anticipates illness or other changes in plans which will necessitate him to discontinue a custom *permanently*. Therefore, in such a case, the custom must be formally annulled.[36]

13:20   An erroneous custom (*minhag ta'uth,* מִנְהָג טָעוּת) does not have to be annulled formally.[37]

13:21   Therefore, if a person erroneously assumes something to be forbidden and accustoms himself accordingly, upon discovering his error, he may abandon his custom without formal annulment.[38] The same is true if one adopts a custom as a safeguard to keep himself from what he erroneously thought to be a serious sin.[39]

33. *Kitzur Shulchan Arukh* 67:7. Cf. *Magen Avraham* 161:13; *Turey Zahav* 161:16.
34. *Dagul Me'rvavah, Yoreh Deah* 214:1; *Pith'chey Teshuvah ibid.* 214:1; *Magen Avraham* 581:12, *Beer Hetiv* 581:12. Other authorities, however, appear to maintain that even a temporary illness is not automatically anticipated; *Sifethey Cohen, Yoreh Deah* 214:2; *Chayay Adam* 127:8.
35. Cf. *Orach Chaim* 568:2 in *Hagah.*
36. *Yoreh Deah* 214:1.
37. Cf. Rashi, *Pesachim* 2b, s.v. *MiShaath.* See *Teshuvoth Rashbam, Orach Chaim* 1 (end).
38. *Yerushalmi, Pesachim* 4:1 (25b); *Yerushalmi, Taanith* 1:6 (6b); *Tosafoth, Pesachim* 51a, s.v. *Iy, Eruvin* 101b, s.v. *Rabbi Yosi, Megillah* 5b, s.v. *Devarim;* Ran, *Pesachim* (Rif 17a), s.v. *Tanya;* cf. *Chulin* 6b; *Yoreh Deah* 214:1, first opinion; HaGra *ad loc.* 214:4; *Pri Chadash, Orach Chaim* 468:4; *Chayay Adam* 127:7. Others, however, require formal annulment in such a case; *Mordecai, Pesachim* 602; *Yoreh Deah* 214:1, second opinion; HaGra *ad loc.* 214:5. See second opinion above in note 30.
39. *Sifethey Cohen, Yoreh Deah* 214:5; *Chayay Adam* 127:7. Cf. *Yoreh Deah* 232:10.

13:22   Likewise, a foolish or unfounded custom, having no true religious significance, can be abandoned without formal annulment.[40]

13:23   Individual customs are only binding on the individuals who adopt them. Therefore, a person's children are not bound to abide by his personal customs, unless they themselves adopt them.[41] Similarly, a community is not bound by the personal customs of its religious leaders, unless they are adopted by the community itself.[42]

13:24   A community custom is binding on all members of the community for all times.[43]

13:25   Therefore, once a custom is established in a community, it is binding upon all future generations, as well as upon all newcomers to the community.[44] The community has the authority to enforce its customs.[45]

13:26   It is a commandment from Biblical tradition[46] to abide by all community customs, as it is written, "Hear, my son, your

40. See below, 13:33.
41. *Teshuvoth Chavath Yair* 126; *Pri Chadash, Orach Chaim* 496, *Diney Minhagey Issur* 7; *Beer Hetiv, Yoreh Deah* 214:5; *Pith'chey Teshuvah* ibid. 214:5; Rabbi Yosef Steinhart, *Zikhron Yosef, Teshuvoth, Yoreh Deah* 14 (Furth, 1733); *Chayay Adam* 127:11. Others, however, maintain that children are bound; *Maasah Melekh* 7:4; *Kenesseth HaGedolah, Yoreh Deah* 214:49; *Pachad Yitzchak,* s.v. *Devarim* (80d)
42. Original.
43. Ramban, *Mishpat HaCherem,* in *Teshuvoth Ramban* 288; *Kol Bo,* end; *Chidushey HaRamban* (Jerusalem, 1928), end of Volume 1; *Teshuvoth Rivash* 399. See next note. Also see Chapter 5, note 33. This is also binding as a vow; *Nedarim* 15a, *Pesachim* 51a, *Teshuvoth Chatham Sofer, Yoreh Deah* 107, s.v. *Shavti.*
44. *Yoreh Deah* 214:2; *Teshuvoth Rivash* 399; *Teshuvoth Rashba* 3:411; *Teshuvoth Tashbatz* 2:132; *Teshuvoth Rabbi Moshe Alshakar* 49. Cf. *Pesachim* 50b.
45. The majority can impose the custom on the minority; *Massa Melekh* 7:12; *Kenesseth HaGedolah, Yoreh Deah* 214:25; *Pachad Yitzchak* s.v. *Devarim* (80c). In some cases, fines can also be imposed; *Yerushalmi, Pesachim* 4:3 (27a); *Tosafoth, Bekhoroth* 2a, s.v. *Konsim.* In some extreme cases, corporal punishment (flogging) can also be imposed; *Yerushalmi, Bikkurim* 1:5 (3b); *Yerushalmi, Kiddushin* 4:6 (46a).
46. *Divrey Kabbalah* (דִּבְרֵי קַבָּלָה), see above, Chapter 8, note 55. See *Chayay Adam* 127:11. Some say that it is an *asmakhta* (see above, Chapter 11, note 75); *Teshuvoth Chavath Yair* 126. See above, note 27. Also see *Chulin* 92a; *Gilyon HaShas, Pesachim* 55a; but see above 13:3.

Father's instruction, and do not forsake your Mother's Torah" (Proverbs 1:8).⁴⁷ It is taught that "Father" in this verse refers to God,⁴⁸ while "Mother" refers to the nation of Israel.⁴⁹

13:27 Our "Mother's Torah" is the Torah created by the Jewish people themselves, namely, their religious customs.⁵⁰ It is therefore taught, "A custom of Israel is Torah."⁵¹ Moreover, just like the Torah itself, a custom is binding for all generations.⁵²

13:28 Only a respectable custom (*minhag chashuv*, מִנְהָג חָשׁוּב) is universally binding.⁵³ This is a custom originated by Torah

47. *Pesachim* 50b; Ran *ad loc* (Rif 17b), s.v. *VeNimtzinu*; *Chulin* 93b; Rashi *ad loc.* s.v. *Al*; *She'iltoth* 67; *Halakhoth Gedolah, Megillah* (end); *Yalkut Shimoni* 1:892 (305c); *Chayay Adam* 127:1. See *Teshuvoth Rashdam, Orach Chaim* 35.

48. And not one's actual father, see above, note 41. Also see Rabbi Shlomo Eiger, *Gilyon Maharsha, Yoreh Deah* 214:2. Cf. *Sifri* on Deuteronomy 32:2; *Shemoth Rabbah* 30:5.

49. *Berakhoth* 35b; *Sanhedrin* 102a; *Yalkut Shimoni* 2:962; *Zohar* 2:85a, 3:213a. In this verse, the word for mother *ima* (אִמָּא) is said to denote one's nation, *umah* (אֻמָּה); *Tanchuma, Re'eh* 14; *Yalkut Shimoni* 1:892 (305c); Bachya, Introduction to *Avoth* (end) (4:526). Also see *Sifra* on Leviticus 9:1 (44c); *Shemoth Rabbah* 25:5; *BaMidbar Rabbah* 12:8; *Shir HaShirim Rabbah* 3:21; Rashi on Song of Songs 3:11; *Pesikta* 1 (4b); *Yalkut Shimoni* 2:986; from Isaiah 51:4; cf. *Minchath Shai ad loc.* Cf. Rashi, *Berakhoth* 54a, s.v. *VeOmer*; Bertenoro on *Berakhoth* 9:5 (end). Some say that, taking the value of the final Kaf (ך) to be 500, the numerical value of *ime-kha* (אִמֶּך) in this verse is the same as that of *Yisrael* (יִשְׂרָאֵל); *Sefer Chasidim* 970; Maharsha, *Berakhoth* 35b, s.v. *Lo Kushia*. Also see *Zohar* 3:55a, 3:197b, 3:277b.

50. Rashi *ad loc.* states that it also refers to rabbinical laws; cf. HaGra *ibid.* Also see Proverbs 6:20; *Sefer Chasidim* 970.

51. *Minhag Yisrael Torah Hi* (מִנְהָג יִשְׂרָאֵל תּוֹרָה הִיא); *Teshuvoth Ramban* 260: Rashba, *Torath HaBayith* 2:3 (Yosefov, 1883), p. 34b; quoted in *Beth Yosef, Yoreh Deah* 39; *Darkey Moshe, Yoreh Deah* 116:5 (end); *Yoreh Deah* 242:14 in *Hagah*; *Matteh Ephraim* 610; *Beth Elohim, Shaar HaYesodoth* 38; *Teshuvoth Maharik* 54:1; Bachya, Introduction to *Avoth* (end) (4:526). There is a similar expression, "The custom of our fathers is Torah;" *Tosafoth, Minachoth* 20b, s.v. *Nifsal; Shiltey Gibborim, Berakhoth* (Rif 39b) 3; *Teshuvoth Maharik* 102:3, *Yoreh Deah* 376:4 in *Hagah*. Also see Rashi, *Pardes* 1, 174 (Warsaw, 1870); *Teshuvoth Rivash* 44; *Teshuvoth Rashba* 3:326; below, note 108.

52. See above, note 43. Also see above, Chapter 5, note 33. See *Teshuvoth Rashba* 3:411; *Teshuvoth Rivash* 399; *Pri Chadash, Orach Chaim* 496, *Diney Minhagey Issur* 7; *Hagahoth Ben HaMechaber, Minchath Chinukh* 467; "*Rav*" *Shulchan Arukh* 468:9. Cf. Judges 21:1. Also see *Yoreh Deah* 228:35; *Beer HaGolah ad loc.* 228:79; HaGra *ad loc.* 228:99; *Teshuvoth HaRosh* 5:4.

53. There is a question as to whether this is the same as a *minhag vathikin*; see note 76.

scholars even as the law itself was.[54] However, a custom initiated by the unlearned masses is considered an inferior custom (*minhag garua* מִנְהָג גָּרוּעַ).[55] Such a custom may be binding on those who observe it, just as any other personal custom, but it does not have the status of a community custom.[56]

13:29   An inferior custom is not binding on newcomers to the community[57] or on future generations[58] unless they themselves adopt the custom.[59]

13:30   Nevertheless, even an inferior custom should never be publicly violated. To do so would cause dissension and also result in the ignorant taking other laws and customs lightly.[60]

13:31   A newcomer to the community, however, may violate inferior customs in the presence of scholars, since it is assumed that these reasons do not apply.[61] Nevertheless, all native residents, including scholars, must abide even by inferior customs, unless they are formally annulled.[62]

54. *Cf.* Hirsch on Numbers 30:2.
55. *Cf.* Rashi, *Taanith* 26b, s.v. *Ora'oy; Teshuvoth Maharik* 171, *Teshuvoth Chavath Yair* 91. See Rashi, *Pesachim* 2b, s.v. *MiShaath.* Also see *Tosafoth, Eruvin* 62b, s.v. *U'Rabbi,* 72a, s.v. *Nagu, Pesachim* 103a, s.v. *VeAmar, Rosh HaShanah* 15b, s.v. *VeKhi, Kethuboth* 3b, s.v. *VeThu;* Maharatz Chajas, *Eruvin* 46b.
56. *Tosafoth, Pesachim* 51a; s.v. *Iy; Rosh, Pesachim* 4:3; Rabbenu Yerocham, *Toledoth Adam VeChavah* 3:5; Rabbi Yitzchak Stein on *Sefer Mitzvoth HaGadol,* Positive Commandments (56c); *Magen Avraham* 468:4; *Sifethey Cohen, Yoreh Deah* 214:7; *"Rav" Shulchan Arukh* 468:16. Others, however, consider all customs binding unless they are patently erroneous as described in 13:20, 13:33; *Ran, Pesachim* (Rif 16a), s.v. *Tanya,* (Rif 17b) s.v. *VeNimtzinu;* Raavad *ibid* (Rif 17a) 2; Ritva, *Pesachim* 51a. See second opinion in note 30. Also see *Tosafoth, Berakhoth* 52b, s.v. *Nahagu; Pachad Yitzchak,* s.v. *Minhag* (138c).
57. See note 56.
58. *Magen Avraham* 468:4; *Pri Megadim ad loc.; "Rav" Shulchan Arukh* 468:17.
59. *"Rav" Shulchan Arukh* 468:17.
60. *Tosafoth, Pesachim* 51a, s.v. *Iy; Sifethey Cohen, Yoreh Deah* 214:7. Cf. *Pesachim* 51a; *Yerushalmi, Pesachim* 4:1 (26a).
61. However, where there is a possibility of dissension, one should keep such customs even in the presence of scholars; *Sifethey Cohen, Yoreh Deah* 214:7.
62. *Tosafoth, Pesachim* 51a, s.v. *Iy; Sifethey Cohen, Yoreh Deah* 214:7; *"Rav", Shulchan Arukh* 268:16. Regarding annulment, see below, 13:51.

13:32   Where it is not known whether a custom was originated by scholars or not, it is assumed that it was, and it is considered a respectable custom. This is especially true if the custom is of long standing.[63]

13:33   In order to qualify as a religious custom, a practice must have some justification, based on the Talmud, Midrash, or other sacred literature. A baseless observance has neither the status of a private or public custom, and may be abandoned without formal annulment.[64] This is especially true if such a practice may lead to a violation of a law.[65] It is also true if because of its stringency, the custom will tend to discourage religious observance.[66]

13:34   Where it is a custom to forbid something due to a *known* lack of information, the prohibition does not extend to newcomers in possession of the required information. Similarly, a resident of a community practicing such a prohibition need not keep it while visiting a community where the required information is available.[67] Nevertheless, the acquisition of the necessary information does not justify

63. Rashba, *Chulin* 18b; *Teshuvoth Rashba* 98; *Pri Chadash, Orach Chaim* 496, *Diney Minhagey Issur* 3; *Massa Melekh* 7:1; *Kenesseth HaGedolah* 214:43; *Pachad Yitzchak*, s.v. *Devarim* (80d); *Birkey Yosef, Yoreh Deah* 214:2. Also see *Beth Yosef, Yoreh Deah* 194, s.v. *Kathav* (74a); Rabbi Elazar (ben Elazar) Kalir, *Or Chadash* on Pesachim 51a (Frankfort am Adar, 1771). Cf. *Teshuvoth Rivash* 44. See below, 13:45, 13:58.
64. *Pri Chadash, Orach Chaim* 496, *Diney Minhagey Issur* 15; *Idem., Orach Chaim* 468:3; from Ran, *Pesachim* (Rif 18a), s.v. *VeLaila; Maggid Mishneh* on *Yad, Yom Tov* 8:19; *Teshuvoth Rivash* 44; *Beth Yosef, Orach Chaim* 670 (end). Cf. Rambam on Mishnah, *Gittin* 5:8; *Yad, Issurey Biyah* 11:14,15. Also see *Teshuvoth Besamim Rosh* 19; *Teshuvoth Rashdam, Orach Chaim* 34; Rabbi Yosef Igres, *Teshuvoth Divrey Yosef* 1 (Livorno, 1742); *Sedey Chemed, Mem* 38, s.v. *U'VeLav* (4:104), s.v. *Shuv* (4:105).
65. *Ibid.* Cf. *Pesachim* 51a; Rabbi Chaim Palaggi, *Massa Chaim, Resh* 222 (Salonika, 1874), p. 60; *Kereithi U'Pelethi, Tifereth Yisrael, Yoreh Deah* 194:2; *Darkey Teshuvah* 194:7. See below, note 71.
66. Cf. *Sefer Chasidim* 362. Also see *Avoth deRabbi Nathan* 1:5.
67. *Chulin* 63a; Rosh, *Chulin* 3:60; *Yoreh Deah* 82:4; HaGra *ad loc.* 82:8; *Sifethey Cohen ad loc.* 82:10; *Turey Zahav* 82:5; *Chokhmath Adam* 36:7.

an entire community to abandon its custom, since it is possible that the custom also involved a safeguard against other prohibitions.[68]

13:35 Wherever there is any question of law and a local or regional custom exists, the custom should be followed.[69] The custom should be observed even if it follows the opinion of a single authority who is disputed by the majority.[70]

13:36 However, where observance of a local or regional custom results in the violation of any law, the custom should be abolished.[71]

68. Rosh, *Chulin* 3:60; *Yoreh Deah* 82:5; HaGra *ad loc.* 82:9; *Sifethey Cohen* 82:11; *Turey Zahav* 82:6; *Yam Shel Shlomo, Chulin* 3:115; *Teshuvoth Nodeh BeYehudah, Tinyana, Yoreh Deah* 29; *Chokhmath Adam* 36:8. Cf. *Teshuvoth HaRosh* 20:20; *Maadney Yom Tov* on Rosh, *Chulin* 3:60 323. Other authorities, however, dispute this; cf. *Yoreh Deah* 82:5, HaGra *ad loc.* 82:9, from *Niddah* 7b.
69. *Yerushalmi, Peah* 7:5 (34b); *Yerushalmi, Maaser Sheni* 5:2 (30a); *Yerushalmi, Yevamoth* 7:3 (40a). Also see *Berakhoth* 45a; *Pesachim* 54a; *Menachoth* 35b; *Orach Chaim* 3:11 in *Hagah; Choshen Mishpat* 409:3 in *Hagah; Teshuvoth Rabbi Yaakov (Mahari) Weil* 70 (Venice, 1513); *Teshuvoth Maharik* 54:1, 102:2; *Teshuvoth Ramban* 260; Rashi, *Chulin* 18b, s.v. *Nahara; Pri Chadash, Orach Chaim* 496, *Diney Minhagey Issur* 10; Rabbi Chaim Abulafia, *Mikra'ey Kodesh, Orach Chaim* 496 (Ismir, 1729); Chida, *LeDavid Emeth, Kuntres Acharon* 21; *Sedey Chemed, Peh* 23 (4:463). See above, Chapter 12, note 12.
70. *Magen Avraham* 690:22; *Beer Hetiv* 690:14; *Pri Chadash, Orach Chaim* 496, *Diney Minhagey Issur* 11; *Teshuvoth Maharil* 37. See above, 12:33. Also see *Eruvin* 62b, 72a; *Rosh HaShanah* 15b; *Tosafoth ad loc.* s.v. *VeKhi; Darkey HaHorah* 3 (p. 226); Rabbi Aryeh Leib Tzintz, *Magen HaElef* (with *Sar HaElef, Shem Chadash,* Novidvar-Warsaw, 1817) 489; *Sedey Chemed, Mem* 38, s.v. *VeHisagti,* s.v. *VeAl* (4:90). Even scholars may keep such a custom; *Teshuvoth Rabbi David Cohen (Radakh)* 5. Others, however, dispute this, and maintain that the majority opinion must be followed completely; *Teshuvoth Rashbash* 419. In any case, this is true if the rabbis of a given region reach a decision in formal session; *Atereth Tz'vi, Mishpatey HaHorah* 5 (in *Kithvey Maharatz Chajas*), p. 380.
71. See above, note 65. Also see *Massa Melekh* 7:7; *Pachad Yitzchak,* s.v. *Minhag* (137c.d); from *Pesachim* 51a; Rabbi Asher (ben Immanuel) Shalem, *Matteh Asher* (Salonika, 1748), p. 130d; *Sedey Chemed, Mem* 38, s.v. *VeHaRav* (4:87). Also see *Teshuvoth HaRosh* 56:5; *Binyamin Zeev* 159, 303, 361; *Teshuvoth Rama* 21; Rabbi Yitzchak Stein on *Sefer Mitzvoth HaGadol,* Positive Commandments (56c); *Magen Avraham* 468:4; Rabbi Barukh (ben Shlomo) Kaley, *Makor Barukh* 35 (Ismir, 1659); *Kenesseth HaGedolah, Yoreh Deah* 214:14; *Pachad Yitzchak,* s.v. *Devarim* (80b); *Chatham Sofer, Orach Chaim* 66. Cf. *Massa Melekh* 7:5; *Pachad Yizchak,* s.v. *Minhag* (137c).

13:37   A local or regional custom should also be abolished if it opposes an unambiguous law.[72] This is even true if such action may result in strife.[73]

13:38   Even if a custom is based on the opinion of earlier authorities, it must be abandoned if present authorities deem it forbidden.[74]

13:39   There is a general principle that custom annuls a law (*minhag mebhatel halakhah*, מִנְהָג מְבַטֵּל הֲלָכָה).[75] This, however, is only true of a custom of pious scholars (*minhag*

---

72. *Sifethey Cohen, Yoreh Deah* 259:8; *Pri Chadash, Orach Chaim* 496, *Diney Minhagey Issur* 10; *Chatham Sofer, Orach Chaim* 690:17; *Beur Halakhah ibid.* Also see *Tosafoth, Rosh HaShanah* 15b, s.v. *VeKhi; Maharatz Chajas ad loc.; Shiltey Gibborim, Pesachim* (Rif 17a) 1; *Teshuvoth Rivash* 49, 122, 388, 389, 390; *Darkey HaHorah* 3 (p. 226). This is certainly true where a Biblical law is violated by the custom; *Massa Melekh* 7:5; *Nachalath Shivah* 27:6; *Pachad Yitzchak,* s.v. *Minhag* (137c, 139d); *Sedey Chemed, Mem* 38, s.v. *U'VeDivrey* (4:89); *Arukh HaShulchan* 651:2, s.v. *VeDa; Pele Yoetz,* s.v. *Minhag.* Also see *Sedey Chemed, Mem* 38 (4:80). There are some cases where people try to justify serious sins on the basis of custom. Regarding this, it is taught that *minhag* (מנהג) spelled backwards is *Gehenom* (גהנם); Rabbenu Tam, quoted in *Teshuvoth Rabbi Moshe Mintz* 67 (Cracow, 1617); *Teshuvoth Binyamin Zeev* 307; *Massa Chaim, Gimel* 29 (p. 49); *Chut HaShani* 56; *Teshuvoth Shevuth Yaakov* 2:6; *Teshuvoth Nachalath Shivah* 78; *Teshuvoth Rabbi Betzalel Ashkenazi* 24; Rabbi Yosef Zechariah (ben Nathan) Stern, *Zekher Yehosef, Orach Chaim* 20 (Warsaw, 1899), p. 36; *Sedey Chemed, Mem* 38, s.v. *Mah* (4:101), s.v. *U'LeKushioth* (4:91). Cf. *Maharil, Hilkhoth Pesach* (Jerusalem, 1969), p. 18b.
73. *Pri Chadash, Orach Chaim* 496, *Diney Minhagey Issur* 16; *Mishnah Berurah* 468:23 (end).
74. *Pri Chadash, Orach Chaim* 496, *Diney Minhagey Issur* 10, quoting *Teshuvoth Radbaz* 73.
75. In the case of business law; *Yerushalmi, Bava Metzia* 7:1 (27b); *Rif, Bava Metzia* 52a. In the case of ritual law; *Yerushalmi, Yevamoth* 12:1 (66a); *Sofrim* 14:18. Cf. *Tosefta, Shevi'ith* 2:8. See *Teshuvoth Maharik* 9:2, 102:2; *Darkey HaHorah* 4 (pp. 228, 230). Some authorities state that the Babylonian Talmud disputes the Yerushalmi; *Teshuvoth Rashbash* 562. However, Rabbenu Tam states explicitly that the Babylonian Talmud also maintains this view; *Sefr HaYashar* (Vienna, 1811), p. 43a; cf. *Rif, Bava Metzia* 52a; also see *Shabbath* 35b; *Eruvin* 104b; *Taanith* 28b. Some authorities dispute this principle completely; *Teshuvoth Rif* 13; *Teshuvoth Rivash* 44, from *Rosh HaShanah* 15b; *Teshuvoth Tashbatz* 3:160. Others say that a custom can only forbid something, but it cannot permit something; *Ritva, Pesachim* 51a; *Teshuvoth Radbaz* 1:359 (end), 3:645 (1070), 4:94 (1165) (end); *Kenesseth HaGedolah, Yoreh Deah* 214:4; *Pachad Yitzchak,* s.v. *Devarim* (80b); *Sedey Chemed, Mem* 38, s.v. *U'VeSethirath* (4:84), s.v. *Gam* (4:109). Cf. *Yad, Shevithath Assar* 3:3; *Teshuvoth Rabbi Yosef ibn Lev* (Rival) 3:14; *Teshuvoth Ralbach* 2:11; *Massa Melekh* 7:14; *Kenesseth HaGedolah, Yoreh Deah* 214:4; *Pachad Yitzchak,* s.v. *Devarim* (80a).

vathikin, מִנְהָג וָתִיקִין),[76] and not of a custom initiated by the common people.[77]

13:40   The principle that custom takes precedent over law applies primarily to the case of business law, and not in questions of ritual law.[78] Where business law is concerned, a custom is like a mutually binding contract.[79]

13:41   Where ritual law is concerned, custom can take precedence over *halakhah* only in the case of a rabbinical

76. Regarding the word *vathikin*, see *Berakhoth* 9b, 25b, 26a; *Rosh HaShanah* 32b; Rashi, *Berakhoth* 9b, s.v. *Vathikin*; *Sefer HaTishbi*, s.v. *Vathak*; *Maadney Yom Tov* on Rosh, *Berakhoth* 1:10, 70 (cf. Rashi, *Gittin* 70a, s.v. *Vathik*); Maharsha, *Shabbath* 105a, s.v. *Vathik*.

77. *Sofrim* 14:18; Mordecai, *Bava Metzia* 366; *Sefer HaAgudah* (Cracow, 1571), p. 228a; *Teshuvoth Maharik* 9:3, 54:2, 102:2; *Teshuvoth Binyamin Zeev* 303, *Tumath Yesharim* 120, 138; *Kenesseth HaGedolah, Yoreh Deah* 214:3; *Pachad Yitzchak*, s.v. *Devarim* (80a); *Teshuvoth Minchath Yaakov* 1 (in *Torath Chatath*); *Darkey HaHorah* 3 (p. 226). Some authorities write that a *minhag vathikin* is one that appears in the codes; *Teshuvoth Nachalath Shivah* 38. There is also an important opinion that a *minhag vathikin* is only one formally instituted by leading rabbis; Ramban, *Bava Bathra* 144b, s.v. *DeAmrinan*; *Numukey Yosef, Bava Bathra* (Rif 67b, end); Ritva, *Kethuboth* 100a; *Bedek HaBayith, Choshen Mishpat* 368:6; *Teshuvoth Radbaz* 3:497 (932); *Massa Chaim* 13 (p. 47); Rabbi Eliahu (ben Moshe) Yisrael, *Kol Eliahu* 1, *Evven HaEzer* 14, s.v. *MeAtah* (Livorno, 1792), p. 66d; Rabbi Raphael Asher Covo, *Shaar Asher, Yoreh Deah* 11 (Salonika, 1877), p. 20c; *Sedey Chemed, Mem* 37, s.v. *U'LeBhatel* (4:76), *Mem* 38, s.v. *VeRa'ithi* (4:81), s.v. *U'BheSiyyum* (4:86). Cf. *Teshuvoth Nachalath Shivah* 78.

78. See above, 13:10. Some say that the rule applies *only* to business law; *Teshuvoth HaRosh* 55:10; *Teshuvoth Radbaz* 359 (end); *Teshuvoth Chavath Yair* 91; Rabbi Chaim Benveneste, *Ba'ay Chayay, Etz HaDaath, Yoreh Deah* 196 (end) (Salonika, 1788); Chidah, *Eyin Zokher, Mem* 179; Rabbi Chaim Palaggi, *Chaim VeShalom* 1:1 (Izmir, 1857); Rabbi Menasheh Sath'hon, *Kenesiah LeShem Shamayim* (Jerusalem, 1874), p. 55b; *Sedey Chemed, Mem* 38, s.v. *Nachzor* (4:91), s.v. *Od* (4:108). Many authorities maintain that even in the case of business law, a custom must be formally enacted; Ramban *Nimukey Yosef*, quoted in note 77; Rabbi Nethanel (ben Aaron Yaakov) Segre, *Teshuvoth Afar Yaakov* 38 (Jewish Theological Seminary, Manuscript 791), quoted in *Pachad Yitzchak*, s.v. *Minhag* (140d); *Sedey Chemed, Mem* 38, s.v. *U'Mah* (4:108). According to these opinions, custom overrides law only when the law is in question; *Teshuvoth HaRosh* 55:10; Rabbi Yitzchak Stein on *Sefer Mitzvoth Gadol*, Positive Commandments (56c); see below, 13:41. Others write that in the case of ritual law, the Babylonian Talmud disputes the Yerushalmi; *Teshuoth Rashbash* 562; see above, note 73. Some authorities, however, dispute this entire opinion, and state that custom overrides law even in the case of ritual law; *Teshuvoth Maharik* 9:3, from *Menachoth* 32a; *Magen Avraham* 690:22.

79. *Teshuvoth HaRosh* 64:4; *Teshuvoth Rashbash* 562; *Teshuvoth Rashdam, Choshen Mishpat* 380; Rabbi Yitzchak Stein on *Sefer Mitzvoth Gadol*, Positive Commandments (56c). see above, note 19.

law.[80] In the case of Biblical law, custom takes precedence only where the law itself is in question.[81]

13:42· Custom takes precedence only if it antedates the final decision of the law. Even when there was initially a question, once a law has been established, a custom cannot be introduced to oppose it.[82] This is especially true if the law has been established, in an accepted code.[83]

13:43 Therefore, even where ancient customs follow opinions disputed in the Talmud, they can be retained.[84] It can be assumed that in places where these customs prevail, the custom was in existence even before the Talmud was accepted by all Israel.[85]

13:44 Ancient customs should therefore be accorded great respect.[86] Wherever possible, effort should be made to justify them according to the law.[87]

80. Raavad on *Yad, Maaser Sheni* 1:3; *Rashdam, Evven HaEzer* 129; *Teshuvoth Rabbi Moshe Mintz* 66:5; *Massa Melekh* 7:6; *Kenesseth HaGedolah, Yoreh Deah* 214:20; *Pachad Yitzchak,* s.v. *Devarim* (80b). Cf. *Teshuvoth Maharik* 9:2; *Maasa Melekh* 7:8; *Pachad Yitzchak,* s.v. *Minhag* (137d); *Sedey Chemed, Mem* 38, s.v. *VeGam* 4:91), s.v. *Gam* (4:108). Some authorities, however, maintain that the principle even applies to Biblical law; *Teshuvoth Tashbatz* 1:153; Rabbi Shimshon Morporgo, *Shemesh Tzadakah* 4 (end) (Venice, 1742), p. 26c, s.v. *Zoth; Ginath Veradim, Orach Chaim* 1:34; Rabbi Chaim Palaggi, *Semikha LeChaim* (Salonika, 1826), p. 9a, s.v. *Pash; Sedey Chemed, Mem* 38, s.v. *VeSefer,* s.v. *VeAl* (4:81), s.v. *U'Bhelnyan* (4:91), s.v. *Minhag* (4:80). Other authorities take the opposite opinion and maintain that it does not even apply in the case of a rabbinical law; *Pri Chadash, Orach Chaim* 496, *Diney Minhagey Issur* 10; cf. *Teshuvoth Rivash* 49, 122. This apparently would also be the opinion that a custom can never permit something, see above, note 75.
81. *Beer Sheva, Teshuvah* 22. See above, note 69.
82. *Teshuvoth Shevuth Yaakov* 2:6; Rabbi Mordecai Barukh Carabellio, *Tosafoth R'em, Chayay Yitzchak* (Livorno, 1761); *Matteh Asher* 28 (p. 136); *Darkey HaHorah* 3 (p. 226); *Sedey Chemed, Mem* 38, s.v. *VeHaHi* (4:90), s.v. *U'LeKushiath* (4:91). But see *Tosafoth, Chulin* 136b, s.v. *KeRabbi.*
83. See above, Chapter 12, note 14.
84. See above, Chapter 12, note 24. See *Darkey HaHorah* 2 (p. 224).
85. Rabbi Yitzchak Stein on *Sefer Mitzvoth Gadol,* Positive Commandments (56c). Cf. *Shabbath* 35b.
86. *Teshuvoth Maharik* 54:2,3; *Orach Chaim* 690:17 in *Hagah; Beth Yosef, Orach Chaim* 690, s.v. *Kathav* (371a); *Magen Avraham* 690:22; *Pachad Yitzchak,* s.v. *Minhag* (13d, 137a); *Darkey HaHorah* 6 (p. 235). Cf. *Rambam, Tosefoth Yom Tov,* on *Berakhoth* 9:5 (end).
87. *Teshuvoth Rabbi Meir (ben Yitzchak) Katzanelenbogen of Padua* 78 (beginning)

13:45 If a custom has been kept by scholars and saints for many generations, it should be retained, even where it appears to contradict a law.[88] It is inconceivable that God would have allowed them constantly to do wrong.[89]

13:46 Hence, any custom followed by all Israel must be retained, even if it appears to go against the law.[90]

13:47 There are many customs which are based on a deeper understanding of the laws as found in the teachings of the Kabbalah (קַבָּלָה). Since the Kabbalah is essentially based on Divine Inspiration, its decisions are not legally binding, and therefore such customs are no more obligatory than any other proper custom.[91]

13:48 Hence, when Kabbalistic customs are in conflict with laws based on the Talmudic authorities, the latter must be followed.[92] However, if there is a dispute among the

(with *Teshuvoth Rabbi Yehudah Mintz*, Venice, 1553); *Massa Chaim* 258; Rabbi Moshe Yisrael, *Masath Moshe* 1, Yoreh Deah 17 (Constantinople, 1734); Rabbi Aaron (ben Chaim Avraham) Perachiah HaCohen; *Perach Matteh Aaron* 1:21 (Amsterdam, 1703); Rabbi Chaim HaCohen Rappaport, *Mayim Chaim, Orach Chaim* 12, s.v. *U'Me'acher; Teshuvoth Rashdam*, Yoreh Deah 193; *Sedey Chemed, Mem* 37, s.v. *Im* (4:78), *Mem* 38, s.v. *VeAfilu* (4:103). Cf. *Tosafoth, Berakhoth* 2a, s.v. *MeEmathai, Shabbath* 48a, s.v. *DeZeythim.* Also see *Beth Hillel, Yoreh Deah* 364:4; *Shemesh Tzadakah, Orach Chaim* 4, s.v. *LeKol; Teshuvoth Chatham Sofer, Orach Chaim* 51, s.v. *Omer.*

88. Mordecai, *Bava Metzia* 366; *Magen Avraham* 690:22; *Teshuvoth Radbaz* 3:532 (967). Cf. *Shabbath* 35b; *Eruvin* 104b; *Taanith* 28b; *Teshuvoth Maharik* 54:2; Rabbi Yitzchak Stein on *Sefer Mitzvoth Gadol*, Positive Commandments (56c); *Orach Chaim* 68; *Sedey Chemed, Mem* 38, s.v. *VeAf* (4:102).

89. *Teshuvoth Maharik* 54:4. See *Yevamoth* 99b; *Kethuboth* 28b; *Gittin* 7a; *Chulin* 5b, 6a, 7a. Cf. *Teshuvoth HaRosh* 55:10.

90. *Teshuvoth Maharik* 54; Rabbi Shmuel (ben Moshe) Kaley, *Mishpatey Sh'muel* 92 (Venice, 1599); *Kenesseth HaGedolah, Yoreh Deah* 214:13; *Ibid., Haguhoth Beth Yosef, Choshen Mishpat* 201; *Pachad Yitzchak*, s.v. *Devarim* (80a,b); Rabbi Yitzchak Abulafia of Damascus, *Peney Yitzchak* 1:7 (Aram Tzova [Aleppo], 1871), p. 31, s.v. *Hiney; Teshuvoth Chatham Sofer, Orach Chaim* 68. Cf. *Yevamoth* 102a; *Menachoth* 32a; *Berakhoth* 22a; *Chulin* 136b. Some authorities maintain that a custom in a major community is as strong as a universal custom; *Tumath Yesharim* 120; *Teshuvoth Chatham Sofer, Orach Chaim* 66.

91. See above, note 5.

92. *Teshuvoth Radbaz* 4:80 (1151); *Beth Yosef, Orach Chaim* 25 s.v. *VeYeBharekh; Kenesseth HaGedolah, Orach Chaim, Kelaley HaPoskim* 1: *Turey Zahav, Orach Chaim* 274:1; *Magen Avraham* 25:20; *Beer Hetiv* 25:14; *Mishnah Berurah* 25:42; "*Rav" Shulchan Arukh* 25:48. Some say, however, that if a law is not mentioned

Talmudic authorities, then the Kabbalistic custom may be followed,[93] just as any other custom.[94]

13:49   A practice only found in the Kabbalah, and not mentioned by Talmudic authorities, may be followed by individuals.[95] However, it cannot be forced upon the community unless it is already an established custom.[96]

13:50   For a practice to be considered a custom, it must occur fairly commonly. However, practices and decisions that are established in individual occurring cases do not establish a custom.[97]

13:51   Any community custom, whether adopted formally or spontaneously, can be annulled.[98] The annulment is

expressly in the Talmud, one may follow the *Zohar*, even against later halakhic authorities; *Beth Yosef, Orach Chaim* 141, s.v. *U'MiTokh* (123b); *Sefer HaYuch'sin* 1, s.v. *Rabbi Shimon* (Jerusalem, 1962), p. 22a. If the *Yerushalmi* dispute the *Zohar*, we follow the *Yerushalmi*; Rabbi Chaim Binyamin Pontromoli, *Pethach HaDevir*, Volume 1 (Izmir, 1855), p. 46c; *Sedey Chemed, Kelaley HaPoskim* 2:9 (9:130). Also see *Pachad Yitzchak*, s.v. *Gemara* (69b).
93. *Teshuvoth Radbaz* 4:36 (1111); *Kenesseth HaGedolah, Orach Chaim, Kelaley HaPoskim* 2; *Magen Avraham* 25:20. Also see Rabbi Chaim Chizkiahu Medini, *Mikhtav LeChizkiahu, Teshuvah* 3 (Izmir, 1866); *Idem., Or Li* 69 (Izmir, 1874); *Pethach HaDevir* 1:46a, 1:115a; Rabbi Chaim Palaggi, *Kol HaChaim* (Izmir, 1834), p. 26b; *Sedey Chemed, Kelaley HaPoskim* 2:13 (9:131), 15:9 (9:173).
94. See above, 13:35.
95. *Teshuvoth Radbaz* 4:80; *Teshuvoth Rabbi Yaakov HaLevi* 41 (Venice, 1514); *Kenesseth HaGedolah, Orach Chaim, Kelaley HaPoskim* 2; *Teshuvoth Chakham Tzvi* 36; *Shaarey Teshuvah, Orach Chaim* 25:11.
96. Rabbi Eliahu Mizrachi, *Teshuvoth She'eloth* 1:1 (Constantinople, 1560); *Kenesseth HaGedolah, Orach Chaim, Kelaley HaPoskim* 2; *Magen Avraham* 25:20.
97. *Terumath HaDeshen* 342; *Teshuvoth Rashdam, Choshen Mishpat* 436; *Teshuvoth Rabbi Yosef ibn Lev (Rival)* 3:30; *Kenesseth HaGedolah, Yoreh Deah* 214:39; *Pri Chadash, Orach Chaim* 496, *Diney Minhagey Issur* 17; *Pachad Yitzchak*, s.v. *Minhag* (136d), s.v. *Devarim* (80c end); *Sedey Chemed, Mem* 37, s.v. *VeKathav* (4:75). Cf. *Tosafoth, Berakhoth* 22b, s.v. *VeNechzey; Yad, Shechitah* 11:3; *Teshuvoth Rivash* 463; *Choshen Mishpat* 331:1 in *Hagah*. A custom must also be unambiguous; *Teshuvoth Rivash* 475; *Teshuvoth Rashdam, Choshen Mishpat* 33. Regarding the case where there is a question involving the existence of a custom, see *Birkey Yosef, Yoreh Deah* 214:2; *Massa Chaim* 158 (p. 58); *Nishmath Kol Chai, Yoreh Deah* 66 (103b); *Sedey Chemed, Mem* 37, s.v. *Velm* (4:76), s.v. *Velm* (4:77). However, see *Tosafoth, Pesachim* 55a, s.v. *Amar.*
98. *Yerushalmi, Pesachim* 4:1 (26a); *Tosafoth, Shevuoth* 29b, s.v. *Ki*; *Rosh, Pesachim* 4:3; *Teshuvoth Rashba* 5:234; *Yoreh Deah* 228:25; *Teshuvoth Chavath Yair* 126; *Pri Chadash, Orach Chaim* 496, *Diney Minhagey Issur* 4; *Chayay Adam* 127:9. Also

accomplished by the common consent of the majority of the community[99] or their elected leaders.[100] Such action requires neither formal grounds[101] nor action by a rabbinical court.[102]

13:52   Just as a community can annul customs initiated by themselves, later generations can annul customs initiated by their ancestors.[103]

13:53   A custom is only binding on the community as a whole. Therefore, when the majority of the community agrees to

see *Teshuvoth HaGeonim, Shaarey Teshuvah* 139; Raavad, *Tamim Deyim* 192 (Lvov, 1812); *Otzar HaGeonim, Gittin* 36a. There is, however, an opinion that a custom can only be annulled if it involves an error in law; *Teshuvoth Radbaz* 3:527 (962); see second opinion in note 30. If a custom is formally adopted by a community as a safeguard (*seyag*, סיג) to prevent a violation of law, all agree that it cannot be annulled; *Teshuvath Rivash* 178; *Yoreh Deah* 228:28; *Chayay Adam* 127:11. Cf. *Yoreh Deah* 228:15, from *Yerushalmi, Nedarim* 5:4 (18b). The distinction between a spontaneous and a formally adopted custom only applies to those who initiate the custom. Later generations, however, are considered as having spontaneously adopted their fathers' customs, unless they specifically adopted them, or unless the custom was specifically initiated on the condition that it should be binding on future generations; *Teshuvoth HaRosh* 5:4; *Yoreh Deah* 228:35; *Sifethey Cohen ad loc.* 228:94; *Teshuvoth Rabbi Moshe Alshakar* 49; *Chayay Adam* 127:12.

99. *Pri Chadash, Orach Chaim* 496, *Diney Minhagey Issur* 5; *Yoreh Deah* 228:31. Cf. *Horioth* 3b. Also see *Teshuvoth HaRosh* 5:4, 7:5; *Teshuvoth Rivash* 73; *Teshuvoth Tashbatz* 1:123, *Teshuvoth Chavath Yair* 127.

100. Ramban, *Mishpat HaCherem* (see note 43); *Teshuvoth Rashba* 5:234, *Yoreh Deah* 228:31 in *Hagah*; from *Yerushalmi, Megillah* 3:2 (24a). Cf. *Teshuvoth Shevuth Yaakov* 1:74.

101. *Yoreh Deah* 228:25; Rosh, *Shevuoth* 3:23. Cf. *Yoreh Deah* 228:8, HaGra *ad loc.* 228:76.

102. Rosh, *Shevuoth* 3:23; *Teshuvoth Rashba* 5:234; *Yoreh Deah* 228:25. Also see Raavad, *Tamim Deyim* 213; *Teshuvoth Rabbi Yosef ibn Lev* (Rival) 2:72; *Teshuvoth Rabbi Yosef (ben Moshe) Trani* (Maharit) 1:69 (end) (Constantinople, 1641); *Teshuvoth Rabbi Moshe Alshekh* 75; *Teshuvoth Rashdam, Yoreh Deah* 26; *Mishpatey Sh'muel* 69.

103. *Yerushalmi, Pesachim* 4:1 (26a); *Karban HaEdah ad loc.* s.v. *U'Pharekh*; Rosh, *Pesachim* 4:3; *Karban Nethanel ad loc.* 5, 8; *Pri Chadash, Orach Chaim* 496, *Diney Minhagey Issur* 8; Rabbi Raphael Meldula, *Teshuvoth Mayim Rabbim, Yoreh Deah* 65, 66 (Amsterdam, 1737); Rabbi Yosef Steinhart, *Teshuvoth Zikhron Yosef, Yoreh Deah* 14 (Fürth, 1773); *Teshuvoth Chavath Yair* 126; *Pith'chey Teshuvah, Yoreh Deah* 228:30; *Chayay Adam* 127:7. Some authorities maintain that children cannot annul their parents' customs if the custom was initiated as a safeguard (*seyag*); Raavad, *Pesachim* (Rif 16b) 1; *Teshuvoth Rashdam, Yoreh Deah* 40. See above, note 98.

annul a custom, it is no longer binding on the dissenting minority.[104]

13:54   Under no condition can an individual or the minority of a community exempt themselves from a community custom by formal annulment.[105]

13:55   Similarly, a community cannot exempt itself from a custom that is observed over a larger geographical area.[106]

13:56   If a custom is accepted among all Jews, it cannot be annulled in any manner.[107] Such customs are as binding as is the Torah itself.[108]

13:57   If a custom was initiated for a well known specific reason, it is automatically annulled when the reason ceases

---

104. Rabbi Meir (ben Shem Tov) Melamed, *Mishpat Tzedek* 2:47 (Salonika, 1615); *Kenesseth HaGedolah,Yoreh Deah* 214:46; *Pachad Yitzchak*, s.v. *Devarim* (80d); *Pri Chadash, Orach Chaim* 496, *Diney Minhagey Issur* 5. A formally adopted custom, on the other hand, is only annulled to those who agree to annul it. Those who dissent from the annulment remain bound, even if they are a minority of the community; *Teshuvoth HaRosh* 5:4, 7:5; *Teshuvoth Rivash* 73; *Yoreh Deah* 228:31. Cf. *Yoreh Deah* 229:2; Ran, *Nedarim* 27a, s.v. *VeKathav* (end); *Teshuvoth Rivash* 94.

105. *Massa Melekh* 7:6; *Kenesseth HaGedolah, Yoreh Deah* 214:21; *Pri Chadash, Orach Chaim* 496, *Diney Minhagey Issur* 5; *Pachad Yitzchak*, s.v. *Devarim* (80b); *Chayay Adam* 127:9; *Mishnah Berurah* 468:11.

106. *Teshuvoth Chavath Yair* 126; Rabbi Shlomo Eiger, *Gilyon Maharsha, Yoreh Deah* 214:1. To be a regional custom, a practice must be generally observed throughout the entire region; *Yad, Ishuth* 23:12. However, if it is observed in the majority of the region, it is assumed to be observed throughout the region; *Teshuvoth HaRosh* 79:4; *Beth Yosef, Choshen Mishpat* 42:21.

107. *Teshuvoth Maharshal* 7; *Sifethey Cohen, Yoreh Deah* 214:4; *Kenesseth HaGedolah, Yoreh Deah* 214:10; *Pri Chadash, Orach Chaim* 496, *Diney Minhagey Issur* 6; *Pachad Yitzchak*, s.v. *Devarim* (80a); *Chayay Adam* 127:9. Cf. *Teshuvoth Rivash* 99. Also see *Betza* 4b; *Yevamoth* 102a; *Yad, Kiddush HaChodesh* 5:5. Such a custom cannot be annulled by even the greatest rabbis; *Teshuvoth Maharik* 54:4, from *Taanith* 28b; cf. *Sedey Chemed, Mem* 38, s.v. *VeAin* (4:101). Only the Sanhedrin had this power; *Yad, Mamrim* 1:2,3.

108. *Teshuvoth Rashba* 3:236; *Teshuvoth Rivash* 44. Cf. *Chulin* 92b; *Pesachim* 31a, 83b; *Bereshith Rabbah* 78:9; above, note 51.

to exist.[109] This is only true, however, when there is no likelihood of the recurring need for the custom.[110]

13:58   Any custom of long standing should be highly respected and not annulled.[111] This is especially true if it is endorsed by accepted authorities.[112]

13:59   Therefore, long standing customs should not be annulled even if they include practices that normally would not be condoned.[113] Concerning such venerable customs it is written, "Do not remove the ancient landmark which your fathers have set" (Proverbs 22:28).[114]

13:60   If something is forbidden only because of custom, it can be permitted in case of emergency or illness, even when there is no actual danger.[115]

109. *Teshuvoth Maharik* 144; *Teshuvoth Rama* 21; *Magen Avraham* 690:22; *Beer Hetiv* 690:15; *Darkey HaHorah* 5 (p. 232). Cf. *Yoreh Deah* 228:29. See above, 11:55.
110. *Betza* 4b. There is an indication, however, that there was specific legislation to retain this custom; *Yad, Kiddush HaChodesh* 3:3. However, see *Lechem Mishneh, Talmud Torah* 6:14 11.
111. *Yerushalmi, Eruvin* 3:9 (26b); *Yerushalmi, Taanith* 1:6 (6a), *Bereshith Rabbah* 94:4; *Orach Chaim* 690:16 in *Hagah*. It is assumed that such customs were instituted by the sages of old; *Teshuvoth Ramban* 51; *Teshuvoth HaRosh* 55:10; *Teshuvoth Maharik* 102:3. Such respect should be regarded to even a local custom; *Massa Moshe* 7:6; *Kenesseth HaGedolah, Yoreh Deah* 114:37; *Pachad Yitzchak,* s.v. *Devarim* (80c).
112. *Teshuvoth Maharik* 142; *Teshuvoth Rama* 21; *Magen Avraham* 690:22.
113. Cf. *Shabbath* 35b; *Eruvin* 104b; *Taanith* 28b; *Tosafoth, Taanith* 2a, s.v. *MeEimathai.* See above, note 86.
114. *Midrash Mishley,* Rashi, ad loc.; *Yalkut Shimoni* 2:960; *Sefer Chasidim* 114; *Magen Avraham* 68:0; cf. *Peah* 5:6, 7:3; *Tanchuma, VaYishlach* 10. See above Chapter 11, note 95. Other sources derive this from Deuteronomy 19:14, *Torah Temimah* ad loc.; *Tur, Choshen Mishpat* 368 (end); *Teshuvoth HaGeonim, Shaarey Tzedek* 20 (32a); *Otzar HaGeonim, Bava Kama* 114a (p. 105); *Teshuvoth Chut HaMeshulash* 3:24; *Sefer Chasidim* 114; cf. *Shabbath* 85a; *Rif, Bava Kama* 37b.
115. *Massa Melekh* 7:1; *Kenesseth HaGedolah, Yoreh Deah* 214:42; *Pachad Yitzchak,* s.v. *Devarim* (80d); *Chayay Adam* 127:6. Also see Rabbi Avraham (ben Nachman) HaCohen, *Tohorath HaMayim* 49 (Leghorn, 1879), p. 95; Rabbi Sh'muel Yitzchak, *Ne'eman Sh'muel* 10 (Salonika, 1723); *Sedey Chemed, Mem* 37, s.v. *Davar* (4:80). Cf. *Orach Chaim* 462:4 in *Hagah; Chayay Adam* 126:7; and *Orach Chaim* 686:1 in *Hagah,* from *Taanith* 14a. See above, 13:19.

13:61   If a community has a practice to follow a certain opinion in a question of law, it is considered the acceptance of that opinion as law, rather than as mere custom.[116] Therefore, such a practice can never be annulled.[117] However, since every community is bound to follow its own religious leadership,[118] it can abandon such a practice on the basis of its rabbi's judgment.[119]

13:62   If a community has an established custom to follow the opinion of one authority, it may do so, even when that opinion is the lenient one and opposes a majority.[120] Nevertheless, a community should not initially adopt a minority opinion as their common practice.[121]

13:63   In all cases, a community is bound to abide by the decisions of its duly chosen religious leaders,[122] and their opinions are binding as a custom even after their death.[123] In such cases, however, a later rabbi can overturn the decisions of his predecessors.[124]

13:64   A person must always abide by the customs of his home community even while temporarily residing elsewhere.[125]

116. Cf. *Sifethey Cohen, Choshen Mishpat* 25:10.
117. Ran, *Pesachim* (Rif 17b); s.v. *VeNimtzinu*; Ritva, *Pesachim* 51a; *Massa Melekh* 7:1; *Kenesseth HaGedolah, Yoreh Deah* 114:11; *Pachad Yitzchak*, s.v. *Devarim* (80a), s.v. *Minhag* (137c); *Pri Chadash, Orach Chaim* 496, *Diney Minhagey Issur* 2; *Chayay Adam* 127:10. Cf. *Teshuvoth Rashba* 3:236; *Teshuvoth Rashdam, Yoreh Deah* 40, 129. Some authorities, however, maintain that even such a custom can be annulled; *Teshuvoth Rabbi Sh'lomo (ben Avraham) Cohen (Rashakh)* 1:178; *Mishpat Tzedek* 1:32.
118. See above, 12:30.
119. *Teshuvoth Radbaz* 359 (end); *Pri Chadash, Orach Chaim* 496, *Diney Minhagey Issur* 2. Cf. *Chulin* 6b. See above, note 107, that no rabbi can annul a universal custom.
120. *Pri Chadash, Orach Chaim* 496, *Diney Minhagey Issur* 11; *Magen Avraham* 690:22; *Beer Hetiv* 690:14. Cf. *Rosh HaShanah* 15b.
121. *Pri Chadash, loc. cit.* Cf. *Taanith* 26b.
122. *Ibid.* See above, 12:30.
123. *Shiltey Gibborim, Avodah Zarah* (Rif 2a).
124. *Pri Chadash, loc. cit.* See above, 12:31.
125. *Pesachim* 4:1 (50a), 51a; *Chulin* 18b, 117a; *Tosafoth, Chulin* 93b, s.v. *MiShum;*

13:65 Similarly, a person is exempt from abiding by the customs of any community where he may be visiting or residing temporarily,[126] as long as he has the intention of returning home.[127]

13:66 Although a visitor or temporary resident is not bound by the customs of the community in which he is staying, he must nevertheless have respect for the sensibilities of the people.[128] Therefore, he should refrain from violating any local customs in the presence of any area residents.[129] Similarly, he should refrain from publicly observing his own customs,[130] unless he can do so unobtrusively.[131]

13:67 Activities which cannot be effectively concealed, such as manual labor, may not be done in violation of local custom, even in private.[132] However, they are permitted outside the city,[133] or away from Jewish habitation.[134]

Ran, *Pesachim* (Rif 16b), s.v. *HaHolekh;* Rosh, *Pesachim* 4:4; *Shiltey Gibborim, Avodah Zarah* (Rif 2a); *Yad, Yom Tov* 8:20; *Orach Chaim* 468:4, 574:1; *Chayay Adam* 127:9; *Mishnah Berurah* 468:13,14.

126. *Pri Chadash* 468:4; *"Rav" Shulchan Arukh* 468:10. Others, however, distinguish between a visitor and a temporary resident in this case; *Teshuvoth Radbaz* 73.

127. There are various opinions regarding this; *Beur Halakhah* 468:4, s.v. *HaHolekh.*

128. *Pesachim* 4:1 (50b); *Bava Metzia* 86b; *Bereshith Rabbah* 48:16; *Shemoth Rabbah* 47:6; *Tanchuma, VaYera* 11; *Zohar* 1:144a.

129. *Tosafoth, Pesachim* 51a, s.v. *Iy;* Ran, *Pesachim* (Rif 16b), s.v. *HaHolekh,* (Rif 16b,), s.v. *U'Rabbah,* s.v. *VeNimtzinu; HaMaor HaKatan, Pesachim* (Rif 16b), s.v. *Makom;* Rosh, *Pesachim* 4:4; *Yad, Yom Tov* 8:20; *Orach Chaim* 486:4; *Magen Avraham* 468:10; *"Rav" Shulchan Arukh* 468:11; *Mishnah Berurah* 468:13. Cf. *Orach Chaim* 572:2; *Magen Avraham,* 574:2.

130. *Yad, Yom Tov* 8;20; Rosh, *Pesachim* 4:4; *Magen Avraham* 468:11; *"Rav" Shulchan Arukh* 468:13.

131. Cf. *Pesachim* 51b.

132. *Tosafoth, Pesachim* 52a, s.v. *BaYishuv;* Ran, *Pesachim* (Rif 17b), s.v. *U'Rabbah; Orach Chaim* 468:4; *Magen Avraham* 468:7,12; *"Rav" Shulchan Arukh* 468:10; *Mishnah Berurah* 468:13,17.

133. *Pesachim* 52a; *Magen Avraham* 468:8; *Mishnah Berurah* 468:18.

134. *Magen Avraham* 496:5; *Mishnah Berurah* 496:10.

13:68   When a person establishes permanent residence in a community he is considered a member of that community with regard to all questions of custom[135] and practice.[136]

13:69   Therefore, when a person moves to a new community, he must abide by all its customs.[137] He is likewise absolved from the observances of the customs of the community from which he came.[138]

13:70 . If a person intends to settle in a new community and never return home, he establishes residence as soon as he enters the suburbs of the city to which he is moving.[139] Similarly, he establishes residence in a nation as soon as he reaches the first inhabited area,[140] even if it is inhabited by non-Jews.[141]

135. *Pesachim* 51a; *Chulin* 18b; Ran, *Pesachim* (Rif 17a), s.v. *U'Rabbah; Orach Chaim* 468:4, 496:3; *Yoreh Deah* 214:2.
136. *Shiltey Gibborim, Avodah Zarah* (Rif 2a); *Teshuvoth Rabbi David Cohen (Radakh)* 14.
137. This does not include inferior customs, see above, 13:29-31.
138. *Kenesseth HaGedolah, Yoreh Deah* 214:12; *Pachad Yitzchak*, s.v. *Devarim* (80a); *Magen Avraham* 468:9,12; *HaGra* ibid.; *"Rav" Shulchan Arukh* 468:9,12; *Mishnah Berurah* 468:13; *Beur Halakhah* ibid. Others,however, maintain that one is never absolved of his native customs; *Tosafoth, Chulin* 18b, s.v. *Hani; Sifethey Cohen, Yoreh Deah* 214:8; *Pri Chadash, Orach Chaim* 468:4; *Pri Megadim, Eshel Avraham* 468:9; *Beur Halakhah* loc. cit.; *Iggereth Moshe, Orach Chaim* 158. Some say that where it does not cause dissent, one should keep his native stringencies; *Massa Melekh* 7:40; *Kenesseth HaGedolah, Yoreh Deah* 214:22; *Pachad Yitzchak*, s.v. *Devarim* (80b).
139. *Magen Avraham* 468:8, 496:5; *Mishnah Berurah* 468:13, 496:10. Cf. *Chulin* 110a; Ran, *Pesachim* (Rif 17a), s.v. *U'Rabbah; HaMaor HaKatan, Pesachim* (Rif 16b), s.v. *Avel*. Also see *Teshuvoth Rashba* 3:414; *Yerushalmi, Yoma* 6:6 (34b); *Gilyoney HaShas, Pesachim* 51a. Some say that there are cases where one must live in an area for twelve months before accepting its leniencies; *Teshuvoth Geoney Mizrach U'Maarev* 39; *Maaseh HaGeonim* 31 (p. 47); *Otzar HaGeonim, Pesachim* 51a (p. 72); cf. *Teshuvoth Rashba* 337. See *Bava Bathra* 1:5 (7b); *Pachad Yitzchak* s.v. *Ore'ach* (39c).
140. *Orach Chaim* 496:3; *Teshuvoth Radbaz* 4:73; *Teshuvoth Rashdam, Orach Chaim* 15; *Teshuvoth Mabit* 2:149; *Magen Avraham* 496:4. Cf. *Pesachim* 52a; Ran, *Pesachim* (Rif 17a), s.v. *U'Rabbah; HaMaor HaKatan, Pesachim* (Rif 16b), s.v. *Avel*.
141. *Teshuvoth Radbaz* 4:73; *Magen Avraham* 496:6; *Mishnah Berurah* 496:11. Some authorities dispute this; cf. *Bigdey Yesha* ibid.

13:71   As soon as a person establishes residence in a community he is bound by all its customs, even if he immediately leaves the area.[142]

13:72   When a family moves its complete household to a new community, they establish residence there even if they plan to return to their home community.[143] Nevertheless, a person can make a permanent move and establish new residence even if he is not accompanied by his family.[144]

13:73   A student retains the residence of his parents, even though he may be away at school for many years.[145] However, if he has clear intentions of permanently residing where he is studying, he can establish residence there.[146]

13:74   When a woman marries, she adopts the customs of her husband.[147]

13:75   A person is absolved from keeping his home town customs only when there is a definite alternate custom in the place where he establishes residence. However, if a definite custom does not exist, he must adhere to the custom of his home community.[148]

142. "Rav" Shulchan Arukh 468:10; Mishnah Berurah 468:14.
143. Teshuvoth Radbaz 4:73; Magen Avraham 496:7; Pri Chadash 468,4; "Rav" Shulchan Arukh 496:10; Beer Hetiv 496.5, Mishnah Berurah 496:13. Also see Ran, Pesachim (Rif 17b), s.v. VeNimtzinu; Teshuvoth Ginath Veradim, Orach Chaim 4:17; Rabbi Avraham Yitzchaki; Teshuvoth Zera Avraham, Orach Chaim 9,10 (Constantinople, 1732); Teshuvoth Rabbi Yosef Trani (Maharit) 19; Teshuvoth Rabbi Shlomo Cohen (Rashakh) 2:26; Teshuvoth Rabbi Shlomo (ben Yitzchak) HaLevi 68 (Salonika, 1690). However,if they have definite, established plans to return, they may retain their native customs.
144. Teshuvoth Mishpat Tzedek 2:49; Magen Avraham 496:7; Pri Chadash 468:4.
145. Teshuvoth Radbaz 73; Magen Avraham 468:12; Teshuvoth Halakhoth Ketanoth 4.
146. Shaarey Teshuvah, Orach Chaim 496:2.
147. Rabbi Moshe Feinstein שליט״א, Iggereth Moshe, Orach Chaim 158. See Rabbi Yaakov ben Abba Mari, Sefer HaMelamed, quoted in Kol Bo 73 (beginning).
148. Teshuvoth Rabbi Yosef Trani (Maharit) 19; Pri Chadash, Orach Chaim 468:4; "Rav" Shulchan Arukh 468:15; Beur Halakhah 468:4, s.v. VeChomrey. Cf. Yerushalmi, Berakhoth 2:2 (19b).

13:76   Therefore, if people settle where there is no existing[149] Jewish community, they must adhere to the customs of their place of origin.[150] If they come from places with different customs, they must adhere to the custom of the majority.[151] If there is no clear majority, each group may follow its native customs until an agreement is reached, or until an indigenous custom develops.[152]

13:77   However, if any Jewish community at all exists in a place, all newcomers are obliged by its customs, even if the newcomers vastly outnumber the original inhabitants.[153]

13:78   If many people from one community settle in another, and wish to maintain their identity, they may form a separate congregationwher ethey can adhere to their original customs.[154] Under no conditions, however, may they impose their customs on the original inhabitants of the community, even if the newcomers vastly outnumber them.[155]

13:79   Every congregation is considered to be a separate community and each may therefore have its own customs.[156]

---

149. Regarding the rule when an earlier community existed but was destroyed or abandoned, see *Shiltey Gibborim, Avodah Zarah* (Rif 2a); *Magen Avraham* 493:6; *Pri Megadim, Eshel Avraham* 468:12; *Beer Hetiv, Yoreh Deah* 214:5; *Beur Halakhah* 468:4; *Teshuvoth Chavath Yair* 126.
150. *Bava Metzia* 83b; *Rashba, Ran, ad loc.; Choshen Mishpat* 331:1 in *Hagah*. Cf. *Yerushalmi, Pesachim* 4:1 (26a); *Pri Chadash, Orach Chaim* 496, *Diney Minhagey Issur* 19; *Massa Melekh* 7:11; *Pachad Yitzchak, s.v. Minhag* (137d); *Teshuvoth Maharik* 102:2.
151. *Nimukey Yosef, Bava Metzia* (Rif 52a), s.v. *BeLikutey*.
152. *Pri Chadash, Orach Chaim* 496, *Diney Minhagey Issur* 19; from *Bava Metzia* 83b.
153. *Teshuvoth Rabbi Yosef ibn Lev (Rival)* 3:14; *Massa Melekh* 7:11; *Kenesseth HaGedolah, Yoreh Deah* 214:9; *Pri Chadash, Orach Chaim* 496, *Diney Minhagey Issur* 19; *Pachad Yitzchak, s.v. Devarim* (80a), s.v. *Minhag* (137d).
154. *Ibid.* Also see *Rabbi Eliahu Mizrachi, Teshuvoth She'eloth* 1:13; *Teshuvoth Rabbi Yosef ibn Lev (Rival)* 3:10; *Teshuvoth Rashdam, Yoreh Deah* 40. The same is true in a new community where many groups come from different places; *Tumath Yesharim* 168; *Kenesseth HaGedolah, Yoreh Deah* 214:7.
155. *Teshuvoth Rabbi David Cohen (Radakh)* 13; *Rabbi Yitzchak (ben Sh'muel) Adrabi, Divrey Rivoth* 162 (Salonika, 1582); *Pri Chadash, Orach Chaim* 496, *Diney Minhagey Issur* 19; *Pachad Yitzchak, s.v. Lo Thithgodedu* (8a). See above, 12:37.
156. Above, 12:37.

Therefore, as soon as a person joins a congregation, he must abide by all its customs.[157]

13:80   In order to qualify as an autonomous community, a place must have a quorum (*minyan*, מִנְיָן) of observant adult males, as well as its own synagogue and rabbi. Otherwise, the community is not considered autonomous, and must follow the customs of the nearest large community.[158]

13:81   In each community, everyone is obliged to abide by the customs of the majority.[159] However, if it is a practice for some to observe stricter customs out of personal piety, they may do so, as long as there is no danger of dissension.[160]

13:82   There are many lofty concepts that seem highly desirable in theory, but work out very poorly in practice. Judaism, however, consists of practice rather than theory, and therefore, God decreed that its final form be established by those who practice it. It is for this reason that we are constantly warned to abide by custom.

13:83   It is also for this reason that we are warned of the great punishment for ignoring a custom.[161] The initial breaking of minor customs often led entire communities completely away from Torah and Judaism.[162]

---

157. Rabbi Eliahu Mizrachi, *Teshuvoth She'eloth* 1:13; *Magen Avraham* 493:6; *Pri Chadash, Orach Chaim* 496, *Diney Minhagey Issur* 20.
158. *Beur Halakhah* 468:4, s.v. *HaHolekh.*
159. See above, 12:39.
160. *Magen Avraham* 493:6; *Eshel Avraham* ad loc. Cf. *Teshuvoth Rabbi Yosef ibn Lev (Rival)* 3:14; *Teshuvoth Ralbach* 2:11; *Massa Melekh* 7:14; *Kenesseth HaGedolah, Yoreh Deah* 214:4; *Pachad Yitzchak,* s.v. *Devarim* (80a), s.v. *Minhag* (138a).
161. *Sefer Chasidim* 607; *Sefer Maharil, Hilkhoth Yom Kippur* (47b); Rabbi Mikhel of Arapchik, *Minchah Chadashah* on *Avoth,* end (Cracow, 1576); *Maaver Yaakov, Minchath Aaron* 7. There is also a curse that he be bitten by a snake (Ecclesiastes 10:8); Rashba, *Torath HaBayith* 2:3 (34a); *Yoreh Deah* 196:13 in *Hagah.* See above, 11:29. Also see *Pesachim* 52a; *Yad, Talmud Torah* 6:14 11; *Lechem Mishneh* ad loc.
162. Cf. *Teshuvoth Ralbach, Chatham Sofer, Orach Chaim* 28; *Beur Halakhah* 150:5, s.v. *BeEmtza.*

13:84   One of the fundamental unvoiced concepts of Judaism is
that God reveals His will to us, not only through prophecy,
but in the common destiny of all who seek Him. Therefore,
even such seemingly prosaic concepts as legal decisions and
customs partake of God's continuous process of revelation.[163]

163. Cf. *Tanchuma, Shemoth* 18.

INDEX

BIBLICAL QUOTATIONS

37:12	136
38:8	61
38:30	115
41:38	91
43:14	91
46:23	115
49:22	108

Exodus

1:5	48
1:7	50
2:2	122
2:24	52
3:2	17, 93, 103
3:4	93
3:5	122
3:13	146
3:15	20, 146, 147
3:16	156, 210
4:5	152
4:9	156
4:29	156, 210
6:5	52
6:7	53
6:24	113
7:3	34
9:15	11
10:23	50
12:21	156, 210
12:26	80
12:37	53, 135
12:40	50
12:48	63
13:8	80
13:14	80
13:18	50
13:21	16
14:23	153
14:27	152
15:2	108, 110
15:18	30
15:20	111
15:25	61, 62
16:4	34
16:5	61
16:8	122
16:29	61
17:6	210
17:7	157
18:12	210
18:20	231

18:21	200
18:22	214
19:4	124
19:5	54
19:9	99, 124, 158
19:11	109
19:14	63
19:17	106
19:18	107
20:2	2, 52
20:2—14	66
20:3	3
20:13	157
20:17	35
20:23	207, 208
21:1	70, 207
21:14	207, 208
22:19	3
23:2	217, 244
23:13	164
24:1	127, 181, 198, 200, 210
24:3	63, 70
24:4	127, 128
24:5	136, 137
24:5—8	63
24:7	54, 63, 68, 127, 128
24:8	63
24:9	210
24:12	61, 67, 177
24:18	61
24:27	62
25—28	98
25:8,9	165
25:16	130
25:22	67
26:33	67
28:9	105
28:21	95
28:30	88, 94, 239
30:6	67
30:26	67
31:18	67, 68
32:13	48
32:15	67
32:19	67
33:11	123
33:16,17	98
33:17	99
33:18	12
33:20	12, 17
33:21	10, 20, 146
33:23	12
34:1	67

Notes

Notes

Notes

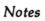

Notes

Notes